THE WALLS AROUND OPPORTUNITY

OUR
COMPELLING
INTERESTS

AN INITIATIVE OF THE
UNIVERSITY OF MICHIGAN
WITH SUPPORT FROM THE
ANDREW W. MELLON FOUNDATION

Earl Lewis and Nancy Cantor, Series Editors

Other books in this series:
Eboo Patel,
  Out of Many Faiths: Religious Diversity and the American Promise
Scott E. Page,
  The Diversity Bonus: How Great Teams Pay Off in the Knowledge Economy
Earl Lewis and Nancy Cantor, editors,
  *Our Compelling Interests: The Value of Diversity for Democracy and
  a Prosperous Society*

The Walls around Opportunity

THE FAILURE OF COLORBLIND POLICY FOR HIGHER EDUCATION

GARY ORFIELD

With a new afterword by the author

PRINCETON UNIVERSITY PRESS

PRINCETON & OXFORD

Published by Princeton University Press
41 William Street, Princeton, New Jersey 08540
99 Banbury Road, Oxford OX2 6JX

press.princeton.edu

First paperback edition, with a new afterword by the author, 2024
Paperback ISBN 978-0-691-23919-4
ISBN (e-book) 978-0-691-26087-7
Library of Congress Control Number: 2023950656

British Library Cataloging-in-Publication Data is available

Editorial: Eric Crahan, Barbara Shi
Jacket/Cover Design: Lauren Smith
Production: Danielle Amatucci
Publicity: Julia Haav, Kate Farquhar-Thomson
Copyeditor: Ashley Moore

This book has been composed in Arno

CONTENTS

AUTHOR'S NOTE

AMERICAN COLLEGES and universities are institutions of immense, sometimes transformative, power, but they are doing far too little to help resolve the dangerous stratification and racial divisions in our society as it goes through the last stage of a white majority. The failure is long-standing and severe, and it may be getting even worse. It cannot be changed without making equity in our colleges a central commitment and working hard to devise means that will actually change the opportunities and outcomes. Affirmative action is a limited policy but is under severe threat in the Supreme Court. Our high schools are resegregated after the courts terminated integration plans, and offer too little support to students of color. Many good people are doing something to address equity on campus and in policy. Things would certainly be even worse without those efforts, and they have created models of what could bring larger changes, but it's not enough to overcome the powerful sorting pressures of our stratified society and its weak current policies. Major new energy or resources have not been put into civil rights policies for a generation. I know the transformative power of college in my own life, with my own students, and in my research, and I know we can do much more to bring into the center of our society and economy the major groups that have always been on the margin.

I was the first one in my family to go to college. I understand in a special way how transformative it can be. My grandfather was an immigrant from a farm in Norway with an elementary education. My father and mother were very talented but were only able to go through high school during the Great Depression. I became a professor at several of the world's great universities. I did not do it on my own. I had a loving, supportive family, and my dad worked hard to be able to live in an area with good schools. I went to one of the best high schools in my state. There was a great low-cost public university, the University of Minnesota, with talented and supportive professors, so I could live at home, pay modest tuition, commute, and be ready for great graduate schools. I went to college with almost a year of credits from high school. I had saved more than two years' tuition from my grocery store work, I got scholarships, and could pay my other costs with summer jobs. My first survey research was about a proposal to raise the tuition at the university. I was in student government and we systematically surveyed students about their economic situation and what would happen if the tuition went up. Though tuition was at what we'd now consider an extremely low level, two-thirds of the students were commuters and many reported that they were struggling and would have to drop out. We sent the report to the state legislature and were stunned when they voted the tuition hike down, putting me in conflict with the university's administrators but maybe saving college access for a number of students. It was my first lesson in the power of research for equity. It showed me that what administrators considered insignificant was a major barrier for many.

I have written extensively about civil rights issues in colleges, public schools, and other institutions; been actively involved as a witness and a court-appointed expert in major civil rights cases; and participated in admissions decisions. I had opportunities to study community colleges and universities in metro Chicago with a wonderful team of University of Chicago students when I was teaching there, to carry out a statewide study of opportunity in high schools and colleges across Indiana, and to do studies of the Atlanta region and other major metro areas. There have been many opportunities since. It has been very depressing to observe, decade after decade, stratification intensifying leaving largely untouched university policies that have the effect of perpetuating inequalities as higher education becomes ever more critical to family and community success.

I believe higher education policy is one of the most important forces that shape our society, but it is usually out of public sight. Often higher education policy is managed in ways that all institutions get something and the status quo is not really challenged. That's not good enough. My work focuses on issues of racial equity. It is clear that our higher education policies are not closing the racial gaps in our society and are, in some ways, legitimating and even intensifying them. I'm glad that higher education was a major issue in the 2020 campaign, but I think too much of the attention was on the admittedly important issue of student debt held by graduates and on community college tuition, not the factors that most directly affect the future of equity on our campuses.

I loved college so much that I never wanted to leave higher education, and my life at six great universities has been richly fulfilling. I have seen so many times, in the lives of my own students, how something that happened on campus has opened up an engaged life of real contributions. I have many academic "grandchildren" (students of my students) around the country and abroad and a long line of former students who are doing great work. We have institutions that have real power in a deeply separated society. Universities have trained leaders and pioneers of color, but access to these opportunities has, in some ways, become even more unequal.

In this last generation of a white majority in American society, I am angry and worried about the failure of our schools and colleges to contribute more to a just society that promises equal opportunity but has never delivered it. I benefited from the strength of an excellent high school, but millions of students of color attend high schools where the path to college hardly exists. Far too often many in higher education and our schools simply assume that what we do is good by definition and that we are expanding opportunity when we are not, in spite of statements of good intentions and a list of programs.

Our recent past in national politics has shown with stunning clarity that our society is still severely threated by racial stereotypes and hate. Education is one of the only remedies we offer. I'm convinced we can do much better, but not on the path we're on now. It is bad enough to reflect and reinforce a highly unequal society; even worse to compound its inequality. We made a big step forward a half century ago in the civil rights era, but we stagnated and then went backward. It is time for the people and the leaders who make higher education and high school policies to think hard about where we are and to actually change outcomes. I know there are many other challenges to our colleges and schools, but we have only one society and we need our key institutions to help it heal its dangerously damaging divisions.

I've tried to make this book as nontechnical and jargon-free as possible, but let me clarify a couple of points about usage. I use the terms *race conscious* and *race sensitive* repeatedly. *Race conscious* refers to a policy that takes race directly into account, such as affirmative action. *Race sensitive* refers to a policy that is designed with understanding of the issues that especially affect students and families of color, such as the necessity of students to help support parents and siblings even during college because of problems at home. Such policies are not overtly race conscious, but they are designed with real understanding of the realities of race.

Terms matter. Here are the decisions that I've made that you need to understand as you read the book. I do not use the term *Latinx* because survey research shows that less than a tenth of Latinos and Hispanics prefer it and it makes no sense in Spanish (and my wife is a Latina). If people change, so will I. I understand that scholars are trying to be respectful, to use current academic terminology, and to be sensitive to gender, and that such terms may be best in the context of their work. I usually use the term *Indian* because the people usually use it. When I was in college, I ran a program on Indian reservations, my MA thesis was about Indian policy, the National Congress of American Indians is a great national organization, a national newspaper is called *Indian Country Today*, the Bureau of Indian Affairs is the key federal agency, and so on. Often, of course, people identify themselves by their tribe or use other terms. In both cases I respect the variations the people and scholars use but try to use one term here to avoid confusion.

I use the terms *people of color* and *students of color* to refer to Black, Latino, and Indian people collectively. I do not include Asians because Asians, as a group, are neither segregated nor unequal in American society today (though they surely were in the past and there are still stereotypes about Asians, stirred up by President Donald Trump, and terrible cases of violence and harassment). There are some struggling Asian subgroups that deserve help, but on average, Asians are the most highly educated and affluent population in America, substantially exceeding average white levels. There is still racial prejudice against Asians, but they are very well represented in the strongest public schools and in higher education. I use *students of color* to cover what are often called underrepresented minority students in academic literature and some official reports. No one ever calls himself or herself an underrepresented minority, and in increasing parts of the U.S. they are not minorities. So please remember this definition as you read the statistics.

I am a political scientist who has taught and researched in political science and education as well as in law and public policy, and I have been directing or codirecting a center of civil rights research for a quarter century. In contrast to economists and sociologists, in my work I often deal directly with policy and legal issues in a country where state governments and federal aid strongly shape higher education and the courts set key parameters. Unlike some of my social science colleagues, I believe that it is very important to understand the historical dimensions because much of the inequality we must address is rooted in a history of intergenerational inequality and stereotypes and the origin of inequality is of great importance in establishing legal rights. We need insights from all disciplines. I believe that our responsibility as scholars is to present evidence and tell the truth as best we understand it. We are also citizens, and we need to take what we learn into the great debates in our society. We have the important protection of academic freedom, and we should use it to discuss not only what is feasible in this moment but what is actually necessary. We never would have had a civil rights movement if its leaders had limited their work to things practical at the time. Academics have special privileges and resources, we don't have to get elected, and our worth to society comes from trying to advance knowledge and telling the truth as best we can find it. The truth is that we are not on a workable path. I'm honored that you are reading this book. I hope it will help move readers toward understanding and action.

After a half century of increasingly conservative Republican politics interrupted by moderate Democratic administrations, the Democratic Party came to office in 2021 after a mass social and political movement, committed to racial equity. The Democratic campaign and platform called for large increases in college aid and debt forgiveness. Under fierce cross pressures to limit expenditures and address an array of major gaps in the social safety net, as well as the world's environmental crisis, what came out of the legislative struggle in 2021 was a modest increase in the Pell Grant, leaving it far too low to make four-year college feasible for millions of families; some aid to institutions educating many students of color; no debt relief legislation; and no "free community college." Other progressive provisions very significantly aid preschool education, child care, housing, and the economic crisis facing low income families, all good and important steps toward equity, and make a major commitment to limiting the environmental disasters threatening the rising generation. There was not enough money left, even in the largest bill in U.S. history, to significantly move the dial on the issues of systematically unequal college preparation and financial aid at the core of this book. Those did not turn out to be top priorities. Administrative and civil rights enforcement actions can significantly help, but much more is needed. The big issues were left for another day, as they have been decade after decade. If we want a less stratified society with more equal opportunity to develop the talents of our students of color, it has to become a fundamental priority and we must build out policies and practices that overcome the actual barriers in the lives of students and families. Too often, in spite of good intentions, our schools and colleges are still perpetuating or even strengthening stratification. We must do better.

I would like to thank the Mellon Foundation, which has made great contributions to higher education policy, for financial support; Earl Lewis, Nancy Cantor, and Doreen Tinajero, for guiding this book through; the Center for Social Solutions at the University of Michigan; and Caroline Peelle, for her always careful editing. Princeton University Press's reviewers offered many helpful suggestions, and the Westchester copyeditor was excellent. This work would have been impossible, especially in the pandemic period, without the constant support, good ideas, and endlessly interesting company of my wife, colleague, and dear partner in all, Patricia Gándara, another first-generation college student, who has worked very hard in her teaching, research, and advocacy to extend to others the opportunities that transformed her life.

INTRODUCTION

Earl Lewis and Nancy Cantor

As we mark the 65th anniversary of Brown, there have been many changes since the ruling, but intense levels of segregation—which had decreased markedly after 1954 for black students—are on the rise once again.[1]

Research shows that segregation has strong, negative relationships with the achievement, college success, long-term employment and income of students of color.[2]

Separate is still unequal. If we are serious about reducing racial inequality in educational opportunity, then, we must address racial segregation among schools. This we do know how to do, or at least we once did.[3]

WHEN THURGOOD MARSHALL and cocounsels first stood before the justices of the U.S. Supreme Court in 1952 and uttered the words that start every case in the highest chamber, "May it please the Court," more than school segregation proved at stake. After a generation of legal contestation, with one precedent following another, the whole logic of segregation or separate but equal appeared up for nullification or recertification. Before the landmark *Brown* decision (1954), segregation had a deadly hold on all facets of life. It determined where one could live, whom one could marry, where one could learn, and with whom one could drink, eat, or be buried. Through accident of birth, segregation increased or reduced life expectancy, made property profitable or valueless,

1. Erica Frankenberg et al., *Harming Our Common Future: America's Segregated Schools 65 Years after Brown* (Los Angeles: Civil Rights Project, 2019), 4.

2. Frankenberg et al., 4.

3. Sean Reardon et al., "Is Separate Still Unequal? New Evidence on School Segregation and Racial Academic Achievement Gaps," Center for Education Policy Analysis Working Paper No. 19-06, Stanford University, September 2019, 35.

or pronounced one socially able and beautiful or unacceptable and ugly. From the vantage point of 2020, it is easy to forget how much was at stake when the Court ruled segregation, and the doctrine of separate but equal, unconstitutional because it violated the Fourteenth Amendment to the Constitution.[4]

The fight to truly desegregate America's classrooms and end all vestiges of segregation faced many more skirmishes before we declared a transitional victory. Linda Brown and her contemporaries may have lent their names and circumstances to the facts that produced the landmark decision, but few of them directly benefited, ironically. Across the South and throughout much of the North and West, school systems reacted gradually, if at all, to mandates to end segregation. Massive resistance, interposition, and other tactics surfaced as public policy alternatives, delaying by as long as a decade and a half the complete end of state-sanctioned racial segregation in public education. It would be 1971–72 before most school districts in the South fully committed themselves to desegregating. Elsewhere, de facto segregation born out of state-enforced housing segregation ensured the need for busing and other tactics to create a proportionately mixed learning environment.

If the period from 1954 to 1971 can be thought of as the last gasp of Jim Crow, and the years between 1971 and 1978 can be viewed as the period when racial restitution mattered most, the years since the 1978 *Bakke* decision, which established that race can be one of several factors in composing a higher education class, may be viewed as the time when race blindness outlasted race awareness.[5] The implications are profound and troubling when we look at the consequences for individuals and our nation. That conundrum—race neutrality in a race-conscious world—is the focus of Gary Orfield's important new volume.

In it we are reminded that we go to school where we live, and this has sealed the educational fate of generations of students educated in low-resource, underperforming schools doubly segregated by race and class, and cut off for the most part from realistic pathways to college and jobs that foster intergenerational prosperity. Why? The American narrative has been written in color since its

---

4. The *Brown* case, which amounted to the bundling of five cases in total, was first argued before the Supreme Court in December 1952 and reargued in December 1953. Before the second round of arguments was heard and a ruling rendered, Chief Justice Fred Vinson Jr. died of a heart attack. His replacement was Earl Warren, former governor of California. The Court rendered its decision on May 17, 1954, in *Brown v. Board of Education*, 347 U.S. 483.

5. See Earl Lewis, "History and the Common Good: Scholarship in the Public Eye," presidential address, *Journal of American History* 106, no. 3 (December 2019): 577–90.

founding days, and colorblind rhetoric aside, it still is, as Khalil Muhammad asserts: "No Racial Barriers Left to Break (Except All of Them)."[6] Every aspect of our history and our contemporary social fabric is shaded by an apparent inability and lack of will to live and learn together on any remotely level playing field. Whether we are speaking of de facto or de jure segregation, across the centuries, we have erected laws, policies, and practices. Sometimes we acted harshly and violently, many times much more routinely, even papering over practices that separated and disadvantaged with lofty rhetoric. The result was the architecture of segregation from the South to the North, stamped with the force of the "color of law." It is seen in group contexts that range from Native American reservations to migrant farm communities, from rural coal-mining towns to red-lined urban public housing.[7] Moreover, when we do not live together, we, by necessity of long-accepted public policy, do not learn together either.[8] Unlike the civic-religious space that Eboo Patel, in our last volume in this series,[9] identified as a possible common ground for the hard work of civic pluralism, schools are not typically open to redesign, except by law, and that history is painfully full of the fits and starts that this volume documents, across the ups and downs that have charted the unfinished dreams of Linda Brown and her peers.[10]

Nonetheless, as relentless as this narrative of educational segregation has been and still is today, there have been small windows of sunlight through an otherwise silhouetted opening, moments when the value of integration, from housing to schools to universities, has shown through in policy and practice, and even in law. We have all experienced these windows of possibility, some firsthand, and we have seen them close as well. One of us grew up in a Southern state and directly experienced the hazards of a segregated learning environment, as well as the benefits of active integration. Born just in time for the *Brown* II (1955) decision that instructed Southern schools to desegregate "with all deliberate speed," he attended segregated schools in Virginia until the fall of 1971. His classmates

6. Khalil Muhammad, "No Racial Barriers Left to Break (Except All of Them)," *New York Times*, January 14, 2017.

7. Richard Rothstein, *The Color of Law: A Forgotten History of How Our Government Segregated America* (New York: Norton, 2017).

8. P. Jargowsky, *The Architecture of Segregation: Civil Unrest, the Concentration of Poverty, and Public Policy* (Washington, DC: Century Foundation, 2015).

9. Eboo Patel, *Out of Many Faiths: Religious Diversity and the American Promise* (Princeton, NJ: Princeton University Press, 2018).

10. Elise Boddie and Dennis Parker, "Linda Brown and the Unfinished Work of School Integration," *New York Times*, March 30, 2018.

represented the transitional generation, Blacks, whites, and others, who went to segregated schools most of their lives and then became a part of the cohort that massively desegregated the South's public schools. After 250 years of slavery and nearly one hundred years of segregation, reform in the civil rights era assumed color-conscious policies to redress old wrongs. These policies aimed to put in place *Brown*'s promise of integration and not just desegregation. Integration, after all, required the sharing of power and not just the removal of obstacles to mixed school attendance.[11] One of us lives in a Northern state where the state constitution actually strongly outlaws separate and unequal schools, along with the housing policies that often promote such segregation. Repeated lawsuits in that state, including one very recently, have put a spotlight on just how hard it has been to realize that constitutional protection even with the best of intentions.[12]

Nor are the assaults on the color-conscious policies that grew out of years of slavery and segregation limited to primary and secondary education. The *Bakke* doctrine's preference for diversity subordinated and nearly removed any hint of the significance of race in America's past and present—in social and public policy as well as attitudes and behavior. That said, both of us understand the social choices at stake. We understand the value of diversity for improving the learning experiences of majority and nonmajority learners. We know that students who learn in such environments go on to play a more active role in the civic interests of the nation, exhibit a higher tolerance for competing viewpoints, and know how to work better in groups. We also know the consequences that arose when the Supreme Court allowed a major midwestern public university to pursue affirmative action in college admissions, only to see it dismantled by a state-level referendum.[13]

We also appreciate what's at stake for the country and our democracy. As William Frey has chronicled, over the last several decades we have witnessed

11. Genevieve Segal-Hawley, *Miles to Go: A Report on School Segregation in Virginia, 1989–2010*, with Jennifer Ayscue, John Kuscera, and Gary Orfield (Los Angeles: Civil Rights Project, March 13, 2013). See also Lewis, "History and the Common Good," 583–85; and Rucker C. Johnson, *Children of the Dream: Why School Integration Works*, with Alexander Nazaryan (New York: Basic Books, 2019).

12. Boddie and Parker, "Linda Brown"; Gary Orfield, Jongyeon Ee, and Ryan Coughlin, *New Jersey's Segregated Schools: Trends and Paths Forward* (Los Angeles: Civil Rights Project, November 2017).

13. Patricia Gurin, Jeffrey S. Lehman, and Earl Lewis, *Defending Diversity: Affirmative Action at the University of Michigan*, with Eric Dey, Gerald Gurin, and Sylvia Hurtado (Ann Arbor: University of Michigan Press, 2004).

an explosion in the diversity of talent ready and wanting cultivation.[14] Yet we must all worry about our ability to handle this assignment, faithfully and effectively. Old assumptions about who's eligible for admission may need to give way to new methods of identifying and developing talent. What if our testing moved from a focus on institutional access to success once one gains admission? This is not a vacuous question. Higher education, especially public higher education, must fulfill the task of serving as an engine of opportunity and social mobility for what is quickly becoming the new majority (of our populace).[15]

We have argued throughout this book series that the compelling interests of diversity and inclusion, for civil rights, for social connectedness, and for full participation, especially in the face of that demographic explosion, could not be more critical than they are today,[16] and maximizing educational opportunity is at their very core. Orfield makes just this point throughout the present volume, forcefully reminding us of the steep challenge we face. He does so by juxtaposing an analysis of the short-lived successes of the color-conscious school integration era with the four (colorblind) decades that followed. The measurable, material outcomes bear tangible implications for individuals, communities, and the broader society. As Orfield has said, "A society which fails to develop the talents of a vast share of its people and creates a permanent reality of racial and ethnic subordination is a society with wasted possibilities and a threatened future." As stark as is that diagnosis, it comes with evidence that cannot and should not be ignored. This is particularly so in a knowledge economy in which education and prosperity are inextricably intertwined. For as Scott Page demonstrated in his volume in this series, success for all depends on reaping the diversity bonus that comes from the collective intelligence of full participation.[17]

14. William Frey, *Diversity Explosion: How New Racial Demographics Are Remaking America* (Washington, DC: Brookings Institution, 2015).

15. Anthony P. Carnevale et al., *Our Separate and Unequal Public Colleges: How Public Colleges Reinforce White Privilege and Marginalize Black and Latino Students* (Washington, DC: Center on Education and the Workforce, Georgetown University, 2018); Raj Chetty et al., "Mobility Report Cards: The Role of Colleges in Intergenerational Mobility," NBER Working Paper No. 23618, National Bureau of Economic Research, Cambridge, MA, July 2017, https://opportunityinsights.org/wp-content/uploads/2018/03/coll_mrc_paper.pdf.

16. Earl Lewis and Nancy Cantor, eds., *Our Compelling Interests: The Value of Diversity for Democracy and a Prosperous Society* (Princeton, NJ: Princeton University Press, 2016).

17. Scott E. Page, *The Diversity Bonus: How Great Teams Pay Off in the Knowledge Economy* (Princeton, NJ: Princeton University Press, 2017).

Succeeding in a Very Short Time of Race Consciousness

Yet what is less often told these days (in our aspirational "colorblind" world), and what Orfield importantly emphasizes in this volume, is the force (albeit short-lived) and effectiveness of the (civil rights movement–inspired) federal interventions of the decade of the 1960s. While those interventions requiring school desegregation plans principally had their effects on the educational opportunities of Black students in the South—ignoring, by contrast, Native Americans in isolated reservation schools and never reaching waves of Latinx immigrating into doubly segregated low-resource communities—they had a very real impact. As Orfield notes, "Within the space of five years of active enforcement, the schools of the South had become the most integrated in the nation."

The effectiveness of that brief period of government interventions delivers a powerful message to keep in mind today. Not that long ago, students from less advantageous family backgrounds had multiple pathways to securing top-flight educational opportunities. In recent years several factors coalesced to stymie those advances, be they the courts, the appeal of neighborhood schools shaped by unchecked housing segregation, or an overreliance on standardized testing. Indeed, we now see court cases dismantling even voluntary desegregation plans (*Parents Involved*),[18] and the composition of Northern schools is following divides along classic lines of race and class. Even highly selective public high schools in otherwise liberal cities like New York City fall prey to the disparate impact of standardized admissions testing on the racial and socioeconomic diversity of their enrollees. Consider, as just one example, the fact that magnet public high schools, which have traditionally been an enormously important road to social mobility in New York City, are no longer populated by large numbers of Black and Latinx students. For example, Stuyvesant High School has gone from enrolling 10.3 percent Black students in 1971 to only 0.8 percent now.[19] Similarly, in neighboring New Jersey, a highly diverse and immigration-dense state, the suburban-urban divide has taken its toll on school integration, such that it now is home to the sixth most segregated school in the country for

18. Parents Involved in Community Schools v. Seattle School District No. 1 et al., 551 U.S. 701 (June 28, 2007).

19. Eliza Shapiro, "Only 7 Black Students Got into Stuyvesant, N.Y.'s Most Selective High School, Out of 895 Spots," *New York Times*, March 18, 2019; Eliza Shapiro and K. K. Rebecca Lai, "How New York's Elite Public Schools Lost Their Black and Hispanic Students," *New York Times*, June 3, 2019.

Black youth and the seventh for Latinx youth, while 80 percent of Black and Latinx students in racially segregated schools in the state come from low-income families.[20] And we know double segregation by race and class is a poor prognosis for educational attainment down the line, as Sean Reardon and his colleagues preview in a recent comprehensive study of eight years of data from all public school districts in the U.S. To quote their conclusion directly, "If it were possible to create equal educational opportunity under conditions of segregation and economic inequality, some community—among the thousands of districts in the country—would have done so. None have."[21]

Turning Our Backs on Linda Brown's Dream of Educational Opportunity

How, then, did we, a country built on the aspiration of *E pluribus unum* and the strength to be garnered in civic life from unity in diversity, come to turn our backs so sharply on Linda Brown's dream in the education of our future majority? How is it now that public schools like Stuyvesant and scores of others from South to North, West to East, no longer can be counted on to ensure the educational road to full participation of our increasingly diverse generations on a path to college in our knowledge economy, signaling a distinct problem for the prosperity of our nation going forward? The answer, as Orfield compellingly tells us in this volume, rests in large part on three elements: First is the forty-year myth of the merit of colorblind educational policies and practices for primary and secondary schooling. Second, colorblind policies and practices are further hampered by the tenacity of residential segregation in the United States and the concomitant segregation of the nation's public schools. And third, there is no escaping the cumulative racial inequalities and concentration of poverty that take such a toll on children and families and that then spill over to define life at school. As he says, schools are supposed to be the equalizer, but they are not anymore. "The fact that a very large share of Black, Latino, and Indian students are concentrated in the schools dealing with the constant challenges of students and families devastated by

20. Gary Orfield, Jongyeon Ee, and Ryan Coughlan, *New Jersey's Segregated Schools: Trends and Paths Forward* (Los Angeles: Civil Rights Project, November 2017).
21. Reardon et al., "Is Separate Still Unequal?," 35.

poverty, and often almost totally isolated from middle-class students and families, is an incredible obstacle on a path to college."

It is precisely that path to college that must now be reconstructed, but it will not happen if we close our eyes to the realities of race in America. It will not happen if, instead of engaging in activism reminiscent of the civil rights era, we show a relentless penchant for blaming achievement gaps on the very children, teachers, and schools that suffer under the colorblindness that has dominated since the Reagan administration's turn away from school integration starting in 1981. We need, rather, to face the ways in which we as a nation have condoned persistent opportunity gaps and turned our backs on the color-conscious policies and practices that created a generation of "children of the dream," profiled by Rucker Johnson in his account of the successful paths of Black students in the integrated schools of the South, during the brief life-span of civil rights progress.[22] We need, as Orfield outlines in this volume, color-conscious policies that systematically create learning environments, especially in high schools, with college-preparatory curriculum, strong and consistent teaching, college counseling, peer expectations for college, and early exposure to college life. We know how to create these learning environments, and study after study shows how the school choice landscape of the past several decades has led even outspokenly progressive parents of white students understandably to choose those largely segregated but successful learning environments for their sons and daughters,[23] while neighborhood-based district policies result in the double segregation by race and class that persistently derails students of color from the pathway to college and upward social mobility. As this volume asks, are we ready as a nation to systematically change policies and practices in order to embrace the talents of the new majority?

Showing the National Courage to Embrace Our Diverse Future

This book series, Our Compelling Interests, is built on the aspirational premise that diversity is an opportunity, one that our nation ignores at its own peril, and as Orfield convincingly articulates, we simply cannot go forward leaving

22. Rucker C. Johnson, *Children of the Dream: Why School Integration Works* with Alexander Nazaryan, (New York: Basic Books; Russell Sage Foundation, 2019).

23. Christina A. Samuels, "White Parents Say They Value Integrated Schools. Their Actions Speak Differently," *Education Week*, February 5, 2020.

so many on the sidelines of educational attainment and therefore without a fighting chance at economic prosperity. If the inequality gap between the richest and poorest households in the United States now stands at a fifty-year high,[24] and inequities in access to good jobs by race and ethnicity have substantially grown in recent decades,[25] just imagine what it will look like as Frey's "diversity explosion" continues to remake the face of America and yet we do nothing affirmative about educating the very groups that are growing and that have historically been excluded. We need instead a policy about-face on the order of the 1960s civil rights and war on poverty platforms. We need new approaches to districting to desegregate our schools while we also work to revamp the learning environments in our neighborhood schools. We need colleges and universities, especially public institutions, to engage in expansive talent search and support programs that reach what Anthony Carnevale and his colleagues say is already an available pool of Black and Latinx college-qualified students. Such an effort would help equalize representation by race and ethnicity at selective public colleges,[26] so long as state and federal financial aid policies shift back to take the burden of higher education off the backs of low-income families. And yes, all of this and the many other specific suggestions in this volume will take hard work and collective commitment, but do we have a choice? How can a nation imagine a future without educational opportunity broadly spread to change the equation for the Black and Latinx children of urban metros, the poor white students in rural Appalachia, or the Native Americans forgotten and isolated in reservation communities across their rightful land? Moreover, as John B. King Jr., former secretary of education, reminds us pointedly, "Diversity is no longer a luxury; it's essential for helping our students get ready for the world they will encounter after high school and, increasingly, throughout their lives."[27] It is our collective responsibility to step to the plate as we once did, and perhaps then we too can make pivotal changes like those that were achieved in a decade that empowered a generation long grown of children of the dream.

24. Chris Lu and Harin Contractor, "Donald Trump's Economic Record Isn't What He Says It Is," *Washington Monthly*, February 5, 2020.

25. Anthony Carnevale et al., *The Unequal Race for Good Jobs* (Washington, DC: Center on Education and Workforce, Georgetown University, 2019).

26. Carnevale et al., *Our Separate and Unequal*.

27. Alyson Klein, "Ed. Sec. John B. King, Jr to PTA: Diversity in Schools Benefits All Students," *Education Week*, July 12, 2016.

1

Colorblind Higher Education Policy in a Racially Stratified Society

AMERICAN SOCIETY is well along in a great transition, nearing the end of its white European majority, but it is failing to educate its future majority. If our society is to succeed, the country and its institutions, including its colleges, must find ways to offer real opportunities to groups they have historically subordinated and discriminated against. There is no real alternative, given the birth and migration patterns that have been changing our communities for a half century. White birthrates have been below the replacement level for four decades, and immigration is the reason we have not aged out as drastically as many peer nations. Our colleges need to reflect a changing nation. The great wave of immigration from the 1970s until the Great Recession was overwhelmingly nonwhite, something we've never experienced before, though it was restricted at least for a time under Donald Trump.[1] College enrollment has declined since 2010. We have campuses that were designed to serve the white middle-class society of the past and are now challenged to adapt. If we are to have the educated workers and leaders an advanced economy demands, we have to reach groups that have long been neglected. If we want to bring together our polarized communities, sharing higher education can be a powerful tool. We have never achieved higher education equity for Black Americans or for our native peoples. The children of a vast immigration from Latin America have become our largest minority and have not received equal opportunity. Since 2000, three-fifths of the nation's most selective public universities have had a decline in Black enrollment and Latino students' access has declined relative to their growing population.[2] How can the higher education system respond? Do we understand the roots of the crisis? Is there any plan?

Americans see college as decisive in the lives of students. You can see the clear pattern in Gallup polls across the decades. In 1978 more than a third of the public thought college was very important, which rose to 58 percent in the early 1980s and 70 percent by 2013. College education came under attack by sectors of the rising conservative populist movement in the Trump administration, and the number saying it was very important dropped somewhat, but only 11 percent, one person in nine, said it was not important.[3] Blacks and Latinos were most likely to say it was very important.

The social and economic impacts of higher education are dramatic, and the inequality of opportunity for students of color[4] and those from poor families is systemic. Typically, college completion makes a major difference in terms of employment, earnings, wealth, and even the probability of marriage and good health. It is strongly related to voting and public involvement, thus to power in the political system and to the health of democracy. In 2016, in a period of unusually low unemployment, among people aged twenty-five to sixty-four, 84 percent of college graduates were working, compared with 68 percent of high school grads and 55 percent of dropouts. Among Blacks the numbers were even more dramatic: 85 percent of college grads had jobs, but only 61 percent of high school grads and a dismal 39 percent of dropouts did. Latino college grads had about the same level of employment as their white and Black counterparts, 84 percent, and their employment shares with less education were the highest—72 percent for high school graduates and 65 percent for dropouts—but the quality of the jobs and incomes were low.[5] The problem for Latinos is the low level of degree attainment. The situation is particularly threatening for males of color. College-age Black males are about one-seventh of the nation's male population but they receive one-twelfth of the college degrees (8.5 percent). Latino males are more than a fourth of the nation's college-age males but they receive one-ninth of the degrees (11.2 percent).[6] The huge gap in college attainment for men of color is a basic cause of poor employment and income, low levels of marriage, involvement in the criminal economy, and many other problems that affect not only the men themselves but also their families and their communities.

There are gaps at every stage. People of color are less likely to graduate from high school, less likely to immediately enroll in college, less likely to go to a four-year college, substantially less likely to graduate from college within six years, far less likely to get increasingly important postgraduate degrees, and less likely to be employed or get equal wages afterward. If colleges are to help heal the wounds of separation and inequality in U.S. society, better policies are needed at many levels.

College education is critical in America's twenty-first-century society. It is the key to opportunity and the pathway to a middle-class life. It has become, for most, the boundary between a life of possibilities and resources and a life of struggle and immobility. In our recessions, college graduates are largely protected while others suffer; in times of prosperity, they get a greatly disproportionate share of the gains. There are, of course, nongraduates in fields like the skilled trades, small business, or good union jobs who do well, but the overall pattern is clear, and college is the high road to success. If the huge gap in college completion continues between whites and Asians and other students of color, wide racial differences will be perpetuated into the rising generation. Since college is so critical to their families, the advantage will pass into children's lives. Students of color have the desire and make the attempt, but they often do not have the preparation and means for success.

Students from all groups have been starting college at higher levels than in the past, but the gaps in completion are actually widening. Starting college somewhere is good, but where you start matters. After enrolling, students must succeed and have the financial means to continue if they are to reap the gains that come from completion. Admitting a student with severely defective preparation or who cannot pay the coming bills often leads to an academic tragedy. A big loan debt without a degree can be crippling. Weak preparation in clearly inferior schools where almost no one is well prepared is a huge barrier. Very capable students find they simply haven't been given the academic skills other students have received. Starting without the means or extended family support to pay college bills, even with student loans, may make success impossible. These are the second and third walls that must be crossed if we are to move toward equity and real development of students' capacity.

The First Wall: Admissions
and the Affirmative Action Struggle

America's selective colleges, both the private ones and the strong public flagship universities, were overwhelmingly white institutions throughout their history until the civil rights movement. Almost nothing serious had been done to integrate U.S. colleges before the movement, which reached its peak in the mid-1960s. In 1965, the year of the Selma march, the Voting Rights Act, and the first large urban riot, the selective schools of New England, for example, professed their readiness to welcome Black students but had only 1 percent Black enrollment.[7] Students, faculty, and local community organizations identified with the great movement for racial justice developing in the South and put pressure on their institutions to take action. Affirmative action became a central tool when selective colleges recognized that their normal processes had never produced significantly integrated campuses and classes and that it would not happen without making it a clear goal and changing policies and practices as needed to make it happen.

The reality was that admissions on the basis of a traditional formula for "merit" and the special treatment of children of alumni and other groups who had special skills, often fostered by special opportunities, guaranteed that there would be little representation of students of color who were being ill-prepared in highly unequal segregated schools and whose parents were not alumni and had limited resources.[8] Test scores were relied on, but scores are very strongly linked to family income and parent education. Privileged children gained from family and school educational resources and experiences.[9] In a society where housing is strongly related to the quality of school opportunity and families of color lack the income and savings or housing equity of whites and Asians and often face housing discrimination, unequal local schooling is built into the racial structure of communities. We have had a strong, deeply rooted, long-established web of inequality, and it did not change itself. Waiting for more traditional students who simply had a different skin color wasn't a workable model. To overcome those and other realities, colleges had to try to assess factors such as teacher recommendations, commitment, and desire to learn, and actively recruit unprecedented numbers of students of color to their campuses. In our extremely unequal society, colleges found that they must consider the circumstances of students of color to fairly assess them and also institute a variety of support efforts on campus.

Colleges had to face the hard realities of race if they were to become diverse. Most Black, Latino, and Native students were from families and schools with more limited resources and did not have the preparation needed to score well on the standardized tests. Many lacked normal prerequisites because of their school's limited curriculum or weak counseling. Their families, on average, had much lower incomes and vastly lower wealth, as well as different needs from those of traditional students. That meant that the normal financial aid policies and assumptions often wouldn't work. They had to convince the students of color to come to campuses where they would be isolated in an overwhelmingly white population with white student organizations and, often, some racial hostility. They had to plan academic support. This was the situation in the Ivy League, the competitive public flagships, and strong private colleges and universities. The response to the demands of the civil rights era was voluntary race-conscious action, and it soon began to make a significant difference, moving colleges from virtually all white to a modest level of diversity.[10] In the South, the passage of the 1964 Civil Rights Act and the 1965 Higher Education Act meant that there were more federal funds and that universities segregated by law could put their federal dollars at risk if they did not take positive action, though that received little attention until the 1970s when a court ordered the Nixon administration to take action to enforce the 1964 law.[11]

It was obvious at the outset that all kinds of adjustments had to be made if the campuses were to integrate and students were to succeed. The hope was that the enforcement of civil rights changes and the many social reforms of the Great Society would help solve the underlying problems of inequality over time, but the country took a long, sharp turn in a conservative direction. Many of the domestic programs were drastically cut back and progress on various fronts stalled or even reversed. The Supreme Court, changed by conservative appointments, became far less supportive of broad race-conscious remedies after President Richard Nixon was able to appoint four justices. By the 1980s, under President Ronald Reagan, the country faced a sharp reversal in both civil rights and social programs.[12] It has yet to recover.

Although the affirmative action policies became rooted in many campuses and the failure to close huge racial gaps made it apparent that the underlying problems were not solving themselves, affirmative action was repeatedly challenged. The ideas that civil rights policies were unnecessary and amounted to discrimination against whites produced continuous challenges. The battles surfaced in three crucial Supreme Court decisions from 1978 to 2016, in each of which affirmative action survived by a single vote in a deeply divided Court. Two of the cases were argued and decided during administrations working to end affirmative action. In the first great decision, the 1978 decision in *University of California Board of Regents v. Bakke*, the Court prohibited setting aside a specific number of seats for students of color, a quota, but held, by a single vote, that universities could consider racial diversity as a "plus factor" because of the educational value of diverse experiences to the university and all students.

As the courts became far more conservative in the 1990s, there was a major attack. A striking decision by a court of appeals, *Hopwood v. Texas*,[13] ruled that affirmative action in Texas was unconstitutional. The same year, the voters of California passed a state constitutional amendment that outlawed affirmative action,[14] which stimulated similar action in nine other states. Two lawsuits against the University of Michigan brought the issues back to the Supreme Court in 2003. The Court held, by a single vote, that it was illegal to simply add points for race in a mechanical admissions formula but that an individualized comprehensive admissions policy considering race as one of several factors was legal.[15] The Court ruled that there was convincing evidence that racial diversity was an educational benefit and a compelling interest that justified this limited consideration.[16] There was a major mobilization of higher education in defense of the university. (After winning the case, however, Michigan opponents succeeded in enacting a state referendum barring affirmative action, and the referendum was upheld by the Supreme Court.)[17]

The issue came back to the Court twice in two decisions in the case of *Fisher v. University of Texas*. The university was widely believed to have the strongest existing alternative to race-conscious admissions, the 10 percent plan, in spite of analyses showing its shortcomings.[18] The 2003 *Grutter* decision had recognized and relied on all the research concluding that campus diversity was a "compelling interest" in enriching the educational process, and the Supreme Court agreed in the *Fisher* cases.[19] Now the question was whether there was a workable alternative that would produce diversity without considering race. In the first decision, the Court accepted the idea that there was a legitimate compelling educational interest in campus diversity but concluded that the lower courts had not demanded sufficient proof from the university that there was no colorblind way to achieve the needed diversity.[20] After serious documentation by the university, the Supreme Court ruled that there was sufficient evidence of the absence of a workable alternative and upheld the university's affirmative plan by a single vote in a 2016 decision written by Justice Anthony Kennedy.[21]

Affirmative action was, in practice, an important but modest policy. It never came anywhere close to producing proportionate representation of students of color in selective universities. Stanford professor Sean Reardon and associates concluded that in spite of affirmative action, whites were five times as likely as Blacks to attend selective campuses.[22] As student demand for the most selective campuses soared, students of color were more squeezed out. A 2015 report of a national survey of admissions offices showed that the large majority of selective campuses, except for public institutions in states where it was illegal, found it was crucial to continue affirmative action. Affirmative action for low-income students was not seen as a substitute. In fact campuses practicing affirmative action for race were also practicing it simultaneously for students from low-income families.[23] Extensive research analyzing admissions variables, considering many alternatives and combinations of variables, found no feasible alternatives that would produce anything like the results of affirmative action at a cost that universities could manage.[24] Although it affects a small share of students, it has a substantial impact on the institutions that train most American leaders and the students of color who would have been excluded but show that they can meet the requirements and become important leaders in many institutions.

The Harvard Case

The second Texas decision seemed to settle the legal challenges for the time, but Justice Kennedy, who had provided the decisive vote, left the Supreme Court. President Trump was able to name three justices and push the Court further right than at any time in the last several generations. The same organization that had masterminded the two Texas challenges was in court challenging the Harvard University affirmative action plan, claiming that it discriminates against potential Asian students with higher test scores. In November 2020 the Court of Appeals for the First Circuit ruled in favor of Harvard, holding that the university had not discriminated and that its plan complied with the standards in the Michigan and Texas decisions. In its ruling the court cited Harvard estimates that its enrollment of Black, Latino, and Native students would fall by 45 percent if it could not practice affirmative action.[25] This decision headed to a very conservative Supreme Court in 2021.[26] In mid-2021 the Supreme Court asked the Justice Department for its views on the Harvard case, making it likely that it would be heard. If affirmative action is ruled illegal and declared a form of discrimination, it would be prohibited by the 1964 Civil Rights Act and consequently prohibited at all public universities, and private universities would also have to stop using it because they would risk losing federal funds—something none could afford—and face massive lawsuits.

During the civil rights era, the courts had made a sharp legal distinction between conscious efforts to exclude students on the basis of race, which were illegal, and conscious efforts to bring them in to reduce segregation, which were fine, a necessary part of a remedy that worked. As the courts became more conservative, any consideration of race, for positive or for negative results, was considered highly suspect. The two sides saw two different Americas. The affirmative action supporters saw a society torn by deep and persisting divisions that could not be repaired without an intentional systemic and persistent effort, and they read the Fourteenth Amendment's guarantee of "equal protection of the law" as the basis for positive remedies for groups that had long experienced systemic discrimination in society. The opponents saw a society that had once had serious discrimination that had been solved by civil rights law, and now had no major racial problems; a society where there was danger of being unfair to whites. This division in the courts is echoed in public opinion.

I am convinced that affirmative action is crucial for both student and faculty diversity. Without serious plans, universities tend to favor the best-prepared students and faculties tend to replicate themselves. I have witnessed in so many ways the powerful benefits of diversity in the six research universities where I have been privileged to teach and conduct research. Before affirmative action, the admissions wall in selective colleges was a formidable barrier for students of color. Affirmative action opened some very important gates at least part way. I have edited two books on the issues of diversity and alternatives,[27] one of which was cited by the Supreme Court in the *Grutter* decision, and done a great deal of other research on the subject. This book was conceived when affirmative action seemed secure at least for a time, but now, with the three very conservative justices nominated by President Trump, it is likely that universities will be forbidden to implement race-conscious policies. This book is part of a long intellectual, legal, and political debate over how to fix the large gaps in educational success that tend to exclude the great majority of Black, Latino, and Native people from most of American society's best opportunities.

Affirmative action, in any case, dealt with only one of the three great barriers considered here. Recent trends indicate that affirmative action is needed and needs to be strengthened even to avoid going backward. But it has always been only one of the needed solutions and substantially affects only a small sector, less than a fifth of U.S. colleges, since most campuses admit most or nearly all of their applicants. The other walls discussed here are important at all campuses and in all systems.

The civil rights movement led to the first major breakthrough in the history of exclusion in higher education and continues to have an impact. Selective colleges went from virtually all-white student bodies to a significant presence of nonwhite students. The initial focus was on Black students, but it expanded to include Latinos and American Indian students. In some places Asian students or Asian subgroups were included. Much of the largest change happened in the South under strong pressure from federal civil rights officials and courts. In other places, it was voluntary, often in reaction to protests by students of color and their supporters on the campuses. The new status quo that emerged a half century ago was one of modest voluntary diversity efforts, except in the states where any kind of race-conscious policy was prohibited. It continued over the years, but there were no new major goals. Many of the racially targeted support programs and financial aid efforts were abandoned as the attacks on race-conscious programs intensified. As the nonwhite share of young people grew substantially, the colleges fell behind in maintaining their level of access. The pattern of faculty diversity followed a similar course. The reality was limited access and representation and little priority for the effort, but a desire to continue it if possible. Things were much better than before affirmative action but far from full integration. Colleges did not have another plan that could maintain or expand the existing level of success.

Our colleges are powerful institutions, respected across the globe, institutions that change the lives of individuals and communities. We are falling behind in the rising levels of education across the world, largely because of our failure to educate nonwhite and poor students. There are deep divisions concerning how we can change the outcomes and whether success will require policies that explicitly take race into account. If the Supreme Court abolishes affirmative action, the best evidence shows that leading colleges will be substantially more unequal. Civil rights advocates will need to struggle to get it back. If a change in Court membership can discard a precedent reaching back more than four decades, another change could bring it back.

Colorblind or Color Conscious?

Since the Reagan administration, the basic approach to fixing racial inequality in the U.S. has been to deny that it is racial and to insist that it is the result of nonracial forces and that colorblind solutions will be fair to everyone. The historic 2020 Black Lives Matter protests across the U.S. challenged those assumptions and both affected the incoming Biden administration's civil rights proposals and triggered a fierce reaction, with many conservative states adopting policies prohibiting teaching about negative aspects of U.S. race relations.[28] In a society where winning racial remedies rest on an understanding of the origins and persistence of discrimination, history has a powerful impact, and prohibiting serious discussion of racial history is part of an effort to erase critical understandings.

There are deep partisan, regional, and racial differences in beliefs about the nature of racial inequality.[29] Even among those who perceive discrimination, there is no consensus about positive steps to take. Among white Americans, there has long been more willingness to recognize that there are racial problems than to support any concrete solutions.[30] There were no major expansions of civil rights or urban policy laws enacted between the early 1970s and the Biden administration. The policy arguments are about what the problem is, what is necessary to produce significant changes, and what is permissible under the prevailing current constitutional doctrines. Underlying the debate are theories and beliefs about the nature of racial inequality in our society, the history and roles of our institutions, and the effectiveness of different policies.

This book is part of that debate. It examines evidence on the degree to which inequalities are race based, critically examines the historical role of higher education in relation to our racial divisions, and discusses the policy history and current needs. The book comes in the wake of the largest demonstrations against racial discrimination in U.S. history, the 2020 Black Lives Matter movement, and after four years of profound racial division in national politics during Trump's administration, a government that fiercely opposed race-conscious policies, appointed hundreds of new conservative judges, and wanted to end affirmative action and prevent colleges from teaching about race. It comes after a national election in which the winning party promised large new investments to make college affordable and relieve debt. The hope that we had become a postracial society was dashed by the Trump period. Many had said that the election of President Barack Obama showed that race did not matter, but he was followed by a president whose campaign from the first day was about racial fears and stereotypes.[31] There was a frightening resurgence of armed white supremacy groups, some advocating violence to try to keep Trump in power after he lost the 2020 election and invading the U.S. Capitol to try to block the electoral votes from being recorded. The U.S. has not arrived at a nonracial place.

After more than a half century seriously discussing minority access to college, a time with much rhetoric about racial justice in higher education, there have been some real successes, but policy has stagnated with the job less than half done. This book is written with the conviction that the goal of racial equity is essential and requires different outcomes from our colleges and universities and more effective strategies from the policy makers who have power over them. Many agree with this goal of equalizing college opportunity, but since the end of the civil rights movement in the early 1970s, there has been little focus on directly addressing the racial dimensions of systemically unequal education. The Supreme Court rejected efforts to equalize school spending and most school desegregation efforts were abandoned in the 1990s. We have been, with the exception of affirmative action admissions, trying to solve racial inequality indirectly through policies that operate as if race is irrelevant. It is like trying to use a broom to bail out a boat that has taken on water.

Major breakthroughs toward equity in education require race-conscious and race-sensitive policies. Policies that falsely assume that all groups have equal chances to prepare and ignore deep differences in background, re-sources, and support make the policy problem like trying to find your way through a maze in a blindfold. All of the normal complexities are taken to a new level. Leaders promise to create equality but the solutions fail. Reports are written, sometimes there are protests, mission statements are adopted, but the inequality persists.

Racial inequality has always been a basic structure of American society, and trying to change the outcomes as if that were not true has failed. Obviously, we have not broken the cycle of intergenerational inequality. Children of well-to-do families with college experience, strong local schools, and substantial resources grow up in a different world from the one inhabited by poor children in inner-city neighborhoods of concentrated poverty and weak schools. Although affirmative action is important, admission is not the only barrier block-ing students of color from college success. Each of the barriers should be at-tacked with an understanding of the reality of race in students' lives. That can bring light into the maze.

Race-conscious policy is urgently needed, and largely lacking, in two other powerful dimensions—preparation in high school and college financing, the second and third walls blocking success. Students and families of color face different needs and obstacles that must be understood and addressed to sub-stantially alter the outcomes. Policy must not assume that all groups of stu-dents face similar realities when, obviously, they do not. As affirmative action encounters continuing threats, addressing the other two barriers becomes even more important. To succeed in college, you must be reasonably prepared to do the work, able to be admitted to a college that can foster your success, and have the resources to pay the large costs so you can study and return each fall. Lacking any one of the three is crippling.

Colorblindness as a Solution?

The absence of policies designed in light of the realities students of color face has been justified by the claim that our policies are colorblind, that they are designed and implemented as if color were irrelevant, and that this is the best, and even the only, legitimate way to design college diversity policies. This theory and the affirmative action bans in several states assume that sufficient diversity will just happen. The continuing efforts to overturn affirmative action nationally are based on a conservative assumption that it is unfair to whites and Asians. This is the view of many Americans who believe that the society is basically fair. This book argues, however, that in the generations before the civil rights revolution, we did not have what some remember as an idyllic condition of fairness and equity in our colleges. Exclusion, not colorblindness, was the basic reality until there were civil rights policies. Diversity happened when leaders and institutions decided that it must happen and took positive steps to make it happen, steps designed to directly change racial outcomes. Since the conservative movement, colorblind policy has been dominant and it has failed. It has failed because the assumptions on which it is based are incorrect. Racial stratification in the U.S. is systemic and has powerful self-sustaining processes. Where there was active color- and class-conscious policy in the civil rights era, large progress was made. Ignoring race means accepting ongoing inequality.

Colorblindness is a subject much discussed in sociology and in critical legal scholarship, where it is often treated as a destructive white misinterpretation of a racially polarized society in which many whites assume that systemic racial discrimination and inequality have been solved, that things are basically OK, and that policies ignoring race will suffice. If it is claimed that there is a level playing field, when that is clearly incorrect, the resulting policies will not only fail but actually be used to shift the blame for continuing inequality to the victims, justifying racial subordination. Often in critical scholarship, color-blindness is described as a tactic for protecting white privilege. On the conservative side, in sharp contrast, color-conscious policy is considered anti-white racism, illegal, and unnecessary since the inequalities are not caused by race.

Colorblind policy means that policy makers refuse to consider inequalities by race as justifying special attention to nonwhite groups. Colorblind policy can be based either on the assumption that there are no longer legitimate issues of race that policy makers need to respond to or, in other cases, on a philosophical or legal theory that is radically individualistic, insisting on individual responsibility for one's own destiny free of government interference as the basic proposition of American society. Although it is now impossible for even the most fervent conservatives to deny that there are long histories of slavery and segregation by law or that there are large gaps in college attainment, they assume that racial discrimination is no longer a significant reality and that racial problems were cured as much as possible by the enactment of the antidiscrimination laws and court decisions long ago. Advocates of colorblind policy often claim that when they look at people they "don't see color," meaning that they have no views or stereotypes triggered by color and they look at individuals without any distortions. When faced with obvious inequality in college opportunity, they tend to blame individual shortcomings or cultural inferiority of the groups left behind.

Conservative legal theorists maintain that race-conscious remedies violate basic principles of equal treatment and that any such policy corrupts the political and social order and discriminates against whites and Asians. Opponents of race-conscious policies tend to blame the continuing inequalities, easy to see in American communities and institutions, on deficiencies of institutions serving people of color and differing economic conditions, not something wrong with society. They hail nonwhite individuals or institutions that perform well with no special support, using their success against the odds to describe large inequalities as simply problems of will and grit. Implicitly, those who do not succeed in spite of multiple obstacles are assumed to not be trying hard enough. If anyone can succeed against all the odds, then everyone should. Often the resulting policies attempt to punish the minority-serving schools and colleges that fail to succeed, assuming that there is no racial barrier and they are not trying hard enough. This was a basic assumption of the No Child Left Behind law of 2002, which dominated public school policy for thirteen years and continues to be the basic assumption of many state education policies.

Colorblind policies assume that looking at individual accomplishments and ignoring race in making educational decisions is fair. Their proponents argue that the failure of students of color could be caused by too much pampering by low standards and by what they see as a big welfare state. All of these claims are widely shared and articulated by conservative policy makers, in the courts, and by one of our national political parties. President Ronald Reagan's first inaugural address, for example, called for a dramatic turn away from social programs after a campaign and a history critical of civil rights. In his address,

Reagan said, "Government is not the solution to our problem; government is the problem." He attacked too much focus on helping any one "special interest" group and promised to make all the working people his special interest group. He warned of "unnecessary and excessive growth of government" and called for reliance on individuals and the market.[32] His government cut and reversed social programs and civil rights programs, sometimes going into court to do so. Often the colorblind argument contains an implicit or explicit claim that civil rights policies discriminate against whites and Asians who have higher average test scores.

Opponents of race-conscious policies argue that the only fair way to select students is to compare their individual accomplishments. They see high scores as products of superior talent and hard work and discount the role of family and school advantages. They ignore structure and think that whatever comes out of the market is best, allowing people to buy advantages. They see nothing illegitimate in providing very different high schools to people who live in different areas, even when those areas were, in fact, defined by racial practices in zoning, land use, mortgage discrimination, realtor steering, and so on (they tend to attribute residential location to choice, not discrimination). If school differences mean that some groups get better preparation and a much higher share of admissions to strong colleges, then it must be because they have more individual merit. Their individual accomplishments, measured by test results, entitle them to the best college opportunities since there are no systemic problems that require attention. The arguments become an endless circle: If systemic racial discrimination is excluded, then those who receive the bulk of the strong college opportunities (disproportionately white and Asian students from higher-income, more highly educated families) are more deserving. People of color, unfortunately, have less merit. That is not a racial problem. Individuals and communities of color need to work harder to seize what opponents of race-conscious policies see as abundant and fair opportunities.

The Intellectual Framework of the Debate

Both the nature of academic research and the kind of scholarship that becomes very visible and is celebrated in a given period significantly reflect the ideology of those controlling the government, funding much of the research, and holding the power podiums for publicizing and rewarding research and using it to justify policies. During the height of the civil rights movement in the Kennedy-Johnson period, there was strong focus on research on race and poverty.

Government and foundations funded and publicized it. Beginning in the 1968 election with Richard Nixon's "Southern strategy" and lasting to the present, the Republicans have had an agenda about rolling back civil rights policy and shrinking domestic social programs. When conservatives control government and set the agenda, they spotlight research adopting the colorblind perspective. Democratic liberal presidential candidates (Hubert Humphrey, Walter Mondale, John Kerry, and Michael Dukakis) lost elections, and winning candidates (Jimmy Carter and Bill Clinton) eschewed liberalism and adopted moderate policies in the political climate created by twelve years of strong conservative dominance under Reagan and George H. W. Bush. Democrats wanted to stay away from the sensitive racial issues that had divided their coalition, and they shifted to issues of the suburban middle class. During this period a variety of academic and quasi-academic arguments justifying colorblindness received a great deal of attention in the media and in politics. When President Barack Obama took office, he largely avoided explicitly racial policies.

Writers produced works that either directly attacked race-conscious civil rights policy as an attack on the rights of whites or argued that it was unnecessary from a more class-based or ethnic orientation (such as Black Power), or they presented data criticizing government action on civil rights and poverty, favoring nongovernmental solutions. Most of the colorblind arguments came from the Right and were linked to the issues pressed by the Reagan administration, which saw targeted social policies as paternalistic and ineffective and advocated cutting social programs and forcing people to make it on their own. Some researchers assumed that the jobless had not tried hard enough. There were widely publicized researchers who argued that welfare dependence was destroying initiative and families.[33] Schools were failing, according to one prominent argument, because they were subject to control by elected officials and too influenced by powerful unions. The cure was nonpublic education.[34] Another set of studies claimed that public schools were failing because they did not have the moral and communitarian values of private religious schools; this research was used to support vouchers.[35]

A major national report from the Reagan administration claimed that educational achievement had plummeted because the schools that were failing (largely minority schools) had lowered their standards and must be held accountable.[36] The claim of academic decline was shown by later analyses to be seriously inaccurate,[37] but almost all states raised testing and accountability following publication of that report. This was the dominant educational policy from the 1980s through the Obama administration. From a more progressive perspective, there were prominent authors of color who insisted that enough was known to educate all students well, whatever their circumstances, implying that when schools were turned over to leaders of color who cared more about students, performance would be much higher.[38] Sociologist William Julius Wilson became famous for *The Declining Significance of Race*, a book that argued that it was a mistake to focus strongly on race-oriented issues and that the basic problem was a collapse of the Black community because of economic conditions that could be cured by tight labor markets.[39] An argument favored by Black conservative writers claimed that affirmative action was destructive because it created stigma, devaluing the accomplishments of all Blacks.[40] The ultimate step in the retrogression from the ideas of the 1960s was the resurfacing of the idea of genetic inferiority in a highly publicized 1994 book, *The Bell Curve: Intelligence and Class Structure in American Life*, coauthored by a Harvard professor.[41] Though there were books making quite different arguments, in this period the government, much of the press, business leaders, and others hailed critical works blaming the schools and government programs, not the society or discrimination; this was seen as cutting-edge and realistic work. There was little attention and little support for those arguing for more race-conscious policies. And there was little progress.

During this long conservative and "neoliberal" era, when white public opinion held that there was no need for further action and the conservatives in power were dismantling civil rights policies, these works had widespread influence and supported the proposition that race-conscious civil rights policies were counterproductive and unnecessary, that the obvious inequalities in outcomes were not the responsibility of society or major institutions but of the communities of color themselves and the institutions that worked with them. The major thrust was to trust the market and private institutions, end civil rights policies, and oppose both race-conscious and social welfare programs, which, they said, were actually destructive, needlessly harming whites.

The conservative presence in politics and Republican governments and the ideology they espoused was considerably strengthened by the creation of think tanks and legal action organizations explicitly dedicated to their cause. Back in the 1960s, the centrist Brookings Institution was the only major think tank in Washington, but large resources were poured into the expansion of insistently conservative think tanks—the American Enterprise Institute, the Heritage Foundation, the Cato Institute, and dozens of counterpart institutions in a number of states and regions. Conservatives opposed to civil rights and expansive court protections developed great power in the Federalist Society and in a series of litigation organizations modeled on the NAACP Legal Defense Fund, which has done powerful work in expanding civil rights. These organizations were deeply influential in generating both program ideas and support for conservative administrations and in changing the composition of the courts and the direction of constitutional law. The net effect, according to author Jason Stahl, was to shift "the whole plane of political debate rightward—foreclosing nearly any policy possibility to the left of the 'New Democrat' position on a whole host of issues."[42] Affirmative action was a major target of these groups, which were amply funded by a network of conservative foundations and major donors.[43] The heavy investments in think tanks and related institutions changed the balance of power and the range of political discourse and made it commonplace for news coverage to present the neoliberal policy as one side of the debate and the conservative side as the other, basically excluding policies that reflected the findings of a growing number of major university researchers as well as the positions of civil rights lawyers in battles in the courts and agencies. Beginning in 1972, Republican appointees had the majority on the Supreme Court, an increasingly conservative majority, reaching a peak under President Trump.

From Nixon's rise in 1968 until the 2020 election, there was no successful presidential candidate advocating major new policies of racial justice. Color-conscious remedies were being dismantled in the courts. The Democratic Party establishment largely adopted the "neoliberal" strategy of the Democratic Leadership Council, which staffed much of the Clinton and Obama administrations. In that period, traditional liberalism (sometimes called the "L word" to denote its political toxicity) was considered politically obsolete. The arguments of the progressives, in sharp disagreement with neoliberalism, insisted that colorblindness and the main lines of neoliberal arguments were factually absurd—that opportunities are still systematically denied to Black, Brown, and Indian students who are so separated from and negatively perceived in the mainstream that they face extra obstacles at every step. The relationships were not hidden. You could walk from a school in a ghetto or barrio community to a nearby middle-class white community or suburb and go into what was theoretically the same class and see obvious differences. Those arguments were largely ignored for decades. Empirical evidence was accumulating, much of it ignored for the time, that race remained a fundamental problem and that ignoring it or trying to force change while ignoring its realities through colorblind policy generally produced well-meaning failures.

When I was in graduate school at the University of Chicago, Professor John Hope Franklin, the great historian of Black America, would talk about how after Reconstruction ended, white research on Black rights largely disappeared for generations and the consensus developed that it had been a mistake to try to achieve equality for the freed slaves. Scholars became famous for books in which they depicted the restoration of segregation and subordination as a natural and acceptable outcome and criticized the Reconstruction for disrupting the white society of the South. Much the same thing happened in the recent conservative era.

Race-Conscious Research

There were, however, scholars of all races who did keep working, often with limited attention to race-conscious policy. During this period, integrationist policies were being dismantled in the right-wing courts and often dismissed as old-fashioned in the media and on campus. For example, J. Anthony Lukas's *Common Ground: A Turbulent Decade in the Lives of Three American Families*, presenting the Boston school desegregation conflict, which was probably the worst in the U.S., got the Pulitzer Prize and far more attention than all the writing on the more positive experiences in many parts of the country and, later, even in Boston.[44] It was a message welcomed by the Reagan administration, which was changing the courts and asking them to dissolve desegregation plans.

Throughout this period there were scholars, civil rights lawyers, and others examining data and historical records that undermined the colorblind assumptions and theories, but they seldom got major grants or attention from public officials of either party and were rarely featured in the media. They confronted courts that were being staffed with conservative judges and justices who increasingly embraced colorblind theories as a basis for cutting back or reversing civil rights policies. There were civil rights lawyers and Black and Latino leaders working to call the nation's attention to what they saw as blatant violations of equity for people of color. In many cases they found such compelling evidence that they were able to defend civil rights policies in many communities until the Supreme Court turned further right in the late 1980s and early 1990s. Douglas Massey and Nancy Denton's *American Apartheid* and other works showed how strongly unequal opportunities were linked to residential segregation.[45] Lee Rainwater and others documented the social disaster created by public housing projects that concentrated very large numbers of very poor people of color in areas without jobs or schools that worked.[46] Urban historians were documenting the history of ghettos and barrios, showing how they had been created and how they were treated by public officials.[47] *The Closing Door: Conservative Policy and Black Opportunity* explored Wilson's theory that tight labor markets would be a solution and showed that the Atlanta boom produced good jobs and education for whites but that they were not shared with Blacks.[48] There were studies of the frustrations of the long struggles for educational equity.[49] Thomas Carter, Roberto Segura, and the U.S. Commission on Civil Rights did pioneering work on the discrimination and inequality facing Mexican Americans.[50] Mary Pattillo-McCoy documented how even successful middle-class Black families faced strong obstacles that middle-class whites did not.[51] There were studies showing that the race-conscious remedies in the Voting Rights Act had profound effects on Black political participation in the South.[52] Melvin Oliver and Thomas Shapiro showed how the enormous difference in wealth by race related to previous discrimination and profoundly shaped family resources and opportunities.[53] Scholars including Robert Crain and Thomas Pettigrew produced important works on educational segregation and the conditions for positive race relations.[54] Until it was taken over by conservatives under Reagan, the U.S. Commission on Civil Rights continued to document racial inequality and the federal failure to fully enforce civil rights laws.

Most of the work of scholars whose research supported the need for further civil rights efforts was ignored in national politics and, increasingly, in courts, but as the affirmative action showdown headed toward the Supreme Court, there was a powerful mobilization across disciplinary lines, producing evidence for the educational benefits of diverse education, and it did make a difference. The University of Michigan invested heavily in supporting research, scholars from across the country produced studies, and leading national scholarly associations submitted a joint brief summarizing relevant research to the Supreme Court.[55] William Bowen and Derek Bok's book, *The Shape of the River*, provided key evidence on the long-term success and careers of beneficiaries of affirmative action in terms of the high level of academic success and lifetime contributions. When the decision was handed down in 2003, the Court's opinion written by a conservative justice, Sandra Day O'Connor, relied directly on published scholarly books and the brief of the social research organizations in establishing the compelling justification for diversity policies, a rare event in the Supreme Court.[56] That decision provided the basis for preserving affirmative action till the present.

The affirmative action success in the Court in 2003 was an important but isolated victory. The Supreme Court was limiting a wide range of civil rights policies on school integration, voting rights, minority contracting, and others, relying on colorblind assumptions. There would not be a significant pro–civil rights change in political climate until the 2020 election. The Democratic primaries that year included major candidates on the left and historic demonstrations against discrimination taking place in all parts of the U.S. The election of a moderate candidate, Joe Biden, whose nomination was determined by Black leaders and voters, and the explosion of the largest racial justice protest movement in American history moved national public opinion about the need for action. But the colorblind philosophy was still widespread and deeply entrenched in the judiciary, which had been transformed by Trump appointments, and in many state governments and school systems. Worse, the demonization of people of color by Trump's political movement stimulated a substantial expansion of white nationalism.

The period between the Reagan presidency and the Trump presidency was a time in which the Democratic Party had increasingly abandoned liberal ideas and formulated a strategy designed to win the suburban middle class, which now had the balance of electoral power. The Democratic Leadership Council was formed in 1985 to move the party to the center, deemphasizing race and poverty issues and focusing on struggling middle-class families.[57] Arkansas governor Bill Clinton became its leader. It led to at least partial acceptance of many conservative policies in areas such as welfare cuts, increased incarceration levels, and social program cutbacks. Both the Clinton and Obama administrations continued the Reagan-era test-driven, high-accountability standards as the basic strategy for schools and increased tax subsidies for middle-class college costs. In education, increased funds went to charter schools while public magnet school funding, intended to foster diversity, was minimized. Accountability was central. Proposals for requiring equal opportunity to learn were rejected. The institutional status quo was largely accepted. The federal government stopped filing new school integration litigation. The basic public school educational policy dominant from 2001 to 2015 was No Child Left Behind—requiring that schools meet strict yearly gains for all racial groups and punishing them harshly if they did not. In higher education, this period brought a focus on outcomes, graduation rates, and repayment levels of student loans.[58] The Obama administration, until its final year, followed the same basic policy line.

Academic Attack on Colorblindness

Eduardo Bonilla-Silva's 1997 article "Rethinking Racism: Toward a Structural Interpretation" and his 2003 book, *Racism without Racists: Color-Blind Racism and the Persistence of Racial Inequality in the United States*, offered an interpretation of the great disjuncture between the evidence of inequality almost wherever researchers looked and the commitment of the basic institutions to denial of the importance of race. After studying the language and beliefs whites used to oppose the need for civil rights remedies while expressing abstract support for minority rights, he found that there was a white insistence on viewing racial issues at the level of overt individual offenses against minorities and not seeing the consequences of systems and beliefs that perpetuated subordination even without any visible individual acts of discrimination. Whites, he said, were very open to other explanations. "Whites rationalize minorities' status as the product of market dynamics, naturally occurring phenomena, and blacks' imputed cultural limitations." There was a dominant ideology that "explains contemporary racial inequality as the result of nonracial dynamics."[59]

Increasingly in the following years, critical scholars would picture colorblindness not as an innocent reality but as a strategy to protect white advantages and block change. Public opinion studies find that white and nonwhite people see the issues of race very differently. For whites they only rarely appear on the list of most important issues that the Gallup Poll tracks over the years, usually in response to a crisis. Whites over time are more accepting of rights for nonwhites in general, but they usually think that enough has been done and rarely favor any expansion of the actions.[60] In terms of race-conscious policies of affirmative action in college admissions and employment, fair housing, and school desegregation, there is usually division and no desire for further action. Blacks and Latinos, on the other hand, tend to perceive serious inequality and far more discrimination and tend to be far more supportive of positive governmental action. This book does not rely on any claim that whites are a unified group that has a strategy of "opportunity hoarding" and wishes to subordinate people of color. Proving intent is very difficult, and any student of public opinion knows that most Americans have little specific information about policies or history. And it is clear that white Democrats and Republicans have dramatically different views on race. It is enough for this book to document actions, outcomes, and policies that have racial effects, whatever their intent might have been. Policies ignoring race and embracing inaction in the face of evidence of systemic inequality do have the impact of protecting white advantages, whatever the intent.

The reality is that the colorblind approach is strongly connected to basic elements of American ideology that usually limit both the perception of systemic discrimination and the need for strong governmental action to repair the damage. We are a racially stratified country with a strong ideology of individualism and suspicion of government. That may not be logical, but it is true. It is an ideology embraced by a great majority of whites. People of color are more in favor of government action for civil rights, but a significant share of all racial groups share the ideology. As documented in his classic *Democracy in America*,[61] Alexis de Tocqueville traveled through the young nation studying its values and institutions and observed that, in a society that had successfully defeated an autocracy, government was limited, mostly operating in localities. Classic nineteenth- and early twentieth-century commentaries on American society and its institutions noted the same qualities. James Bryce, in his *American Commonwealth*, observed, "Everything tends to make the individual independent and self-reliant. He goes early into the world; he is left to make his way alone; he tries one occupation after another, if the first or second venture does not prosper; he gets to think that each man is his own best helper and advisor."[62] Herbert Croly, in *The Promise of American Life*, writes about how America was seen by the European immigrant as a land of economic opportunity where one could "enjoy the fruits of his own labor," "a New World in which economic opportunities are much more abundant and accessible." Similarly, native-born Americans believed in a future of expanding opportunity.[63]

The U.S., from its foundation, tended to embrace a set of beliefs often described as the American dream—the idea, described as "rugged individualism," that the society was open, that a person could make it on his or her own, as in the Horatio Alger story of poor boys who work hard, find a way, and eventually, through their determination and effort, achieve the dream. Since the great majority of white Americans are descended from various streams of immigration, many families have a highly valued story of struggle and success in their histories and myths. The Black migrants from the South to the North and West had such dreams as well, and so do many in the huge migrations from Latin America and Asia since the 1970s. In spite of evidence that inequality is deeply embedded even among whites and mobility now is less than in a number of peer nations, this dream is still widespread. In a society with limited social policies, Americans focus on the belief that people can and should acquire enough education to make their dream come true.[64] When there is a basic belief that people can and should make it on their own and that all have a reasonable chance, it makes it difficult to argue that there is systemic discrimination and that problems should be treated as a group rather than among individuals. So the call for systemic remedies to racial discrimination is an uphill battle working against strong ideological currents. The realities of society, however, diverge very sharply from this ideology. In his Howard University speech, President Lyndon Johnson made that case and spelled out its implications:

> You do not take a person who, for years, has been hobbled by chains and liberate him, bring him up to the starting line of a race and then say, "you are free to compete with all the others," and still justly believe that you have been completely fair.
>
> Thus it is not enough just to open the gates of opportunity. All our citizens must have the ability to walk through those gates.
>
> This is the next and the more profound stage of the battle for civil rights. We seek not just freedom but opportunity. We seek not just legal equity . . . but equality as a fact and equality as a result.[65]

That speech, however, was an outlier, and those ideas were strongly rejected by the conservative movement and the neoliberals. We did not hear speeches like Johnson's from the White House again until the early Biden administration when the president discussed the deep and continuing impact of racism.

The measures normally used to evaluate individual success are not, in reality, measures of individual merit but are heavily weighted by group advantages in opportunity. Good jobs and high incomes reflect not only hard work but initial advantages and connections that are strongly related to race. Fairness requires adjustments and supports to take into account the barriers to the development of individual talent. Progressives maintain that what the opponents see as measures of merit are actually strongly related to privilege. They are reflections of advantages of family, community, and school resources, which should not be used in ways that perpetuate and justify inequality and punish the victims of discrimination today who suffer the intergenerational effects of past discrimination. Progressives hold that there is strong evidence that race-conscious policies including voting rights, college affirmative action, and school integration have clear benefits for people of color, take nothing away from whites, and foster more positive race relations.

Social scientists played a major role in some of the epic struggles occurring in the courts as the political tide turned against civil rights. Increasingly, researchers worked to dissect the assumptions of the colorblind ideas that were fueling the abandonment of civil rights remedies. Conservatives hold that there was a point at which discrimination was cured and, as a systemic force, ended. Civil rights advocates concede that positive policies, when implemented, produce important gains, but that those policies have been largely abandoned and were, in any case, not nearly powerful enough for long enough to substantially break the intergenerational inheritance of unequal starts reinforced by the continuing inequality of opportunities. Progressives argue that there has never been a break in the chain of inequality and that the intergenerational effects of parents' education, their access to buying homes in desirable communities, and their employment and income are powerful transmitters of advantage to successive generations.

Race shapes lives in many ways, and students of color face inequality from the earliest parts of their lives. The data show that racial inequality is many sided and involves life before school, family resources, quality of schooling from the beginning, segregation in unequal schools, very different opportunities and preparation in high school, the massive financial inequalities that affect children and their choices, and other aspects of life.

This book begins with stark data on inequality. It moves beyond the issue of access and admissions, the great issue of affirmative action, to the issues of systematically unequal preparation and profoundly unequal financial circumstances, the second and third walls that have to be overcome for college success. It looks at the history of policy along these dimensions, showing that, as high schools and colleges emerged in American society, they were designed for and largely educated middle-class white students. It shows that, apart from the brief period of the civil rights revolution, our educational system has worked more to embody and perpetuate racial inequality than to overcome it, apart from affirmative action in the highly selective colleges.

At present, unequal treatment by race and different outcomes persist. Colleges, in spite of positive efforts, are part of the problem. Though universities and higher education organizations are fighting to preserve affirmative action in selective colleges, those programs are limited in scope and clearly inadequate. Affirmative action has been outlawed in two of the nation's three largest states, California and Florida, and eight others. As the country has changed, there have been no major additional race-based initiatives since the civil rights era, and affirmative action is threatened again by lawsuits and a solidly conservative Supreme Court. The enormous changes brought by huge Latino immigrations have been largely ignored in civil rights policy.

This book argues that the current failure of higher education policy is rooted in an inadequate understanding of the realities of racial inequalities, all the racial inequalities outside the schools, and the widespread assumption that policies that ignore race can solve problems rooted in race. When policy is designed with the assumption that you can ignore race and be fair, it fails because the situations of different racial groups are distinctive in ways that must be considered to produce successful options. Since whites and Asians, for example, have, on average, many times more wealth than people of color, a well-intended college finance policy written by those with wealth and a margin of long-term resources will seldom be written in ways that make sense for those who have very low or negative net worth (more debts than total assets). Success requires effective policies before college as well as at the entrance to college and on campus. If your school did not provide training in basic precollegiate skills, the chance for success in a strong college is much lower. If you have the ability to succeed but do not have the money to go, you are much more likely to fail to enroll or be unable to continue. In my final chapter I outline what I believe are the most effective policies to move higher education forward.

For a half century the policy battle on higher education for students of color has been focused on the admissions issue. But the two other large walls block many students of color and the admissions gains are strongly threatened. The second wall is inadequate preparation to succeed in college, and the third is getting enough money to actually go to a school of promise and persist to graduation. The wall of admissions is, of course, critical for the minority of powerful and influential institutions with significantly selective admissions and requirements, some of which have enough money to give those admitted full support. The great majority of those institutions decided long ago that they have to consider race as part of their recruitment and admissions policies to create an integrated student body. Though most also practice affirmative action for low-income students, direct consideration of race is seen as necessary to the creation of significantly interracial student bodies. For the other institutions and the other two walls, there is no parallel set of practices, and today's policies are colorblind.

Because civil rights groups and higher education advocates have had to spend so much time trying to defend and keep existing programs, there has been far too little thought about what is actually needed to provide equitable education in a polarized society where most whites do not see a serious racial problem. Many believe that whites are actually discriminated against. White racial fear and stereotypes erupted in the 2016 election. Much existing education policy is based on a tacit assumption that racial animus has been largely cured and has no continuing effects that policy needs to address. These assumptions were sharply challenged in the 2020 protests across the nation.

Why Not Give Up on Race Policy and Just Focus on Poverty?

If it is too hard to deal directly with race, can't we figure out another way to solve the problems without raising the political and legal challenges to solving racial problems? Some assume that equal access can be solved indirectly by concentrating on poverty and that it would be much easier politically. Richard Kahlenberg of the Century Foundation has made this argument repeatedly, even sending amicus briefs advising the Supreme Court to take this course on school integration and affirmative action. Conservatives often suggest this approach. Since some of the problems confronting students of color are economic, wouldn't it work to simply have affirmative action for children from low-income families? The critical assumptions are that political leaders and the public would be much more ready to support this solution and to put up the funds to do it because, in college admissions, the most expensive students to aid are those with no family resources and those are also students likely to have weak schooling and need serious academic support. But in reality, conservative governments have cut back help to the poor and, in the gigantic Bush and Trump tax reforms, sharply reduced revenue for social programs through large tax cuts for the rich and corporations, increasing inequality. Reagan ended the War on Poverty in 1981. The federal government simply surrendered.

Although many colleges seek to help low-income students, very few are able to meet the full financial need that would actually permit more students in poverty to attend. Admitting students from families without any money and sending them aid packages that have an unrealistic "family contribution" and a large unmet need either keeps the students away or presents them with terrible choices. Unquestionably, programs are needed for the poor, and clearly there has not been any great impulse for sustained action on poverty. With many colleges in financial trouble and most unable to afford to meet the aid needs of existing students, it is highly unlikely that they will make targeted recruitment of those who need much more and can pay little or nothing. For these colleges to say that you can only pursue racial diversity by admitting students in poverty is to say that you cannot do it on any scale in most colleges.

Advocates favoring a shift to a poverty focus often discuss it as if people of color are all poor. However, though they are far more likely to be poor than whites, the substantial majority of Blacks and Latinos are above the federal poverty line but still experience unequal treatment on many levels. In 2016 more than a third of Black children (34 percent) and more than a fourth of Latino children (28 percent) were classified as poor, but only one-eighth of white and Asian children (12 percent).[66] A 2021 Census report showed that Black families were far more likely than others to experience persistent poverty. It's true that Black and Latino children were about twice as likely as whites to be in families with a high housing cost burden in 2016, meaning that they often had much less money to spend on other things, including education and health,[67] but it's also true that many millions of nonwhite families are homeowners but, because of housing segregation, often do not get the same opportunities as their white counterparts or the same gains in housing equity. Even when they are safely out of poverty, students of color face obstacles much more serious than those affecting whites.

Focusing on poverty would include many whites who are not poor in the same way as poor families of color. Many whites live in poverty for a time, when they are studying, sick, looking for a new job, recently divorced, caring for a new baby, and so on, but it is often a spell of poverty rather than a life in poverty. A 2021 Census Bureau report shows a highly significant racial gap in long-term poverty.[68] Obviously poverty has many dimensions with quite different meanings and consequences, and there are strong intergenerational effects of deep concentrated, persistent poverty, which is far more likely for families of color. A poverty definition would also bring in many children of recent immigrants whose parents have not yet found good U.S. incomes but have higher education in their native countries, strong educational capital for their children, and strong long-term prospects—not the kind of U.S. minority colleges especially want to help.

Victims of racial discrimination include many people who are not poor. Many middle-class people of color often experience discrimination and unequal treatment that has nothing to do with poverty but much to do with stereotypes and discrimination—things such as police stops, differential treatment of job applications, and many others. When I taught big graduate school classes at Harvard, sometimes I would ask, "Who has been followed by a security guard in a store in Cambridge recently?" It was always Black men, people with excellent records training for future leadership at Harvard. There is an overlap between race and poverty, but full treatment of race issues cannot, in its nature, be reduced to poverty. A focus on a simple current income definition of poverty will direct attention to include a much larger population from groups not experiencing the distinctive racial obstacles and thus reach a smaller number of students of color or cost a great deal more to admit the same number of students of color. Because the best-prepared students of color are not likely to be the poorest, class-based policy excludes many who might have greater likelihood of success on campus. If campuses only use poverty to indirectly identify students of color, the students of color they admit are likely to reinforce campus stereotypes that students of color are poor and to deny the campus community an understanding of the rich diversity within as well as among racial groups in the U.S.

There are very important historical and legal reasons to focus on race. Racial subordination was fundamental from the earliest days of European settlement. Race discrimination is forbidden by the Constitution in amendments that are one of the principal results of the Civil War. Unequal treatment by income is not unconstitutional. Race is an immutable characteristic outside the control of individuals. Income is not. Slavery was about race, not class, and slavery was a fundamental shaper of the nation. Conquest and subordination of Mexicans and Indians after the conquest of their lands was about race and ethnicity, not class. For most of our history we have had almost caste-like racial separation and intense stereotypes. In Trump we had a twenty-first-century president who trafficked in inflaming racial stereotypes. We are only one generation away from the operation of racially separate public universities in nineteen of our states. Because of these basic features of history and law, race discrimination occupies a special position.

A troubling part of the debate regarding a focus on race versus poverty is the assumption that advocates should be forced to choose one or the other. But there have been no large initiatives on either front for decades, even as the society reached extremes of economic inequality. Policy makers and researchers debate what should come first. Should there be more money for segregated schools, for example, or more efforts to open the doors of white and Asian schools? Should college admissions pay most attention to one or the other? This book will show that in times when there was serious attention to race, there was also serious attention to poverty. In times when civil rights efforts were reversed, there were also cuts in the programs aimed at the poor. It has not been either-or but both-and or neither.

This book shows that class is not race and race is not class, though they overlap and both are important. The origin of severe persisting poverty for families of color was often racial discrimination in earlier generations, which produced diminished opportunity over time. Conservatives tend to assume that racial discrimination is like a bacterial infection that was treated and goes away with time, but it is actually a serious chronic condition that requires continuing treatment and surgery. Of course, poverty, lack of a home, lack of wealth, and many other inequalities are both important and profoundly related to the history of racial and ethnic inequality in the U.S. Students of color who are in the middle class often face inequality and discrimination on multiple dimensions. And there are students whose families have low income but strong social capital and support systems, such as new immigrants with well-educated parents currently earning little. We have a complex society, and it pays to look carefully at simple claims of equivalence.

There are important aspects of contemporary social science methods that can lead to a serious underestimation of the importance of race in shaping unequal outcomes. Most social research is contemporary. It is looking at a cross section of variables at a recent point in time and exploring the statistical relationships among them, sometimes with very complex mathematical modeling. If the discrimination occurred long ago, it was not measured, and if is not actively present today, it is easy to think that the differences are not caused by racial factors, though they actually were. A cross section is a photo of a moment. An analysis rooted in history and longitudinal data is a movie, something that better shows origins, development, and dynamics. This book examines a wide range of data and research on persisting racial differences in many aspects of life as well as historical data on gaps and the persisting nature of colorblind policy in our divided society. The second and related obstacle is that so many people of color, particularly those with negative outcomes in education, are both poor and nonwhite. When you are doing the analysis, you want to control for one variable when estimating the impact of the other. When they both are present in the same people, what you choose to subtract from the equation matters. If you subtract the relationship between poverty and failure to earn a college degree from your estimate of the impact of race, it becomes much smaller and vice versa. If poverty is treated as an independent variable and the reason for the poverty (often, for people of color, earlier racial experiences) is not known, you may get a serious underestimate of the overall effect of race.

A major study following people through multiple surveys over eighteen years in Chicago highlighted the weakness of much contemporary work on race that grows out of failing to deal with the dimensions of time and history.

"Despite theoretical motivation stemming from assertions of the importance of 'cycles of deprivation' in earlier classic studies," Kristin Perkins and Robert Sampson write, "the trend in poverty research in recent years has been to dissect individual components and to estimate the effects of specific dimensions of poverty." They argue that we must learn what happens to real people over time. The research showed that the inequality was more tied to race than income. Whatever their income level, Blacks were much more likely to live in areas with higher joblessness and concentrated poverty. Blacks who were not poor lived in less organized communities than poor whites. When looking at multiple inequalities, "compounded deprivation" was "virtually nonexistent" for whites, worse for Latinos, and "far more serious" for Blacks. The evidence, Perkins and Sampson suggest, means that "common strategies to dissect or tease apart the effects of what are closely linked social realities that unfold in interconnected form over time do not capture the true impact of race."[69]

Those issues are central to the theme of this book. Discrimination operates over time, and there has never been a decisive break in the endless chain of inequality. There has never been a period when these groups have had income or education or health care or housing that was equal to that enjoyed by whites. There are many obvious ways in which the impact of past discrimination causes conditions such as poverty that should not be used as "controls" in estimating the impact of race because they are, in substantial measure, the product of earlier discrimination and inequality. This may seem like a technical question, but it can lead to a gross underestimation of the impact of race.

Situating the Problem

This book shows that both the preparation for college and the ability to afford college are profoundly related to race, and always have been, in a society of deeply segregated schools and vast differences in wealth by race. Making race invisible and adopting colorblind policies came with a concerted attack on systemic civil rights and educational policies beginning in the early 1970s and reaching a high point in the Reagan-Bush period. Under Reagan the Justice Department became an advocate of reversing color-conscious rights policies. The department's staff included now Chief Justice John Roberts and Justice Samuel Alito, strong affirmative action opponents. Clarence Thomas had experience in reversing civil rights policies in the Education Department and in employment discrimination before being named to the Court. Now we have several justices on the Supreme Court who worked in conservative battles, both state and national, against civil rights policies.[70] It was a period when a basic goal was to deflect the blame for minority inequality and the responsibility for fixing it from white society to the victims. The public discourse has been impoverished ever since.

This book looks at race in many ways. It confronts at the outset the idea that race is no longer a problem. I argue that race is fundamental to the college access crisis and that the financial and other issues are not the same across racial and ethnic lines and cannot be solved without understanding the highly consequential differences. This book documents very important racial differences in many aspects of life, differences that have educational impacts and cannot be solved unless they are explicitly addressed. It shows that the existing colorblind remedies are far from sufficient. It shows still pervasive inequality in many aspects of American life that mean that Black, Latino, and Indian students have little chance to be equally prepared for the college success that they and their families want.

Policy has been very sharply constrained by ideas of what is politically feasible and by conservative control of the courts for several decades. What is "feasible" often does not work. This book is focused on what would. It gives special attention to two aspects of an unequal system—the highly segregated and unequal high schools that prepare students for success or failure in college, and the financial barriers that are often insurmountable for families of color who have lower incomes, dramatically less wealth, less information, weaker networks, and responsibilities that white families often do not face because they are in an extended network of need rather than support. The conservatives who organized to reverse the civil rights revolution did not look at what was feasible at that time but at what they believed. They won key elections and made key appointments, and we live with the consequences of their success. People and institutions concerned with racial justice need to undertake similar long-term efforts and to base them on awareness of the real problems and solutions derived from evidence.

High Schools Must Be Part of the Solution

Weak preparation can destroy the chance for college success. Colleges aspire to be the answer to equal opportunity and mobility, but in general, in spite of some excellent efforts, they are a major part of a system that perpetuates intergenerational inequality for students of color. Extremely unequal secondary preparation and deep financial inequalities by race must be confronted to produce better outcomes.

The tacit assumption in the higher education policy debate is that, in general, policy can ignore race except in the case of modest positive consideration in college admissions at selective colleges. This book argues that race is fundamental to the crisis, that the experience of students from different races is profoundly different, and that financial differences, segregated and unequal schools, and other issues are not the same across racial and ethnic lines and cannot be solved without understanding and fixing the consequential differences. At a time when the one surviving race-based policy, affirmative action, is under fierce attack, this book argues that race-based and race-sensitive policies must be extended much more clearly into high school preparation and college financing. If the Supreme Court moves against affirmative action, keeping these issues in focus will become even more important.

American society has always been racially separated and unequal and has always had stereotypes and discrimination, both individual and institutional. Usually, as is evident in public opinion polls and political agendas, civil rights issues receive very low priority, and most Americans, especially most white Americans, do not see more efforts as necessary. Most people of color disagree.[71] Sometimes racial stereotypes and the idea that people of color get special treatment are used to trigger conservative votes, as in the Nixon, Reagan, and Trump campaigns.

Schools and colleges are the largest public investments in our society. Back in the 1960s, when civil rights was a basic issue, policy was largely about ending overt discrimination against African Americans and other excluded groups, getting rid of traditional Southern laws and practices, and giving Blacks and other people of color a chance for fair treatment in education, jobs, housing, and voting. Major new funding was provided for high-poverty schools and for financial aid for poor students to go to college. Sweeping civil rights policies were enforced for a time. As the 1960s ended, the country was going through urban riots, and the civil rights struggle, which Martin Luther King Jr. brought to Chicago, was focusing on the problems of urban decay and segregation. The Black Power movement and the Vietnam War struggles divided civil rights advocates. The country took a sharp turn away from civil rights with the election of Nixon, whose campaign featured searing film of Black rioters and embraced anti–civil rights conservatives in the "Southern strategy." By the time of Reagan, there were sharp reversals, with the president attacking "welfare queens" and insisting that sanctions and markets would solve educational inequality and that no focus on race or expansion of social policy was needed. Government was defined as the problem, not the solution. Government withdrew. People began to assume that race-conscious policies had failed and there was a better answer and that it was wrong or even illegal to focus on race, though race was the underlying problem. Far too often people assume that policies that were discarded by conservative governments and courts had failed. In shaping the future, it is essential to examine the best evidence on what actually happened. Most readers of this book, more than they might realize, have been immersed in a post–civil rights politics. Civil rights advocates don't assume that any policy will produce huge changes in the short run. Students of color are, on average, seriously lagging in preparation as they approach college. This book summarizes very powerful data documenting persisting group inequalities in opportunity that affect preparation.

Deepening Consequences

As times have changed, the success of families in the economy has become more and more linked to a higher education system, which is not free and open but increasingly selective, with costs rising far more rapidly than family incomes. Educators see their values as far more egalitarian than those in corporate America, but too often education is stratifying and legitimating stratification and conferring advantage on the advantaged through its credentialing systems. The society has been changing more rapidly than people can keep up with as older whites from the last period of rapid family growth, the postwar baby boom, are retiring and being replaced by less educated people from less privileged groups, very often people of color. Our politics have ignored these basic facts and provided more resources and opportunities for the most privileged groups, as in the highly skewed 2017 tax reform and the tax subsidies for college directed mostly at those who actually are able to go to college and have enough income to make tax-based subsidies valuable. The debates on the cost of college in the 2020 primaries suggested that the issues of access and support are becoming more central.

Apart from limited strategies by individual institutions and limited initiatives in a few states, there is no credible plan to move the country toward truly equal educational opportunity in the public schools. Four decades of claiming that it could be done by ignoring race and putting intense pressure on schools to raise test scores have failed.

The Stakes

The U.S. developed as a white society with a significant Black minority concentrated in the South and a few big cities outside it. It developed as a society where higher education was not very important. Its civil rights policies came out of a great movement, mostly in the South, sixty years ago. What it is, what it's becoming, and what our economy needs have changed beyond recognition since we created our major civil rights laws and policies. Higher education policy focuses mostly on aid to students and help with debts and on meeting institutions' budgets. Leaders want diversity, but it's usually a secondary issue and many institutions have not made substantial admissions policy revisions as the population changed. If a plan was adopted by a state university back when 10 percent of students in the state were Black and very few were Latino, it hardly makes sense when the state's college-age population has become 15 percent Black and 25 percent Latino. Such a campus is likely to think that it is doing a good job in civil rights. Like any important educational policy, affirmative action needs to be updated periodically, at a minimum raising its diversity goals as the population changes. Leaders have to be accountable.

The civil rights movement was basically about a battle to end legal and institutional discrimination excluding African Americans from the largely white mainstream of the society. Latinos were then a regional minority accounting for only about 5 percent of students and were not even seriously counted by the Census until 1980. Their issues seemed important only in the Southwest and in the greater New York and Chicago areas. In educational terms, the civil rights era was about access to the better opportunities available to whites and integrating largely white institutions.

There is no national initiative now to give Black and Latino families access to the more successful public schools, particularly those families living both within the large sections of concentrated nonwhite enrollment in the highly concentrated poverty areas within central cities and within racially changing suburbs. From 1980 until 2015, federal policy bet on test-driven accountability policies that did not work. Most of the states continue to operate similar policies.

Giving up on a vision of shared opportunity as schools resegregated and civil rights efforts were abandoned, many privileged white and Asian families have opted out to find areas with strong public schools in expensive outer suburban communities or gain access to high-performing magnet or charter schools or, in some states, use vouchers and tax subsidies to enroll children in nonpublic schools at public expense. In higher education the shift has been from an overwhelming focus on aid to the poorest students and trying to keep tuition down, to letting tuitions soar as public financing shrinks after tax cuts slash public revenue. Policies shifted more aid dollars to tax subsidies serving higher-income groups.

Between 1991 and 2007 the U.S. Supreme Court gave up on the goal of the *Brown* decision—to end separate and unequal education by race—and prohibited even the major forms of voluntary local integration strategies that the courts had encouraged for decades. Segregation has intensified, and efforts to open the best schools to students of color have disappeared in many places. Earlier, the Court had decided that the federal Constitution created no right to equal spending on schools, something that state courts have found in some state constitutions. At the federal level there was no right to access for students of color to the stronger white and Asian schools and no right to equal funding or programs. By the 1980s most of the major social policy and urban policy efforts to improve the situation of poor families and communities had been either sharply reduced or eliminated. Race-specific efforts such as requirements that middle-class suburbs approve some subsidized low-income housing have been abandoned, to say nothing of plans to not only create but also integrate such developments. In the economy the inequality of incomes has reached historic highs and the inequalities of wealth by race have soared to shocking levels.

The U.S. had a special situation in terms of the supply of students for colleges and workers for its economy. It was younger than counterpart countries, largely because of immigration, and it had groups of low-paid workers of color who could be called into the labor market when the economy needed more workers. As these policy trends have unfolded, the stakes have steadily grown because the rapid expansion of the U.S. population has ended, the birth rates have fallen far below reproduction levels, and the declining population of young whites in many areas has been mostly replaced by Latinos. The population of high school graduates entering the labor market or college is now past its peak. We cannot count on growth to cover up our failures. If we do not figure out how to educate the people we have, things will deteriorate.

Most discussion about higher education policy is about students who get to college and is limited to what happens in college. There is very little about those who never go, those who go very briefly and leave, those who go to an ineffective community college or a destructive for-profit school, or those who run out of money, get into dangerous levels of debt, work too much, or cannot hold things together when their lives are squeezed from all sides. We need to focus on all young people and especially those who could benefit who don't go or can't stay.

By the time they finish high school, some students seem marked with destiny, some are moving steadily on a clear path, and others have no plan and little preparation. Unfortunately, but very clearly, these differences are related to race and poverty and they matter. Usually, in the development of policy in recent decades, these differences have been treated with more pressure, requirements, and sanctions. The diagnosis has been that they have been the fault of a system that has not put enough pressure on the faculty and the students. It is much more than that.

In the reality of students' lives, for college success, students have to move successfully into and through high school and into and through higher education. High schools and colleges are part of a process that has to fit together for the students. For successful students in middle-class high schools, the fit is built in and usually works well. At its best it is a superhighway from academically intense high schools with strong teachers and curriculum and excellent college connections right into adult life. Millions of students of color, however, mostly from weak public schools, arrive already far behind, entering high schools that have the most inexperienced teachers, unprepared fellow students, and a limited curriculum taught at a less challenging level because student preparation and teacher quality are so inadequate. High schools are blatantly unequal in every important way as launching pads for college, yet the colleges often select and place students as if they all had a fair chance to get ready. Many high schools do not know what happens to their students when they go to college, and colleges give little or no feedback to high schools.

This book argues that the unequal path to college is fundamentally related to race and that the abandonment of desegregation policies that gave millions of students of color access to stronger, whiter schools has made a bad situation significantly worse. In this book I offer a broad exploration of the race-related barriers and inequalities and discuss ways they might be addressed and ways in which colleges can take them into account so that students of color will not be punished for the harm that was inflicted on them. This book shows how the whole process is infected with many types of race-based or race-connected barriers and influences, and how policy and practices that assume that the society has reached a colorblind stage of equal opportunity compound the inequality and blame the victims.

Public schools take children all the way from preschool through high school completion, with a single district normally dealing with stages of life that have remarkably different learning goals and conditions. There is a lot of exchange among schools and staffs from different levels in the system, and there is one superintendent and board who control it all (subject to state requirements). Leaders often have worked at various levels, and many have trained in the same local colleges.

Suddenly, when it comes to the transition from high school to college, a transition the large majority of high school graduates now try to make, none of these conditions are present. College faculty and school officials come from very different backgrounds, they never have the same governing body, and careers take place on one side or another of that dividing line. In higher education there is a robust sector of private colleges but much less in the precollege systems, and most of the private schools have a religious orientation. Each college campus tends to have a good deal of autonomy, and they often compete for students and resources. Students have a right to a public school education. Colleges have far more control over who enrolls, but most colleges admit most applicants. Most students who go to selective colleges come from high schools that serve successful communities with resources and that are organized with curriculum and processes designed to meet college requirements. These are schools where teachers serious about their subject love to teach. They have students who are prepared, and the schools have a serious academic atmosphere. They have college connections and are respected by college admissions staffs. They are institutions with a relatively clear and well-understood mission and operate it with a good deal of success.

At the other extreme there are high schools where most of the students are years behind grade levels, where there are more students in special education, where attendance is a problem, and which have a hard time attracting and holding strong teachers. These are schools where few students are performing at a strong precollegiate level and there are relatively few advanced classes offered because there is limited demand and it is hard to attract specialized teachers. These are schools where there are many students who have been in contact with the criminal justice system and that, sometimes, have gang problems. They are often in parts of town with limited resources where teachers do not want to work. Few of the parents have college degrees and understand what their children need to be college ready. Strong colleges seldom recruit there. These schools often have most of the students of color in the community, and many of those students are from families struggling with poverty and the problems that come from poverty.

In between there are many generally comprehensive schools that try to offer something for everyone. Although they seldom have formal tracks or levels these days, they have courses and teachers that sort out the students. There often are a few advanced and AP courses for the best students and experienced teachers. They also have less competitive students heading for the local community college and jobs in the community. And they may have low-level general courses for those who struggle to finish high school. These schools have complex schedules and choices many students do not understand, but the course choices can make a big difference. Often the students of color end up in the less competitive courses, sometimes because of counselors' stereotypes, sometimes to be in courses with their friends, sometimes because no one notices and no one tells them they have college potential.

The schools in most districts are segregated by race and class, and Black, Latino, and Indian students tend to end up in schools with few white and middle-class students, less expert teachers, and more limited curriculum. Some districts also have magnet schools, district-wide schools with special offerings. Many of these schools were established during the desegregation era with specific recruitment and selection mechanisms to guarantee that they were highly diverse, and the stronger magnets had good reputations and clear paths to college as well as highly motivating special foci and activities. Those schools gave some low-income students of color the kinds of opportunities students in affluent suburbs have. After the local desegregation plans were dropped following the Supreme Court decisions in the early 1990s, many of these schools became colorblind and selected students on the basis of tests and other academic criteria without any focus on racial diversity. In such schools, the number of students of color dropped seriously.

Policy, research, and even data systems tend to treat high schools and colleges as fundamentally different, separate, and independent systems, and while they are institutionally separate and run by people trained in different ways, they are intimately connected through the lives of students who must pass from one to the other. In important ways, high schools are the foundation for advanced work, but many students are not in schools that lay a strong foundation for or have real bridges to college. Most studies of college success start with students who have survived high school and have enrolled in college. Often they only deal with those who have enrolled in four-year colleges. Students who don't make it into or rapidly leave community colleges or go to for-profit schools or into the military thinking they will go to college later are often ignored. Those students, however, make up a large share of students of color, and what happens to those who don't make it or only last for a term or two, or go to a dysfunctional institution, has a big impact on the future of communities of color.

To change college success for students of color, we need policies that strengthen their high school preparation and give them more access to good high schools that are more effective. The last place where we observe the entire population of the age group, because of dropouts, is in the early grades of high school. There are a very limited number of longitudinal studies following cohorts through high schools and for years afterward, and they ask limited questions. Some states have had student identifiers for decades and have data that can track students through high school and into college, but most do not, and the vast majority of research and policy focuses on either high schools or colleges, not their interactions and barriers. Public school research and policy has focused largely on the early years of schooling, much less on high schools, which is much more complex and difficult to research or change. The implicit assumption of policy has been that changes have to be made far before high school rather than to try to alter the education practices of the high schools. The Biden administration's strong emphasis on preschool, which is important but not sufficient, continues this practice.

All stages of life, of course, are crucial for children's futures. For more than fifty years, federal higher education policy has focused largely on the elementary school and preschool. These are very important years. In truth, however, what really immediately matters for college is the high school experience and, in spite of considerable efforts, the test outcomes of high school students have little changed in nearly a half century and the academic gaps between Blacks, Indians, and Latinos and whites and Asians remain very large.

Reforming high schools is more difficult for a number of reasons. Adolescence is a difficult period even for privileged children and is exceptionally difficult for many students of color in concentrated-poverty schools in neighborhoods immersed in poverty. Few students from those schools experience success in four-year colleges. By high school, the racial and socioeconomic status gaps in student preparation are large, often two or three grade levels in achievement scores. Students of color in weak high schools usually lack key college skills such as researching, writing clear narrative prose, using formal English, developing and explaining arguments, and dealing with diverse perspectives.

High schools are large, visible, important institutions with many functions, including preparing students for college and jobs, facilitating social development as adolescents move toward adulthood, enabling participation in activities that develop future talents, helping students build networks and friendships that will last, providing counseling and support to students facing challenges, and many others. We have high schools that are seen very positively by colleges across the country and others that recruiters very rarely visit, ones where almost everyone goes to four-year colleges and others where those who go to college enroll in the local community colleges, many of which lose a large fraction of new students from Black or Latino high schools in the first months.

We have high schools where students drive late-model cars and high schools where it is unsafe for teachers to park their cars and where many students don't have enough to eat. In the first set, going to a four-year college is the default. In the second, those who graduate may try a local community college. The first is overwhelmingly white and Asian, the second, largely Latino and African American and poor. In between these extremes there are a broad variety of schools of all levels and compositions, most offering many of the same courses but taught at different levels and with widely divergent results. Though there have been a variety of ways to try to force changes in curriculum and testing, no administration has proposed or provided incentives for changing the basic system of stratification for a half century. For many students of color, high school is the last chance to prepare for college after weak elementary and middle schools.

The system of stratified high schools radically limits the future prospects of most students of color. If high schools are so unequal, why don't we have serious policies about giving students of color access to the high schools that are most successful in preparing for college? This discussion was virtually killed by the Supreme Court decisions dissolving desegregation plans in the 1990s. School districts could open opportunities. Why don't we have programs to investigate and develop remedies in high schools where very few of the students of color are enrolled in the best courses for the college bound? Why don't we have funds to give college counseling from the beginning of high school to students of color whose families may not know what their children need for college? These will be questions for the final chapter.

Distributing College Opportunity by Money

Higher education, like health care in America, provides world-class opportunities, particularly at its higher levels. But it is very complex and the choices are very different at different economic levels. In this system, money matters greatly. Most families of color do not have substantial college savings and many have none. The lack of money can be decisive, even when the student has great talent and desire. Money and information are both critical. If a family has neither, the student's chances are severely limited. Families with college-graduate parents who have resources and investments can plan ahead, accumulate money in tax-sheltered stock accounts, and often engage in fiercely competitive behavior to ensure that their children get into and go to the best colleges. Colleges have become very expensive but have insufficient aid. Often the barrier of cost is so serious that students and their families never even consider the kind of four-year public university where students are likely to graduate and to be prepared for a good job or professional education.

Families with money see the best possible college as a great investment, the best way to transmit advantage to the next generation. Families without college savings, with moderate incomes, and with little wealth see college choices in a far more limited way, hoping for a scholarship, limiting possibilities to local public institutions, putting the burden on the student to qualify for some help and to take on debt to meet the costs and, often, work during college. For low-income families who rent their homes and have little or no cash in the bank, college depends on a low-cost local community college or a for-profit school that tells them they can go by signing over the proceeds of their Federal Pell Grant and taking out a guaranteed student loan, a complex package that few students understand but that can tie them up in debt for decades. Those with talent hope for the rare chance for an athletic scholarship. Many just look at the costs and decide college is impossible. Often students decide to enroll in the military to qualify for college aid later. These programs do offer significant aid, but as students age, form families, and have other responsibilities or need to work full time, it often is not used. Too often veterans who do use them sign up and use their eligibility at for-profit schools with poor completion and job placement records.

College is a complicated, expensive market in which knowledge and connections matter. Since families with resources tend to have more personal experiences and much better information as well as considerably greater resources, it is a highly skewed market. The published cost of college, known in the trade as the sticker price, appears as the actual cost to many families and seems totally unattainable. To more sophisticated families or those who have assistance from a hired counselor, their high school, or other informants, the published price is just the starting point, since colleges often give most admitted students a scholarship of some sort (a discount) and provide them with an aid package offering some help to meet the costs. For students the college is eager to attract, this can be a radically lower actual net cost of attendance. Some states offer "merit scholarships" for students with a certain level of success in high school and, sometimes, on entrance exams. Students of color are very underrepresented among the recipients of these scholarships, which often go to students without financial need.

Colleges want to offer a chance for all, but in this game, families with resources have enormous advantages. The differences are strongly related to race because of the economics of race and the deep inequalities in the information that families have. In a very complex market, information is power and options. Those from the families with the most resources also have the best information and support in moving through the complex process. At the upper income levels, families can increase the probability of admissions and aid with expensive test preparation courses from groups like the Princeton Review, help in filling out applications and writing personal essays, and a variety of other related services. Probably the most important advantage comes from going to excellent schools with talented and experienced teachers, good college counseling, and strong connections with colleges. If the parents are alumni of or substantial contributors to a college, their children's applications often get special attention. It is a pathway with obstacles, walls, and special shortcuts for some. Money matters very much and is a basic lubricant in this market.

To go to college requires not only tuition, fees, housing and food, and books, computers, and supplies but other living costs. Many students try to offset some of those costs by working. Working more than fifteen hours or so a week can seriously damage academic performance. Many students work too much. Students with full-time jobs often drop out or delay completion, sacrificing years of potential earnings.

Success in college requires not only enough money to get started but enough to continue each year, and students of color tend to take longer to complete. If they do not have enough money to come back, the path is shattered, students have to find a new place and transfer credits, and the chance of finishing somewhere else is lower.

In higher education the basic aid for low-income students, the Pell Grant, fell very far below what was needed to support access to four-year colleges for students with no family resources, even with federal student loans. Many colleges are not focusing their aid on the poor or nonwhites but using what aid they have to drive up the average test scores of their students to improve their reputation and rating or for enrollment management—getting enough students who can pay enough of the sticker price to keep the college functioning. Students who apply to public universities in other states or countries may get admissions preference because they can pay the full fare and colleges in financial squeezes need the money.

We are a market-oriented, capitalist society that values competition and often measures results in terms of money. Policy changes in U.S. higher education since 1980 have dramatically raised the price of college, and stagnant incomes and growing economic inequality have diminished the ability of students of color and their families to pay it. There are predictable racial effects. Controlling for test scores, students from the higher income quartiles have much higher chances of finishing college than similar students in the lowest income quartile, where many families of color are located.

Native American, Black, and Latino families often face financial burdens and have attitudes toward cost and debt that are different from those of white and Asian families with far stronger financial resources. For example, students much more likely to be from single-parent families without adequate medical insurance often are not receiving family money but are called on to help even during college because someone in their family has an urgent need and there is no other source of funds. Those students are much less likely to have grandparents or other relatives who can help. Understanding the financial situations of families of color and how those realities affect the possibilities, perceptions, and consequences of college success is critical to changing the outcomes. If you give students of color aid from a formula worked out for white students, it simply may fail.

Making Higher Educational Opportunity Fair

This book was written with a sense of urgency because things are not getting better over time. Gaps are huge, segregation in unequal schools is intensifying, costs are soaring, and the gaps matter greatly in getting access to college and to jobs. The crises of college costs and student debts became major national issues in the 2020 presidential campaign and the early legislative battles of the Biden administration. The administration acted in its first year to forgive some student debt for some groups of students, tried to make free community college the center of its largest legislative initiative, and requested an increase in Pell Grants. It reversed Trump policy to strongly support affirmative action in pending litigation. It did not propose any major initiatives for four-year colleges or high schools. The community college proposal failed.

This book was also written because of limits in the existing research and policy. Sadly, college and high school systems often operate as if they were on separate planets, under control of authorities who do not communicate well, especially for students of color. Even the researchers and educational leaders tend to focus only on one set of institutions, not the path between them that students must traverse to have a viable future in contemporary U.S society. This is not a problem for students lucky enough to have families and schools that put them on the academic superhighway that goes directly to good colleges, but it is an enormous problem for students who have neither. To create more equity in college, we need to make high schools and their impact on college more equitable and to create more access for students of color to high schools that have a college prep default. Especially for students without advantages, sometimes facing discrimination, it is essential to build well-marked paths where there are no paths.

This book cannot accurately measure the net impact of race on college access—no one can, because of the multiple ways in which race works in society and the limited longitudinal data on many intergenerational factors—but it can lay out many of the race-related dimensions of inequality in preparation and outcomes. Good policy requires broader awareness of the complex power of race in our institutions so that both school and college policy makers at both levels of education may devise race-specific remedies likely to address the real issues that a great many students of color face. Facially positive policies must be analyzed in light of racial realities or they will often unintentionally make things more unequal. If a higher education policy gives substantially more new aid to those who managed to enroll in four-year colleges while ignoring those who saw a weak local community college as their only choice, it will reinforce subordination. We often give the least support to those who have the least and face the greatest barriers. Crossing those barriers requires a much deeper understanding of how they work for students and families of color and readiness to act on that knowledge.

There is a deep concern now about college access by American families. The danger is that in our eagerness to help, we will unintentionally do something that fails. It's easy to assume that if we identify and act on one dimension, such as college debt, it will help all, especially students of color, who tend to end up with high debts if they go to college. Relieving debt takes revenue that comes from all and gives it to students fortunate to have had college experiences, but this does nothing for those who did not go, those who were enrolled in a very weak low-cost institution, or those who were quickly flushed out. If we are to be equitable, we have to take a broader view. The truth is that we have, in important respects, many separate communities and separate social realities with divisions so deep that without knowing about the realities of race, nothing is likely to work as we would wish. The persistence of inequalities in what is rapidly becoming a predominantly nonwhite society will have unacceptable costs and risks if it is not addressed.

The next chapter attempts to widen the lens, tapping into a rich body of research on profound inequalities in many aspects of society that shape the path from birth to college and adult success. We will then take a historical journey that challenges the delusion that we had an earlier period when colorblindness worked, examining what actually happened in the civil rights revolution and why its momentum was lost. The investigation of the many years of the era of colorblind policy that took hold in the 1980s and continues to have large impacts intends to challenge the received wisdom on which many assumptions are based. The last chapter will explore race-conscious and race-sensitive policies that could better address the multiple dimensions of inequality in higher education and make our colleges a far stronger force for equity.

2

Cumulative Racial Inequalities and the Path to College

LIFE IS UNEQUAL for most Black, Latino, and American Indian students in ways that have not been recognized or seriously addressed in our policies for college access. The differences are not in one or two arenas but in many, and at all stages of life, and these differences create barriers and obstacles on the path to college and during college. Racial inequality, racial discrimination, racial segregation, and racial stereotypes and attitudes are basic structures of our society, though many Americans do not see them or even accept their existence. Civil rights opponents often simply insist that equal opportunity is a reality today. Generations of research and national data sources, however, document systemic differences from preschool to family and community opportunities, through college and into adult lives. Students of color are born and develop within systems of multidimensional, cumulative disadvantage. Although this book is about college opportunity and two major forces most directly related to it—secondary education and the ability of students and families to overcome the growing financial barriers—it is essential to understand the depth and range of the forces holding back students of color. Inequality starts long before conception in the experiences of the parents. It carries through until early deaths.

Many Americans are aware of some kinds of inequality, but whites are far less likely to see inequalities than people of color or to understand their depth. Often there are reports on individual issues, but it is important to think about the broader picture. In considering the policy changes discussed later, the many impacts of a complex web of inequalities will help make it clear why so much is needed to overcome the cumulative racial differences. The interventions in high school and college need to be strong because they have a great deal to overcome at a relatively late period of students' development. It is particularly important to keep these realities in mind when analyzing ideas and policies of conservative governments and of substantial portions of the white public that simply deny that there are any persisting racial problems that need to be addressed. At worst, they believe that people of color are getting so many advantages from government that they are harming opportunities for whites, a belief that has been fanned by claims dating back to the campaign of President Ronald Reagan in 1980, which featured discussions of Black "welfare queens" and promised to roll back civil rights policies it said were unfair to whites. People of color, of course, saw a different reality.

Many policy discussions touch on race in relationship to one particular problem or program. Fewer Black students, for example, get AP courses in high school. Cumulative disadvantage is something very different. It is true and important that students of color have lower-quality preschool than white and Asian children do and that the quality of preschool matters. So the natural response is to propose more funding for preschool for communities of color or for all children. In reality this is only a small part of the problems these children and their families face, and providing preschool for all would not ensure that what was provided was equal. Many students of color do not have a stable place to live, a significant share go to bed hungry at night, experienced teachers may not want to work in their neighborhood, there may be no books or educational materials at home, they may live somewhere where it is not safe to play outside, their neighborhood may be a "food desert" where stores don't have fruits and vegetables they need, they may face racist comments or treatment in their school, and children may be constantly worried that their parents may be picked up by immigration authorities while they are at school and deported. Too many children grow up in a world of trouble. Preschool funds are nice, but all the other conditions will remain even if preschool is expanded. The preschool gains, research shows, are likely to vanish in weak elementary schools in their neighborhoods. These children need to be understood in the context of their lives, and remedies need to be considered in that light. Policy makers thinking about the roots of and solutions to their problems need to understand what it means to grow up Black or Latino or Indian in today's society. Otherwise they are likely to fixate on a solution that may be well meaning but may be insignificant or even counterproductive. At worst it would be a solution that made sense in the white middle-class community the policy makers live in but was pointless or even harmful in a very different context.

This chapter injects into the discussion uncomfortable facts on many dimensions of contemporary racial and ethnic inequality. Some facts are taken from careful research studies; others simply reflect basic data taken from public documents on school enrollments, the income and job data of households across the country, and birth statistics. Census data on neighborhoods and cities, public health data, vital statistics, and so on are simply facts. Of course there are many other dimensions of racial inequality. Children and families that always live in unequal conditions often internalize that inequality and lower their aspirations, and that has many consequences. There is what Martin Luther King Jr. called the false assumption of superiority by those on the white side of segregated communities and schools and the false assumption of inferiority among those excluded and confined largely to ghettos and barrios and weak segregated schools. This chapter does not attempt to probe various complex and controversial theories. It is about sad facts that educators and policy makers need to keep in mind as they make decisions where these realities are often not considered.

Research tends to be on single dimensions and directed to specialists interested in that particular field or policy. One study looks at lead poisoning in old houses, another looks at exposure to violence, and a third at the lack of books in poor homes. This chapter shows that for the typical students of color and families of color, it is not one key thing missing but a sequence of obstacles and, often, multiple harmful factors operating simultaneously over time. Most popular "solutions" to racial inequality focus on a single problem and a single solution, such as the three decades of intense focus on the high-stakes standards and sanctions of No Child Left Behind requiring that students of color all be proficient at a fixed time or else very heavy sanctions would be visited on schools and teachers. That was a long, very expensive effort that finally collapsed in 2015, when the whole policy, which had been an overwhelming failure, was almost unanimously abandoned by Congress with the enactment of the Every Student Succeeds Act, which simply punted the problem to the states.

Creating greater equity in higher education access, changing the path to college and bringing greater success in college, requires that we understand the effects of profoundly different resources, unequal information, and discrimination. In a world where success usually requires college, it is not fair to ignore the circumstances of groups that are systematically treated unequally in selecting and supporting students. One of the possible advantages of reforming higher education institutions is that more of those who make decisions are actually interested in data and may sometimes act in response to powerful facts. The intent of this chapter is to help those thinking about increasing college opportunity for students of color to understand the many-sided inequalities over many years that shape the lives of too many of those students.

The inequalities reported here cannot, of course, be addressed only by educational institutions. Facing all the dimensions of racial inequality calls for action also by others to provide more viable opportunities for students to prepare for college and to deal with college costs. Affirmative action was a major breakthrough of voluntary action at elite colleges in the 1960s, but we haven't moved much beyond it. We need policies that start earlier and go far beyond that effort. This book is not about solving all these problems, which involve many basic aspects of American social and economic policy. It is about taking these realities into account in providing realistic preparation for college in high school and in helping families and students in very different situations deal with the rising financial barriers to higher education. For educators and those concerned about educational policy, it should encourage their involvement in those broader discussions.

Research documents powerful relationships between the situation of children's families and communities and the nature of their childhood experiences and the impact of those experiences on later life. A 2019 National Academies of Sciences, Engineering, and Medicine report concludes, "The unfortunate truth is that these striking differences in opportunity are associated with striking differences in outcomes—in health, safety, well-being, and educational and occupational attainment—and in trajectories over the life course. To the extent that these disadvantageous conditions have already impeded healthy development during childhood, failure to address the resulting deficiencies during adolescence represents a missed opportunity."[1] It is essential that the educational interventions to offset some of the negative impacts begin far before college.

The reality is that students of color are much more likely to be exposed to damaging conditions and far less likely to experience the kind of supports needed for eventual academic success.[2] Racial inequality is deeply built into our society, but most high school and college policies are colorblind. We act as if it is fair to ignore realities that often directly affect many young people of color. Whether this is caused by racial animus or simply by policy makers' lack of real understanding of the situation, the impact is the same. Students are judged, and their destiny is often shaped under the tacit assumption that they've had a fair chance. That assumption is wrong and becomes even more mistaken as economic inequality and racial polarization grow. Facing facts involves learning and speaking out on the inequalities on the path to college. Some of these inequalities are caused by poverty, and poverty is often the result of racial discrimination, past or present, but there are others that are simply caused by race and hit people of color of every social and economic level. The offense of "driving while Black," the different exposure to police violence, and the stopping of people who look Latino, demanding documents, along the southern border are among many examples. When I taught a large graduate class at Harvard for many years and asked which students had been followed by security guards in stores in Harvard Square in the last week, it was almost always Black male Harvard graduate students.

A History Whose Impacts Endure

Racial exclusion and discrimination were basic structures of our society from the beginning, and we have never broken the chain of intergenerational impacts and racial stereotypes that continues to shape our society and the development of children within it. There is powerful research showing that students' lives are strongly influenced not only by the situation of their parents but also by that of their grandparents. There is a widespread assumption in the policy mainstream that with the passage of time, things became equal. Though progress was made on some important fronts against racial discrimination, there was also strong resistance and serious backward movements. The more correct general assumption is that inequality tends to be self-perpetuating in the absence of strong countermeasures.

As the great author William Faulkner said, "The past is never dead. It's not even past." This is especially true about race, as Southern writers and historians know so well. So too, those who write about our southern border and the Southwest or trace the history of Indian tribes. American children are not born into a hypothetical society where everyone starts out even but into an ongoing history of racial inequality and subordination that has existed for four hundred years, since the beginning of colonial settlement. Most adults were born after the civil rights era in a time of policy reversals, not in an imaginary time when racial equality had been achieved.

The American pioneers did not merge with the native population as happened in Mexico and Central America but rather saw natives as enemies and warred against them, driving them out of their settlements and taking their land and their rights, sometimes practicing genocide. Slavery came to Virginia from the earliest days and shaped the society and economy of large sections of the country, and rigid racial subordination with Jim Crow was reestablished after the brief period of Reconstruction. Both Indians and Blacks were long excluded from white conceptions of democratic rights, and the acceptance of slavery was fundamental to the bargain that produced the Constitution, a failed bargain, eventually leading to the Civil War. Indian tribes were conquered and forced to accept treaties that were not honored as they were pushed aside and their economies and cultures destroyed. We had many state laws forbidding people of different races from marrying and preventing them from voting until the mid-1960s. Our first president, George Washington, and the primary author of the Declaration of Independence, Thomas Jefferson, were slave masters, as were ten more presidents. Little more than a half century after the Constitution was adopted, a war with Mexico brought under U.S. control half of the territory of Mexico. Although the rights of Mexicans were guaranteed by treaty, their land and wealth were seized, largely through court actions that they did not understand, and Mexicans were driven into subordination and segregation in the Southwest.[3] These conditions went on for many generations without serious challenge, and they became baked into our society and its institutions and beliefs. The resting social decay and poor health in communities of color were treated as signs of inferiority.

A common assumption, particularly among conservatives, is that racial inequalities were largely cured by civil rights laws. But racial subordination was and is the norm, though its form has mutated and is often invisible to those in white communities. Sometimes overt racial discrimination is controlled, but it can burst out again with the igniting of racial fears.

The only two sustained national efforts in U.S. history to break patterns of exclusion and segregation came for a decade after the Civil War and during the decade of the civil rights era from the early 1960s to the early 1970s. After both reform periods, conservative Supreme Courts interpreted away many of the rights that had been established in the periods of reform.

There is little general awareness today that the increasingly conservative Supreme Court since 1980 has interpreted away many of the rights won in the civil rights era.[4] Immediately following the enactment of the major civil rights laws in the 1960s, a sustained effort to roll them back mobilized and has been a central goal of our conservative party since then.[5] The movement to roll back civil rights and to strengthen racial stereotypes reached a peak in the 2016 election, and the Trump administration gained three Supreme Court appointments that created the most unfavorable court for civil rights in generations.

The conceit that centuries of racial subordination were cured by the few years of the civil rights era a half century ago and that we now live in a society of equal opportunity is simply wrong. This idea is accepted by much of the white public and by conservative courts but, as this chapter will show, is inconsistent with scientific research and data collected in many fields.

Education statistics show that there have always been massive educational gaps between Blacks, Hispanics, and Indians and the white population in spite of numerous colorblind policies that leaders claimed would end inequality but failed.

Educational inequality has powerful intergenerational effects that perpetuate inequality even without contemporary discrimination. The grandparents and parents of the students in our schools now did not live and develop in a context of equal opportunity.[6] Most grew up in communities that have always been far behind economically and educationally and were not able to realize their potential, thus raising the next generation with fewer resources.[7] The cycle of discrimination and inequality transfers the inequality of one generation to the next and then to yet another.

School-age children of color have parents with far lower levels of educational attainment in spite of generations of struggle. The levels of all groups have increased, but the gaps are massive (table 1). Over 90 percent of White, Black, and Asian parents were high school graduates by 2019. Almost a fourth of Latinos had not completed high school and a ninth of Indians are dropouts as well. More than a fourth of Blacks, Latinos, and Indians finished with high school. Fifty-four percent of whites and 70 percent of Asians have a bachelor's degree or higher, compared with about a fourth of Blacks, Latinos, and Indians. Post-bachelor's degrees have increased substantially, and Latinos and Indians have had limited success there while Asians have soared, with one in

TABLE 1. Highest Education Level of Parents of Children under Age 18, 2019, by Race (%)

	Less Than High School	High School	AA	BA	MA	Doctoral
White	3.1	14.1	11.0	28.3	17.8	7.8
Black	8.2	26.0	11.1	15.3	9.8	2.7
Latino	22.0	26.5	8.5	13.8	6.1	2.2
Asian	6.3	9.0	5.7	29.5	26.4	14.5
Indian	10.9	25.7	10.6	14.3	8.5	1.6

Source: Digest of Education Statistics, 2020 (Washington, DC: National Center for Education Statistics, 2020), table 104.70, 52.

seven receiving a doctoral degree, and whites are far ahead of people of color. These differences reflect the different human capital of parents of color and have strong intergenerational consequences.

Patterns of Inequality

Families of color are less likely to be married, far more likely to have babies as single parents, and much less likely to have a good job, to own their own home, or to have any significant net worth in our capitalistic society where money matters greatly. Often money and credit mean choices, and lack of resources means having no choices. Children born into single-parent families in poor neighborhoods face much greater challenges in a society with very weak child-care provisions. There is not time to go into the roots of all these inequalities that exist before a child is born, but for instance, people with more education and good incomes are much more likely to marry and raise children in a stable setting, which produces notably greater success for children.[8] People who own homes are more attached to communities and less likely to need to move often. Moving homes tends to disrupt educational progress.[9] People with higher education and wealth are more able to afford high-quality medical care and not have to choose between paying the doctor and paying the rent. Other families are more likely to have children with untreated chronic health problems. People who live with resources and good choices in communities with good support systems usually cannot comprehend what it is like to raise a family with none of those things.[10] The very high degree of separation in our society makes it all too easy for whites to accept the claim that issues of discrimination have been solved or that they are due to personal and cultural failings of nonwhites.

A basic result of previous educational inequality is that the parents of students of color, on average, have far less education than white and Asian[11] parents.[12] White parents are twice as likely as Blacks to have college degrees and two and a half times more likely than Latinos and Indians, which has a dramatic impact on family income and ability to help children in many important ways. For many reasons, parents' education is related not only to their own economic success but to the opportunities and achievement of their children. College degrees are strongly related to higher income, the chance to own your own home in an area with good schools, more stable marriages, better health, and many other factors creating better conditions for children. These are the principal ways in which racial inequality is perpetuated across generations.

The fact that, in spite of subgroup differences, Asian parents—the product of the most educated large immigration in U.S. history—are, on average, substantially more likely than whites to be college graduates means that their children start with great advantages and do better at school.

The long list of racial inequalities that often severely limit the development of students of color on the path to college include the following: (1) Because of growing up in homes with minimal economic and social resources and great stressors, students are far behind before their first day of education. (2) They attend the weakest preschools and elementary schools. (3) They are affected by worsening isolation in segregated, concentrated-poverty neighborhoods and schools, which limits resources and opportunities and increases risks. (4) Their families lack significant wealth, and housing market discrimination isolates the families and their children from strong schools and districts. (5) Children of color have more developmental problems and chronic untreated medical problems. (6) They have the least experienced teachers, often from the least rigorous colleges. (7) Their peer groups are far less prepared, which slows instruction and limits both curriculum and level of instruction. (8) The students face more residential instability and homelessness, which profoundly disrupt schooling. (9) They have more exposure to violence and crime. (10) The transition to high school often is difficult and produces rapid failure. (11) School suspension is very damaging and disproportionately affects young men of color. (12) The schools often must cope with overwhelmed single parents or grandparents and family disorganization. (13) Students and their families have far less information about college. (14) Choice systems typically favor middle-class families and students. (15) There are few teachers of students' own race or ethnicity. (16) Students face discrimination by teachers and school staff. (17) A disproportionate share of students face incarceration in institutions where the education is weak and there are few supports for reentry in regular high schools. (18) Children of immigrants often face the threat or reality of losing parents by sudden deportation. (19) Schools are not organized to produce the levels of academic English and basic study, research, and writing skills needed in college. (20) Schools often lack the needed level of AP and strong honors programs that prepare for college study. (21) High schools usually have weak relationships with colleges and severely inadequate counseling resources. (22) Families have only a very small fraction of the resources whites and Asians, on average, have for college and little understanding of the financial aid, testing, and application processes.

Just reading through this list and comparing it with the typical middle-class white experience is sobering. There are, of course, poor, uneducated whites and Asians, and a small proportion experience some of these conditions, though they are much more likely to be temporary. They rarely live in areas of highly concentrated poverty or simultaneously face multiple barriers. Many have a network of family resources. There are, of course, highly educated, high-income Blacks and Latinos who have more resources and opportunities, but they often experience discrimination anyway and often face obstacles in gaining access to the neighborhoods of whites with similar credentials.

When you add these things up, they amount to a web of great strength holding back the development of the full potential of students of color. They mean that, on average, students of color coming into high school and college have been repeatedly harmed in their development by a wide variety of unequal opportunities and conditions. For them to have the kind of support they need to succeed in college, it is very important that policies specifically targeting these groups be designed with understanding of these realities.

Lasting Damage Starts Very Early

This book is not about solutions to all of the cumulative impacts of systemic differences on families and communities but rather about what students of color have lived through and live with along the path to college and, often, during their college experience. Children whose basic needs have been cared for, who learn to socialize in positive environments, and whose curiosity and creativity are stimulated and rewarded take that with them into adolescence and college. Children who have been hungry, who have been kept in custodial settings with few resources, who have grown up without a stable home and community, who have been treated as inadequate or frightening by strangers, who go to dismal schools and whose friends are living with similar conditions, carry that with them.

Even before they are born, people of color often suffer from unequal prenatal care, worst for Black and Indian women facing the stress and risks of unsupported pregnancies.[13] Black women were significantly more likely than whites to have preterm babies, limiting their development (13.9 percent vs. 9.1 percent). A seventh of Black women, compared with half as many white women, had low-birth-weight babies.[14] Both of these statistics show that Black children were far more likely to be exposed to inadequate development in the womb, which is extremely important for later health and development.[15]

Babies develop their mental capacities very rapidly in the right environments. Anyone who has had a baby or been close to one sees how intensely newborns and toddlers try to comprehend the world and learn about it and how interactive they soon become. The Harvard Center on the Developing Child concludes, "Babies' brains require stable, caring, interactive relationships with adults. . . . Science clearly demonstrates that, in situations where toxic stress is likely, intervening as early as possible is critical to achieving the best outcomes."[16] Obviously highly educated parents who have time and resources are an enormous advantage to children, and trained professional preschool educators can have a large and lasting impact.

People who live in poverty, insecurity, and instability love their children but often cannot afford decent homes or the basic essentials for their children. They cannot give them the same time and preparation.[17] Many are in contingent work schedules where they cannot even plan their work and home hours from day to day. In 2018 69 percent of Black children and 68 percent of Indian children were born to single moms, compared with 52 percent of Latinos and 28 percent of whites.[18] Single mothers on average have much lower household incomes and face many challenges. One study reports that the average income of a single parent was only a third (31 percent) of the two-parent level.[19] The impact of thousands of days of very different experiences and interactions with parents in fundamentally different circumstances on the basic cognitive and emotional development of children is massive.

Preschool Is Important and Highly Unequal

Preschool is seen by many policy makers as the magic bullet for equal opportunity. However, children of color are the least likely to have the kind of high-quality education with professional teachers and support services that can make a long-term difference. A recent study of school quality concluded that the average Black child was in a preschool whose quality was a large 0.55 standard deviations below that of the preschool attended by the typical white child, and there was a substantial Hispanic-white gap as well.[20] A 2018 study showed that the racial gaps were related to the peer groups in the preschool and to the level of segregation in the states. When little children are in groups where the other children are behind, they tend to learn less rapidly.[21] By preschool, we already clearly see the diverging educational patterns. Students of color in communities of concentrated poverty get the worst quality of education, and students from affluent white and Asian communities get the best, a process that cumulates into profound inequality over the years of schooling.

Nobel Prize–winning economist James Heckman reached the influential conclusion that high-quality preschool can have lifelong impacts,[22] but decades of research show that the kind of preschool most children receive is not of that quality and has only a temporary impact that fades in a few years.[23] Vanderbilt University researchers evaluating Tennessee's massive preschool program were disappointed to find that by the end of third grade, the initial gains were gone and the students were actually behind those who had not attended. They found that good teachers tend to leave concentrated-poverty schools and that a weak first-grade teacher can quickly eliminate any lasting benefits of preschool, something that many other researchers have documented elsewhere.[24] Spending a day visiting typical preschools of both the upper-middle class and the poor is enough to see huge early gaps. Inexperienced and less effective teachers tend to be concentrated in schools of racial and economic double segregation. A study by the American Enterprise Institute concludes that the most important need is not preschool but "to improve child care and support parents in better fulfilling their role as their children's first teachers,"[25] something more powerful than the current focus on expansion of preschool.

In truth, a much more comprehensive approach is needed in a nation with weak childcare systems and millions of families without resources, where we send the children who have had the fewest opportunities and support to the worst schools and their mothers into entry-level contingent jobs with chaotic schedules that often create impossible choices. The reality that so many children of color are in families struggling with one parent in inadequate housing and experiencing hunger is related to the fact that a very disproportionate share of young fathers of color are incarcerated by young adulthood.

The worst outcome would be to conclude that we have given students of color a good start and they have blown it, when the reality is that, even if they went to a strong preschool, we then promptly plugged them into profoundly inadequate subsequent grades—which is what usually happens for students of color. People want to believe that there is a magic time for inoculation against inequality, and, of course, very young children are not blamed for their own problems, so helping them is good politics and, if done well, a good investment. The reality is that children can be helped at any age, but the education and support have to be good and continuous. If they are usually weak, even if policy creates bright spots, the students will lose a great deal over time.

The Health and Nutrition Gap

If you do not get good nutrition and health care, you are less likely to learn. Children of color are much more likely to go to bed hungry, without adequate nutrition. All of these things matter greatly. The share of nonwhite families who run out of food is vastly higher than for whites. In addition, as former first lady Michelle Obama notes, many low-income communities of color are "food deserts" with little stores selling high-cost, unhealthy packaged goods and high-calorie snacks with no nutritional value but without access to the variety of fresh and healthy foods available in supermarkets.[26] It is clear that students of color have less access to health care, fall behind in key ways that damage their education, and are exposed to untreated long-term harm, including mental health damage from their high level of exposure to disruptive situations and events.[27]

The inequality in health conditions and health care takes many dimensions. Children of color are more exposed to a variety of physical threats such as lead poisoning, which is much more common in old and deteriorating urban buildings with layers of old lead paint.[28] They and their parents receive less adequate care for mental health issues, which are very present in American society and have powerful impacts on successful development and family life as well as education. When there is care, it is often of low quality.[29] Many children in poor nonwhite areas have untreated vision problems that affect their academic success. If a child cannot see the blackboard or focus his or her eyes on lines of print, it is a huge barrier to learning.[30] In general the provision and the quality of medical care in nonwhite neighborhoods are seriously deficient. Students of color are very seriously underrepresented in medical training, and few white and Asian doctors choose to practice in Black, Latino, and Indian communities, a key reason for the strong support for diversity at leading medical schools. The list could go on and on and, in the aggregate, these issues can have devastating consequences. When students fall behind because of health issues, there often is no recovery.

Family Poverty as a Fundamental Force

U.S. children of color are far more likely to live in poverty than white children, and their poverty is much more likely to be persistent and isolated, both of which deepen its impact. The U.S. poverty standard is very low compared with most Western democracies, where it is typically something like half the

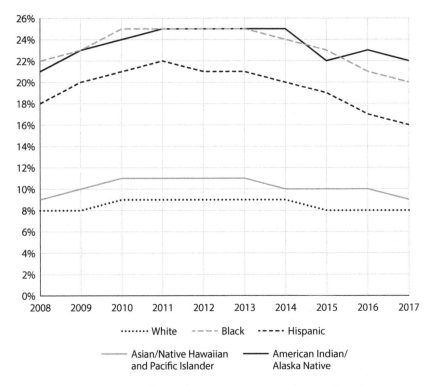

FIGURE 1. Poverty rate by race/ethnicity, 2008–2017. Kids Count Data Center

average annual income, which is about twice the U.S. level.[31] So what we consider just above poverty here would be well below in most of our peer nations. Figure 1 shows that, over a decade, there has consistently been a large racial gap between two sectors—whites and Asians have only about a tenth of people living in poverty, but Blacks, Latinos, and Indians have far higher levels of poverty during all parts of the economic cycle. Black and Native American poverty rates are consistently the highest, though the Latino numbers rose dramatically during the Great Recession but then recovered significantly.

There are, of course, spells of poverty for many families of all races because of unexpected life changes, such as losing a job or a business, a divorce, a serious illness, the time needed to learn English to qualify for a decent job, and other conditions that may be temporary, such as being a graduate student. Some people, when they are poor, receive help from relatives and others to tide them over. They may be without income but sharing someone else's good housing, as happens to many young college graduates. But people without a safety net can be forced into the very bottom of the housing market, in dangerous neighborhoods, or, at worst, into homelessness when they lose a job. Some families where one or both parents are undocumented live in permanent fear of deportation, of armed Immigration and Customs Enforcement agents hammering on their doors and taking parents away from their young children, who are citizens born in the U.S. but often go with deported parents. Many parents without papers must accept off-the-books jobs with low incomes and bad work conditions. If they protest, the owner can report them and have them expelled from the country.

Research on the impact of housing subsidy programs shows that as they are usually administered, they concentrate poor people of color in areas segregated by race and poverty, usually with weak schools and job markets, which cut off the chance of escaping poverty.[32] We have a massive shortage of affordable housing in the country, and families remain on waiting lists and take anything that becomes available in the subsidized sector. Compared with other nations, we have a tiny share of our housing stock in the subsidized sector in spite of our unusually high percentage of families living in poverty and unable to find housing they can afford. Unfortunately, although the construction of subsidized housing, the vast majority of which is owned by private businesses, is very expensive, there are no serious policies to place it in communities with viable schools. Often it is exactly the opposite. Families desperately needing housing have to live in isolated, concentrated-poverty communities without decent educational opportunities for their children, often communities where their children will be exposed to negative conditions and peers. The schools serving areas of concentrated subsidized housing are often extremely segregated by race and poverty and are among the lowest performing in the region.

Although many people experience temporary spells of poverty, some experience lasting poverty that shapes their lives for year after year. For some young people, an early struggle with poverty while going to college, starting a business, doing military service, or working flipping burgers or folding clothes in an inexpensive store is a stage of life, sometimes romanticized in retrospect. For others it is an endless reality. Equating the two by simply looking at cross-sectional data leads to highly misleading conclusions. It is people of color and their children who are most likely to be deeply affected by long-term debilitating poverty in a concentrated-poverty community with no real ties to the middle class. It is they who were most affected, for example, when the federal government blocked all efforts to raise the federal minimum wage from 2009 to 2020. Concentrated-poverty communities, often almost entirely nonwhite, have the weakest schools.

Isolated long-term poverty causes cumulative damage and affects only a tiny minority of white and Asian families. In other words, this experience of concentrated-poverty communities, which affects about one-eighth of all U.S. children, is only one-third as likely to affect whites and half as likely to shape the experience of Asian children but twice as likely to affect African American and Native American youngsters.[33] Concentrated long-term poverty and all its harms were largely irrelevant for the racial groups far more likely to complete college but a very severe barrier for students of color. The lifetime impact of such experiences shapes millions of students' development even when they have the capacity to perform at a very high level.[34] Families with money living in communities with money, in important ways, live in a different society. Ignoring that reality leads to policies that perpetuate it.

Schooling Disparities

American public education is supposed to be the answer to inherited inequality, a goal that is fervently espoused by many educators and parents. So even after considering the very apparent inequality in our communities, we hope that the schools will be the equalizer. In a society where there is no long-term agreement on social policy except for support of the elderly, the schools are supposed to be the default. The problem is that the stratification of society is reflected in and often exacerbated by the stratification of our public schools and the small private sector that serves less than a tenth of high school students.

The schools that have the highest achievement, graduation, and college-going levels are the fifth (20 percent) of U.S. schools that have at least three-fourths middle-class students. In 2015, in a rapidly growing economy, 28 percent of whites and 37 percent of Asians attended such schools but only 7 percent of Blacks, 8 percent of Latinos, and 9 percent of Indians.[35] The fact that a very large share of Black, Latino, and Indian students are concentrated in the schools dealing with the constant challenges of students and families devastated by poverty, and often almost totally isolated from middle-class students and families, is an incredible obstacle on a path to college. For students whose home language is not English, attending schools with few native speakers of English limits their acquisition of the fluent academic English that is a key for testing and college success.

In neighborhoods where the parents are college graduates, they have much more knowledge of what is needed to prepare for college and expect their schools to provide it. And they have power to demand changes if the school falls short. Children from middle-class families grow up with friends who are planning on college and in communities that have a lot of information about college. Students who grow up in communities with low educational levels tend to have neither. Students in the schools of the middle class are seen as future college students. Students in concentrated-poverty schools often are not, either in the neighborhood or in their schools.

School assignment and choice policies either can open access to better schools, which are usually predominantly white middle-class schools, to students from historically excluded groups or can actually intensify the segregation already built into the structure of neighborhoods and communities. The idea of *Brown v. Board of Education* and civil rights policies was to remedy the history of discrimination and segregation by requiring school districts to use student assignment policies to produce racially integrated schools. This produced new opportunities in previously inaccessible schools for students of color (though, of course, the changes were imperfect and the children not always welcomed by teachers and fellow students). These policies increased the probability that students of color would attend better schools and that the faculties would be integrated and trained to respond to all children's needs. These were required elements of desegregation plans. This effort was largely focused on the seventeen states with a history of mandatory segregation laws. The big changes took place before the massive Latino immigration, and Black students in those states were most affected. It made a large difference there. It was applied only in limited and shorter periods in the North and West because of limits imposed by the Supreme Court after the appointment of four justices by President Nixon.

Latino students, for generations, were often assumed not to be going to college. Attention turned to the rapidly growing Latino population only a generation after *Brown*, near the end of the civil rights period, and the rights recognized were never seriously enforced.[36] Latinos, who had made up only a twentieth of U.S. students in 1968, became more than a fourth by 2014, so the combination of failure to initiate new cases, the dissolution of existing desegregation plans, and the enormous increase in their numbers produced a steady increase in segregation by ethnicity and poverty from the time national data on Latinos were first systematically collected in 1968.

The growth of segregation was very dramatic as the great migration of Latinos developed in the 1980s and 1990s. There had always been serious segregation in the more traditional parts of the Southwest, particularly Texas, but in California in 1970, the typical Latino had been in a majority-white school. That changed. On average, California Latino students now attend schools with only about a sixth whites and a great majority of fellow students living in poverty.[37] If you look at the way the state's schools are rated by the state, only about a twentieth of Latino students are in the top quintile of schools, the schools that are likely to provide access to a four-year public college in a very stratified state higher education system. This segregation by ethnicity, by poverty, and sometimes by home language serves to keep the students off the path to college.[38] The Supreme Court in *Brown v. Board of Education* said segregation caused "irreversible" harm, but the country has bet on a succession of policies that promised that the separate schools could be made equal. This effort has persisted in spite of the lack of any significant evidence of success. The least success in producing gains has occurred for high schools, which are much more difficult to reform than elementary schools. High schools and colleges have to work hard to try to reverse the "irreversible" damage if students of color are to have an equal chance to develop their potential, but they often fail.

School segregation for both Blacks and Latinos has continuously increased since 1991, when the Supreme Court established policies to terminate desegregation orders of federal courts even if racial integration and more equitable outcomes had not been fully achieved, even for a brief period, and even if school officials then adopted policies such as neighborhood schools that would inevitably increase segregation by race and poverty given the nature of residential patterns.[39] In the following decade most major desegregation plans were dissolved; magnet schools and choice plans lost their desegregation requirements and became stratified, with fewer students of color being admitted to the strong schools. Beginning with the 1991 Supreme Court decision on ending desegregation orders, segregation began to rise year after year for both Blacks and Latinos, producing greater racial and economic separation in the schools as economic inequality deepened.[40] In its five-to-four decision in the 2007 *Parents Involved* case, the Supreme Court prohibited many forms of voluntary desegregation plans that school districts were pursuing on their own without a court order because they believed it strengthened education. The decision ruled that no children could be assigned to schools based on their race even if the purpose was to create integrated education.[41] In a school choice context, it is difficult to produce substantial and lasting integration without the goal being firmly built into the operation of the choice process, with diversity goals, targeted recruitment, admissions by choice rather than tests, fair lotteries, free transportation, and other policies designed to foster integration. Typically, parents and teachers of all racial and ethnic groups like substantial lasting integration but not resegregation, which triggers fear of academic decline. Not only are there few remaining major plans for school diversity in major districts, but many of the good schools of choice that offer rare opportunities to ambitious students in decaying cities are now adopting admissions and test requirements that turn them into special opportunities for children from educated, connected middle-class families. This raises more barriers for students of color.[42]

School integration was an educationally successful and durable reform until the policies were first limited and then reversed. Desegregation continued to rise right through the hostile Nixon and Reagan administrations because the courts protected desegregation plans and residential segregation became less extreme for Blacks, particularly in areas with desegregated schools. Federal policy changed from active work on integration to opposition under conservative administrations and to a dismantling of legal requirements by the transformed Supreme Court. President Lyndon Johnson was committed to serious enforcement of desegregation law. President Richard Nixon was an active critic, changing the balance of the Supreme Court with four appointments, and his Justice Department and Office for Civil Rights stopped enforcing the law.[43] In this period the record of unanimous decisions for desegregation changed to a sharply divided court. In 1974, by a single vote, the Court declared that desegregation must stop at the city-suburban line, locking in segregation for millions of students of color living in central cities. In another five-to-four decision, the Court ruled that there was no federal right to equal school resources.[44] Those decisions have profoundly limited school equalization efforts for a half century. A period of major focus on equity gave way to policies that insisted that separate and less funded schools must perform much better or face harsh sanctions.

At the peak of school desegregation in the South, where most of the enforcement was focused, the region had changed from almost total segregation to operating the most integrated schools in the country, bringing a surge of Black educational achievement. It did not end racial gaps in achievement, but it was far more successful than segregation, even segregation with extra money. Although most of the studies focused on the relationship between school composition and test scores (the most readily available data), the strongest long-term effects were not on test scores but on life chances—future higher

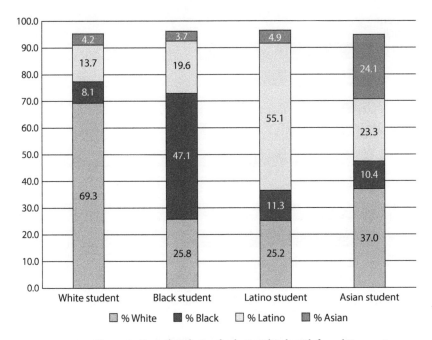

FIGURE 2. Concentration of students of color in schools with few whites, 2016.
Civil Rights Project at UCLA

education success, success in the job market, changes in racial attitudes for both nonwhite and white students, and other important long-term effects.[45]

A 2019 report showed that in the most recent data (2016–17 school year), the nation's Black and Latino students were, on average, attending schools that were three-fourths nonwhite and with substantial majorities of children living in poverty, while white and Asian students were in middle-class schools. Double segregation and all the inequalities in educational opportunities and outcomes associated with it shaped the experience of millions of children of color.[46] Both Black and Latino students attended schools where whites were only a fourth of the total enrollment. Whites were in schools that were over 60 percent white and Asian and both had far more Latino than Black classmates (figure 2).

These were two different worlds of schooling in which virtually all the major inputs and outcomes were far weaker in the schools segregated by race and poverty. The interaction between race and poverty compounds the barriers facing students. They are doubly segregated, in a society where whites and Asians are concentrated in the middle class and students of color face both race prejudice and the pervasive impact of poverty on family resources,

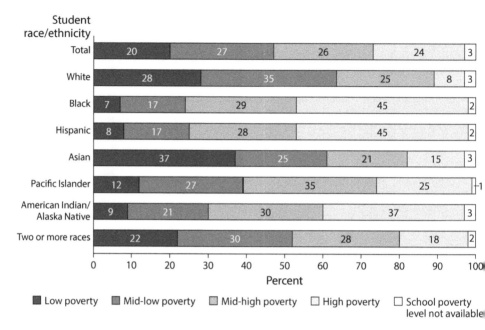

FIGURE 3. Low access to middle-class schools for students of color.
Civil Rights Project at UCLA

connections, and instability. Only one in twelve whites and one in seven
Asians attend the high-poverty schools where 45 percent of Blacks and Latinos
are enrolled (figure 3).

If college admissions are to be fair, this must be taken into account. It is not
fair to hold such a systemic inequality against the victims of segregation or to
ignore realities this critical in educational development. If we are to have just
results and build positive intergenerational gains, students who have never
been given a fair chance must receive one that is more fair, as their last chance,
in higher education.

Higher education selection and support mechanisms designed to enhance
equity need to evaluate students for college on the basis of what they have
been able to accomplish with what opportunities they've been given, and that
should play a significant part in admissions and support. The alternative is to
concentrate on those from families with resources, educated in strong college-
oriented schools, and to blame a great many students of color for not learning
many skills they were never seriously taught.

A very important analysis of lifetime effects of segregated high-poverty
schools by Berkeley professor Rucker Johnson focused directly on the long-term

comparative impact of segregated and integrated schools. Johnson combined data sets covering generations of experience, comparing those who had serious experience with integration with those who got most or all of their education in segregated schools. He notes in his 2019 book, *Children of the Dream*, "a striking increase in educational attainment for black children that grows as the number of years of exposure to school desegregation increases ... with stronger effects for those exposed to integration for more of their school-age years, particularly beginning in the elementary school years. . . . Compared to black children who were not exposed to integration, black children who were exposed throughout their K–12 years had significantly higher educational attainment, including greater college attendance and completion rates, not to mention attendance at more selective colleges." He points out that there had been an amazing gain in college access in the civil rights era, when, "by the late 1970s and early 1980s, college enrollment for black eighteen- to nineteen-year-olds rose to rates similar to those for white students," which, according to his statistical model, was largely the impact of desegregation.[47] Because his project combined data sets that looked at a much longer time and outcomes outside of academic outcomes, it showed that "the average effects of a five-year exposure to court-ordered deseg-regation led to ... a 30 percent increase in annual earnings." It also was related to an 11 percent drop in the incidence of poverty in adulthood. Early desegregation was related to a shared 22 percent decline in the "probability of adult incarcera-tion."[48] There were also significant relationships with more positive adult health outcomes.[49] Obviously there are always disputes about causation and unexam-ined factors, but these findings command serious attention.

Although the evidence on the impacts of segregation is increasingly com-pelling, policy has moved in the direction of increasing segregation. College officials need to take into account the impact of profound and enduring edu-cational segregation for most students of color. Universities have been harmed by the increasing inequality of the schools, which has increased as the non-white share of the college-age population has grown so dramatically.

In a historic civil rights trial in Connecticut, Columbia University professor Gary Natriello "summarized the average makeup of a Hartford classroom with 23 students—8 to 15, his data showed, were likely to be living in poverty; 3 to have been born to mothers on drugs; 15 to live with single parents; 9 to have parents who did not work; 8 to live in inadequate housing; and 9 to have par-ents without high-school diplomas." English was not the native language for a substantial share of the students. He observed, "We organize schools on the assumption that students will come for the most part in good shape, that they will have slept the night before, that they have a place to do homework, that they have parents at home."[50] These Hartford schools, doubly segregated by race and poverty, were spending far above the national norm and had scores of special programs but were nearly dead last in the state in achievement. Susan Eaton studied the children in one classroom in Hartford in her book *The Children in Room E4*. The school was focusing fierce energy on getting them to pass the state tests. She showed the incredible instability and obstacles many children were facing in their communities and in their often disorganized and difficult family lives.[51] Problems outside school draw down the teachers' energy, and the lack of a core of high-achieving students to model and support learning in the classroom makes things much harder for both teachers and students.[52]

As a researcher familiar with data sets from many parts of the country, it is always depressing to see the high statistical relationship between race, poverty, and low achievement and other key outcomes. These relationships have not been effectively addressed in policy for a half century or more and were documented in all the high-stakes test and accountability data from the policies that have dominated our schools since 1980. Wave after wave of reforms have produced massive disappointment. Education officials have continually reported gains, but most of the gains are on local or state tests that are heavily drilled, and do not appear on other tests that have not been coached. This means that they were more the result of test prep than true learning. Educators work hard to create the appearance of gains, but the students are far behind when they get to college. Most of the billions of dollars of programs set up to improve schools of concentrated poverty, the basic goal of federal policies for a half century, have not worked. When the federal government set up the What Works Clearinghouse to carry out serious independent evaluation of the data from a myriad of programs, the great majority showed no significant impact. There have been persistent large racial achievement gaps, particularly at twelfth grade, the most relevant level for assessing college preparation. Students coming to college from these schools serving students of color and poverty are not ready and, though they enroll somewhere, they do not receive degrees.

The Residential Inequality Perpetuation Machine

Neighborhoods matter greatly in the development of students, and major research is documenting the way communities shape the destiny and eventual success of students. Under the normal pattern of school attendance zones, growing up in segregated neighborhoods means attending a segregated, high-poverty school as well as other limitations. Leading recent economic research on racial inequality has focused on the lasting impacts of neighborhood segregation and the impact of policies that have led to severe segregation in cities and growing sectors of suburban rings. Normally, econometric studies of vast data sets over generations are doomed to live and die in economics journals. But recent studies, including those by some of the nation's most prominent younger economists, have shown with shocking clarity that where you grow up deeply shapes your life chances and that residential segregation is particularly harmful for students of color. Using truly massive data sets covering a large time span, these studies have shown lifelong consequences of the racial composition of neighborhoods. A major 2018 study by scholars at Harvard, Stanford, and the U.S. Census Bureau led by Professor Raj Chetty found that people of various races do better in neighborhoods with more successful residents and that moving to such a neighborhood, especially as a young child, substantially improves life chances, even though significant racial gaps remain, especially for Black men. The most positive outcomes come from selective neighborhoods with more positive racial attitudes, but only a very small share of Blacks are able to live in such communities. The analysis found that Black males do best in communities with low poverty rates and where more than half of Blacks live with their fathers, but only 4 percent of Black children, compared with 63 percent of white children, grow up in such conditions, conditions with major intergenerational benefits.[53] One of the basic findings of the historic 1966 Coleman report was that a child's peer group in his or her school was strongly related to academic success.[54] Neighborhood segregation affects peer groups in and out of school and, of course, teens in high school are deeply affected by peer groups as they become more independent of their parents.

Some think it would be easier to change educational opportunity by changing the housing opportunities for families of color. For schools this could certainly be part of the solution, if there were a feasible policy, since we normally allocate schooling opportunities by residential areas through attendance areas and district boundaries. But residents of desirable communities with strong schools usually strongly resist any significant effort to develop affordable housing or to allow students from other areas to attend their schools, so there are massive barriers.

People get access to communities by buying homes. Many communities with the best schools have almost no affordable rental housing big enough for families. They zone to keep lower-income families out to avoid the cost of educating children whose families do not pay enough in property taxes, and they totally exclude subsidized housing. The workers who keep the community operating and safe and educate its children often cannot live there. Unless these policies are substantially changed, the only way to get access to the best schools for significant numbers of students of color would be through plans that let them transfer there or come together in regional magnet schools. Housing policies reinforce the stratification of schooling. If you look at the high schools with the most resources and highest-scoring students, they tend to be in affluent white and Asian suburbs. These areas also have barriers even for families of color with sufficient money to buy or rent there, including discrimination by real estate and rental agents, by landlords, and by mortgage lenders.[55] There is also the continuing impact of earlier discrimination over time. People normally move into areas they have knowledge about and where they have contacts and feel they would be welcome.[56] This means that they usually move nearby or to an adjacent community, which, in the long run, tends to spread segregation.

Students are deeply affected by schools, but they spend the great majority of their hours outside schools in their homes and communities.[57] The school issue often becomes capitalized into housing costs and leads parents to accept very long commutes to work and high mortgage and property tax payments in order to try to give their children educational advantages. Realtors use school quality, often measured by average test scores on state tests featured on websites, to market housing. Test scores are highly correlated with family income, so this is a force for deepening inequality. Those who can afford to buy into the most desirable school areas are also buying into areas that often have rapidly rising housing prices, creating a major barrier for those without wealth and increasing wealth in housing value for those who have high incomes and housing equity. Families whose parents or relatives can help with down payments are, of course, families whose parents had better education and jobs, and this help gives them more access to the best schools in this cycle of inequality. Those communities tend to engage in "exclusionary zoning," which largely forbids rental housing (a large majority of nonwhite families are renters) and sets building requirements so that only expensive single-family homes can be constructed. California made major changes in 2021.

The initial development of suburbia operated under a variety of policies and practices that made it easy for white families to become homeowners in affordable but rapidly appreciating suburban housing developments but virtually impossible for families of color. Housing wealth cumulates, so that a family who bought a $20,000 suburban home after World War II, with no down payment and low interest in the Veterans Administration mortgage guarantee program, often saw it double in value ten years later, providing the equity and credit rating to trade it up to a $400,000 home later. Most of those postwar subdivisions made the housing available to whites only during the baby boom. Families who got in had wealth they could borrow against for college costs and credit ratings that could support loans. The great suburban expansion happened before the federal fair housing law was passed, and most of the new suburban developers did not sell to nonwhites in their new developments. Housing equity is the only significant source of wealth for most families. Wealth breeds wealth and flows through generations. Relatively low-achieving students from high-wealth families have a much better chance of finishing college than high-achieving students from low-income, low-wealth families. In a market society, wealth is capital and capital invested creates more wealth. Wealth is choices, often choices to increase the success of children.

Discrimination meant that those nonwhites who were able to buy housing often got it with more costly and risky predatory mortgages in areas with much less effective schools with less qualified and experienced teachers, who often transferred out. These areas were subject to increasing influxes of low-income students of color, and the ghettoization process continued there.[58] Because families usually look for housing in areas near where they live, housing segregation had long-term impacts even when overt discrimination by realtors declined significantly. In educational terms, this cut access to powerful schools.

Eleven million households face severely excessive housing costs, spending more than half of their income on housing (when anything beyond 30 percent is considered too high to manage given other necessary costs), and the racial disproportions are stunning. The number of cost-burdened families tripled from 2001 to 2016 while the supply of subsidized housing was virtually unchanged, meaning that three-fourths of those needing assistance did not get it. Over three decades the number of very low-income families in the U.S. had grown by six million but the supply of federally subsidized units had increased by less than one million.[59] There has been very limited construction of subsidized housing for low-income families since 1980, and much of what has been built has gone up to house poor people of color in doubly segregated areas with "dropout factory" schools where large shares of students fail to graduate.

After a major effort in the 1990s, heavily promoted by President George H. W. Bush and mortgage lending companies offering risky predatory mortgages, many nonwhite families invested all they could to become homeowners before the housing market collapsed in the Great Recession. The failure to regulate mortgage lenders produced a speculative frenzy and risky predatory mortgages that would only work out if housing prices continued to soar. Many of those who held risky mortgages (very disproportionately families of color) lost their homes as they were denied the refinancing needed for a long-term mortgage or faced impossible interest payments. The homeownership rate fell sharply, most dramatically for Blacks. The white level of homeownership is 26 percent higher than Black levels and 17 percent higher than Latino levels, and those families of color who have homes have much less valuable homes. The Great Recession was a wealth disaster for many. Home equity is, by far, the largest share of family wealth, which matters greatly in choosing colleges, being adequately financed during college, and not finishing with crippling debt that drastically limits future choices, including graduate and professional education.

The worst damage to education comes at the extreme of the housing crisis—homelessness, something that used to be rare in the U.S. but now is painfully visible and hitting families. A 2018 study of homelessness in New York found that the city had 111,500 students who had been without a home of their own sometime during the previous year. And among 102 middle schools in New York City with high rates of suspension, the researchers reported that the typical homeless student missed twenty days of school and that about a seventh of homeless students were suspended from school, deepening their awful problems. For Black homeless students and those living in homeless shelters, the rates were even higher. Almost a fourth (22 percent) of homeless Black boys in the schools studied were suspended during that single year.[60] And this was before high school, where many of the most severe classroom conflicts occur. Housing crises create extreme instability in schooling because students must move from one community and school to another, sometimes more than once during a school year. That can bring jarring changes in learning materials and classroom practices, and there is often nowhere to do homework at night. Sometimes we are applying high-stakes test-driven requirements to children who have no place to study, no real home. Then we blame the children and their schools for their scores. Severe housing costs force families to choose between making their rent or mortgage payments and losing housing. As a result, they sharply cut what they spend on food, educational costs, and medical services, harming students on other dimensions.[61]

School authorities cannot change housing policies, but they need to understand their impact, and education and civil rights groups need to challenge housing and municipal officials to foster more diverse neighborhoods, since schools pay the price for the damage of growing up in isolated, segregated communities. Creating magnet schools can make neighborhoods more attractive in the housing market and can expand the opportunities for integrated education, especially if combined with housing policies that use subsidy money to give longtime residents the ability to remain as the neighborhood strengthens. Colleges and universities also are often very important forces in their neighborhoods or communities, and they have expertise in housing and urban development. They should speak out on the issues, especially in their own areas, and take those realities affecting many students of color into consideration in assessing and supporting students.

People who would be outraged by any law that distributed opportunity on the basis of race or ethnicity are all too willing to ignore similar results rooted in a system of housing discrimination and land use policies preventing the construction of affordable housing in the areas of job growth and good schools. The housing system has many of the same general consequences as a law distributing school opportunity by race would have. Maps showing the racial composition of neighborhoods are maps of the opportunity systems of metro areas. It is long past time for a very serious discussion of the consequences of a profoundly polarized society that excludes the majority of youths of color from a real chance and washes its hands of any responsibility. Decisions about housing policy are decisions about opportunity.

Incarceration and Education

The largest social policy change affecting young people of color in the post–civil rights era was a commitment to extremely harsh punishment of nonviolent drug-related offenses. Richard Nixon made "crime in the streets" a central issue and turned the country in the direction of massive long-term jailing of young men of color. He ran ominous campaign ads showing dangerous Black rioters and promising to reinforce police. A series of presidents and Congresses from 1980 to 2008 engaged in the war on crime and the war on drugs in a competition to raise sentences, including lifetime jailing for "three strikes" even for minor nonviolent offenses. In the short term these policies conveyed a dramatic image of action, but in the long term they proved to be prohibitively costly in money and social damage as states found themselves paying more for prisons than higher education. Generations of young men of color were harmed as these policies determined their lives and those of their children because of the racial bias in arrests, prosecutions, and sentences,[62] as well as the relationship between criminal records, poverty, and job opportunities.[63]

The crack cocaine scare led to extreme sentences for young men of color, and the law imposed much harsher sentences on crack, sold and used far more by people of color than the powder form of cocaine, more used by higher-income whites.[64] Incarceration of a substantial share of young men of color meant that generations of children have grown up without dads, and mothers are on their own, assailed by negative forces. The statistics are particularly grim for African Americans and American Indians. National statistics show that a third of young African American males could expect to be imprisoned at least once in their lives. Arrested men are often parents of young children and cannot support their children, who are often exposed to arrests and violence. Many children end up in unstable foster care or with some other relative. Parents and other caregivers often feel judged harshly by school staffs and worry about having their children taken and put into foster care.[65] When the incarcerated parent comes out of prison or jail, he or she has a criminal record, which makes it much harder to get a job, especially for Black men,[66] and, on average, the jobs are very low paying. Some landlords and public housing agencies will not rent to or will evict offenders or ex-convicts.[67] With incarceration a norm in many of the poorest communities, Black young men hardened in prison and often unemployable come back to their communities facing deeper poverty and instability as ex-offenders.

School shootings, though typically carried out by whites, spurred "zero tolerance" restrictions on school violence, and the introduction of police and armed guards into schools spread rapidly, especially in minority schools. As police moved into schools, so did criminal arrests and prosecutions of students and the creation of criminal records for the kind of conflicts that had normally been resolved informally within the confines of the school.[68] As educators expelled and suspended more students or sent them to separate alternative schools where few graduated and none prepared for college, still more young men of color were further separated from normal schooling. The result was to destroy the educational possibilities for what became a very significant share in many communities. The Great Recession decimated state budgets, eliminated much of the rehab for prisoners, and led to contracting out the operation of prisons to for-profit businesses, which made them even worse environments. Recently the huge costs helped trigger reforms, including the 2019 First Step Act, but the damage has been long and severe.

Children of color usually come to school behind and attend the weakest schools, and they and their families confront many problems and stresses middle-class families normally avoid. They often bring those problems to school. If they are excluded from school, even for a brief period, they are much more likely to fail within the school or to drop out and are much more likely to end up in the criminal justice system. Often they receive neither good education in detention or a positive reconnection with good schooling when released.[69] Students of color with criminal records are being radically devalued.[70] Each sentence, in important ways, is a life sentence (though reformers are working to purge records of nonviolent crimes). There is no significant welfare for young men not raising families, and their only options may be in the criminal economy that is often very present in the communities they return to. Some students live in communities where gangs control streets and young men must decide to join for protection or take on personal risk.[71]

Adolescents, even from successful families, often make mistakes and do things that are reckless, disruptive, and even illegal, but those in privileged settings tend to have families and are connected to institutions with resources to protect them. They get help and a second chance or a third chance. For those from families of color without resources, there is often no safety net and no real second chance in agencies with few resources to help and practices that deeply stigmatize ex-offenders. The racial impact damages the next generation.

Discrimination and Inequality inside the Schools

Often we have political struggles about schools that focus on two things— spending and achievement levels measured by standardized tests. What students of color need goes way beyond what can be easily bought—they need the educational experiences middle-class white and Asian students normally get. Creating all of those elements in segregated high-poverty schools or programs is very difficult. An October 2019 *New York Times* analysis concludes, "Students, no matter how capable, who attend low-performing high schools are often held to lower standards that make success in college nearly out of reach."[72] In other words, students need classes with students and teachers performing at higher levels or some kind of massive intervention to replace their absence.

Central city schools have been under relentless pressure to make their children score higher on standardized tests or face a variety of personal or school consequences, including the loss of jobs and even the shutting down of entire schools.[73] There are rare examples of schools that met the proficiency standards, but the vast majority of concentrated-poverty schools could not do so in spite of intense pressure and threats, as they usually lacked the most important things that are found in schools where the students succeed and are well prepared for college—strong, experienced teachers and administrators who know their subjects and identify with and care about the students, and groups of fellow students above grade level who create a community of learners. Successful schools are overwhelmingly middle class and seen as good places to work by experienced teachers and administrators. Segregated, concentrated-poverty schools often have classes that fail to provide the key precollegiate skills, including critical reading, strong analytical writing, original researching, and knowledge of advanced math. The students typically enter college far behind those in middle-class schools and fall further behind as the years pass. Where there are systems of school choice in the community, students and families in communities of color tend to get the least information about choices. They have the least chance of enrollment in the most desirable and educationally powerful schools, especially when the schools adopt entrance requirements.

Some students face special external problems even though their own families are successful. Mary Pattillo-McCoy's important book *Black Picket Fences: Privilege and Peril among the Black Middle Class* shows that, in contrast to many white families who have extended families with resources who help support them, successful Black families often have relations who need support from them.[74] Students of color often confront situations in which their family needs and their values lead them to make decisions, such as leaving school for a time, that harm their long-term prospects. They may face dangerous and sometimes seductive activities that white middle-class students rarely encounter, as well as greater likelihood that a mistake will be prosecuted. Research clearly shows that there is a substantially greater risk of intergenerational downward mobility among people of color.

The broader network of unequal opportunities, external prejudice, and negative family and neighborhood realities makes middle-class status far less secure and comes with burdens of extended family support rather than family safety nets.[75] For example, many children of families with wealth and strong credit get decisive help from their families in securing loans and getting mortgages that bring them into homeownership or businesses earlier and with less stress than similar families who have to do it on their own.[76] Such opportunities improve their children's opportunities.

School Suspensions

Students of color, most notably Black boys, are suspended from school at very disproportionate rates. Black boys, the most educationally vulnerable group, are often suspended at least twice as often as whites. It is often an arbitrary and biased process that badly damages the future prospects of students who already have a sketchy connection with school. It makes school staff see them negatively and deepens the negative views of students about school. It is part of the "school-to-prison pipeline" that makes small problems into changes in life pathways. Fortunately, major research showing the inequities and the lifetime costs of suspension and documenting better alternatives has significantly reduced suspension recently, but it is still disproportionately directed at students of color.[77]

Lack of Faculty Diversity and Limited Preparation of Teachers and Staff

There is an increasingly powerful body of research showing that faculty of color stimulate stronger performance from students of color. In racially polarized schools, having faculty whose personal experience helps them understand and identify positively with students of color and their parents is a clear advantage.[78] Although these realities have been recognized for at least a half century and the desegregation plans required both actual desegregation of teachers and, often, affirmative action plans to hire more teachers of color, as well as race relations training for existing staff, these issues have been neglected now for decades, even as the nation's school population has undergone fundamental racial and ethnic changes.

The great migration of middle-class families of color to sectors of suburbia took hold in the 1970s, and much of the rising diversity in schools happens in historically white communities where a substantial number of Latinos or African Americans are moving in. This is often not lasting integration but a transitional phase in which many white families and teachers may leave.[79] These schools need a diverse and stable faculty with training in equity policies. Since boys of color experience more educational reversals and often lack male models at home, adult mentors of color in schools can be critical.

Tracking

From the early days, American high schools were open to a wider range of students than those in Europe, but they were also stratified internally. The idea was to educate all interested students but to provide different levels for those most prepared and for those who were lagging or not interested in higher education. Schools had an internal system of separation that had major consequences. In our stratified communities, students from nonwhite families were often not seen as candidates for the upper-level courses and programs. In the past these were often whole sets of courses, tracks that created, in essence, a set of parallel schools in the same building. Scholars, including Jeannie Oakes in her classic *Keeping Track*,[80] pointed out that there were courses and teachers for the "smart kids" who were going to college, and midlevel, undemanding classes for the "general" students not preparing for college. There were also low-level "gut" or remedial classes for students just trying to somehow get a high school diploma. Students of color were disproportionately in the lower tracks. And for students judged not to be able to function in regular schools, including ex-offenders, there were alternative schools where few would graduate or be prepared for any job. The tracks provided systematically unequal preparation in math and science.[81] The clear racial differences in access to the college-going tracks stirred efforts at reform. Reforms, however, met major resistance from both teachers and parents who were accustomed to the sorting process.[82] There were many attempts to limit or overcome tracking, and it now happens much more through course selection than through entire separate programs, but it is still prevalent. Discrimination in counseling can easily set students of color on a dead-end pathway through weak courses where they get so far behind that there is no way to get back on the college path. One remarkable example of success in ending stratification showed that it took years of very skillful work, both educationally and politically, but paid solid dividends in that small district.[83]

The research shows that placement in lower-level courses harms students. Teachers often support tracking because teaching is less demanding when the range of students' background is narrower. Teachers with seniority tend to be awarded with high-achieving students, while new and less experienced teachers are often assigned to the bottom-level classes.

On top of this whole system, many high schools have a substantial offering of Advanced Placement classes, which often yield college credit for successful students and raise their grade point average because AP courses usually get special weighting in calculating the GPA. An Educational Testing Service report showed that nearly half of Black and low-income students attended schools where there was no AP or very little. At the other extreme, 83 percent of Asian students were in high-AP schools, compared with 56 percent of Black students. To get college credit, you must take the exam and score at a specific level. At the time of the study, 10 percent of Asian American students were taking the exam, compared with 5 percent of whites, 2 percent of Latinos, and 0.5 percent of African Americans and Indians.[84] Even when there are teachers who are highly motivated to implement new AP classes in concentrated-poverty, segregated schools and there are students signing up, there are real limits, especially in the more creative and analytic tasks, for which, the teachers say, their students are unprepared.[85] The good students in successful schools may acquire as much as a full year of college credits and preference in admissions. This sorting can enable some students to graduate in three years, saving a year of college costs.

In many schools the differentiated classes have very different racial and ethnic compositions. The special education class in the basement may be mostly young men of color, while the AP calculus class may be almost all white and Asian. Highly talented Black and Latino students may not be recruited or counseled into the demanding classes or may feel uncomfortable in classes where they are a token. Diverse faculty, counselors, and staff can help. Though the harm has been quite clear for decades, remedies are hard. Many teachers were trained within these systems of sorting and differential treatment, and the parents of high-track kids want to preserve their advantages and often fight change.[86] Black and Latino students are predominantly in schools that are highly isolated from white and Asian students and middle-class students. Even those who are not, who are in diverse or largely white schools, tend to be seriously underrepresented in the classes that are most directly linked to college preparation.

Parents with less education often do not understand the consequences of course selection and may encounter stereotypes and discrimination from counselors. At the same time, the students of color who are placed in and succeed in the advanced courses do acquire a college-going peer group, favorable treatment by teachers and counselors and college recruiters, and very tangible advantages. Increasingly, after the end of desegregation efforts, gifted and talented classes and other special opportunities dropped policies that intentionally favored diversity. Elite courses tended to be a potent mechanism for perpetuating and legitimating racial stratification. To break the self-perpetuating cycle, it is necessary to have diversity as an explicit basic goal and the resources and policy to pursue it.

Why Attention Must Turn to High School

While a great deal of attention has been paid to early education, high schools have received little of the funds set aside to help disadvantaged children's education. Apart from adding more math and science courses and increasing pressure for high school completion, little has been delivered. Many states raised high school graduation requirements and created high school exit tests. Vocational education was widely cut back because there was not space for it in a curriculum with more academic requirements, in spite of the fact that the great majority of lower-income and nonwhite students do not complete college. It was expected that the increased requirements and assessments would raise the achievement and success of students at the bottom.[87] Unfortunately the most important national testing system, the National Assessment of Educational Progress, showed few significant high school gains over four decades.[88] There is also evidence that the increased requirements increased the dropout rate for disadvantaged students.[89] The 2019 Programme for International Student Assessment international report comparing advanced societies across the world showed almost no significant gains for U.S. adolescents over several decades.[90]

The U.S. was the only major Western nation where the high school graduation rate was not rising for decades, though that has finally changed significantly.[91] So in an important sense, the costs and barriers had been raised and heavy pressure was put on school staffs and students. More requirements and tests have not changed the situation much. The accountability policies failed to solve the large racial gaps in preparation.

The basic reality in education, however, is that it is never too early and never too late. The idea both of desegregation and of choice programs and college prep programs of the last half century is that if you transfer a student who has had weak preparation to a school with much stronger classes and peers, she or he will do much better. There is good evidence that this is true on average, though, of course, no policy works for everyone. Both in the great desegregation experiences and in special programs like Prep for Prep, which takes adolescents of color from weak schools and brings them into some of the most competitive private schools, and in many high school magnet schools, this hope has been borne out. One of the major discoveries of the implementation of affirmative action in selective colleges was that many students of color from weaker backgrounds who might previously have been assumed to be unable to manage some of the world's best universities succeeded.[92] Much the same happened in many of the nation's experiences with school desegregation under very difficult circumstances in the civil rights era. Such challenging changes are difficult and do not work for everyone, and do not close all gaps, but it is obvious that educational fate can change at any age given the right opportunities and support. A major 2019 National Academies of Sciences, Engineering, and Medicine report that combines research on brain development, psychology, and social structure concludes that "although each stage of life depends on what has come before, redirection, recovery and resilience are possible, and windows of plasticity that make this possible are to be found across the entire life course."[93] Students are going through very important changes in high school, and it is a place where inequalities can be addressed, the last good chance to reduce racial inequalities in college preparation.

The Dangerous Transition to High School

Ninth-grade students with weak educational backgrounds often confront a crisis when they begin high school. Students who fail classes in ninth grade are much more likely to drop out, eliminating their chance for college. Repeating the same grade already failed in a humiliating situation is not a recipe for success. Flunking students seems tough-minded but actually tends to compound educational problems.[94]

High schools are much less flexible than middle schools and often have extremely little counseling and support. Faculty are much more focused on a particular subject and have less chance to get to know individual students. Students begin to fail important courses in the first semester. Often inexperienced teachers are assigned to teach ninth grade, and stronger teachers get more desirable assignments to teach honors courses in the upper grades. This means that poorly prepared students, disproportionately nonwhite and boys, are suddenly facing demands they cannot meet in classes taught by teachers who have little experience, expertise, or training to help them. These students can suddenly face the possibility of flunking out and get so far behind on credits that they can never catch up with their classmates. Large shares of students in central city high schools fail at least one course in ninth grade. A study in Los Angeles found that students who passed ninth-grade algebra were twice as likely to graduate as those who failed it. More than a tenth of students nationally flunk ninth grade and have to repeat it, and the rate is half again as high for Black and Latino students.[95] Transitions are particularly dangerous for students who are marginal academically.[96]

Information, Contacts, and Counseling

College access is about a very complex market with millions applying to thousands of colleges and universities. If students are to be ready, they must first successfully navigate the often fateful choices within high school. Readers of this book are very likely to be college grads, often from families where the parents were college grads, and to have grown up in a community where there was lots of information and discussion of college. Families in such communities have a sense of what courses students need to take, and the schools are organized to get almost all students prepared. Students, unless they mess up, are often on a virtual glide path to college. They are likely to have the right courses, the right level of instruction, and the needed precollegiate skills; to know about and prepare for high-stakes tests; and to be taken to visit college campuses. Recruiters from good colleges visit these schools. Even with all of this, the process of selecting and applying to college demands a good deal of attention and hard work. Schools serving these communities are organized to get out letters of recommendation and materials the students need. Parents fill out the complex financial aid forms, and many have the resources to help their children.

In contrast, there are schools and communities that are virtual information deserts where neither students nor their parents nor their peer groups understand the process, their choices, or the key deadlines. They tend to have very little accurate information about college costs and aid and even less about the landscape of grants and loans. Few have significant savings to help and many face very difficult financial challenges of their own and expect children to help pay family costs. Often these families consider only the local community college or think that their children will have to go into the military to afford college later, unless they get athletic scholarships. In such contexts, information and good advice are crucial but scarce. Counselors have many other assignments, such as dealing with testing and special education, working with students with bad problems at home, and coordinating with social work and other agencies. For schools that rarely send students to four-year colleges, there is often very little information about those choices, and the colleges often do not visit or have contacts with the school. In those schools, families often assume that college aid comes only with high grades, knowing little or nothing about need-based aid, and think that they have no choices. Neither students nor parents know about the large risks of starting in a weak community college or putting off college for a few years, both of which seriously lower the probability of completion. Most students apply to only one college.

The higher education system often involves financial dimensions that are very hard for many to understand and large debts that cannot be forgiven even in a future bankruptcy of the student or parents who cosign loans. The least prepared students from the families with the fewest resources often find out too late that they made bad decisions at earlier stages in the process. If you make a mistake, the opportunity may never be recovered. Information is crucial, especially for students whose parents have not had the experience. Children of college graduates in communities of college graduates, with siblings who have gone to college, are often in schools where almost everyone is going to college and are exposed to a great deal of information. Students and parents without any such contacts often make the worst decisions.

Very little attention or priority is given, in the making of education policy, to counselors, though they are often the only resource of higher education information for nonwhite and poor students. A 2018 report concluded that the average U.S. ratio of students to counselors was 482 to 1.[97] Though the ratio is modestly better in high school, it is an impossible job since many students need help at all stages of high school and timely advice to be on track for all the crucial stages of college applications, testing, applying for financial aid, and other steps. Adding a single counselor to a high school can significantly increase enrollment in four-year colleges, and a single one-to-one meeting with a counselor about financial aid, the research found, increased the likelihood that a student's family would apply for federal aid by sevenfold.[98] Most students attend schools where at least 80 percent of the time the small counseling staff is devoted to issues other than college advising.[99] The reality is that students from disadvantaged families and communities get little help unless there are special programs or some teacher takes a special interest.

Testing

Issues related to testing deeply influence students' opportunities, the instruction and preparation they receive, and their standing in the competition for positions in selective colleges. One of the primary motivations for the creation of college testing was the desire to identify deserving students outside the normal recruitment paths, but it has been used to sort and select students. A leading national testing expert, Daniel Koretz, describes in his influential 2017 book, *The Testing Charade: Pretending to Make Schools Better*, the profoundly inaccurate conclusions that policy makers have drawn about students and schools from tests that are, in their nature, highly limited and strongly reflect the advantages students have had, not merely their own efforts.[100] Test scores have been equated with the student's "merit" but, in fact, are strongly related to parents' resources and education, and the student's previous schooling advantages. Tests are often used by counselors to recommend courses to students, thus shutting down chances. Tests are often treated as if they are a valid, neutral measure of a student's capability to succeed in college, but they only assess a particular set of skills and knowledge at a particular point in a student's development. If tests are, to a substantial degree, actually a measure of privilege and not of individual effort, then allocating important opportunities on the basis of tests rewards those to whom much has already been given. When educational pathways to college are opened and closed on such data, the decisions perpetuate and even intensify inequality that is embedded in a highly polarized society. Leading admissions tests do have some power in predicting student performance and provide useful information, but it is extremely important to recognize their limits and to select and support students who have talent but never had a chance to develop it in weak schools.

College entrance testing has played a central role in admissions and counseling for many years but is one area where the pandemic of 2020–21 actually brought substantial changes. Many colleges suspended requirements during the disruption of 2020, and the largest research university system, the University of California, suspended admissions test requirements, as did many other campuses, producing an unprecedented drop in the share of students submitting test scores with their college applications even to the most highly rated campuses. Some campuses reported a simultaneous surge in applications from students of color. A fall 2021 national survey of college admissions offices showed that more than 95 percent reported that their campuses were test optional or did not use testing as a criterion. More than half said that they were admitting more students of color. Most favored permanent change. It is too soon to assess the consequences, but this could be a substantial benefit of the pandemic crisis.[101]

The Complexities of Choice

Given the systematic concentration of students of color in schools segregated by race and poverty that offer inadequate preparation for college, and given the current lack of race-conscious desegregation plans, school choice is often the only possible route for students of color to get into a high school that trains students at a strong precollegiate level in classes taught by experienced teachers with college-bound peers. There has been a great expansion of school choice since the 1970s, particularly with magnet and charter schools, and choice systems sometimes include schools with excellent track records in preparing students for good colleges. Unfortunately, the choice systems that were created in many magnet schools and transfer plans to integrate students of color are not working today because of policy reversals, and colorblind choice plans may even increase inequality.

Historically, in American public schools there was no choice about where your child went to school—defined attendance boundaries determined your child's assignment. There were a small number of special schools, mostly vocational schools and schools for the handicapped. There were also a few examination schools like Boston Latin and Bronx Science, but most schools served everyone who lived in the zone, with the great exception of the seventeen states where, until well after the *Brown* decision, children in the same area would be assigned to separate Black and white schools. Outside the South, the attendance boundaries for schools were often gerrymandered along racial lines.

Choice emerged as a serious possibility for students only during the desegregation struggles. First, a policy called "freedom of choice" emerged as the South's leading strategy to preserve the basic structure of school segregation.[102] The idea was to give Black students a "choice" to attend white schools and offer the same choice to whites. Since no whites chose to transfer, Black schools remained entirely segregated. Investigations showed that Black students who transferred faced isolation and bad treatment in virtually all-white schools and their parents often faced retribution. Transfer students would go into a school with an all-white faculty where their cost for a more competitive education was often isolation and hostility. The policy left the structure of segregation virtually untouched and defended it as a product of "choices." A decade after *Brown*, 98 percent of Southern Blacks were still in totally segregated schools. The idea that this was an adequate remedy for a history of discrimination was struck down by a unanimous Supreme Court in the 1968 *Green v. New Kent County* decision.[103]

When serious urban desegregation came in the 1970s, a new form, more positive, of choice arose. When urban school systems were sued over segregation, there was abundant proof of historical violations in virtually every district sued, so they would be ordered to take action. Once the Supreme Court

blocked the inclusion of the suburbs in desegregation plans in 1974,[104] a growing number of districts developed "magnet schools," which offered a special
curriculum to attract voluntary transfers of both races and had explicit integration goals and a series of policies to make them work.[105] These policies actually
produced substantial desegregation in some cities using voluntary methods,
and they created some of the nation's most respected schools.

Beginning in 1991, however, a new form of choice emerged—charter
schools—that were strongly embraced by many federal and state policy makers for three decades. These schools typically had no diversity policies and
turned out to be even more segregated than regular public schools. In spite of
some high-performing schools, the research showed that they performed no
better, on average, than regular public schools and they tended to underserve
special education and language minority students.[106] In the meantime, as the
court-ordered desegregation plans were dropped and the civil rights policies
that had been an integral part of magnet development were lifted, the magnet
schools were pressured by middle-class parents and elected officials to drop
desegregation goals and become increasingly selective, often instituting exams
and other entrance requirements that made them into institutions of stratification rather than places of diversity. They had been created on the basis of student interest, building pathways to college for students from ghetto and barrio
neighborhoods. Choice without diversity goals, without special outreach for
families with less information, without welcoming limited-English children,
without transportation, and with entrance requirements will stratify children,
and the best choices are available to the most educated and connected families.
On the other extreme, choice embodying the best of the race-conscious policies of magnet schools that succeeded for decades can be an important channel of opportunities to a significant number of students.[107]

Since the end of desegregation plans and court orders, the growth of choice
and the rise of charter schools have been largely colorblind and, therefore, part
of a system of stratification.[108] It is all about the policies, and the policies that
would open pathways for more students of color have been losing out to policies that foster stratification, using tests to measure who deserves good choices.
A recent study of a Buffalo, New York, choice program found that when the
desegregation policy was dropped, the strongest high school, City Honors,
became a school with a very small Black enrollment in a majority-Black school
district.[109] Many cities have responded to budget pressures by eliminating free
transportation to some of their schools of choice. This policy is, of course,
strongly discriminatory against families without the time and resources to

transport their children to and from school every day. It means no choice for those who need it the most.

Making good choices and understanding and acting within complex choice systems requires information. Those with the best information and connections tend to get the best choices. It is clear that families of color typically have far less information.[110] There need to be real choices for those who have none, not simply good subsidized special opportunities for the most privileged. There needs to be a choice mechanism that ensures opportunity for the neighborhoods and groups that are the most disadvantaged and a way to get to the schools of choice.

Because of the restrictions on voluntary plans for integrated schools imposed by the Supreme Court in the 2007 *Parents Involved* case, the stakes in doing choice equitably have become much higher. The Court forbade the common magnet school practice of holding seats for and recruiting a portion of students of color for the desirable magnets. A choice plan, however, is often the only way for students of color in low-performing schools to enroll in a school that has a strong path to college. There are methods of running choice programs to expand opportunity that, for example, give preference to students from segregated nonwhite neighborhoods, but without explicit focus on the integration goal, choice plans are quite likely to make things worse. To help create viable paths to college for poor families of color, it needs to be an explicit goal, seriously planned for and carefully monitored. It needs to be race conscious. When this is done well, there tends to be high demand for spaces across race lines, so it is important to expand the offerings to avoid fighting over insufficient spaces.

Can It Be Solved by Focusing on Poverty?

Poverty and race are, of course, significantly related, and that leads some policy makers and researchers to argue that poverty is the underlying factor and that if it were addressed, it would produce real access for students of color. Poverty has many meanings, differs by race, and has degrees of severity. Black family poverty is related to present and past discrimination based on color and involves long-term confinement to neighborhoods and schools with almost no middle-class population. The poverty of Black families and Latino families is much more concentrated in high-poverty communities that concentrate related social problems and offer less mobility. Black, Latino, and Indian poverty is far less likely to be a spell of poverty and more likely to be a life of poverty.

Few white and Asian middle-class children face any significant risk of falling back into poverty. It is much more likely for young Blacks and Latinos. If we were a society in which poverty had not always been related to race, this would not be the case. But we are not and never have been.

More important, research shows that using poverty as a proxy for race fails on a number of fronts. First, it does not effectively target Black and Latino students, especially if it is combined with any other sorting mechanism like grades or test scores. If you look for low-income students with high test scores, which colleges would want, you are likely to bring in many white and Asian students who have been to better schools and have a stronger peer group but are poor for particular reasons—death or divorce of a parent, family health crisis, being a new immigrant—though they have significant human capital, not students from very weak segregated schools with parents or guardians who have less knowledge and contacts. At the other end, focusing on poverty ignores the fact that there are, in the aggregate, large Black and Latino middle classes whose members often experience various forms of race discrimination. They are often the students of color most prepared to succeed in a demanding college. From the perspective of the college or the selective high school, if the only diversity comes from students of color in poverty, there will be an unhealthy tendency to equate race and class and the white students will be less likely to encounter the better-prepared students of color and their families. College diversity efforts should undermine stereotypes, not reinforce them. Powerful research shows that using class for school desegregation or for higher education admissions would produce far less integration at a far higher cost since aid would have to be provided for many nonminority students who are affected by a spell of poverty at any point in time.[111]

Summary

At every stage of life, and even before children are born, opportunities are not equal across color lines. Policies that assume that we've achieved equal opportunity and that race can be ignored are built on profoundly inadequate foundations and are often counterproductive. If we make decisions about students for college based on the assumption that everyone has a reasonably equal chance and their current situation is the result of choices they and their families have made, we are operating in an alternative reality. Our society is so stratified by race and so burdened by the continuing effect of a long history of rigid racial subordination that the current colorblind assumptions are simply blind. Though there were major changes in the 1960s and prejudice has declined on some important measures, there has never been a time without large racial gaps in the major opportunities and outcomes of our institutions. The dismantling of the policies of the civil rights era has been evolving for decades. What we learned in a shocking way in the Trump campaign in 2016 is that it is easy to reactivate racial stereotypes and fears that policy makers had implicitly assumed were things of the past. Obviously, they are not. They are a persisting threat to American society.

People of color living today, even those who have never encountered overt discrimination, live in a world where African Americans, Latinos, and Indians have a tiny fraction of the average wealth of whites, where the great majority of their families never had the same opportunities, where their schools are separate and widely seen as inferior, and where there are persisting stereotypes leading to different treatment and lower expectations. Failing to think seriously about race in high school is simply bad educational practice. It will perpetuate deeply unequal preparation for college. Thinking that students are just making different choices on the same path with the same information is simply wrong.

Clearly, good policy means asking middle- and upper-class educators and policy makers who come overwhelmingly from very different lives and often have few real interracial contacts to understand the depth of these differences and discard simplistic assumptions. Understanding is essential, as is support for solutions strong enough to make a difference in developing our talent and becoming an equitable society. Some solutions must take race explicitly into account. Others need to be sensitive to the realities and develop race-sensitive policies aimed at unequal communities and schools, and look for and take into account very different life experiences that are rooted in race. Those policies need to explicitly address conditions that differ widely by race.

If very large communities historically discriminated against are more and more concentrated in segregated schools that are less and less able to prepare students for college, our colleges, without major changes, will not be able to meet the country's need for an educated workforce and citizenry. This generation and those that are coming no longer have the kind of white middle-class majority that our educational institutions were designed to serve, and we must learn to better evaluate and educate the people we actually have. More fundamentally, continuing on the existing path means the perpetuation of a deeply unequal society where opportunities and destinies are often determined by race. It will mean accepting continuation of failing policies in a time when the stakes have become much higher. Since whites have already become the minority in the precollegiate population and the number of college-age students reached a plateau in 2011 and is down more than two million students, failure to make major adjustments will mean that, in many parts of the country, we are making policies that cannot effectively reach the future majority of our communities or prepare our young for the kind of a society and advancing economy where they will live the rest of their lives. Educators are trying to steer our colleges and universities through a fundamentally transformed society in a time of great racial polarization with little help and some intentional disruption in our divided politics. This is a challenge worthy of a generation of rising leaders of our public schools and colleges.

The election of President Joe Biden and a Democratic Congress in 2020 opened the possibility of addressing some long-neglected racial inequalities in the society. The Biden program, as it passed through an extremely closely divided Congress, came to focus on the needs of young children and their families. The provision of two years of federally supported preschool was a major breakthrough, as were support for child care and basic family needs. The expanded earned income tax credit and other policies were sufficient to lift most poor families over the poverty line. Substantial payments for parents raising children brought a common European safety net into the United States, and expanding affordable health insurance addressed another key need. The program was not racially targeted, but was sensitive to barriers facing many people of color. The program certainly would be invaluable to millions of families of color, especially if the changes became permanent. A major cautionary note, however, was the unanimous opposition of the Republicans in Congress. The gains, however, did not include any significant support for adolescents or high schools, or more than a modest increase in maximum college aid for the poor. It was a historic step but left much to do.

3

The Tradition of Exclusion

SUPPORTERS OF TODAY's colorblind school and college policies often describe them as a return to our true colorblind traditions of individualism and individual merit before the civil rights revolution. But this was not the true tradition around which our high schools and colleges developed. The actual tradition was one of serving middle-class and affluent whites, with little focus on racial minorities or the poor. The real tradition was exclusion.

Educational policy and practice generally reflect the nature of a society. Our institutions operate in a society in which racial separation, subordination, and inequality have always been major features, usually denied or rationalized. Some Americans believe that those conditions have been solved, but the evidence is very different. As the last chapter showed, almost all stages of life in our society still have quite dramatic differences in opportunities by race. A major 2019 National Academies of Sciences, Engineering, and Medicine report outlined the dimensions of educational opportunity and summarized the "key indicators of disparities in access to educational opportunities." It pointed to the following critical dimensions: segregation by race, ethnicity, and poverty; the lack of "high quality learning programs"; the lack of access to high-quality pre-K programs; the lack of access to high-quality courses and instruction, strong teachers, and rigorous courses; the lack of a supportive environment; and inadequate provision of nonacademic supports for other problems that affect education.[1] Along all of the key dimensions, Blacks, Latinos, and Indians are denied equality.

They were denied it historically and they are denied it now, though the mechanisms and severity have changed. To achieve more equity in higher education, it is essential that policy be based on an understanding of the historical roots of our institutions, practices, and beliefs that have perpetuated inequality. The history of public schools and financial aid policies shows that

that understanding has usually been absent. This chapter explores the implications of the original traditions of exclusion for college opportunity.

The contemporary argument in politics and in the courts for colorblind policies assumes that the race-conscious remedies created in the civil rights era—intentional school desegregation, affirmative action in employment and housing, the Voting Rights Act, minority contracting policies, and others—were deviations from a tradition of colorblind policy that conservatives claim to be fighting to restore. The actual tradition, however, was color-conscious action by white institutions and policy makers that excluded people of color. Historically it included a widespread belief that students of color were inferior.

That tradition existed from the earliest settlements until the civil rights revolution of the 1960s, when it was strongly challenged. The civil rights policies adopted then were implemented because the segregation, stereotypes, and unequal conditions of people of color were so deeply rooted that trying to prosecute individual cases produced no significant changes—the classic attempt to empty out a river with a teaspoon. The violations and the practices were not about individuals; they were against all members of certain racial and ethnic groups, and they were broadly supported in many institutions, so the remedies had to be proportionate. The turn toward colorblind policies in the 1980s was a turn against successful civil rights policies. Policies were frozen or even reversed.

In a way it was a restoration of tradition, but the tradition of exclusion.

This chapter explores the pre–civil rights practices, with a special focus on high schools and public colleges as they developed from the beginnings in the 1800s to the time of the civil rights revolution in the 1960s, a period of more than a century in which high schools and public colleges were created and expanded across the continent.

We need to think about how high schools and colleges were created and grew and how they became important to the future of students and communities. The central reality is that they were created in an overwhelmingly white, racially polarized society and very little attention was paid to nonwhites as the institutions grew and became critical for social and economic mobility. For generations the dominant idea was that high school and college education were not necessary or feasible for students of color. The history of high schools is critical since they are the pathway directly into higher education, a pathway that can work very well, especially for middle-class white students.

Our educational institutions were formed in a society where white superiority was assumed by those who controlled major institutions and was deeply institutionalized in the development and operation of these key institutions. Though there were a small number of notable exceptions, the record is dismally clear. People of color were not regarded as having higher intelligence and were confined very largely to menial work requiring little education. It was, according to those beliefs, senseless to try to educate at a high level a group of people with limited capacity and who could not, in any case, get the jobs such education might qualify them for. There were caste-like barriers both in the society and in the institutions. American slavery had been a particularly vicious type of slave system.[2] The social separation was so thorough that we did not get anything like the vast mestizo population of Mexico or the creoles of the West Indies but rather a culture that generated mob lynchings of people of color who were accused of crossing the race line, a culture that saw segregation of groups defined as inferior as a basic norm that could be enforced by violence that white juries would never punish.

From the beginning, families and students of color have experienced different treatment. The Constitution of the U.S. included provisions accepting slavery, denying rights to Indians, and counting slaves as three-fifths of a person for the purpose of apportioning representation that increased the power of slave owners. Many of the Founding Fathers were slaveholders and held much of their wealth in slaves. Slaves had no enforceable rights. In the eastern U.S., the basic practice with the existing Native societies was ethnic cleansing. Indian societies were conquered and their land taken, and thousands were driven across the country on the tragic Trail of Tears, where many died. Early on, "the image of the native as hostile inferior creature became indelibly printed on the white mind. . . . He was uncivilized, and, it was generally concluded, incapable of civilization as Europeans defined it."[3] Just decades after Mexican independence, the U.S. invasion conquered and took half of the nation's land mass and signed a treaty guaranteeing to respect the rights of the residents of the conquered land. The Indian and Mexican treaties have been largely ignored.

Blacks, Indians, and Mexicans were confined largely to physical labor by job discrimination, and they were widely believed to be incapable of serious education. These assumptions were very widespread among whites, and racial stereotypes are still strong in the twenty-first century. In the Great Depression, Black men lost their jobs as the economy constricted and Black women were reduced to being servants.[4] Much earlier, whites turned violently against the Chinese, and the federal government banned them. President Theodore Roosevelt negotiated the Gentlemen's Agreement, in which the Japanese government agreed to block immigration in response to a fierce battle over access to schools in San Francisco.[5] Belief in the genetic superiority of northern Europeans was fundamental to the very restrictive immigration law adopted in 1924.[6]

Significant immigration did not resume until the 1965 immigration law, passed during the civil rights era, opened the door. The devastating conditions that had produced the epic floods of poor people from Ireland, Scandinavia, and elsewhere before World War I had ended. During the Depression and World War II, immigration was low, and the percentage of the U.S. population who were immigrants reached a low point at midcentury as the baby boom produced rapid population gains.

The Development of Secondary Education: Historical Roots of Unequal High Schools

The idea of free public high schools for local students emerged in Boston in the mid-nineteenth century. The schools developed around an American ideology of access for all, at least for all white students who were able to dedicate four or more years to significant academic study. Before there were public high schools, there were private schools emphasizing the classics and private academies that focused less on Greek and Latin and the ancient world and more on modern subjects, with emphasis on English, history, science, and other subjects. Those flexible American models did not assume that their students were headed to college, and this was definitely true of the new public high schools.[7]

The idea of free public high schools was a small part of the general national movement for the creation of state systems of free public education. After the public high school originated in Boston, "it quickly developed into a public institution offering the option of an English or a classical curriculum. It was copied in many other communities." It began to spread in the 1820s but grew significantly only after the Civil War. Public high schools made "available to local students at modest cost or gratis what had formerly been available to boarding students. . . . Where a local high school developed as a continuation of the primary or grammar or intermediate school, it constituted an additional rung on what was increasingly perceived as an American education ladder, or unitary school system, in contradistinction to the dual school systems of England, France, and Prussia," where only a "small minority of young people" were prepared "for further education in the university."[8] High schools were the last stage of an enormous expansion of public education in the U.S. in the nineteenth century and would become a dominant institution in the first half of the twentieth. The development of this democratic access to secondary education was an example to the world, but for a long time, it had limited meaning for the poor and far less for African Americans, Latinos, and Native Americans.

The growth was amazing. Since there was no national education agency or policy, schools developed at the state and local levels. Across the country, communities built impressive school buildings that often became great centers of community activity and sports. They developed without any federal policy except the creation of small vocational education grants in 1917. As the first public high schools emerged, it was clear that they would offer a broad range of subjects, with college preparation only for a few. This major democratic innovation reflected an optimistic society with a dynamic economy and a belief in mobility through education—a society that did not believe in sorting most students into vocational schools or apprenticeships at ten or eleven years old, as was normal in Europe. The U.S. was distinctive in creating what was then the broadest access to secondary education. This development would be of great value in producing economic growth and mobility. For a long time, however, these schools were largely irrelevant for students of color.

High schools were created in many places, but it was unclear how best to organize the new schools. In the absence of any national education authority, the educators and their organizations set up the powerful Committee of Ten, chaired by Harvard president Charles Elliot, with prominent educators from across the nation appointed by the National Education Association to figure out how to organize the schools. The committee's 1894 report established the basic framework calling for four years of courses, outlined basic required courses and the number needed, provided room for student choices, and addressed many other issues. The report had very long-lasting impacts that are still apparent in schools 125 years later.

A second very influential national report, the 1918 *Cardinal Principles of Secondary Education*, outlined a much broader and less focused role for high schools.[9] The report spelled out a wide range of basic goals, including "health, command of fundamental processes, worthy home membership, vocation, citizenship, worthy use of leisure and ethical character." In academic terms, the report was committed to a broad range of courses and approaches for an extremely diverse body of students. In practice, this definition was flexible and well accepted by educational leaders since it gave them broad discretion. It was at the polar extreme from traditional classic schools with a fixed curriculum. It was a move toward something for all. The tension between a rigorous academic core and very diverse offerings reflected deep differences that constantly recur in debates over secondary education. In fact, many commentators see the "excellence" movement that took hold in the 1980s, which raised course requirements and dominated policy well in the twenty-first century, as a kind of return to the original, more academic conception that is much less focused on the diversity of student needs.[10]

The high schools took hold first in big cities in the East and Midwest and then spread. For the white population, the development of free high schools that were not limited to a small elite was a quite remarkable expansion of schooling. As the great educational historian Lawrence Cremin observes, "The high school came into its own during the decades after 1876 [as] enrollment in public high schools began to exceed enrollments in private secondary schools . . . during the late 1800's. From 1890 to 1930, public high school enrollments virtually doubled every decade."[11] Decade by decade, the growth was amazing. From just 2 percent enrolling shortly after the Civil War and less than 7 percent in the 1889–90 school year, enrollment reached 11 percent ten years later, soared to 32 percent in 1919–20 as World War I ended, and reached an incredible 73 percent in 1939–40 during the Great Depression, when the lack of work created an incentive to stay in school.[12] The world had never seen this kind of mass secondary educational enrollment (though graduation rates lagged far behind).

High schools did not screen students; they could enroll but often did not stay or graduate. From the beginning, public high schools had classes that were aimed at college, which a small share of students took, and many others that had no connection with higher education. It was a time when few went to college. The students most likely to enroll in high school, most likely to graduate, and most likely to go to college were overwhelmingly from middle- and upper-class families. A history of Chicago and San Francisco public schools notes that "the early high schools . . . were initiated by school professionals who explicitly aimed to serve the well-to-do." The San Francisco superintendent stated, "The high school elevates and gives character to the city, making it attractive to a better class of citizens who may be seeking a home."[13]

Research shows that, from the beginning, there was a major class division between those who went to high school and those who did not. High school students were overwhelmingly from middle-class, white-collar families,[14] but the schools were open to children from the working class who wanted to try.

It was still a predominantly rural nation, and many young people were committed to work on the land. Black, Latino, and Indian students had very low levels of participation and graduation for generations.[15] The reality was that "many children could neither afford the time nor meet the examination requirements to attend." Those who could were divided "according to their courses of study."[16]

Serious large-scale social science was only just emerging in the early twentieth century in the U.S., and regular collection of systematic data by race in public schools came much later. One pioneering study of the life of a typical American city was carried out by Robert and Helen Lynd and reported in their influential 1929 book, *Middletown: A Study in Contemporary American Culture*. Their detailed examination of the growing small industrial city of Muncie, Indiana, included substantial discussion of the role of the high schools, pointing out that they were much more than precollegiate institutions and had come to play a powerful role in the socialization of adolescents who could afford to go and in the sports and cultural life of the city. Poor people often could not afford to go and felt excluded from the social life of the schools. The high schools were dominated by and very important for the "business" class, the white-collar workers and managers in the city, and were seen as very important for economic and social mobility even by those who could not go.[17] During this period, child labor laws were breaking the very common practice of children working full time, and compulsory attendance and truancy laws were keeping children in school longer, meaning that larger shares of the age group were at least starting high school.

New York State education officials commissioned a large study of the factors related to success and dropping out in high schools across the state during the Great Depression of the 1930s, a period in which the lack of jobs and the rise of compulsory attendance laws produced a large increase in high school enrollment but the persistence of a high level of dropouts. This study covered fifty-one communities with detailed information from 62 schools. Eventually 420 schools, almost half of the state's high schools, provided some information.[18] The study collected a great deal of data and showed quite clearly that success in completing high school and, especially, in finishing the more demanding precollege program that educated only a small share of high school students was strongly related to race and family economic situation.[19] It also showed that dropouts were prevalent among those in the general curriculum but uncommon among those enrolled in the "classic" or "college entrance" tracks.[20] Dropping out was directly related to economic status. "Almost two out of every three pupils who drop out of school below the ninth grade come from homes rated as poor or on relief." The college entrance students were "drawn from the more privileged classes, and those in vocational courses from the lowest ones."[21] Students of color were rare in high schools, which were 98 percent white in the state. Most of the students of color dropped out, many early in high school. The study noted, "All races, of course, many not be equally competent at present to profit by advanced work, but there is at least cause for concern in the fact that nurture now operates so consistently to increase whatever differences exist in native ability."[22]

Completion of high school was an uncommon accomplishment for white adults in 1940 and rare for Blacks. About a fourth of white adults had finished high school, compared with less than a twelfth of Blacks (7.7 percent). By midcentury it was more than a third of whites (36.4 percent) and almost a seventh of Blacks (13.7 percent). This was where the country was when *Brown v. Board of Education* came before the Supreme Court. By 1960 the Black rate had climbed to 23.5 percent, while 43.2 percent of white adults had high school diplomas. In 1940 less than a twentieth of white adults had college degrees (4.9 percent) and only one in a hundred Blacks (1.3 percent). By 1960, on the eve of the civil rights revolution, it was about a fifth of whites (21.7 percent) and one Black in thirty (3.5 percent).[23]

The enrollment of Indians and Latinos was very low. The great majority of African Americans lived in states where it was illegal for them to enroll in white schools, even if one was next door, and there was little change until well after the *Brown* decision made segregation by law illegal. From Baltimore to Miami, from Wilmington to Houston and across all of Texas, the doors to the high schools that prepared students seriously for college were shut for Blacks, and neither Latinos nor Native Americans were there in any significant number. In the big cities there were a few well-known Black schools, like Dunbar in Washington, with strong students and an excellent staff, made possible by the intense forced residential segregation of Black middle-class families and the very limited job opportunities for skilled Black professionals.

This happened as high school education was becoming more necessary for middle-class success and as rural jobs and physical labor gave way to large industries with millions of white-collar and clerical jobs. In some cities, including Saint Louis and Kansas City, Blacks who lived in communities in what became the suburban rings had to move into segregated areas of the central cities to have access to a high school that would enroll their children. On the nation's many Indian reservations, high schools were very rare, and students often were taken from families to go to one of the infamous "Indian boarding schools" for any secondary education. In white towns on reservation borders, there was often intense racial prejudice.

The federal data systems did not systematically collect Latino data until 1980 (except for counting "Spanish surname" in parts of the country). Researchers often reported that the data on Native students were so unreliable and they had such insignificant representation in national surveys that statistics and research were extremely difficult, but all the available data suggested grave problems.

As the 1960s began, high school attainment was rising but graduates were a small minority within Black, Latino, and Native American populations. With the long years of the Great Depression followed by the massive demands of World War II, there was not much money and not much focus on high school policy. Nevertheless, high school attendance became the norm for white students during the 1930s. States were adopting child labor laws and compulsory attendance laws that strongly encouraged secondary education. Serious attention to policy would come back in the 1950s, when the historic postwar baby boom headed toward the schools, the white suburbs exploded, the U.S. took on a new role as the superpower leading the West in a great world conflict, and the space age arrived, all of which combined to create demands for national action. Any white American with ability, a willingness to work, and time could get a reasonably good education, and many continued in the expanding public colleges. Issues of minorities had been largely ignored or excluded, and long-established racial patterns continued.[24]

The 1950s were a period of consolidation of the ideas of large comprehensive high schools, growing concern about the international standing of our system, and the beginning of serious court attention on issues of racial equity in education for the first time since the end of Reconstruction in the 1870s. A former Harvard president, James Bryant Conant, a preeminent leader of American science, received large Carnegie grants to do a comprehensive study of American high schools, which involved visits and surveys across the country and led to the 1959 publication of *The American High School Today*, an extremely influential study. He recommended large comprehensive high schools and reorganization of school districts to meet the enrollment size he defined as essential for the offering of an adequate range of sufficiently rigorous courses. He was strongly in favor of assessing, sorting, and tracking students by their level of talent. The book encouraged the development of large regional high schools with an extraordinary range of courses and a good deal of stratification. Many small rural districts were consolidated. Conant was strongly against small high schools with limited curriculum.[25] He advocated large schools offering a full range of subjects and drawing students from what had been several independent school districts. While some of these schools became famous and were able to give remarkable preparation to their students, for disadvantaged students who could become lost and were often ignored in these large institutions, it was a different story, later stimulating various reform efforts to personalize secondary schooling.

As the urban ghettos and barrios grew, residential segregation produced many segregated, concentrated-poverty high schools with weak educational results. The basic idea was that the schools should offer something for everyone and a strong academic pathway to those who were ready for it. This led to rigid tracking within the schools and to a major controversy later about the consequences of sorting students. When disadvantaged students in comprehensive schools were placed in dead-end tracks, they were often given weak instruction in the "general" track and dropped out or were left unprepared for anything.[26]

When the Soviet Union successfully launched Sputnik in 1957, the world's first orbiting satellite, and showed the world that the USSR had surpassed the U.S. technologically in the space race, the nation was shocked. In the midst of the Cold War, a world political battle for influence between democratic capitalism and communist dictatorships, this was a huge threat, and attention turned immediately to the schools and the colleges. Congress approved the National Defense Education Act, which targeted funds on science and critical languages. Funding was sharply increased for the National Science Foundation's educational efforts. In his State of the Union address in 1958, President Dwight D. Eisenhower sounded the call: "With this kind of all-inclusive campaign, I have no doubt that we can create the intellectual capital we need for the years ahead, invest it in the right places—and do all this, not as regimented pawns, but as free men and women!"[27] The science and technology issues would recur time and again in the succeeding decades. Coming just two years after Sputnik as suburbanization was running full tilt, the Conant report and reformers had a great opening. The science theme would be a major focus from the later part of the century to the present. It has been a period in which educators have often been devalued and business leaders have a large influence on policy, usually in terms of instituting more demanding curriculum, especially in math, computing, and science. The mid-twentieth century was a period with little concern by policy makers about equity.

Education had been considered something for state and local govern-ments, not a national policy concern. There was no significant federal role in public schooling and, although federal land grants had been crucial in launch-ing public universities, they were basically state institutions. The universities had become crucial national resources for defense in World War II, which massively expanded research funding, and the GI Bill began to greatly in-crease their reach. With the Sputnik crisis, the country recognized an urgent need to upgrade science and math training to catch up in the technological race. But the idea of a large continuing federal role in education centered on equity was a product of the 1960s, the civil rights revolution, and the tide of Great Society education and social legislation passed by the most liberal Con-gress in generations.

The federal role in higher education had been limited. The land-grant colleges were a very important product of the First and Second Morrill Acts, which spurred the creation of what became the great flagship public univer-sities, but they were basically supported by state governments and modest tuitions. The federal government fostered research during the World War II period, and the officer corps came largely out of universities. The GI Bill was part of the federal government's plan for the demobilization of the vast war-time military forces. In 1944, when President Franklin Roosevelt signed the GI Bill of Rights, he guaranteed that qualifying veterans would receive free years of college—up to $500 a year ($6,800 in today's dollars).[28] This deci-sion, based in part on the fear that it would be impossible for the economy to absorb millions of veterans returning at once, turned out to have very large impacts on moving toward the concept of broader college going, suc-cessfully educating many students who would not have likely attended in the past.[29] "In the peak year of 1947, Veterans accounted for 49 percent of college admissions. By the time the original GI Bill ended on July 25, 1956, 7.8 mil-lion of 16 million World War II Veterans had participated in an education or training program."[30] Although there had been a million Blacks in service, the GI Bill had substantially greater benefits for whites. Most Blacks returned to the South, where the colleges were still segregated and there were far fewer opportunities, so this race-neutral policy actually led to a widening of the racial gap in college going.[31] It was a striking example of how a progressive race-neutral policy could have counterproductive impacts if it did not come to terms with underlying racial structures. The GI Bill was an important in-novation, but it did not produce any general aid for college students. That would come in the 1960s.

Students of Color and Moving beyond Grade School

After the Civil War, Congress enacted constitutional amendments and Reconstruction laws to end slavery, guarantee fair treatment of emancipated slaves, protect their right to vote, and provide "equal protection of the laws" by state and local governments. The Thirteenth, Fourteenth, and Fifteenth Amendments were a fundamental change in the Constitution. Enforcing the Reconstruction policies produced a rush of freedmen into schools, election of Blacks to Congress, and many other changes. But it also generated fierce resistance and white "redeemer" politicians who used governmental power and terror from the Ku Klux Klan and other organizations to fight for a return to white supremacy. After a decade, following the 1876 election, a deadlock in the Electoral College was resolved by an agreement to give the presidency to a Republican in exchange for a withdrawal of federal troops who had been enforcing civil rights in the South.[32] After this bargain, white proponents of rigid segregation and subordination of Blacks took control of the South and Black rights largely disappeared. Reconstruction lasted only about a decade. In the following decades, the Supreme Court interpreted away most of the power of the civil rights laws and constitutional amendments. The 1896 *Plessy v. Ferguson* "separate but equal" decision authorized overt segregation in all aspects of life and did not define the "equal" part or how to enforce it. The decision was written as if it were a colorblind doctrine concluding that segregation was natural and that each race would enjoy equality in the law in their separate institutions, ignoring completely the structure of the society and that whites controlled all the levers of power. What followed was six decades of rigid segregation and repression enforced by state laws. The "equal" part of the doctrine turned out to have virtually no enforcement, so the policy was really to separate the races and allow whatever the state and local politicians decided to do in a situation in which Blacks had virtually no power and their right to vote was largely lost. Segregation and inequality were not substantially changed for a decade after *Brown* until the 1964 Civil Rights Act became law and far-reaching requirements were imposed by the Supreme Court, which ended the gradualism it had long accepted.

Outside the South, the cities with significant populations of nonwhite students were long segregated by neighborhood and school attendance boundaries backed by white political control and strong support for segregation. There were individual schools and small communities where these problems were not severe, but they were minor exceptions. Housing segregation was extremely high and reinforced by legally enforceable whites-only covenants prohibiting sales or rental of housing to people of color. Public officials and courts usually rejected or refused to even consider demands for changing policies or even acknowledging obvious inequities in the schools, maintaining that they were colorblind and no racial data needed to be collected or released. This was the basic policy of the U.S. from the 1870s until the 1960s when the great civil rights laws were enacted.

It is important to be aware that the color-conscious policies of segregation and exclusion were not simply written in the laws; they were enforced during that period with the full force of state and local law, and violence in their defense was widely tolerated. These were policies that were built into the structure of life and fully supported by the institutions and leaders. They were built into long-fixed ideas about white intellectual superiority.

As high schools developed, about nine-tenths of young Blacks were growing up in the South, in states with mandatory segregation laws where disenfranchisement laws and practices were limiting or excluding Black voting, so the key decisions were made in virtually all-white governments. Well after the end of slavery, there were high levels of illiteracy among African Americans, many of whom never went to school at all. Just after the Civil War, in 1870, as high schools were developing in the North, less than a tenth of Black children in the South were in school at all, rising to 45 percent by 1910.[33] In 1890 fewer than half of Black children over ten years old were literate, which rose to four-fifths by 1930.[34] There was rigid segregation in employment, so the job opportunities for Blacks who gained more education were very limited. It was no accident that so much talent went into education and ministry in segregated communities, given the exclusion from so many good jobs.

Given white beliefs in Black inferiority, the total segregation of schools, and white unwillingness to spend on Black children, the development of high schools for Blacks in the South came late and was limited. The first schools were often the products not of local school boards but of philanthropy from the North. The General Education Board, the Slater Fund, and the Jeanes Fund played a very important role in stimulating and supporting the creation of county training schools that were aimed at giving practical, work-oriented training to African American students, not emphasizing academic preparation. Later, the Rosenwald Fund, founded by the president of Sears Roebuck, Julius Rosenwald, stimulated the creation of more than five thousand schools across the South.[35] These efforts could not change the race relations of the Southern states, but they did begin to provide some opportunities where there had been none. However, the segregated public schools for Blacks had far less money, drastically lower teacher salaries, shorter academic years, and many other forms of inequality.[36]

The basic institutions of secondary and higher education developed in a situation of denial of racial inequality. In developing education policy, the courts' and federal officials' idea was to pay no attention to the special circumstances of the Blacks in the South or the Mexican Americans or Indians in the Southwest and the West and simply accept whatever kind of schools state and local authorities found appropriate.

There was virtually no attention to higher education for people of color, who were believed to be unable to benefit. A pioneering study by the great Black sociologist W.E.B. DuBois actually counted all the Blacks who had ever graduated from college by 1910, concluding that there had been just 693 from all the white schools in all of U.S. history. Columbia University had had 3; the University of Illinois, 1; the University of California, 2; and Princeton and Johns Hopkins, 0. There were only a few U.S. colleges that had more than a handful in their entire history.[37] Booker T. Washington and his famous Tuskegee Institute were celebrated by white leaders for his philosophy of training Blacks with skills that could get them jobs in the segregated labor market, not providing them with academic preparation that, it was thought, would make them ill-suited for those jobs. The Black colleges of the South began to expand after the Civil War, initially under the initiatives of religious groups and philanthropists. In 1890 the Second Morrill Act, which helped finance the nation's land-grant colleges, allowed states to exclude Blacks from white land-grant colleges and create separate Black schools, spurring the creation of a number of Black public colleges, but there was no enforcement of equity among the systems and they were fundamentally different.

There were individual campuses outside the South known to be open to students of color but in very small numbers. The society of college was a white society, as anyone who looks at old photos or movies of college life before the 1960s can see. Everything from the faculty to the student activities (except for sports in some places) to the curriculum was white. Outside the relatively small and poorly funded historically Black colleges and universities in the South (a product of Northern philanthropy, religious organizations, and the "separate but equal" provisions of the land-grant Morrill Act), there was extremely little provision in higher education for Blacks, and even less for Latinos and Indians. The historically Black colleges and universities played a critical role in creating a small but crucial population of college graduates.

White beliefs in the inferior intelligence of students of color, and the realities of employers' unwillingness to hire people of color for anything but menial labor, combined to focus attention on elementary education. A historian of Mexican American education writing about the early twentieth century concludes that there was "negligible" concern from white leaders: "Attitudes were tinged with racial prejudice, and the literature on the subject emphasized the inadequacies of the child of Mexican descent. The typical low IQ test scores . . . were considered evidence of innate intellectual inferiority, which in turn was thought to justify segregating the schools. Mexicans were said to be capable only of manual labor, and in fact farmers were afraid that education would make them useless even for farm work."[38] The IQ test was long seen as a neutral measure of ability to learn, not something strongly influenced by opportunity, so the test scores would be used to reinforce stereotypes.

We don't have national surveys of racial attitudes in first decades of the twentieth century when the country passively accepted increasingly rigid segregation of Blacks, when ghetto systems, enforced by discrimination, law, and violence, developed in the cities. Survey research had not yet developed. Our secondary and postsecondary institutions were evolving in an era of overt racism. Woodrow Wilson, elected in 1912, instituted segregation in the federal government and showed at the White House the famous film *The Birth of a Nation*, which glorified the Ku Klux Klan and portrayed it as saving the country from the savagery of freed slaves and the Union Army in the South and extolled the heroism of the white-power terrorist organization in restoring white control.[39] It was the first movie ever shown at the White House. The film was credited with a huge expansion of the Ku Klux Klan, which became a political power in many states. It was a period of white race riots in which Black communities were attacked in cities, including Chicago, Tulsa, East Saint Louis, and elsewhere, and hundreds of mob lynchings of Blacks who were accused of violating local values.[40] Bombings were common in cities when Blacks tried to move out of ghetto areas. The tradition was one of overt racism.

In the 1924 Immigration Act, extremely restrictive immigration policies, including installation of the first border controls with Mexico, were adopted in part on the widespread belief that northern European whites were the superior race and that other groups were inherently inferior. Immigration quotas were set very low or at zero for non-European countries in a system that lasted without basic changes until 1965. Virtually no immigration was allowed from Asia and Africa.[41] The first known national survey on the issue in 1939, in the early days of serious survey research, found that 71 percent of the public said

Blacks were less intelligent than whites, and 44 percent of those holding that opinion said that the inferiority was innate.[42]

U.S. schools and colleges developed and operated in a climate hostile to people of color. They formed images, traditions, and practices in a climate of segregated and unequal lives. The conditions were most rigid in the seventeen historical slave states; in other parts of the country with substantial nonwhite populations, the practice was to keep things separate and to have laws that ignored race—colorblind laws—and to collect no data, do no investigations, and deny any problems. By denying discrimination and blocking the collection of data, the status quo could be maintained.

Outside the South, the high schools and colleges were, in theory, colorblind but, in practice, built around middle-class white culture for white students. Up through the mid-twentieth century, only a small minority of students of color were finishing high school, and they had only token presence in higher education, except in the small historically Black colleges, many of which were founded by religious and other private organizations, or by state governments in the nineteen states required by the federal law to provide something separate for Black students. In 1900 nine-tenths of the Blacks (who made up an eighth of the national total enrollment) lived in the South, where public high schools for Blacks were rare. High school was considered, by white leadership, to be unnecessary for Blacks. To make the situation very clear, the U.S. Supreme Court unanimously decided in 1899 that its "separate but equal" decision, handed down just three years before, did not mean that there had to be high schools for Blacks—whatever the local officials decided was equal enough.[43] In the South, public high schools were developed in most regions for whites only until public high schools for Blacks began to expand significantly in the 1920s. Two decades after *Plessy*, many of the large cities in the South, including New Orleans, Charlotte, Mobile, and Atlanta, had no public high school education for Black students.[44] When Black public high schools came to the region, they often reflected the idea that Black students should be trained for practical work, the kind of lower-level jobs Blacks could get in an intensely segregated labor market. In a few cities with significant concentrations of educated Blacks, some strong high schools emerged, employing well-trained faculty who could not get jobs elsewhere and serving the emerging Black middle class.

As the great Black migration northward took hold in the early twentieth century, families of color arriving in the great industrial cities of the North lived in very difficult conditions. Students were isolated by housing discrimination and by a variety of discriminatory location, zoning, and enrollment policies and local resistance and violence that prevented moves into white areas. When the histories of many northern and western cities were examined much later by federal judges in civil rights cases, the courts found compelling evidence that virtually all school districts had used a variety of public policies to reinforce segregation, including drawing physical boundary lines through zoning, planning highways to separate whites from nonwhites, gerrymandering school attendance boundaries to preserve racial separation, locating schools in segregated areas, hiring no teachers of color for white schools, and using the courts to prevent minorities from buying housing or getting mortgages in white areas by enforcing racial covenants, all of which produced a very high level of racial separation in unequal schools.[45] Segregation was not an accident of the markets or a product of choice by nonwhite families. It was planned and enforced by white institutions. It produced schools that were unequal in all critical respects and students who were unequally prepared for success in high school and for college.

In other words, color-conscious policies restricting educational opportunities for students of color were very powerful for much of our history. School policies were designed to segregate, as were housing policies. Neighborhoods segregated by discrimination in housing created segregated education, and the pattern was reinforced by boundaries of individual schools, by the selection of school sites designed to be segregated, and by some kinds of choice mechanisms. Police practice kept crime out of white areas and concentrated vice in neighborhoods of color. There were few stably integrated neighborhoods in the U.S. in the mid-twentieth century. Once a neighborhood began to change, racial steering and panic peddling among whites usually produced rapid resegregation.[46] All-white suburbanization encouraged by federal policies was the major reality of the baby boom era after World War II.[47] In the cities with large nonwhite populations, segregation was often almost total.[48] This process of virtually all-white suburbanization was dominant until the 1970s, when significant Black suburbanization took hold in some metros following the passage of fair housing laws.

The periods of imposed segregation were far longer than those of active school desegregation and affirmative action. Segregationist policies reached many more people and were much more seriously enforced than desegregation issues either in the schools and colleges or in the housing market. Apart from a few university towns, almost no major school district seriously desegregated its schools without a legal mandate, and most soon abandoned such efforts after court orders were lifted.

In discussions of institutional development, Native education is usually neglected. The issues are complex, requiring understanding of the differing patterns of reservation, border town, and urban Indian settlement. The statistics are hard to obtain and interpret, with considerable confusion about the use of terms that in Indian Country are about tribal membership but in surveys are about self-identification. But the issues are too important to neglect. The available statistics consistently show patterns as devastating as those that affect Black Americans. In important ways, Indian education has almost always been a forgotten promise. Indians tend to go to school on reservations, or in racially polarized reservation towns, or in big cities where they are either treated badly when they are a visible presence or ignored or uncounted.[49]

Latino students, particularly in the Southwest, faced many problems of discrimination and segregation similar to those faced by Black students, as the Supreme Court recognized in the 1973 *Keyes* decision. There was a long-held belief that nonwhite students had inferior capacities and did not need to be provided equivalent education or access to white schools. In 1859 California's state superintendent noted, "If this attempt to force Africans, Chinese, and Diggers into one school is persisted in it must result in the ruin of the schools. The Great mass of our citizens will not associate on terms of equality with these inferior races; nor will they consent that their children should do so."[50] The Mexican American population of California dropped to a very low share as the state's white population exploded decade after decade. The wartime labor demand stirred immigration during World War I, and there was still an open border. When the Great Depression hit, however, there was large-scale deportation of Mexicans and even Mexican Americans by local officials. Latino children were seldom educated beyond the early elementary grades. Low scores on English-language IQ tests "were considered evidence of innate intellectual inferiority, which in turn was thought to justify segregating the schools."[51] A researcher in 1914 wrote, "Like the Negro, the Mexicans are a child-race without the generations of civilization and culture back of them which support the people of the United States."[52] Mexican Americans in the Southwest faced signs in restaurants and stores that said, "No dogs or Mexicans allowed." Their children were often sent to separate schools or "Mexican rooms" in schools where they received a much more limited curriculum. In the mid-1940s a study of Texas education reported that nearly half (47 percent) of Mexican American children received no education at all, and the great majority of the students were in the first three grades. A study of Austin showed that the public schools of the state capital were graduating an average of eight Mexican American students a year in a ten-year period.[53] In 1950, among adult Latinos in the Southwest, the average education level was less than sixth grade (5.4), and it was only seventh grade in 1960 when the civil rights movement hit.[54]

The pattern of segregation of Black and Latino students was first documented with federal statistics in the 1960s when school districts were required under the Civil Rights Act to report these data. The U.S. Commission on Civil Rights reported that in the early 1960s, two-thirds of Black first-grade children were in schools that were 90–100 percent Black, while 80 percent of whites were in schools that were 90–100 percent white a decade after the *Brown* decision. By 1960 four in five Blacks in major metro areas were in city schools, while more than two-thirds of whites were already in the suburbs. In the big central cities, three-fourths of Black students were in schools that were 90–100 percent Black.[55] The commission reported a strong correlation between the racial composition of schools and the performance of Black students.[56]

In the exodus from the South, Blacks came to very difficult conditions in the great cities of the North, which were rigidly segregated in housing and in jobs.[57] As families of color crowded into cities in search of jobs, intense overcrowding of housing and schools developed as local officials, realtors, and others "protected" white neighborhoods. Often there would be half-empty white schools losing students to the suburbs very close to Black or Latino schools bursting at the seams with playgrounds full of temporary classrooms, all to maintain separation. When many of the nation's largest cities faced desegregation lawsuits in the 1960s and 1970s, the courts outside the South could not order desegregation unless there was convincing proof of officials' action producing segregated schools, a difficult and costly process to investigate in the face of local resistance. Nevertheless, the courts found substantial documented proof of discrimination and policies producing segregation in virtually every case. Schools offered different educational programs with extreme differences in curriculum and teachers' levels of experience and qualifications. Segregated housing projects sometimes had their own schools to keep students separate.[58]

The reality is that, for generations, the education of Blacks, Indians, and Latinos was extremely unequal and often in obviously inferior segregated settings. Only a small fraction were able to graduate from high school. Apart from the all-Black or reservation Indian schools, which were much weaker in educational resources, the schools did not see students of color as their mission.

For generations the story of the nation's high schools was an overwhelmingly white story. This was a period in which the civil rights reforms of Reconstruction had been largely eliminated by conservative courts.[59] The courts did nothing to enforce equality for generations while local and state officials strongly enforced separation. In many places nonwhite students were assumed to be intellectually inferior and destined for menial jobs, mostly physical labor.[60] Many job categories were rigidly segregated in all parts of the country.[61] The institutionalization of American secondary and postsecondary education was carried out by whites and designed to serve white children and white communities. Where most people of color lived, in the South and the Southwest, they were often overtly excluded from white institutions. Elsewhere, a variety of policies and practices accomplished much the same in cities where there was a significant share of students of color. Where separate schools were created, they had far more limited resources. In fact, there were many decades of unsuccessful struggles to equalize resources before the National Association for the Advancement of Colored People (NAACP) decided it would never happen and launched a frontal attack on segregation itself.[62]

Higher education in the mid-twentieth century was segregated for Black students in the public colleges of nineteen states that had separate state universities for Blacks, seventeen of them by law, before *Brown*. In the rest of the country, there was no legally imposed segregation but there were virtually all-white traditions, many racial barriers, and forms of discrimination in admissions, housing, and other aspects of life. Racist attitudes and practices were common on campus as in the rest of the society, including the military. In the early twentieth century the Ku Klux Klan was a recognized student organization on some campuses. There were tiny changes in public colleges and some private ones, but real change would come much later.

For centuries, color-conscious policies—white-conscious policies—were thorough and serious in public schools, and people who tried to cross the lines often faced impossible resistance. Immediately after *Brown* there was the rise of "colorblind" choice systems, but they failed very badly. Colorblindness emerged as a way to try to block desegregation, then came back and has remained as a justification for the dismantling of civil rights policies. Colorblind choice often relies on a very idealized and inaccurate view of the working of markets and choice systems.

Delegitimizing the Racial System of
Seventeen States Where Most Black Students
Lived and Were Segregated by Law

The segregated and disgraceful conditions confronting students of color led civil rights organizations to focus great attention on educational issues, trying for decades to obtain more equal conditions. Finally Blacks, through the NAACP, engaged in an organized strategy to attack segregation itself, first in Southern universities and then in the public schools themselves.

A half century of legal struggles by the NAACP, and by Black communities and their allies, led up to *Brown v. Board of Education*. The first great victories in the early 1950s were about access to graduate education in the seventeen states with segregation laws where only whites could go to the law school or the medical school. In the University of Texas case of *Sweatt v. Painter*,[63] the Supreme Court faced the question of whether a segregated law school set up just for Blacks could ever equal a flagship university law school that trained the state's legal leadership. It concluded that it could not, helping set the stage for the great battle over school segregation.

The legal revolution began with the *Brown* case in 1954 and the related higher education decisions. *Brown* held that segregation was "inherently unequal" and ordered the federal courts to take some unspecified action to end it with "all deliberate speed." It was the first fundamental challenge to the social structure of the states with segregation laws in nearly ninety years, but the resistance was so strong that simply declaring the principle was insufficient to produce more than token change, justified by a colorblind policy known as "freedom of choice," which allowed all children to choose between the white and Black school systems. The policy, spelled out in a key lower-court decision, *Briggs v. Elliott*, held that school systems could fulfill the constitutional requirements of *Brown* by offering Black students who complied with local requirements a choice to transfer to white schools. The idea was that since white students were also free to transfer to Black schools (though none ever did), it was a perfect colorblind policy. One of the difficulties with the colorblind theory in an extremely unequal society is the creation of policies that sound equitable on their face but in the actual context of the society are meaningless, such as the idea of choice as if there were no social pressures or stereotypes drastically limiting real choice. As far as desegregating the schools, choice was, with very few exceptions, an abysmal failure. The Black schools remained totally segregated but lost a few of their stronger students. The Black students who transferred and their parents often faced harassment and isolation in white schools. Nine years after *Brown*, when President John F. Kennedy sent what became the 1964 Civil Rights Act to Congress, 99 percent of Black students were still in totally segregated schools in the South. "Freedom of choice" in reality was freedom to segregate, a little veil over controlling barriers to change.[64]

The experience was an important lesson about a how a colorblind choice system works in a stratified, polarized society. The first reality was that it left the historically Black schools totally segregated while making that unchanged reality, in theory, a product of choice. Few Black families and students in polarized communities chose to transfer to what were often obviously better white schools. This was because the choice was not really free and there were high costs for many of the choosers. Because the Black students were entering schools that had always been white in a climate where state and local leaders were mostly segregationists, they often faced hostility in school and pressures on their parents. Especially at first, it took courage and there were real risks. Saying there is a choice without doing anything to change long-established racially polarized institutions leaves the status quo largely intact. Often families who chose to transfer faced pressure in their jobs and elsewhere. Within a decade it became apparent that this form of choice would leave the status quo almost untouched and would even legitimate it. By the early 1960s, when the civil rights movement exploded in the South, it was clear to civil rights advocates that the colorblind policies needed to be replaced by something fundamentally different. Choice and markets work best when there are not serious constraints, and they work best for those with the best information, the most resources, and the most contacts. They work worst for those without information and resources, who often face active resistance when they exercise their choices. In this case something far stronger than colorblind choice would be required to actually change the schools.

Brown was hailed as a revolutionary decision when it was handed down. All of a sudden white schools and colleges no longer had the right to refuse to educate students of color. But the extreme resistance of the white politicians and the communities was so serious that *Brown*, as implemented by the often recalcitrant federal courts,[65] hadn't moved even 1 percent of Black students in the segregated states into white schools by the end of the 1950s. The traditional practices and the racial politics of state and local elections undid this monumental Supreme Court decision until the great events of the civil rights movement and congressional passage of unprecedented new laws produced real progress.

The tradition of American high schools and colleges was one of creating white schools and public colleges that served and expanded opportunity for white students. In the Southern states and the historical slave states outside the South, the racial character of the schools was established by law until *Brown*. For Indians and Mexican Americans, it was mostly by local and state practice. There was a widespread assumption that secondary and higher education were not appropriate for students of color. In the Black schools and colleges, there was profound inequality, and local and state officials were unwilling to seriously address the issue. In most of the North, there were few college students of color. In spite of the great success of the GI Bill, there was no significant movement for general aid to low-income students. When the large migrations came during World War I and II, meeting demand for workers, segregation was intensified by a variety of local practices and did not become a serious issue until the 1960s. In the states whose policies had been overruled by *Brown*, the fierce resistance of local officials virtually reduced that powerful constitutional decision to insignificance for a decade. Discrimination in housing and employment was rampant. The tradition, largely intact, at the beginning of the civil rights era was one of separate and unequal education with limited opportunity for students of color to prepare for white colleges that, with few exceptions, showed little interest in serving them. There were few signs that large changes were coming. In many ways, the system was color conscious, but in whites' favor.

The experience of a war against the racist Nazi government, the commitment of President Harry S. Truman and the Democratic Party to take the party's first major steps to support serious federal civil rights laws, and the accumulating evidence of injustice in society helped set the stage for the 1954 *Brown* decision, which undermined the legality of segregated education and the whole Southern system of racial stratification by law and spurred movements across the country. But even that remarkable decision was largely frustrated by the intense white resistance. Segregation was fiercely defended by the leaders of the segregated states, and it took a great social movement and a decisive change in political leadership to produce the tools that could actually change a tradition of racial subordination and exclusion that had always existed, in one form or another, in U.S. history.

As the civil rights revolution began to take shape in the early 1960s, the country still faced extreme educational stratification and exclusion. Directly challenging that and creating opportunities previously unknown on a large scale in U.S. history was a central goal of the civil rights movement. First becoming visible with the Montgomery bus boycott and beginning to develop momentum with the student sit-ins and the Freedom Rides early in the decade, the revolution led to the first major effort to change the nation's tradition of educational exclusion since the end of Reconstruction, eight decades earlier.

When opponents of race-conscious policies refer to a tradition of a historical time when race did not matter, when colorblind policies and beliefs led to the equitable treatment of all, they are discussing not actual history but an ideologically constructed memory. The tradition was not colorblindness and, certainly, that was not the reality in schools and colleges. It was a form of willful blindness that functioned to keep the issues out of the public and the white institutions protected from any change the white communities did not favor. The true tradition was white-conscious exclusion, transcended only by the hard-earned accomplishments of the small minority of students of color who succeeded in spite of the array of barriers. Thinking about the long arc of educational policy in the U.S., it is important to keep the true tradition in mind, since it is a tradition that was rooted in the very structure of our educational institutions.

4

The Civil Rights Revolution
and the War on Poverty

A COLOR-CONSCIOUS RIGHTS
POLICY WORKED

THE 1960s were a decade of astonishing social change and breakthroughs for civil rights and social policy reforms emphasizing equal opportunity for the poor and justice for people of color. In the space of a decade, we went from separation and discrimination to the adoption of antidiscrimination laws, to the realization that we needed laws and policies that were intentionally aimed at changing racial conditions, and to an array of policies strongly aiding families and students living in poverty. The federal role changed from largely passive acceptance of notoriously unequal situations to recognition of the inequalities and, finally, to genuinely effective action. Historic changes in schools and colleges happened quickly. It was the peak of the judicial development of civil rights law in the final stage of the Warren Court. In the space of a few years, the rigid structure of segregation by public officials in the seventeen de jure segregated states was substantially dismantled in many institutions. The Johnson administration's Great Society agenda had wide range from the creation of Medicaid for poor children, to the Head Start preschool program, to ambitious housing and urban programs designed to upgrade poor neighborhoods, to the affirmative employment programs designed to bring down racial barriers and expand the nonwhite middle class. It was the only time in American history that a coordinated attack on discrimination and poverty was launched by the federal government. As a radical change, it triggered strong resistance, resistance that has already lasted a half century on some fronts.

During the 1960s, government decided to confront segregation and poverty through a great expansion of the federal role in supporting schools of children in poverty and children of color. The changes were embodied in four legislative changes: the creation of the War on Poverty in 1964, the enactment of the 1964 Civil Rights Act, the passage of the first general federal aid to schools in American history, the Elementary and Secondary Education Act, and the creation of a critical new role for the government in colleges with the enactment of the Higher Education Act.[1] The laws made the federal government an unprecedented force in education and defined the basic responsibility of federal education policy to be not passively distributing money to local institutions and elites but equalizing opportunities by ending exclusion and supporting the students and the schools and colleges that served minorities and the poor. These were historic changes, and they came in a remarkably short period. By the end of the decade, however, the new policies were under a fierce attack; a harsh opponent, Richard Nixon, was president; and the Supreme Court was becoming far more conservative. An administration hostile to civil rights was taking power.

The largest and most influential social protest movement in American history—a dignified and powerful nonviolent movement with strong religious dimensions and eloquent leadership—emerged in the early 1960s and its protests aroused the conscience of the country and led to large racial changes. The killing of a popular president shortly after he had asked for unprecedented civil rights reforms, and the ascent of a president with unique legislative skills and determination who won a landslide election and brought in the century's most liberal Congress, opened the door for rapid change. For a few years all three branches of the federal government worked in tandem on major changes increasing racial equity in American education. The government enacted and exercised strong civil rights enforcement powers that had not existed before. A great deal was done in a few years. Some of the changes were irreversible but divisions soon opened, white resistance grew, and the entire effort got tangled up with and derailed by an increasingly unpopular war in Vietnam, urban riots, and division during the Black Power movement, which divided the broad political coalition that had driven the civil rights and antipoverty reforms and drove President Lyndon Johnson from office.[2]

The 1950s were shaped by the postwar baby boom and the creation of vast suburban developments. It was a period of return to traditional families, a growing economy, and conformity. The U.S. had become the world's dominant nation and was in the midst of a cold war with the USSR. President John F.

Kennedy had been elected by a very narrow margin in 1960, and there had been no major social issues in the campaign. It was a generational-change election, but Kennedy had been cautious on civil rights. There had been a shift toward more support for him from the Black community when he called Martin Luther King Jr.'s wife to express sympathy for her husband, who was jailed during a great protest campaign. It was a symbolic gesture but a powerful one to Black Americans, though civil rights was not Kennedy's priority.

The election was very close, and there was no mandate for big changes. Many of the most powerful chairs in Congress were Southern conservative Democrats strongly opposed to change in the South's deeply rooted practices of racial subordination. The energy came from what became a major social movement rising from the Black South.[3] As the decade opened, there were stirrings of civil rights struggles across the South. King had become a major national spokesman through the 1957 Montgomery bus boycott, Black students were sitting in at lunch counters and demanding to be served, and the Freedom Riders would soon be defying Southern bus segregation laws and provoking confrontations across the South.[4] There were small cracks in the walls of segregation in schools and colleges across the region.

Kennedy had not been a civil rights liberal as a senator, and his priorities were traditional Democratic goals. He initially pressed for only a very modest civil rights law focusing on voting, a law that turned out to be too weak to produce significant change. In spite of campaign promises, he delayed issuing an executive order on housing discrimination.[5] Kennedy had to send federal authorities into Mississippi and Alabama to defend courts requiring slight integration of the major public universities. Things were stirring, but the Democrats did not want to disrupt congressional action on other bills by raising issues that would damage their coalition, which still included many powerful Southern conservative lawmakers. Kennedy even successfully pressed Black leaders to keep civil rights issues out of his pending education bill. He wanted to control tensions, negotiate solutions, and concentrate on other issues. History intervened and a remarkable social movement met by brutal Southern resistance moved the president and Congress.

As the 1960s began, the federal government was almost powerless to act against the blatant segregation and discrimination shaping the lives of millions of families of color. There had been no tradition of strong positive federal action for racial justice since Reconstruction, and the government had limited authority to act on the issues. Its major social expenditures, products of Franklin D. Roosevelt's New Deal, were Social Security and related social insurance systems such as unemployment insurance. There was no significant federal role in education or health care, no major urban policies, and limited involvement with local communities. Conservative courts back in the 1880s and 1890s had dismantled what remained of Reconstruction-era civil rights laws, and Southern power in Congress had blocked any significant new ones in spite of comprehensive segregation in seventeen states with blatant inequality. An antilynching bill, proposed in the 1920s, had been blocked. Apart from extremely limited voting rights laws passed in 1957 and 1960, steps toward the desegregation of the army, and the creation of an independent agency, the Commission on Civil Rights, to carry out investigations, there was nothing. There was no legislative authority for the Justice Department to act or to initiate litigation on civil rights. When a Virginia county (Prince Edward County) shut down its public schools to prevent desegregation and funded private school vouchers for whites, all the Justice Department could do was to ask for private philanthropy to provide something for the county's Black children. U.S. international influence was threatened by the blatant discrimination confronting people of color coming to the country. As Western colonialism gave way to independent nations in Africa, their diplomats could not find decent places to stay or eat when driving from Washington embassies to the new United Nations. The administration was increasingly frustrated by Southern political leaders who grandstanded their defiance of federal courts to preserve segregation against even modest changes. The federal government had no funds or authority for training or conciliation of growing racial disputes. The private civil rights groups struggled to make headway with a handful of out-of-state civil rights lawyers who had to appear before largely conservative Southern judges, facing resistance from thousands of school districts. Segregation was illegal in theory but largely untouched. The great decision in *Brown v. Board of Education* was a dead letter in the great majority of school systems after a decade.

A major revolution in U.S. civil rights policy took place between 1963 and 1965, and it coincided with large political changes and an astonishing array of new federal policies. In the spring of 1963 the Southern Christian Leadership Conference organized a campaign against segregation and discrimination in the heart of the Deep South, Birmingham, Alabama.[6] When a peaceful march of protesters, including children dressed in their Sunday best and singing hymns, was attacked by police dogs, women were assaulted by police, and fire hoses were turned on children on national television, people across the country saw the brutality of the local sheriff, "Bull" Connor.[7] The reality of

Southern white resistance and the violence that had always lain behind it became apparent to millions of Americans, and public opinion shifted dramatically with an unprecedented increase in the public identifying civil rights as
the most urgent issue. Civil rights demonstrations sprang up across the U.S.
The protests and the segregationist reaction made conditions very clear to
Congress, where scores of civil rights bills were quickly drafted and intro-
duced. There had been a clear political reason to avoid civil rights battles in
Congress; now it was urgent to show leadership.

President Kennedy sent the most far-reaching civil rights measure in ninety
years to Congress in June 1963. It outlawed discrimination in public accom-
modations such as hotels and restaurants and changed the government from
a neutral bystander of discrimination to a powerful opponent, at least when
government chose to use the act's powers. Most important for education, it
authorized the Justice Department to file civil rights cases for the U.S. government to enforce the Constitution and the laws, and it forbade giving federal
funds to institutions that discriminated. Since that implicated almost all major
educational institutions, it meant that there was massive leverage: all recipients
would have to comply with legal requirements or lose money and still face litigation against the federal government. This power created the possibility of
policies and actions that would simultaneously affect thousands of school districts and colleges. The National Association for the Advancement of Colored
People had been pushing for federal civil rights power like this ever since facing the massive Southern resistance to the *Brown* decision. The 1963 bill faced
powerful resistance. Southern political leaders had been successful in using
the filibuster and other legislative tools to block every significant civil rights
proposal since Reconstruction, including, for example, a proposal by a GOP
president in the 1920s to outlaw racial lynching, which still happened regularly
and was almost never punished in the South. The new legislation had made
limited progress before Kennedy was assassinated in Dallas in November 1963,
profoundly shocking the country.

President Johnson, who had been known as a master of the Senate and who
had not been identified as a civil rights liberal, immediately committed his
administration to enact the law as Kennedy's legacy, and to enact it without
the compromises that had been expected. This triggered the longest Senate
debate in U.S. history as the South tried to block it in an all-out battle, with
senators camped near the chamber for key quorum votes. Religious and other
groups across the U.S. mobilized to urge support from conservative and moderate members. The debate went on for eighty-two days, the filibusters

paralyzing Congress while these vast changes were debated.[8] The law that was passed in 1964 was the decisive defeat of those committed to the old order in the South. It generated quick changes in some important aspects of Southern life but triggered a major realignment of Southern conservatives into the Republican Party by the end of the decade. It was the most decisive act in race relations in ninety years, changing the role of the federal government so that it was possible to implement a fundamental change in basic institutions. A major survey in 1999, a third of a century later, showed that the American public rated the passage of the act as the second most important domestic event of the twentieth century.[9] There has been major controversy over the law since it was enacted.

There was a parallel attack on poverty, though far more limited and less controversial. As the civil rights reforms were developing, the Kennedy administration was working on new approaches to helping the poor and attacking the root causes of poverty, stirred in part by a widely read book, Michael Harrington's *The Other America*,[10] as well as by experiments in high-poverty neighborhoods sponsored by the Ford Foundation, by job training ideas, and by other current reform ideas. The concept of the War on Poverty, enthusiastically embraced by President Johnson, was an effort to identify and address the various conditions that were keeping a large group of Americans outside the economic and social mainstream and presenting them with many barriers and problems in a prosperous nation. As the suburbs exploded and left behind increasingly poor central cities, it was clear that divisions were deepening in the metropolitan areas. Poverty was stubbornly persistent and entrapped millions of people who were not being reached by existing programs. Larger and larger sections of central cities were becoming ghettos and barrios as the explosive growth of white suburbs drew the white middle class out of the cities but blocked families of color through housing discrimination. One of the key dimensions of what became Johnson's War on Poverty was enabling poor communities to organize and have a say in the conditions that affected them through community action agencies. (Johnson ruled out direct federal programs to employ the jobless.) Because of the lethargy of traditional agencies, a new agency, the Office of Economic Opportunity, was created.

Johnson made the War on Poverty a prominent part of his election campaign in 1964, and it was enacted as the Economic Opportunity Act in 1964.[11] The bill was a combination of a variety of programs with limited funding, but it did prove to be a vehicle for both initiating a number of important educational ideas and providing a central idea for broader public school and higher education legislation. The first federal preschool effort, Operation Head Start, was created; Upward Bound and Work-Study were created to help identify and support low-income students; and there were summer jobs designed to encourage students to finish high school.

A far deeper and more lasting impact came from making poverty the central issue in the design of the first program providing general aid to education in U.S. history, the Elementary and Secondary Education Act,[12] and the first general support for college participation by the poor, the Higher Education Act, which funneled federal dollars to schools with concentrations of poor children.[13] This period made helping the poor the priority in federal education policy both in the schools and in higher education. The basic structure of federal aid to higher education came in the form of money going to poor students to pay tuition and costs. At the same time, ideas of equity rights were spreading to other groups—Latinos, Native Americans, and, by 1970, the women's movement.

The initiatives on civil rights and poverty during the brief period of 1963–65 combined to transform the federal role in education and were driven in good part by the understanding that both people of color and people living in poverty were excluded or faced serious barriers to full participation in educational opportunity. The basic funding programs were directly class conscious in funneling resources and opportunities to schools serving concentrations of students in poverty and low-income students struggling to afford college, both disproportionately nonwhite.

The civil rights law forbade discrimination and created powerful tools to act against it. The education laws were not directly color conscious but were intended to bring down the economic barriers that helped produce racial inequality in education. The education aid was targeted at extremely low-income children. Since they were aimed at concentrations of poverty, they were especially important in communities of color. The bills were about replacing a system of entrenched discrimination and exclusion and giving people the supports they needed to take advantage of new opportunities. They were about giving effect to Supreme Court and federal court decisions that were being widely ignored and addressing the social and economic conditions that reinforced and perpetuated the inequality. The central thrust was expanding opportunity for historically neglected students.

Some important civil rights reforms were accomplished rapidly with limited difficulty. For example, restaurants, hotels, hospitals, and other public places in the segregated states largely complied voluntarily. Many of the owners actually saw them as increasing markets. Education was something different. There was determined resistance by political leaders to changing the racial realities of the basic public system of socialization in Southern society (and, later, in Northern cities). Southern states belatedly began physical improvements in shabby Black schools in the hope that that would block integration demands. In the South, there was almost no voluntary compliance with school desegregation, meaning that, until the Civil Rights Act, civil rights lawyers had to sue each community before judges who were themselves part of the white Southern elite.[14] Suddenly, under the new law, lines of caste enforced by law and custom were being powerfully threatened by putting the power and money of the federal government behind demands for change. As that effort became serious and faced the nature of the barriers, and the unwillingness of institutions and leaders to obey the law, the remedies shifted from making voluntary change more systematic and prosecuting outliers to increasing the focus on outcomes. Fiercely resistant state and local officials meant that normal law enforcement processes could not work, given the defiance of voluntary compliance with the law and active multidimensional resistance. To change the realities confronting students of color, policy had to move toward generalized, class action solutions requiring basic institutional change and changes in outcomes. These policies were increasingly color conscious in the sense of establishing the specific rights of all Black students, keeping close track of what was happening to them, and monitoring the progress the schools were duty-bound to make under regulations that became increasingly demanding over time.

The Failure of the Case-by-Case Civil Rights Policies and the Civil Rights Revolution

Because the resistance was too powerful for procedural remedies that relied on voluntary compliance, a direct focus on racial outcomes was the alternative. In its nature, that had to be color conscious. This change did not happen because of ideological reasons. It happened because nothing else was adequate to remedy the generations of active discrimination built into structures and beliefs, and the failure of the responsible institutions to implement real changes until there were unambiguous requirements enforced by severe penalties. That approach, systemic remedies for deeply entrenched discrimination, worked. The alternatives failed.

The futile effort to prosecute individual violators gave way to positive requirements for all institutions. Much the same happened in moving enforcement of voting rights from prosecuting each registrar to requiring federal clearance of state voting policies in resistant areas and in the movement from individual employment discrimination cases to the requirement of affirmative action plans for government contractors. The great expansion of the collection of racial data triggered by the Civil Rights Act and the production of scientific reports on racial equity provided the basis for identifying systemic problems and monitoring policy impacts. Race-conscious changes were seen as necessary to change the basic, deeply rooted dimensions of racial inequality, from affirmative plans for employment for federal contractors to enable a Black business class, to minority contracting provisions in government procurement, to voting rights.

Almost a century after the rights of former slaves to vote were written into the Constitution, nothing had worked since the Federal troops occupying the South were withdrawn and Southern whites were able to take away the right to vote. Southern Blacks were allowed to vote after the enactment of the Fifteenth Amendment during Reconstruction but were disenfranchised in the late 1800s and the early years of the twentieth century after politics and the Supreme Court changed through a combination of state laws, rules of political parties, and violence and intimidation by the Ku Klux Klan and other groups that would terrorize Blacks who tried to vote. In spite of a long and brilliant legal campaign stretching over a half century, civil rights protests, several Supreme Court decisions,[15] and enactment of two modest voting rights laws, few Blacks were able to vote in many parts of the South in the early 1960s. Following the Selma-to-Montgomery march led by Martin Luther King Jr. in Alabama, Congress passed the 1965 Voting Rights Act. In an extraordinary speech to a joint session of Congress, President Johnson said that there was no alternative to a vast expansion of federal authority: "Every device of which human ingenuity is capable has been used to deny this right. . . . Experience has clearly shown that the existing process of law cannot overcome systematic and ingenious discrimination. No law that we now have on the books, and I have helped to put three of them there, can insure the right to vote when local officials are determined to deny it. In such a case, our duty must be clear to all of us. The Constitution says that no person shall be kept from voting because of his race or his color."[16]

The act was based on the premise that states where Blacks had voted in low numbers should be subject to virtual takeover of the registration process by federal officials and that electoral laws should be subject to approval by the Department of Justice. The new law "swept away the primary legal barriers to black registration and voting in the South, eliminating the literacy tests and poll taxes and allowing the Justice Department to dispatch federal registrars and poll watchers and insure the integrity of the voting process."[17] This was a radical expansion of federal power to protect an elemental political right, and it did rapidly produce a great expansion of Black voting, particularly in the most resistant areas. It moved away from requirements that there be proof of intentional violations in each jurisdiction and a remedy limited to that proof toward an assumption that the entire process was corrupted by racial bias and that only structural changes could break the white control and create real opportunity for Black political participation. The results were substantial, particularly in the most conservative areas: "In Mississippi, black registration went from less than 10 percent in 1964 to almost 60 percent in 1968; in Alabama, the figure rose from 24 percent to 57 percent. In the region as a whole, roughly a million new voters were registered . . . bringing African-American registration to a record 62 percent."[18]

When the sweeping changes in the Voting Rights Act were challenged in the Supreme Court, the Court strongly upheld the law, citing the impossibility of achieving justice under the traditional procedures of proving each individual violation. The Court held,

> Despite the earnest efforts of the Justice Department and of many federal judges, these new laws have done little to cure the problem of voting discrimination. According to estimates by the Attorney General during hearings on the Act, registration of voting-age Negroes in Alabama rose only from 14.2% to 19.4% between 1958 and 1964; in Louisiana, it barely inched ahead from 31.7% to 31.8% between 1956 and 1965, and in Mississippi it increased only from 4.4% to 6.4% between 1954 and 1964. In each instance, registration of voting-age whites ran roughly 50 percentage points or more ahead of Negro registration. The previous legislation has proved ineffective for a number of reasons. Voting suits are unusually onerous to prepare, sometimes requiring as many as 6,000 man-hours spent combing through registration records in preparation for trial. Litigation has been exceedingly slow, in part because of the ample opportunities for delay afforded voting officials and others involved in the proceedings. Even when favorable decisions have finally been obtained, some of the States affected have merely switched to discriminatory devices not covered by the federal decrees, or

have enacted difficult new tests designed to prolong the existing disparity between white and Negro registration. Alternatively, certain local officials have defied and evaded court orders or have simply closed their registration offices to freeze the voting rolls. The provision of the 1960 law authorizing registration by federal officers has had little impact on local maladministration, because of its procedural complexities.[19]

The Supreme Court recognized that it was impossible to change fundamental aspects of racial subordination without changing the structures that supported them and that traditional case-by-case, voter-by-voter litigation was futile. The choice was between simply accepting the perpetuation of inequality, on one hand, and, on the other, deciding that the fundamental pattern of exclusion was illegitimate and recognizing the necessity of changing the structures to produce genuine measurable progress toward equal opportunity. The problem to be solved was not individual acts of discrimination; it was about changing the structures deeply enough to actually change outcomes. To actually have the right for Blacks to vote in the most resistant states, the traditional state control of the electoral system had to be changed. The power of courts and administrative agencies to enforce laws rests on the general compliance reinforced by the risk of sanctions against obvious violators. When there is almost universal noncompliance and the state and local officials and private institutions obstruct change and refuse to comply, traditional legal processes do not work. If 99 percent of households refused to file their income taxes and each had to be individually sued, it would be impossible. The practical impossibility of using traditional methods to change such deeply rooted attitudes and the institutions built up around them led to the development of broad class action litigation for entire classes of victims and to the development of sweeping civil rights injunctions[20] and broad results-oriented laws. The Court, Congress, and the executive branch face a very similar challenge in the schools and in the higher education systems in seventeen states with a history of de jure segregation.

The Politics of the Civil Rights Victories

President John F. Kennedy won narrowly with strong Black support, but his administration and the independent Commission on Civil Rights confronted the frustration caused by the unyielding resistance to the *Brown* decision and the failure of the modest civil rights laws (the first since Reconstruction) adopted in 1957 and 1960. The inability of civil rights groups to sue each of the thousands of segregated school districts or of the Justice Department to investigate and prove discrimination by each of the huge numbers of registrars who were refusing to register voters of color made it apparent that it would be impossible to solve discrimination case by case forever. Laws simply forbidding discrimination only work where the great majority are willing to comply, not against strongly defended basic structures.

There was a national wave of support for Kennedy's plans after his assassination. The loss of a popular young leader shocked the country and made him a martyr, producing support that brought quick passage of the War on Poverty plan. Although the program's Office of Economic Opportunity had a modest budget, it quickly initiated the Head Start preschool initiative and launched the Work-Study program to help students work their way through college in campus jobs. Ending poverty became a central theme in education policy.

As Johnson took over and won a landslide election in 1964, the country was prospering, the suburbs were giving new homes to growing postwar baby boom families, the U.S. was the unchallenged leader of the free world, incomes were rising, and poverty and joblessness were declining. There was severe poverty and racial inequality, but it was still an overwhelmingly white society where children could expect to do better than their parents. There was the most socially progressive Supreme Court in U.S. history, and the most important social movement for civil rights was arising out of the heart of the Black South. Conservatives were defeated so badly in the 1964 election that pundits speculated about the end of the Republican Party. President Johnson loved legislative battles and knew more about manipulating Congress than any president except Franklin D. Roosevelt, and his vision was completing the work of the New Deal and Abraham Lincoln. He understood race and poverty and wanted to write great new laws into the nation's books. Money was flowing into the federal government before all the big tax cuts and there were resources to be used. Johnson created a series of commissions to bring him the best ideas and went to work, knowing very well that political cycles were limited.

Under the War on Poverty, an array of programs was aimed at adolescents to give them summer jobs and create connections with colleges. The idea was that deep inequality could be addressed with multiple interventions and that it was the responsibility of a rich society to create real opportunity. Johnson knew he had a historic opportunity and was determined to accomplish everything possible before the backlash he knew would come.[21]

A great historic struggle focused on civil rights. After the longest debate in American history, virtually shutting down Congress for months, Johnson refused to compromise and Congress passed the most far-reaching civil rights law in U.S. history in 1964. It required, in Title VI, that discrimination be ended in all programs and institutions receiving federal assistance, providing powerful leverage as federal aid was dramatically expanded for schools and colleges.[22] It provided two new and powerful tools for forcing compliance, and the administration soon demonstrated its determination to use them in spite of strong political resistance. The law gave the Justice Department the power to file lawsuits against state and local agencies violating civil rights and, more important, gave agencies the power to cut off federal funds for any agency that did not comply.[23] So, in sum, the new laws greatly increased the financial rewards of compliance and threatened agencies not obeying the law with the prospect of losing all their federal funds and, even then, facing the U.S. Justice Department in court, where it almost always won. For the first time, the executive power of the federal government was mobilized on behalf of civil rights changes.

Once these tools were in place and the administration showed that it was ready to use these powers forcefully, things began to change dramatically. The Supreme Court, the most supportive of civil rights in U.S. history under Chief Justice Earl Warren, rapidly rejected challenges to the laws and showed that it would support the agencies administering it. After his landslide election, Johnson gave highest priority to enacting a bill providing general aid to education for the first time in American history. The legislation that emerged, the Elementary and Secondary Education Act, was squarely focused on directing substantial new money to schools where poor children were concentrated, giving massive increases in big cities and in the impoverished sectors of the South. The huge increase in federal education funds gave the government strong leverage when civil rights violations threatened fund cutoffs.[24]

The federal civil rights officials and courts faced the need to devise policies that would actually work, bringing down barriers and producing a major expansion of opportunities. Within a short time, it became apparent that changes were needed, and ones were developed that produced far more progress than the courts had in the previous decade.[25] Two very important changes happened rapidly as the Justice Department was empowered to sue on behalf of civil rights and actual desegregation became a requirement for receiving federal dollars. Before the Civil Rights Act, school districts only had to produce desegregation plans when they were sued, and the cases often dragged on for years and ended with extremely limited remedies. There were thousands of school districts with a history of segregation by law but only a handful of civil rights lawyers. The climate was so hostile that there were entire states where no lawyer in the local bars would take such a case because of the resistance.

Steps toward Color-Conscious Policy

Once the Civil Rights Act was in place and Congress had passed the Elementary and Secondary Education Act, the civil rights officials whom the law required to enforce nondiscrimination in all districts had powerful sanctions and incentives. They had the Justice Department ready to sue those who refused to comply and the threat of losing an unprecedented increase in federal funds. Though some federal officials wanted simply to get an assurance of nondiscrimination from all districts, the administration drafted guidelines and required plans from all districts, as the courts did in systems where there had been a long history of overt discrimination. Federal officials told local school leaders that they must have a desegregation plan and that it must meet standards that had been established by federal courts as constitutionally necessary. At this point, a decade after *Brown*, there were still federal courts that were only requiring that school districts open up for a few voluntary transfers each year, with a twelve-year wait for small changes at all grade levels. These plans did nothing to desegregate the often-inferior segregated Black schools unless some white student might choose to transfer there. And they left the faculties segregated though it was clear to educators that interracial schools needed an interracial faculty. In some places the local school authorities were "desegregating" by sending some Black students to Latino schools or vice versa, combining two minority groups. When the U.S. Commission on Civil Rights sent out investigators, it was clear that the "free choice" often was far from free because both the students and the parents who decided to cross racial lines faced harsh resistance.[26] The initial plans required that all students be given choice forms, that all grades be open, and that free transportation be provided. Southern leaders thought that was all they should have to do.

The school policies stated that in the first year, fall 1965, all districts would be asked at least to create a more serious choice option for Black students to transfer to white schools. The Southern districts wanted to just sign a statement that they would not discriminate anymore but guidelines were issued, all school districts were required to file plans, and the minimum standards were taken from the more forceful federal court decisions. Guidelines were issued in 1965 that required at least the implementation of a more extensive freedom-of-choice plan. That change produced a notable speed-up, doubling the progress achieved in the first decade after *Brown* in a single year, but still left the Black schools almost totally segregated and the schools' faculties almost completely segregated. More than nine-tenths of Southern Black students were still in totally segregated historically Black schools. The most important thing that happened was that thousands of school districts that had done nothing now had a desegregation plan, and an agency had been created that was capable of administering a huge civil rights change in American education. The next key steps were to fix goals and deadlines.

The change was promising compared with the previous decade, but still very disappointing. In hundreds of districts the freedom-of-choice plan left the schools almost all segregated. As small-scale school integration was taking place, Black faculty and administrators were fired in many districts. Educators and school facilities that had been considered fine for Blacks were considered inadequate for schools with whites by local officials. Experts knew that a diverse faculty was an essential part of success in diverse schools, but almost nothing was done about faculty desegregation.

The second year moved toward policies requiring actual results. Choice plans were to be considered unacceptable unless they made significant progress in actually creating diverse schools, moving significantly each year toward a situation in which at least a fifth of the Black students had transferred. School districts were told that they should start on faculty integration, with at least one teacher of the other race in each school. Rather than just filing a plan about procedures, the districts were required to produce progress. That meant, for example, that they might have to seriously recruit students to make integration choices rather than create obstacles. There were thousands of schools where there had never been a Black teacher teaching whites in the history of the community, but now that had to start. After more than a decade of resistance and failure to change, policies became focused on results and performance criteria were emerging. That meant that the goal was to have not a promise to comply but evidence that the plan was actually integrating students across racial lines and beginning to integrate faculties.

The problem was not creating a formal choice plan that might have worked in a very different context but changing institutions and communities with deeply embedded practices. The agencies had determined that color-conscious requirements focused on increasing access to opportunities for students of color were the only way to break the logjam and achieve the goals of *Brown* and the Civil Rights Act. The second year, momentum grew and the percentage of Black students attending integrated schools in the South grew from 6 percent to 16 percent in a year.[27] By the end of the Johnson administration, the policy framework had shifted from increasing choice to abolishing the whole system of segregated schools, integrating the Black schools as well as the white schools and thoroughly integrating faculty, a goal established for the year after the end of the Johnson administration. Beginning in 1966, and accelerated by the election of a more conservative Congress that year, there were growing political attacks on the effort, but it continued until President Richard Nixon was elected.

The goal that emerged was the maximum feasible integration of all the schools and their faculties. The policies were supported by the largest cutoffs of federal aid in any federal grant program's history. Dozens of districts that defied the requirements had their federal funds cut off and, after they lost the funds, they were sued by the Justice Department's Civil Rights Division to force them to comply anyway. When they tried to go to federal courts for protection, the courts upheld the policies.[28] Within the space of five years of active enforcement, the schools of the South had become the most integrated in the nation.

The great success of the effort came when the Supreme Court, in a sweeping 1968 unanimous decision, adopted the standards that had developed in Civil Rights Act enforcement and, for the first time, laid out explicit requirements for desegregation. The *Brown* decision had held segregation unconstitutional but had neither defined nor created a deadline or enforcement process for desegregation. In *Green v. New Kent County*,[29] the Court ruled that desegregation must be immediate and comprehensive, including the maximum feasible reassignment of students and teachers to integrate all the schools so that they no longer had racial identities and there were not separate Black and white schools but "just schools." The Court required that in addition to student and faculty integration, the remedy must consider "staff, transportation, extracurricular activities and facilities." It noted that under the districts' freedom-of-choice plan, no white child had chosen to attend a Black school and 85 percent of Black children were still in all-Black schools, in part because of the harassment of the students who transferred. The Court held that it was not the responsibility of individual students and families to integrate the school; it was the responsibility of the school officials to do whatever was needed to accomplish the goal of integration and to end "racial imbalance" among the schools. In this decision the Court found that only a comprehensive race-conscious policy would produce integration, the same conclusion reached by the executive branch. This decision, coming after the officials enforcing the Civil Rights Act had announced a deadline, produced large breakthroughs.

Desegregation in the South soared during this period. In 1954 one Black student in one hundred thousand attended a white school. Six years after *Brown* it was one in a thousand. In 1964 when the Civil Rights Act passed, it was one in fifty. By 1968 almost a fourth (23.4 percent) were in white schools. By 1972, following the *Green* decision, it reached 36 percent. The truly massive change took place between 1964 and 1970.[30] Color-conscious policies, seriously implemented and backed by powerful sanctions and real resources, accomplished changes that had been unimaginable a decade earlier. These changes did not, of course, solve all problems. When a reform is implemented that people do not support, there are many ways it can be resisted or limited. The Civil Rights Act did include some modest funding for retraining and created the Community Relations Service to help settle conflicts in communities undergoing big changes. But it created fundamental changes and, over time, the attitudes of Southern whites, who were initially overwhelmingly opposed, improved considerably in accepting and even supporting integrated schools over time. In fact, there was significant evidence that even parents whose children were bused to schools under court-ordered desegregation plans reported that it was a positive experience.[31] That did not mean that there was not continuing controversy and litigation against the plans.

The Impact on Opportunity

The effects on the academic opportunities for students of color were substantial and positive, although they fell short of creating equal educational opportunities since they did not address the major out-of-school sources of academic problems. In its nature, civil rights enforcement must rely on changes within the very institutions that had violated the rights. Studies over more than a half century have shown academic gains associated with racial and class diversity in school composition, and they have shown it to be especially powerful for African American students, particularly low-income ones, who likely have had to contend with multiple forms of inequality. Although a great many studies simply compared the test scores before and after integration at the school level or the scores of students attending schools that happened to have different racial compositions at the time they were tested, it has long been apparent that some of the most important impacts have not been on test scores but on what happens in students' lives, particularly in their attainment of higher education and better employment. Long-term research shows major gains in future life, including college going and college completion, community involvement, job and income opportunities, and even better health. There are studies that show that the gains can be enhanced by creating in-school practices and values that foster successful diversity.

There is significant research that shows gains for white and Asian students as well and strong research showing that no group loses from integration experiences. Privileged students tend to be less influenced academically by school and more by their home and peer groups, and they also gain important understandings and relationship skills (the critical "soft" skills) from learning to manage diversity. For the purposes of this book, the effects on high school success and college success are critical.

Berkeley professor Rucker Johnson carried out a remarkable analysis for the National Bureau of Economic Research, which led to his 2019 book.[32] The study involved combining records of the initiation of school desegregation, longitudinal data on students, and measures of school quality, making it possible to consider multiple factors over time and examine multiple outcomes. Given the great complexity of all the forces and changes involved, these estimates are not likely to be precise, but they do give us a vision previously unavailable. The research shows that the students affected got access to schools that had substantially higher levels of support and smaller class sizes than the segregated schools.[33] The more years of desegregated education they had, especially beginning at young ages, the larger the gains Johnson reported and the better the outcomes were. Students with consistent integration experiences "had significantly higher educational attainment, including greater college attendance and completion rates, not to mention attendance at more selective colleges. Specifically, black children exposed to desegregated schools throughout K-12 completed more than a full additional year of education than comparable black children confined to segregated schools throughout their school-age years."[34] His analysis found that experiencing at least five years of desegregated education on average was related to a substantially lower level of poverty or incarceration for Black adults and a sharply higher average annual income.[35] Given the massive battles over change, these are remarkable impacts.

There had been studies for years that examined the relationship between desegregation and "life chances" in later life. In an early 1970 article in the *American Journal of Sociology*, Robert Crain reported that more powerful than the educational effects were the results of creating a much broader network of contacts crossing racial lines that led to better opportunities. A study of Blacks in Northern metro areas showed that friends were a crucial resource for finding jobs and that those who had white friends, controlling for other factors, got better jobs and income and were more likely to have attended college.[36] Jomills Braddock and James McPartland did important early work showing links between school desegregation and adult job opportunity.[37]

With increasingly sophisticated methods of analysis and the current "big data" period of access to very large and more often longitudinal data sets, a more complex and positive assessment of the long-term impacts of school desegregation has emerged in recent decades.[38] During the desegregation era, there was substantial research on the policies and techniques that produce positive racial interaction in schools and on ways in which these experiences can be made more powerful. Some of these were on the impact of the federal desegregation aid program, which supported successful adaptations within schools but was canceled in President Ronald Reagan's first budget and never restored. Some key research dates all the way back to Gordon Allport's classic 1954 book, *The Nature of Prejudice*,[39] which posited the conditions for effective intergroup relationships, including committed leadership, fair rules, and mutual respect. An extraordinary summary of the impact of these conditions in more than five hundred cases across the world has confirmed those basic insights.[40]

This book cannot possibly review the vast literature on this issue over the past six decades. It is fair to say that the policies of the 1960s made a huge change in the historical patterns of total exclusion of African American students from white schools and in the segregation of faculties across seventeen states. This was the direct result of the Civil Rights Act and its enforcement and made the South the most integrated region for decades to come in spite of backward movement after the Supreme Court backed off in 1991. These changes were difficult, but there was a major surge of academic achievement, high school completion, and college going during and after the 1960s. The largest declines in the white-Black and the white-Hispanic gaps on the National Assessment of Educational Progress, the "Nation's Report Card," took place between the first test data in 1971 and the 1986–88 period, after which the gaps began to grow again for a generation.[41] Although the systematic national test was not implemented in the 1960s, careful analysis of existing test data shows that these trends clearly began in that period.[42] Black high school completion rates and college enrollment rates rose dramatically in the 1960s.[43]

Opening Up White Higher Education

The civil rights revolution had major effects on access by minority students to selective colleges and the ability of those colleges to achieve the significant levels of diversity they believed produced a better educational experience for all students, a belief supported by a substantial body of research.[44] Those colleges changed primarily by voluntary action, in a positive civil rights climate at schools. For seventeen states with a history of de jure segregation of higher education, change came through enforcement of the Civil Rights Act and federal court orders. The major changes in both sectors were concentrated in the late 1960s and early 1970s, and affirmative action was a central part of the solutions.

In 1964 there were still five Southern states where at least 97 percent of the Black students were attending Black colleges. More than three-fourths of the Black collegians were in segregated institutions, usually notably inferior, in all of the Southern states.[45] The civil rights revolution made a major difference.

All colleges were affected by the reporting requirements and fair employment requirements of the Civil Rights Act and the Equal Employment Opportunity Commission, created under Title VII of the Civil Rights Act. In the colleges outside the South, mobilization of student movements on campus also played a significant role.

In William Bowen and Derek Bok's major study of the impact of affirmative action in higher education, they describe the increasing attention from the federal government, particularly on their employment practices, requiring "elaborate plans that included goals and timetables for assembling a workforce that reflected the availability of minority employees in the relevant labor markets"[46] and other conditions that led most major universities and colleges outside the South to voluntarily adopt race-conscious affirmative action plans. There had never been significant Black, Latino, or Indian enrollment in the nation's elite private and public universities going into the 1960s, though there were some small recruitment efforts beginning. The leading New England colleges, for example, had only about 1 percent Black students in 1965. Blacks made up less than 1 percent of law and medical students on white campuses. Harvard Law School dean Erwin Griswold, whom President Kennedy had appointed to the Commission on Civil Rights, initiated an affirmative plan to diversify the school through summer training programs and race-conscious admissions.[47] Bowen and Bok note, "Often spurred by student protests on their own campuses, university officials initiated active programs to recruit minority applicants and to take race into account in the admissions process by accepting qualified black students even if they had lower grades and test scores than most white students."[48] Between the late 1960s and mid-1970s, Black enrollments more than doubled in many leading colleges and professional schools. This kind of increase was not to be seen again up until the present, though almost all of the schools expanded affirmative action to include Latinos and Native Americans.[49]

Voluntary affirmative action was upheld by a single vote after a major legal battle in the Supreme Court in the 1978 *Bakke* decision, but the University of California, Davis, was required to end its practice of setting aside some seats for students of color in its medical school, which had never had significant enrollment of students of color, in a state that was becoming far more diverse, with many communities needing doctors of color. The court rejected explicit racial-change goals in higher education and only approved consideration of race as one of many "plus factors" in admissions decisions, not to repair historical exclusion but to provide diverse classes that would enrich all students' education. A limited affirmative consideration was approved but no specific plans. The author of the decisive opinion in the divided court was Lewis Powell, a conservative Virginian appointed by President Nixon.

The nineteen states with separate public Black colleges clearly violated the constitutional prohibition against de jure segregation, and changes were needed, but they initially focused on the worst places that had been completely segregated. Federal civil rights officials were so overwhelmed with school desegregation that they did not take the first steps toward change in higher education until late in the 1960s.

With the election of Nixon, whose administration was opposed, the effort stalled[50] and very little was done, but the federal courts took the extraordinary step of finding federal civil rights agencies guilty of nonenforcement of civil rights law in the *Adams v. Richardson* litigation.[51] The language in the Civil Rights Act did not simply allow federal authorities to take action; it required action against discrimination by systems receiving federal money. A federal district court ruled in November 1972 that the Nixon administration had failed to enforce the Civil Rights Act in the higher education systems of ten states, and it set deadlines for state desegregation of higher education systems. The federal education officials were ordered to produce statewide higher education desegregation plans or face losing critical federal aid. There was a lot of confusion about how to do it since students are not assigned to colleges as they are to public schools. The basic tools were the transfer of attractive programs, the upgrade of long-neglected Black campuses, and merger, since the South had a number of cities with Black and white public colleges in the same community teaching the same courses to segregated groups of students. Eventually, under the Carter administration a set of policies was drawn up to satisfy the courts.[52] The race-conscious policies included upgrading the historically Black campuses, substantially increasing Black enrollment on white campuses and recruiting whites to improved programs on Black campuses, and increasing faculty and staff diversity to reflect the racial proportions of people with the needed credentials. The basic goal was for the colleges to reflect the racial composition of the state's high school graduates.[53]

Several states strongly resisted and sued the federal government. It was soon apparent that progress was slow on both the student and faculty desegregation levels on many campuses.[54] Some states moved toward serious plans under the impetus of continued judicial urgings, even under the Reagan administration, but others became openly resistant. With serious challenges to federal authority, the government moved toward a key test of enforcement in North Carolina. There, the Office for Civil Rights rejected the plan submitted and was engaged in a major conflict likely to influence the entire process. However, when Reagan became president, his administration promoted a plan demanding far less than the one the Carter administration had rejected as insufficient.[55] This signaled that little would be required and results would not matter, a fundamental move back from the systemic remedies of the civil rights era.

But the reforms had created some progress. Between the 1975–76 academic year and the 1980–81 year, the percentage of Southern Black graduates receiving their bachelor's degrees from predominantly white institutions rose by a third, a much more rapid growth in Black degrees in Southern white colleges than outside the South. The elite flagship state universities of the South did become significantly integrated institutions. Because of the impetus for a serious enforcement effort, the South became less segregated than any other region, even though all the other regions had a much lower percentage of Black students.

The desegregation plans adopted by the Southern states and the various campuses had many race-conscious elements, including major upgrading and location of high-demand educational programs on the historically Black campuses to make them attractive to non-Black students. On various white campuses there were special outreach and recruitment efforts that finally came when a federal court found the Department of Health, Education, and Welfare guilty of nonenforcement of the 1964 law and set deadlines for the development of statewide college desegregation plans. Nothing was done about merging campuses, apart from one court order. (I served on an advisory committee, dominated by college officials, named by Department of Health, Education, and Welfare secretary Joseph Califano during the Carter administration and noted the strong lack of interest by either Black or white administrators in giving up power through mergers in spite of the possible savings in eliminating duplication and gains in actually integrating the campuses.)

Making College Accessible to Low-Income and Nonwhite Students

As in public school policy, higher education saw a major expansion of the federal role, which came to focus on issues of access for students of color and those from poor families. The key components were the Civil Rights Act, the Higher Education Act, and the War on Poverty. The basic commitment in the expanded federal role was to bring down the financial and racial barriers to college for large groups that had never had significant access. The War on Poverty quickly identified college access as a key goal and created the college Work-Study program to make it possible for students without money to make it through by working on campus. The Office of Economic Opportunity recognized that there had to be programs to encourage students to hope for college, to acquaint them with college, to help them pay for college, and to get them some of the key skills and preparation.

The Higher Education Act of 1965 was part of the tidal wave of major legislation created after the landslide victory of Johnson in 1964. Johnson called on Congress to enact a program to help low-income students and struggling colleges, and the law was enacted later that year.[56] The most important provision was a federal grant to help students who could not afford to go to college. The grant could be up to $800 (equivalent to $6,600 in 2020 dollars), but if the student was receiving other scholarship aid, it would be no more than half the amount of the financial aid the student was receiving from other sources. There was a bonus for students who earned high grades. This was a substantial help at a time when the average annual tuition of a four-year public university in 1965 was $327, and the total cost including room and board was well under $1,000.[57]

The act also provided funds to identify and support low-income students in high school who were not thinking about or familiar with colleges. Upward Bound funded local programs that served up to one hundred students.[58] Also in the law was what became the Talent Search program, which identified high school and junior high students needing support who were poor and from families with parents lacking college degrees. Both of these programs were to endure across the country, but always funded with budgets that strictly limited their reach. The third important part was Student Support Services, which was designed to help students complete college.

By the 1972 amendments, the financial aid system had become the Pell Grant, which has been the basic element of federal assistance for low-income students ever since. With low public tuitions, substantial federal aid, and the possibility of earning enough to pay a good share of the costs with a summer job, college became genuinely affordable for many students. The 1960s and 1970s were a period of major state investment in the creation and expansion of colleges. In terms of equity, as colleges rapidly expanded and states kept tuition low, and civil rights laws and pressures had created new goals, it is not surprising that the late 1970s brought a historic high point in access (not completion) for students of color. For a brief period in the late 1970s, a Black high school graduate was about as likely as a white one to start college—a major sign of progress.

The Census Bureau reported in 1981 that Black enrollment in college had nearly doubled in the 1970s, passing a million students. "The increases were particularly heavy early in the 1970's," the report showed, and noted, "Since 1976, the proportion of black college students has been at least equal to the proportion of blacks in the college-age population."[59] The reforms of the Great Society education and civil rights policies were related to a great surge of college going, eliminating racial gaps in initial enrollment for a time by the late 1970s. The combination of affirmative race-conscious policies, substantial federal aid for low-income students, support programs, Work-Study, and an expansion of college spaces available at low costs all contributed to a remarkable accomplishment. In reality, of course, there was a huge difference between starting college and completing it: enrollment in community colleges was far less likely to lead to graduation than attendance at a university. But this was a substantial change. The related policies were both race conscious and class conscious. Because of the complexity of higher education, the limits of the *Bakke* decision, and the strong retreat from civil rights in the 1980s, higher education never had the explicit race-conscious requirements for change that made such a difference for the public schools of the de jure segregated states.

Summary

In the civil rights fights in desegregation, voting, and other fields, colorblind policy, which left the basic system largely untouched but provided some limited opportunities, became the central strategy of resistance and was rejected at the height of the movement. After the civil rights era ended and conservatism rose to power, as the next chapter will show, colorblind policy again became dominant. Race-conscious policies were limited or dissolved, the consequences were ignored, and the idea that race-conscious policies violated the Constitution and were unfair to whites, and had not worked, took hold in a substantial segment of the white community.

It was not until national politics was deeply changed by the great civil rights protests, by the sweep of Great Society social and educational legislation, and by passage of the most important civil rights laws that the nature of the overwhelmingly white institutions in higher education began to change. In the midst of a social revolution, institutions that had been satisfied with only tiny nonwhite representation recognized that their traditional processes did not work, and they made a rapid change. The new laws defined the basic responsibility of federal education policy as being to equalize opportunities for students of color and students living in poverty by ending exclusion and supporting the students and the schools and colleges that served them.

The conditions in the mid-1960s were optimal for major changes. It was a society with a large white majority, at the peak of the baby boom, with the world's great industrial economy, with millions of unionized factory jobs that supported middle-class families. There were rising real incomes and a growing middle class as suburbia expanded vastly. Immigration was at a modern low. It had virtually stopped during the Great Depression and World War II, and the restrictive laws of the 1924 Immigration Act, which set "national origins" quotas favoring northern Europeans and virtually banning nonwhites, remained in effect until President Johnson signed the Immigration and Nationality Act of 1965, which abolished the National Origins Formula and opened the door to immigrants from Asia and Africa. It set up family reunification as a top preference, on the idea of supporters that it would reinforce existing ethnic patterns, but turned out to be a key avenue for surging immigration later denounced by President Donald Trump as "chain migration." Though it was expected to have modest effects, it ended up triggering a wave of immigration that deeply altered American society by 2000.[60]

There was the most socially progressive Supreme Court in U.S. history in the 1960s and the most important social movement for civil rights arising out of the Black South. The most liberal Congress of the twentieth century was elected in 1964 and, under the leadership of Johnson, there was a vast expansion of laws and programs aimed at helping nonwhites and poor people.

As the Warren Court came to its final period, the decisions on color-conscious school desegregation remedies became powerful and clear, and the justices unanimously affirmed that it was not possible to undo segregated institutions without establishing specific race-conscious requirements and methods. Decades of attempts with case-by-case antidiscrimination policies had left conditions virtually unchanged. The new policies produced visible and substantial change.

It would be wrong to think that these changes were sufficient or that there had been strong and consistent pressure for change. Even when desegregation and affirmative action plans were in place, they were often limited and "second-generation" challenges remained. Once you create a diverse school or college, then it becomes essential to take steps within the affected institutions and staffs to prevent internal discrimination and realize the potentials. School desegregation was seriously enforced by the federal government for about five years, 1965–70, producing major changes, but active federal support in terms of funds for the desegregation process lasted only until the Reagan administration. It was well understood, even in the creation of the Civil Rights Act, that federal support for schools and colleges would be needed for the educational and social transformations that were sought, and there were never enough such resources. The Civil Rights Act itself contained a small program to help schools with the transition, and the Community Relations Service was intended to help communities solve divisions. At the beginning of the 1970s, Congress and the Nixon administration created what became a large and successful program offering aid to school districts that requested it to help in that transition.[61] Then, at the beginning of the Reagan administration, the federal government eliminated aid for success in diverse schools and actively worked to end desegregation plans.

The largest changes in the civil rights revolution came for Blacks in the South, the group whose movement had sparked large national changes. Legal recognition of the educational rights of Latinos to overcome segregation came two decades after *Brown*, during the Nixon administration, and was never seriously enforced. In the 1973 Denver desegregation case,[62] the Supreme Court held that Latinos had the same rights as Blacks. A small grant

program launched in 1968, the Bilingual Education Act, as well as an important 1974 Supreme Court decision from San Francisco,[63] recognized that
non-English-speaking students had the right to education in a language
they could understand, and created a basis for major change for Latino
children and others. Unfortunately, these reforms came at a time when the
administration was opposed to urban desegregation and working hard to
cut back federal education funding. The bilingual initiative had far more
impact than desegregation, but neither made anything like the major
changes that had happened for Black students in the 1960s. Latinos, whose
numbers were growing rapidly, experienced steady increases in isolation in
concentrated-poverty schools.[64] One very important change was that the
federal government began systematically collecting education data on all
major racial groups.

There were major battles over Indian policy in the late 1960s and early
1970s, including an Indian occupation of the U.S. Department of the Interior.
In 1969 a special Senate Subcommittee on Indian Education published a major
report, *Indian Education: A National Tragedy—a National Challenge*, dealing
with the scandalous conditions. In 1972 Congress passed the Indian Education
Act, providing more aid and strengthening tribal control of reservation schools
and tribal colleges. This legislation did not produce major changes in educational attainment. Coming into the 1980s, all federal programs were threatened
by the intense effort to shrink the government, by the loss of tax revenue
through Reagan's large tax cuts, and by a serious recession. In spite of critically
unequal outcomes, Indian education gets little attention in Congress or in state
governments.

Changes on the Supreme Court under President Nixon severely undermined the race-conscious and class-conscious policies developing in the civil
rights era. Nixon had the rare opportunity to name four justices during his five
years as president, turning the Court in a conservative direction. A five-four
majority in the Court ruled that there was no constitutional right to equal
school resources in the 1973 *Rodriguez*[65] decision. In the 1974 *Milliken v. Bradley*[66]
decision, the Court ruled that the suburbs could not be included in desegregation plans even when that was the only way to remedy a history of segregation.
In the 1978 *Bakke*[67] decision, the Court significantly limited affirmative action
in higher education without closing the door. After a crucial period in which
the Court had been a leading force in moving the country toward race-
conscious policies that actually worked to produce major changes, these and
other decisions showed that the Court was becoming an obstacle, setting

limits, and taking steps that would lead to further reverses and severe rollbacks in the coming decades.

During the 1960s Presidents Kennedy and Johnson invested their power in expanding civil rights, attacking poverty, and pursuing significant racial change. Nixon set the Republican Party and a series of administrations that would follow on a path to limit and reverse major civil rights changes in educational opportunity.

Color-conscious policies changing traditional practices and aimed at actually achieving diversity and equity were mainly a product of a major social movement in the 1960s, and a brief era of civil rights change during strong moderate-liberal control of all branches of government. That period opened gates through the color line on a large scale for Southern Black students in public schools and, at least modestly, for many selective colleges across the U.S. whose students and faculty had been all white. It produced schools and colleges that were more diverse and interracial than had ever been seen before and initiated a definition of the federal role in public schools and colleges that was built around expanding opportunity for poor and nonwhite students. At the time it seemed a historic but incomplete revolution.

5

Colorblindness Reigns

FOUR DECADES OF INEQUALITY
IN A TRANSFORMING SOCIETY

COLORBLINDNESS HAS BEEN THE DOMINANT policy since the Reagan administration took charge in 1981. It was largely unchallenged in national politics until the 2020 presidential campaign raised issues of systemic discrimination and racism in the Democratic primaries. It had been contested during the Nixon, Ford, and Carter administrations. The 1980 election brought a dramatic change in the White House and the Senate and moved what was then the majority party far to the right, setting the stage for a fundamental rejection of the civil rights revolution and the antipoverty programs and policies that had come with it. It brought a time of increasing inequality, economic stratification, resegregation, and a turn against public schools and their social mission. A serious recession triggered negative changes that became locked into federal and state funding. The impact affected generations of students. Policy based on colorblind assumptions has been dominant so long that it is often seen simply as the norm.

History is mostly not about moments. It is usually about long-term trends that become evident in retrospect, though they were more obscure at the time. But sometimes, there are turning points, major reversals and redirections, or large new efforts, changes that have long-term impacts. That is what happened in the 1980s. The 1960s had been a period of dramatic changes won in political, social, and legal movements and battles. A number of the basic laws created in that decade endure, though their meaning and enforcement have changed. The 1980s reshaped educational policy quite quickly and in ways that amounted to clear and dramatic reversals. Similarly, the conservative movement reshaped the law and the courts, another basic source of power and policy ideas within the American system.

Within weeks there were major changes embodied in budget cuts and civil rights reversals. By 1983 the education policy world had been deeply changed, and the changes were to dominate policy for the next four decades. This was an incredible impact for a president who came to office wanting to end the federal role in education and ended up leading the administration that affected the basic goals and discourse in education for generations of students. A central theme was that we had already done too much about race and poverty. New policies assumed that the problems were not with the society but with the schools and teachers serving students of color. The fundamental problem was to find a way to force them to be more effective, because it was their fault. The civil rights reforms had been overdone and were harming whites, the conservative policy makers and advocates argued.

After a generation of increasing opportunity and commitment to higher education by government, there was a sea change that persisted. Where the Great Society had brought a sharp focus of government on inequality and opportunity for excluded groups, and the 1970s had seen a battle of ideas between the center-right and the center, the twelve years of the Reagan-Bush era were a time when government was seen as the enemy, not a tool, and unrestricted markets were seen as the solution for all problems. The idea that the courts were a source of power for equity, dominant in the 1960s, gave way to the reality that the altered courts were a force for limiting and reversing social change.

The two Democratic presidents following Reagan, Bill Clinton and Barack Obama, also generally accepted colorblind policies for public schools and colleges, as well as ending the focus of college aid on the poor and ending significant challenges to segregation. Though they did not propose eliminating programs, supported enforcing civil rights law, and did not try to end surviving policies addressing poverty, policy moved toward increasing aid to the middle class. During the post–Great Recession period, the high school completion and college-going rates rose but the isolation of students of color in doubly segregated schools intensified significantly and the gap in college completion by race, ethnicity, and poverty was large and rising. Students of color were strongly concentrated in high schools that did not prepare them effectively for college, and they remained far behind at the end of high school. Race-conscious solutions for public schools were largely dismantled by the Supreme Court, and federal aid for voluntary efforts to improve race relations was virtually shut down, even for local efforts. Selective colleges were able to maintain a modest consideration of race as one of many factors in college admissions, but race-oriented recruitment and preparation policies were abandoned in many campuses and outlawed in some critical states. Federal financial aid for college was increasingly shifted to loans and tax subsidies. There was no coherent focus on equalizing educational opportunity for students of color.

The History of High School Development

The creation of U.S. high schools had historically greatly expanded opportunity for education, but it was opportunity that came late and remained unequal for students of color. Policy for high schools, except during the civil rights era, basically ignored or even reinforced the severe racial polarization of the society, with the result that policy and practice tended to perpetuate those divisions. Sometimes by putting enormous pressure on the segregated schools serving students of color without addressing the issues that make them unequal, accountability policies since 1980 unintentionally made a bad situation worse. There was a notable change from respecting public schools and teachers to blaming them and fostering nonpublic approaches.

Since the federal government began to take an active role in American education in the 1960s, the basic idea was to try to change the educational trajectory early in the hope that it would persist. This continued in the colorblind period, though the quality of early education differed greatly, was often insufficient, and never became equal. Yet all children must pass through the difficult years of adolescence and cross from childhood to adulthood. They must get on the path to college with preparation and information. In high school, students and families face critical decisions that have large impacts on college and the future. It is a dangerous time, especially threatening for students in poor communities with weak schools, negative peer groups, and single-parent families struggling to survive. High schools are the last good chance to prepare for successful entrance into higher education. The focus of resources on preschool and elementary education has produced some gains at the lower grades but few at the end of high school in the last generation.

Strong high schools, like strong colleges, can change lives, even for students from very limited backgrounds. We have examples of programs and schools in which low-income students of color have had a much better record of preparing for college—many magnet schools, policies that allow transfer to excellent suburban schools,[1] scholarships that send students to elite prep schools, long-standing programs that place students from poor nonwhite communities in selective high schools, and so on. The programs of Prep for Prep[2] and ABC

(A Better Chance) have helped students prepare for college by placing them in far more competitive schools with intense precollegiate organization and goals and giving them the support they need to catch up, putting them in radically different settings, sometimes changing their residence and their life experience—basically moving them to a different context and set of possibilities. There is also an array of intervention programs, such as the special classes for Latino students in the Puente program in a number of Southwest high schools,[3] that create separate supported groups within weak schools. The dual high school–community college programs sometimes have similar effects. The basic idea of the Harlem Children's Zone and similar efforts for multidimensional intervention in poor neighborhoods was to simultaneously address a number of inequalities holding students of color back. The fundamental goal of all of these programs is to get the students off the dead-end path that does not lead to college success for the great majority of the students of color, and to connect them to at least some aspects of the experience middle-class students normally receive. The reality, however, is that few students receive these opportunities, and there is severe concentration of students of color in high schools where few students go on to success in four-year colleges.

Segregating students in weak high schools that do not provide good preparation for college is a central mechanism for the intergenerational perpetuation of racial and ethnic inequality in American society. Our society has an ideal of individual-level opportunity and mobility for each student, but the reality is stratification by race and poverty. In our society, inherited disadvantages or advantages play a key role, and schools of different quality and opportunity are key mechanisms to perpetuate those differences.[4] Money and racial privilege can put children on a superhighway to college in a high school where that is the default. Poverty and segregation can put them on a dead-end path where they will have almost no opportunity to develop their talent.

Without successful high school preparation, students of color are at an enormous disadvantage since most have fewer resources at home and in their neighborhood and have usually been poorly prepared in unequal elementary and middle schools. Obviously, none of those students receive the special admissions treatment many colleges offer to children of alumni and donors. Given the limited ability and resources of most colleges to make up for enormous gaps in educational preparation, colleges often do not enroll or do not graduate many students of color. College recruiters know where their institution has found high school students who succeeded and where it has not, so they often recruit based on experience and, sometimes, on the basis of embedded stereotypes.

Too many students of color are in high schools where very few graduates succeed in completing college, schools written off, often, by their own students. Students in ghetto and barrio schools often know that other schools have much more to offer. Many things about high schools as currently organized tend to transmit rather than remedy inequality. In the civil rights era, high priority was placed on getting access for students of color to the high schools that regularly prepared students effectively for college and on the creation of more such schools through integrated magnet school programs. Then the focus changed to leaving the system unchanged but putting more pressure on the weak schools and their faculties.

The Ideology of the Conservative Era

This period brought a seismic shift in beliefs about the causes of unequal educational opportunity. The conservative campaigns were attacks on government social programs and civil rights policies. The remedies they proposed largely ignored race and poverty, and equity was not a central focus of policy. Treatment for the obvious problems of students in concentrated-poverty schools, which became all the more apparent with the spread of mandatory testing and data releases, featured remedies directed at forcing change in the schools serving nonwhites. At the higher education level, conservative state governments were cutting taxes and greatly expanding incarceration as part of the "tough on crime" strategy, which took a growing share of young men of color out of the educational process and after imprisonment they could work only in the criminal economy.

Federal and state tax cuts and budget cuts meant that there was not enough money for colleges and students. The result was the transfer of higher education costs to families. The conservative political coalitions drew in Southern whites in part through attacks on civil rights policies, and those administrations responded by reversing previous civil rights policy. The basic direction of policy changed from blaming discrimination and inequality in the society for many educational problems to the opposite belief—that discrimination was irrelevant and minorities had already been overcompensated for past discrimination. The new framework blamed the schools and families for the continuing inequality. In higher education, college became unattainable for many lower-income families, but government priorities changed to provide more help for middle-class families through the extension of subsidized loans and tax subsidies. Poverty was blamed, in good part, on welfare and various subsidies undermining the need to work. The cure was to cut or withdraw the programs and create a more urgent need to work. Welfare programs for poor women with children were slashed. The belief in such strategies is deep among conservatives and continues to the present.[5] Civil rights policies were seen as unfair to whites.

Unsurprisingly, there were no racial equity breakthroughs like those of the 1960s as major gaps were perpetuated through more generations of students. One of the great differences, however, was the scale of the social consequences. In the civil rights era, these policies affected the fifth of students who were nonwhite. In the colorblind period, it came to affect about half of the generation of students in a transformed society. As the historic migrations flowed into the country from Mexico and Asia, consequences grew.

Policy now assumed that it was unnecessary to make provision for the special needs of students of color trying to make it in college, even as the composition of the country's schools was changing from what was still a large white majority at the end of the civil rights era to only about half white in the public school population. Policies assumed that colorblind policy would also help students of color. The idea was that serious discrimination was over and everyone had to make it on their own. Blame was redirected from the broader society to the institutions serving students of color. Since, according to the new theory, discrimination had been cured, they and their students had to bear the responsibility.

The share of Black students grew very slowly in the college-age population in this period, but the proportion of white students plunged in the 1968–2016 period (table 2). Immigration was the big story. Latino enrollments soared from two million to thirteen million and became by far the largest nonwhite group. White enrollment dropped by eleven million students. U.S. fertility rates fell far below the replacement level in the early 1970s, and population growth was shaped largely by immigration. Asians, who had very small numbers in the 1960s, surged after the 1965 immigration reform ended a long history of almost total exclusion. By 2010 we were entering a time of shrinking high school and college enrollments with a smaller white proportion year by year.

During this period, economic inequality deepened and became even more related to education levels. As union membership declined to less than a tenth of nongovernmental employees and industrial jobs dropped to a small fraction of the labor force, educational credentials became requirements for more and

TABLE 2. Public School Enrollment by Race (in Millions), 1968 to 2016–17

	1968	1988	2006	2011	2016
White	34.7	23.6	26.9	25.1	23.9
Black	6.3	5.3	8.0	7.5	7.5
Latino	2.0	3.9	9.7	11.4	13.0
Asian	—	1.1	2.2	2.5	2.7
American Indian	—	0.3	0.6	0.5	0.5
Multiracial	—	—	—	1.2	1.8

Sources: U.S. Department of Education, National Center for Education Statistics (NCES), Common Core of Data (CCD), Public Elementary/Secondary School Universe Survey Data, 2016–17, 2011–12, 2006–7, and 1988–89. Data for 1968 were obtained from the analysis of the Office for Civil Rights data in Gary Orfield, *Public School Desegregation in the United States, 1968–1980* (Washington, DC: Joint Center for Political Studies, 1983).

more of the jobs with middle-class incomes. Many of the jobs developing in services were low-wage, low-benefit nonunion jobs, and much of the growth came in anti-union states with limited public sectors. Salaries were strongly linked to education. The federal minimum wage declined dramatically in value during this period without adjustments for inflation, driving many full-time minimum-wage workers into poverty. The number of contingent, part-time jobs was high among less educated workers. Often entry-level jobs did not provide full-time employment or predictable hours.

Throughout the post–civil rights period, there were major racial gaps in test scores and college completion, a chronic shortage of teachers and faculty of color, and many other measures of inequality. Even though the policy discussion of this long period emphasized outcomes, and racial gaps persisted, the major policies were colorblind and the basic assumptions were not critically evaluated.[6] As waves of conservative reforms were implemented, policy makers and educators passively accepted the intense and growing segregation of the schools and the rising barriers to college as if they did not matter. Teachers and leaders of concentrated-poverty schools were told that the problems of their students of color were their fault and were commanded to meet goals that turned out, after years of massive struggles and the expenditure of many billions of dollars, to be impossible. In this period, policy assumed that race and class could be ignored in school policy, that schools had enormous capacity to change outcomes, and that, if commanded and sufficiently threated, they would do it. Each of those assumptions turned out to be wrong.

A Changing Vision

The traditional political ideology of the U.S. is equal opportunity for all, operating through free public schools that give every child a chance to make it in society. The "American dream" is the belief that there is a fair chance to make it into the mainstream, that those who apply themselves in school and work can succeed, and children can do better than their parents. The basic idea is that individuals make it or fail in free competition and that the schools provide everyone the fair opportunity to achieve economic and social mobility.

The reality, however, has been that students of color have always had inferior opportunities. Their communities have asked for more, but white communities and leaders usually insisted that the system is basically fair and no changes directed explicitly at racial or class inequalities are necessary. In the U.S., a central enduring strand of ideology is individualism and self-reliance in what is believed by whites to be a reasonably fair system.[7]

Communities of color continuously point out the contradictions between the dream and actual treatment, but only rarely do the claims of their leaders attract serious attention from government and the white public. The individualistic dream (or hopeful myth) remains powerful even in the face of declining mobility and increasing economic and racial polarization. The dream is shared by many in communities of color.

During the civil rights era, for a few years there had been a widespread recognition that opportunities were not equal, that past and present discrimination were powerful forces, and that strong race-conscious action was needed to generate change. To the civil rights movement's supporters, it was clear that the colorblind approach had failed, could not produce equality, and often masked discrimination. Civil rights advocates, researchers, and progressives called for taking race into account in education, voting, employment, and other arenas in order to ensure that "equal protection of the laws," the promise of the Fourteenth Amendment, was actually accomplished. Opponents saw such actions as a violation of the individualistic beliefs that they believed were central to the Constitution.

By the 1980s the country had turned away from the race-conscious understanding of the civil rights reforms. Colorblind arguments had been consistently used to oppose race-conscious civil rights remedies from the time of *Brown*. The opponents had long insisted that examining individual cases of overt discrimination was the only acceptable approach to civil rights. By the 1980s this became the dominant vision. People expressed beliefs in the *principles* of equal schooling and other civil rights changes. From the 1950s to the

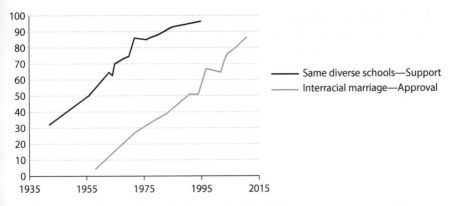

FIGURE 4. White support of the principle of racial equity. M. Krysan and S. Moberg, "Trends in Racial Attitudes," University of Illinois Institute of Government and Public Affairs, August 25, 2016, http://igpa.uillinois.edu/programs/racial-attitudes

early 2000s there was a steady increase in affirmation of equal opportunity, as shown in data reported by University of Illinois scholars.[8] On the other hand, there was a deep division by race in the blame for unequal results and the willingness to commit resources to equalizing opportunity. People of color believed discrimination was serious and continuing and the government needed to act. Many whites disagreed. A continuing dilemma in civil rights policy is that white Americans recognize that there are racial problems but rarely favor any government action to resolve them, as shown in figure 5.

Studies of white opinion over the last half century show that the priority of the issue of racial equity rises over time and sometimes surges at times of crisis, such as when police dogs and fire hoses harmed children in Birmingham, Alabama; violence erupted in response to the Selma march for voting rights; and George Floyd was killed. Sometimes, skilled leadership has helped produce policy changes. Usually, however, the salience does not last, though the support of the principles remains. Generally, when they have been asked, whites say that government is already doing enough and they do not support increased governmental action.

There is a profound racial gap in policy attitudes. Whites usually believe that no additional action on racial equity is needed. People of color disagree strongly, with Blacks seeing the most urgency.

The problems were explained and the contradictions resolved during the conservative era by shifting blame to people of color and arguing that enough, or maybe too much, had already been done. Opposition to civil rights policies was, of course, intensified by politics, especially politics that conveyed the idea that nonwhites were criminal and dangerous and were responsible for the problems whites were facing. Following the civil rights revolution, a virtual consensus developed in terms of desirable goals for racial equity (see figure 4), but except at the high points of the civil rights movement, the white public generally thought that enough had been done and did not favor further initiatives.

Conservative campaigns and administrations argued that discrimination had already been solved, that going too far was counterproductive. In reality, the public turned against any serious effort to enforce racial change. Conservative administrations put strong pressure on the courts and agencies, which were being transformed through appointments, to end race-conscious equity policies. White support for doing anything about school and job discrimination and inequality had radically declined. Support for fair housing climbed rapidly from the passage of the fair housing law in 1968 but leveled off in the 1990s. About half of whites had wanted the government to take action to integrate schools in the 1960s and almost two-fifths to act against job discrimination. By the early 2000s, both had declined to less than a third. Whether it was caused by the way leaders framed the issues or the government was responding to strengthening conservative public attitudes, or both, government and the white public wanted to favor equal rights in theory but to follow colorblind policies with no need for governmental enforcement.

In fact, though whites became far more positive in principle on a number of goals for racial justice, many blamed nonwhites for their own problems and were reluctant to commit resources to help. Believing in the principles and seeing no need for action were part of the colorblind approach. Conservative leaders said that they were opposed to discrimination in individual cases of overt racial rejection, but that people of color had actually been hurt and their self-reliance weakened by too much aid and too much talk about racism, which they considered something that had only been a major problem sometime in the past. Now, they argued, the civil rights agencies and courts were actually making things unfair to whites. Major GOP political campaigns also played on racial stereotypes and white fears and blamed violence and drugs on people of color.[9] Facing obvious inequalities, the strategy was to shift blame to the victims by activating stereotypes. Figure 5 shows the persistence of those beliefs about causes.

Researchers in multiple disciplines have continued to explore empirically the evolution and effects of the colorblind rationale across various contexts— individual decision making, institutional and organizational practices, schools and classrooms—to examine the rhetoric and assumptions of the arguments and explore whether this approach leads to better interracial relationships,

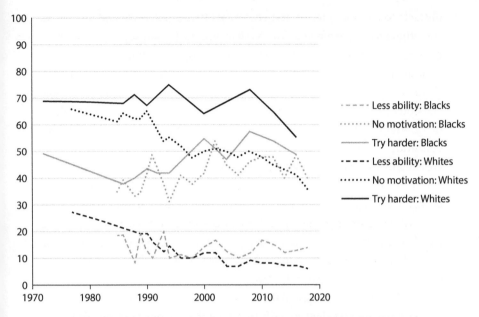

FIGURE 5. Persistent racial differences on causes of racial inequality. M. Krysan and
S. Moberg, "Tracking Trends in Racial Attitudes," Institute of Government and Public Affairs,
University of Illinois System, April 2021, https://igpa.uillinois.edu/programs/racial
_attitudes_2021

student-teacher engagement, and organizational climate and actual opportunities.[10] In this chapter I explore them with reference to high school and college
policy since 1980.

The Reagan-Bush era brought in a time in which race- or class-conscious
policies were widely seen as failures. The basic attitude was "We tried that and
it failed." The criticisms constantly reinforced by government leaders were
widely accepted as the reality. Government policies giving special attention to
Blacks, Latinos, and the poor were seen as nothing more than "excuses" for
failing to take the needed tough steps to return to what conservatives saw as a
far more successful tradition within which nonwhites needed to succeed. Government was spending too much money and getting too big; it needed to give
money back to the people through tax cuts and cut government to help pay
for them. The world-view was individualism within a market system that conservatives saw as fair and positive.

Policy envisaged a society where racial inequality was not a government
responsibility but something created by individual and group failures in communities of color. The conservatives saw too much government as a basic

obstacle to national success and civil rights laws as intrusive and ineffective, something to be terminated. The Reagan administration set out to end race-conscious policies and to reduce expensive college and school aid policies that it thought were unneeded and cost too much. In practical terms, its civil rights policy set in motion resegregation of the public schools, the end of conscious work on race relations, the end of systemic plans for desegregating the colleges of the South, and substantial cuts in school aid and funding for access to higher education. In racial terms, the twelve Reagan-Bush years were a time of increasing inequality and greatly diminished civil rights or social policy interventions for equity. In federal courts, the Justice Department became an enemy of civil rights groups, working to dismantle the color-conscious policies the civil rights struggles had won. College costs soared as family income stagnated. The dominant ideas were that government action for racial equity was unneeded and probably would make things worse and that it was the struggling middle class that most deserved help.

The change was so deep, and the defeat of a succession of progressive Democrats running for president so stark, that it left the way open for centrist Democrats whose emphasis was on the suburban white middle class and who adopted some major elements of the conservative agenda, including an increasingly colorblind policy in education and higher education, major cuts in welfare, and soaring incarceration. The Democratic Leadership Council, organized in 1985, was a consciously moderate organization designed to move the Democratic Party to the political center under an ideology sometimes called neoliberalism, which was a market-oriented strategy that consciously turned away from the controversial issues of the poor and minorities, downplayed the use of government for social change, and built its agenda around the concerns of suburban middle-class families, especially the lower-middle-class whites who had become a key swing group in national politics. In education and social policy, this movement, which was to dominate the Democratic Party from the Bill Clinton campaign in 1992 through the Hillary Clinton campaign twenty-four years later, identified with major themes of the Reagan reforms.[11]

The suburbs now dominated the metro areas where the great majority of Americans lived and were now the fulcrum of politics. Jimmy Carter was a frugal Southern moderate who downplayed racial issues and initiated no major social policies. President Clinton always talked about middle-class families playing by the rules and working hard for a living and needing a little help.[12] His administration would adopt welfare reforms and criminal justice policies embracing conservative Republican ideas. For a generation, efforts to equalize educational resources would diminish following a decisive Supreme Court defeat in the 1973 *Rodriguez* decision,[13] and the blame for inequality would be shifted from the society and the government to the institutions—the schools and colleges—that served people of color. During this period liberalism would lose influence, and the basic political and legal battles would be between increasingly conservative Republicans and centrist Democrats. President Clinton called it "triangulation," which involved major compromises with the conservatives.

Dropping and often attacking the previous focus on race did not bring an increased focus on poverty, though critics of race-based programs argued that would happen. Programs for the poor were also cut back or eliminated in the Republican periods. The primary focus of the federal government in higher education changed from giving scholarships to the poor to giving larger and larger subsidized loans to the middle class as well as very expensive tax benefits. Political priority shifted from helping the poor and the nonwhite to supporting middle-class families in the less affluent suburban communities that often held the balance of political power, people who had no savings for college and, often, had left racially changing neighborhoods in the cities.

The policy changes had their ugly side. Negative racial symbols had become increasingly common in politics and provided a justification for policy reversals. Race riots and the rise of the Black Power movement stirred white fear and resistance, which was fanned by the Nixon administration's Southern strategy and realigned politics. His election campaign tried to ignite racial fear and anger with stark images of Black riots and a strong promise of tougher laws.[14] Reagan used the "welfare queen" image in his first campaign, featuring stories about a fat Chicago woman cheating to get multiple subsidies, ripping off what was pictured as a permissive and destructive welfare system wasting taxpayer dollars.[15] George H. W. Bush used a Black rapist released from prison as a central symbol of his campaign against Michael Dukakis, stoking the fear of Black violence and reinforcing belief in the need for harsher sentencing.[16] Stereotypes were used to legitimize policy reversals and generate opposition to integration policies. These were large changes, but they were mild compared with what would come with the 2016 Trump campaign.

Conservatives denounced color-conscious remedies in schools and housing as unfair to whites and ended efforts to use housing subsidies to provide a chance for some low-income people of color to move to the suburbs. President Reagan had strongly opposed the major civil rights laws, did not believe in federal social policies, and fostered an ideology that civil rights were harming whites and did not work. The administration held that all legitimate basic claims of people of color had been settled and that too much focus on civil rights was actually harmful to those it was supposed to help. Reagan made a major speech shortly after his GOP convention nomination in Philadelphia, Mississippi, a place famous for the assassination of three civil rights workers in the 1960s, where he pledged a change, embracing the "states' rights" slogan of the Southern resistance to civil rights:

> I believe that . . . programs like education and others, should be turned back to the states. . . .
>
> I believe in state's rights; I believe in people doing as much as they can for themselves at the community level and at the private level. And I believe that we've distorted the balance of our government today by giving powers that were never intended in the constitution to that federal establishment.[17]

A fundamental goal was to take control of the courts through systematic appointments of young ideologically screened conservatives committed to rolling back the work of the Warren Court and limiting civil rights and social policy, something never done so systematically before. Nixon's four high court appointments had brought an end to the expansion of desegregation requirements and a five-four decision holding that there was no federal right to equal school resources.[18] President Reagan appointed William Rehnquist, a strong opponent of race-conscious civil rights policy, as chief justice, and he would hold that powerful office for nearly two decades, until his death in 2005. By the end of the Reagan administration and early George H. W. Bush administration, the Court was actively narrowing minority rights and reversing or terminating earlier policies.[19] Over the sixty years following 1968, Democrats were able to name only four justices to the Supreme Court.

Since Reagan, the basic education policies in the nation have been color-blind and made without serious consideration of racial realities. They were often modeled on what policy makers incorrectly thought was a better past with higher standards and accountability. The policy changes largely ignored nonwhite leaders. White politicians assumed that they knew better. Policy was made as if there were no color-related factors that needed to be taken into account. The one exception was limited affirmative action admissions, implemented voluntarily in most highly selective colleges, except in the nine states where it is forbidden in public institutions.

Segregation Soars

We learned in the 1960s that if you focus consciously on bringing down racial barriers to white schools, which typically have stronger academic outcomes, you can, with strong enforcement measures, achieve rapid and sweeping increases in diversity and opportunity. Research showed that it benefited students of color, that it did no harm to white students in their test scores, and that all students gained in racial attitudes, understanding, and relationships. We created diverse institutions in a still segregated society. The hope was that integrating one major set of institutions in education would be a key move toward a genuinely integrated society. In fact, however, policy worked to reverse much of what had been attained. In the post–civil rights colorblind period, we found out what would happen if government dismantled enforcement processes and operated schools as if color were irrelevant in an outside world that was highly stratified and unequal. The result was steadily increasing segregation. It was segregation by race and class, and it was strongly related to educational opportunities and outcomes. In the colorblind period, the new policy framework actually focused sanctions on the schools with double segregation of race and poverty, adding insult to injury. If race were irrelevant and a high-stakes, high-sanction policy were implemented, policy makers assumed, it might end racial difference in outcomes. But if you assume race is irrelevant when it is still highly relevant, then you end up blaming the victims of racial inequality. That is what happened.

Desegregation had turned out to be a durable policy. Its momentum was strong enough that the level of Black-white segregation reached its low point near the end of the Reagan administration in 1988, after two decades of conservative opposition. In spite of administration opposition, the Supreme Court did not roll back the basic legal requirements until 1991 in the *Dowell* decision,[20] the culmination of a long-term legal strategy by conservatives and judicial appointments that changed the composition of the Court. The *Dowell* decision defined desegregation plans as temporary, not lasting responsibilities. After the courts dropped the plans, local school officials were free to take actions that would predictably segregate the schools so long as they did not say that was their goal. After 1991 there was a steady rise in segregation in all parts of the country. The Court's premise was that racial problems had been solved and there was no more need for policies sending students of color to the better white schools. Because the share of low-income students in U.S. schools was increasing, the rising racial segregation also meant that the large majority of

TABLE 3. Percentage of Black Students in 90–100 Percent Nonwhite Schools, by Region, 1968–2016

	1968	1988	2001	2006	2011	2016	Change between 1988 and 2016
Northeast	42.7	48.0	51.2	50.8	51.4	51.5	3.5
South	77.8	24.0	31.0	32.9	34.2	36.4	12.4
Border	60.2	34.5	41.6	40.9	40.9	42.2	7.7
Midwest	58.0	41.8	46.8	45.8	43.1	42.0	0.2
West	50.8	28.6	30.0	30.1	34.0	37.7	9.1
National	64.3	32.1	37.4	38.5	38.8	40.1	8.0

Sources: NCES CCD, Public Elementary/Secondary School Universe Survey Data, 2016–17, 2011–12, 2006–7, 2001–2, and 1988–89. Data for 1968 were obtained from the analysis of the Office for Civil Rights data in Orfield, *Public School Desegregation.*

racially or ethnically segregated Black and Latino schools had concentrated poverty. On average only about a third of the students in their schools were from families able to pay for school lunches. The proportion of poor was twice as high as in majority-white schools, which, on average, had clear middle-class majorities. So students of color were doubly isolated.

The resegregation of Black students, as the courts changed, was most notable in the South, the region where civil rights policies had produced the greatest diversity. In 1968, the year the Supreme Court had greatly increased the requirements, 77 percent of Black students in the South were in highly segregated schools. By 1988 the share had dropped by two-thirds, down to 24 percent. By 2016 it was back up to 36 percent. The share of Black students in majority-white schools, which had greatly increased, declined rapidly (table 3). The courts had never ordered desegregation in most of the North and West because of limits in the Supreme Court decisions, so the declines there were more modest. The Supreme Court did not set rules for desegregation cases outside the South or for Latinos until 1973,[21] almost two decades after *Brown.* The rules were never seriously enforced by either the Justice Department or the Education Department, both of which were controlled by conservatives for most of the following two decades. The administrations of Clinton and Barack Obama tried to defend existing court orders but came up with no important new initiatives as almost all the major desegregation plans were ended after the Supreme Court changed the rules in 1991.

The growing segregation of Latino students was different. They were never desegregated except in a few localities. Latino students were first counted nationwide in 1968, when national racial data were collected under the Civil Rights

TABLE 4. Percentage of Latino Students in Intensely Segregated, 90–100 Percent Nonwhite Schools, by Region, 1968–2016

	1968	1988	2001	2006	2011	2016	Change between 1988 and 2016
Northeast	44.0	44.2	44.8	44.2	44.1	43.5	−0.7
South	33.7	37.9	39.9	40.3	41.5	41.9	4.0
Border	—	—	14.2	17.6	20.0	24.3	—
Midwest	6.8	24.9	24.6	26.7	26.1	24.9	0.0
West	11.7	27.5	37.4	42.2	44.7	46.2	18.7
National	23.1	33.1	37.4	40.0	41.1	41.6	8.5

Sources: NCES CCD, Public Elementary/Secondary School Universe Survey Data, 2016–17, 2011–12, 2006–7, 2001–2, and 1988–89. Data for 1968 were obtained from the analysis of the Office for Civil Rights data in Orfield, *Public School Desegregation*.

Act, and their segregation had increased to equal the Black rate by 1988. The effects were dramatic in the West, where immigration in the 1980s and 1990s was most massive. This great Latino immigration was largely of poor people with little education, so the future of their families depended on getting access to good schools, but they did not. Latinos had been a small share, about a twentieth, of all national students in the 1960s. Less than an eighth of Latinos in the West attended intensely segregated schools in 1968, but the share more than doubled by 1988, rose sharply by 2001, and continued to rise to 2016 (table 4). What those statistics suggest is that, although the Supreme Court recognized the right of Latinos to desegregated schools in 1973, the policy made it difficult to obtain a remedy and nothing serious was ever done. This rapidly growing group that became the nation's largest nonwhite community became as segregated by ethnicity and poverty as African Americans. Latinos also had the problem of high concentrations in places where access to four-year colleges was limited, especially California, where the state's Master Plan limited four-year public colleges to the top third of students, where affirmative action was outlawed, where there were few private colleges, and where the community colleges had low transfer rates. California had about a third of all Latino students.

Double Segregation and Its Consequences

Black and Latino schools are severely segregated by poverty as well as race, greatly increasing the educational and social impact.[22] If we could eliminate stark racial differences in income and wealth, we would have fewer multidimensional problems. Families of color would live in better neighborhoods and have more educational resources at home and more money to invest in supporting their children's development and higher education. But the schools serving students of color bring together families and communities struggling with far more limited resources. At the beginning of the twenty-first century, in the schools with 90–100 percent Black and Latino students, almost nine-tenths (88 percent) of the students were low income. Very few of the overwhelmingly white schools had high poverty levels.[23] The most isolated students of color had virtually no contact with middle-class students. A decade later, the overlap between racial and low-income concentrations was even more extreme: half of 90–100 percent Black and Latino schools had 90–100 percent students from low-income households. More than a fourth of Black children and a fifth of Latinos lived in areas of concentrated poverty, compared with one in sixteen Asian children and one in twenty-five whites. Residential segregation is strongly related to lifetime success.[24] Researchers often debate whether segregation by poverty or race is most damaging to children, though it is clear that both are strongly related to differential opportunities and outcomes and that poverty is often the result of a history of racial discrimination. The reality is that most students of color experience both and most white and Asian children experience neither. (The small number of concentrated-poverty white schools, which tend to be in places like Appalachia, typically do experience serious educational problems, but many poor whites elsewhere live in communities that do not have concentrated poverty and retain connections with the middle class.)

Double segregation has serious consequences in high schools. The focus of civil rights groups on integration reflected strong preferences, especially among Blacks, who struggled to gain access to more effective schools.[25] Though critics often dismiss it as "sitting next to white kids," the benefits come from escaping schools that are overwhelmed with the problems of poor families and getting access to experienced teachers, strong peer groups, and challenging instruction. The consensus of nearly sixty years of social science research on the harms of school segregation is that racially and socioeconomically isolated schools are strongly related to an array of factors that limit educational opportunities and outcomes, including less experienced and less qualified teachers, high teacher turnover, less successful peer groups, and inadequate facilities and learning materials. Highly qualified and experienced teachers are spread unevenly across schools and are much less likely to remain in segregated or resegregating settings.[26] Students and classes most in need of highly skilled and experienced teachers often have new teachers who have not yet developed the skill that comes with experience and who do not stay long enough to build an effective team.

In California schools, the share of unqualified teachers is 6.75 times higher in high-minority schools (more than 90 percent minority) than in low-minority schools (less than 30 percent nonwhite). Schools serving low-income and segregated neighborhoods have been shown to provide less challenging curricula.[27] High-stakes testing has hurt minority-segregated schools, producing a focus on rote skills and test-taking strategies because the school's future often depends on scores in the required tests. By contrast, students in middle-class schools normally have far less trouble with high-stakes exams, so the schools and teachers are free to broaden the curriculum. Segregated school settings are also significantly less likely than more affluent settings to offer AP or honors courses. Students are more likely to be expelled or to drop out. Dropout rates are significantly higher in segregated and impoverished schools (nearly all of the two thousand "dropout factory" high schools are doubly segregated by race and poverty).[28] Segregated students have less success in college; test scores and graduation rates underscore the negative impact of segregation.

Disappearing High School Opportunities under Colorblind Policies

Higher education officials need to understand that while race-conscious policies have been protected and continued in most selective private universities and in leading public universities in the forty-one states that allow them, there are almost none in high schools, and we have been resegregating our high schools and elementary schools for almost a third of a century. In other words, we have been shrinking the pipeline for students of color. That has radically lowered access to some of our most outstanding public schools, which have changed their focus from conscious efforts to include students of color to rigid test-based admissions. Many of the outstanding urban high schools were created as part of desegregation plans. When magnet high schools were created and expanded rapidly in the 1970s, they were directly related to desegregation, recruited students intentionally to produce and continue substantial diversity, often received special funding under court orders, had no admissions requirements except student interest, provided free transportation, and were often highly popular in both white and nonwhite communities. There are more than two million students attending magnet schools. These schools were far from perfect but offered very important opportunities, including educational programs never before available in the city. In poor school districts with few remaining middle-class students, they were often the only major path left to prepare for selective colleges.

After a series of Supreme Court decisions lifting all race-conscious requirements and outlawing the admission of individual students solely on the basis of their race, many school districts dropped their efforts and did not adopt new policies to implement diversity criteria that were still permitted by the courts. Schools that were created to produce voluntary integration and successful in doing it were often turned into elite white and Asian schools. Communities that wished to continue desegregation policies in their magnets were often challenged by white parents who claimed that their children should have gotten spaces held for minority children. In 2007, in a much-criticized decision, *Parents Involved*, the Supreme Court by a single vote declared the voluntary efforts of local communities illegal if students were selected on the basis of race, even in pursuit of maintaining integration opportunities in largely segregated communities.[29] Methods that had been accepted and even required for decades became illegal. Many school districts responded by abandoning their efforts, even those that were still legal under the decision.

The *New York Times* described the recent history at one of the nation's most famous high schools, Stuyvesant, in New York City, which was never substantially desegregated but was more than a tenth Black in the early 1970s when there was an effort at diversity. "At Stuyvesant High School," the *New York Times* reported in 2019, "out of 895 slots in the freshman class, only seven were offered to black students. And the number of black students is shrinking: There were 10 black students admitted into Stuyvesant last year, and 13 the year before."[30] Stuyvesant is a superhighway to great colleges. For Black students it is now a detour sign. In communities where the magnets had produced substantial integration, which had been acceptable to both sides, often at the fifty-fifty mark, the changes were much larger.[31]

Integrated schooling is only part of what is needed for equal opportunity, but it typically produces gains in college success and in workplaces and neighborhoods later in life. Students from segregated schools, where almost all the students are poor, have to adjust at college to differences in race and class, as well as a peer group that has been better prepared—a hard combination. Integrated schools, on the other hand, may also provide better educational opportunities for the children of those who benefit, creating intergenerational social capital.[32]

The process of stratification, or resegregation, has taken hold in many magnet high schools, which now use academic screening procedures and have no policies to maintain diversity. Since inequality has significantly deepened for high school students of color, it is all the more important that there be policies and programs to support students with potential in inferior, segregated schools. Strong magnet schools (and other schools of choice) that do not provide free transportation exclude the families who cannot afford to live in their regions and are not able to provide or pay for transportation, seriously limiting access for many low-income single-parent families of color. Choice without transportation is often no choice for the poor.

Cutting Resources for Educational Opportunity

The early 1970s saw the cutoff of tools needed to integrate schools in the nation's segregated metro areas, a shutdown of housing integration policies, and a decision that decisively shut the door on the idea that the equal protection clause of the U.S. Constitution mandated equalization of school funds for poor areas, areas with many students of color. In the *Rodriguez* decision in 1973 the Court held that there was no right to equal educational resources in the Constitution.[33] It was widely expected that the Court would require some form of equalization, but the effort failed by a single vote. The case has now slammed the door for at least a half century on efforts to use federal courts to enforce equity within or among the states. Though the decision was based in part on since-disproved research that showed that financial resources are not significantly linked to educational outcomes, lawyers representing poor students and districts have since confronted even more conservative federal courts and have been turned back.

The Constitution says nothing about education, unsurprising considering its origin in what was then a 95 percent rural society dominated by subsistence farmers where public education had not yet been developed. The *Brown* decision was basically about discrimination within public school systems, not about the substance of educational provision. *Plessy*'s right to "separate but equal" had long since been proved a fraud. Just three years after the Supreme Court established the "separate but equal" doctrine in 1896, it ruled unanimously that school districts in the South need not provide any high school education for Black students. There were massive differences in resources provided for Black and white schools for generations. Civil rights groups had tried without success for decades to win equal funding before they decided to demand an end to separate schools. The Supreme Court's *Brown* decision said segregation was "inherently unequal." Since *Rodriguez* there have been many lawsuits under state constitutions and laws that, when successful, on average have significantly lowered the fiscal gap between the poorest and most affluent districts in a state at least for a decade, until the Court turns things back to elected officials. Many decisions leave the top districts largely unchanged but raise dollars for those at the bottom significantly.[34] Some of these orders have been terminated,[35] and other efforts have been rejected by courts.[36] They rarely deal with issues like teacher and curriculum quality, but significant increases in funding can produce gains for students. One major problem is that big city schools, with great majorities of students of color, often are not in the poorest districts because they often have larger tax bases than rural or low-income bedroom suburban districts without viable commercial areas or job centers, they receive streams of money for special education and language instruction, and cities have higher costs, so equalization of funding does not bring substantial benefits in most cases. Few state courts have shown the will and power to equalize opportunities in a meaningful and lasting way.

The net effect of the U.S. Supreme Court decisions meant that neither access for students of color to good suburban schools nor equal resources was a right, except in a few states with stronger fiscal commitments. The assumption underlying many of the colorblind reforms was that segregation and unequal resources really didn't matter, that it was a question of will and sanctions against the schools that fall behind.

The social policy strategy of conservatives managing the federal budget was to "starve the beast." They saw government as the insatiable beast and cutting revenue through major federal and state tax cuts as an effective starvation strategy. David Stockman, the budget director Reagan appointed to control the federal budget cuts, consciously made plans to simply eliminate as many domestic program expenditures and programs as possible, both of these things taking place in two massive laws passed in the first year of Reagan's administration.[37] The administration instituted a massive tax cut, as did a number of states, sharply reducing resources for public-sector expenditures. It turned out that the large "beast" the conservatives across the nation cut most dramatically was higher education, especially at the state level. Part of the state budget problem was caused by the costs of expanding health care and greatly increased incarceration, particularly of minor drug offenses, in the "war on drugs," which had a huge impact on Black men and their families. When the state tax cuts surged, starting with California's Proposition 13 in 1978, and the Reagan cuts in federal tax rates were combined with the sharp reduction in state and federal revenues from a serious recession in the early 1980s, state governments (which have to balance their budgets each year) made sharp cuts in higher education. The cuts were covered, in part, by large and rapid increases in tuition during a bad recession. It seemed to be an adjustment to a crisis, but it was the beginning of a profound and lasting change.

The day he was inaugurated, Reagan announced, "It is time to check and reverse the growth of government," and he pledged to "curb the size and influence of the Federal establishment" and not to let government "ride on our back." The key to American greatness was unleashing "the energy and individual genius of man." There is no need for government to protect and foster equal opportunity. "It is no coincidence that our present troubles parallel and are proportionate to the intervention and intrusion in our lives that result from unnecessary and excessive growth of government."[38]

The conservative vision looked backward to an imagined successful time before civil rights. Historian Meyer Weinberg defines what happened this way: "Federal expenditures fell sharply and were grouped disadvantageously from the viewpoint of poor and minority children. Legislation enacted originally on their behalf . . . was shorn of much financial support. Remaining programs were grouped into block grants and left to the state to apportion as they saw fit. The struggle against school segregation was all but abandoned. . . . Efforts were made . . . to reopen cases decided in favor of civil rights plaintiffs in previous years. Federal financial incentives to school boards to induce them to desegregate . . . were eliminated."[39] The conservative idea was that what was needed was to stop social reforms, enforce traditional basic education concepts, and get rid of civil rights orders. Meanwhile the courts were staffed with young conservatives as judicial appointments were centralized and subjected to an unprecedented and detailed ideological screening designed to "institutionalize the Reagan revolution so it can't be set aside."[40] By the end of twelve years of judicial appointments screened by the right-wing Federalist Society, the federal courts had become a minefield for civil rights and resegregation of schools was under way.

The largest education program that was eliminated in the first Reagan year was the desegregation assistance program—a popular voluntary program of grants to school districts wanting to improve integrated schools, create many new magnet schools, and support other steps many districts wished to pursue. Desegregation aid went from $386 million the previous year to zero within months. Since that time there has been no significant federal funding of desegregation and race-relations efforts. Many education programs were combined into a single block grant, the total budget was cut, and the money was sent to states to do whatever they wanted. Most just tended to send out small per capita grants to districts.[41] Research had demonstrated both academic and race-relations benefits from the desegregation aid program. Early in the Reagan administration, the desegregation studies research advisory group in the National Institute of Education was dissolved and all the pending grants for basic research in the field canceled.[42] Since that time there has been no significant federal money for race relations even as segregation worsened year by year, data accumulated on the educational damage it caused, and the nonwhite share of young Americans soared. (There were proposals for modest efforts in the last year of the Obama administration, which were rejected in Congress.)

The Wall of Cost

In higher education there were quick changes in financing, setting the higher education system on a path to ever-higher tuition. This was happening in a period when almost all the gains in income were going to people with higher education, income inequality was getting steadily worse, and the share of students of color in the college-age population was surging. Sharply diminished state support as states cut taxes and shifted funds to incarceration and health costs led to far higher tuition and fees. The consequence was to continuously shift a higher share of the rapidly rising cost of college to students and parents. This was workable for higher-income families, who were getting most of the gains as economic inequality intensified, but for the majority whose income was not rising significantly as college costs soared, it was a crisis. Higher education increasingly shifted from being seen as a good public investment to being seen as a valuable private good that would produce economic gains, and it was believed that families should bear more and more of the responsibility to pay for it.

College costs became almost impossible for the poor to pay, even with available aid, which fell far behind rising costs, but policy attention shifted from the poor to the middle class. Most middle-income families were not prepared to deal with soaring costs. The theory, as tuitions began to soar, was "high tuition, high aid," but the maximum aid fell further and further behind the costs. Even before these dramatic increases in tuition began, the anxiety of the middle class about college costs was surging as stagnant incomes and low savings were insufficient to manage costs. President Jimmy Carter agreed to extend subsidized student loans to the middle class in the 1978 Middle Income Student Assistance Act, an early sign of what was to come.[43] Loans would eventually grow to be far larger than the Pell Grant, the basic national resource for low-income students. During his administration, Clinton rejected the advice of his experts and accepted the findings of his pollsters, deciding to substantially increase aid to the middle class during his 1996 reelection campaign by adopting tax credits that subsidized mostly higher-income families.[44]

In both administrations these changes were seen as additions to, not substitutes for, aid to the poor. But in fact, budgets are finite and funds were always scarce in a period when Republicans were cutting taxes and resisting policies they said would raise the national debt. Once the tax credits were implemented, they were in permanent legislation as entitlements, in contrast to Pell Grants, which relied on annual appropriations. The resulting tradeoff helped middle-class families continue to access college but, too often, reduced the opportunities for students of color to access, afford, and persist in the kinds of colleges most likely to produce long-term success, strong four-year colleges. Private colleges became far less affordable except for the very small number that gave aid packages meeting full need. There was more demand from the middle class on the strong public universities as private tuitions soared, intensifying competition for scarce seats as campuses stopped expanding. All this happened as incomes for people without higher education were declining and the country was experiencing deindustrialization in major sectors. Historically, as the economic need for further education had grown, so had the provision of free schools and affordable colleges. No more.

A central problem with college financial aid is that the policies are shaped within a constellation of interest groups whose primary interest is in the finances of the institutions they represent, not in focusing financial aid on the most needy students. The interest groups want the policies that work for their colleges. Though college admissions and aid offices want to be able to finance students who most urgently need help, institutional interests are often very different. The students who most need help do not have a lobby or a political force in the process. Suzanne Mettler explains, "The most visible actors on student aid policy have long been the numerous trade associations that represent universities and colleges, and a vast number of professional organizations," many sharing a single building in Washington, DC, 1 Dupont Circle. Universities and higher education systems have Washington lobbyists who are involved with the crucial committees and subcommittees and agency officials who help frame the policies, but "the primary concern of these organizations is with the sustainability of the institutions they represent, not broader issues. . . . They have put a priority on preserving their member institutions' strength and autonomy, rather than pursuing broader goals and new approaches."[45] Many policies are developed over time in what political scientists described as "subgovernments" composed of key congressional committees and staffs, agency leaders and staffs, and the major organized beneficiaries, operating through their organizations and lobbyists.[46] Conspicuously absent is any force representing the interest of unorganized groups with few resources, such as low-income families and students of color. They rarely get much more than modest targeted funds for historically Black colleges and universities and institutions with substantial enrollments of students of color. The log-rolling system works to get something for all the types of institutions, but not to get enough to be workable for the students and families with severe needs.

The contemporary statistics on the striking gaps by race and class in college completion are not an accident. They are often unintended but very real consequences of a third of a century of increasing economic inequality and policy decisions focused especially on low taxes and middle-class aid. The cost of the tax subsidies and loan subsidies became far larger than the total payments for access by low-income students. The gigantic George W. Bush tax cuts included further tax subsidies for student loans, and those became permanent in a budget deal between Obama and congressional Republicans.

The net policy effect of aid changes was neither color conscious nor poverty conscious. It was mostly middle-class and upper-class aid, though this was never the announced goal. That is the consequence of aiding people going to college and people who have enough income and a sufficiently sophisticated understanding to file tax returns with all the deduction categories. Priority shifted from heavily nonwhite recipients to predominantly white and Asian higher-income beneficiaries. Most tax subsidies could, in their nature, only go to families filing detailed tax returns with itemized deductions and credits. Few low-income families filed those forms, and many had income so low that they had no tax liability that could be helped by a deduction or a credit. This situation was bad for all lower-income families but was even worse for very low-income families of color, who typically had no wealth to draw on to make up for inadequate aid packages or high incomes to shelter. Families with accountants were much better situated to claim subsidies than families with incomes low enough to be exempt from federal income taxes.

There were other compounding developments. Beginning with the Georgia HOPE Scholarships, a number of states adopted "merit"-based scholarships given out on the basis of high school grades and test scores, whose renewal was often dependent on achieving a certain grade-point average in college studies, conditions that strongly favored students whose families had resources and who had been to the better high schools.[47] Many aided merit students had families with the means to pay. Many states have no substantial need-based aid. A financial aid administrator at a major Southern state university in a state with merit scholarships told me that the great majority of the students getting the scholarships had not even submitted financial aid applications, while there were few resources for need-based aid.

As college became more and more expensive, both the "sticker price" (published total cost of attendance) and the inadequate aid packages became serious obstacles to students of color. Research has shown that the sticker price discourages many families from even considering four-year colleges, especially the many families who do not understand the complex aid system and do not want to sign up for what seem impossibly large loans that can never be forgiven since Congress decided they could not be canceled in bankruptcy like other debts. Many students apply to only one local low-cost college even when they are eligible for a stronger institution. There is significant analysis of both cross-sectional and over-time studies employing sophisticated economic models that indicates that "increases in net cost over time lead to decreases in enrollment rates for lower-income students." Michael S. McPherson and Morton Owen Shapiro observe that "a consensus in the econometric literature is that a $150 increase in net cost reduces enrollment rates by 1.8%."[48] The lower economic resources of Blacks and Latinos meant that tuitions' far faster growth than the cost of living or of incomes had a specially damaging effect on their college going and helped account for the growing racial and economic gaps after 1980.[49]

Because the population of high school graduates has been declining and the costs are so high, many small colleges, especially private colleges, are devoting a substantial share of their aid to non-need-based scholarships (often called tuition discounting) to attract enough students to fill classes and dormitories from families who can pay at least a good part of the high costs. That money, of course, is not available for institutional scholarships for the students with the greatest need. Very few colleges award packages that cover all costs. This means that colleges routinely make aid offers that require substantially more money than the college's own formula thinks the students could reasonably provide. Students of color often lack the connections, such as other relatives who can come up with more help, that may be available to those with more affluent extended families.

When students are sent their financial aid letters, most schools provide a calculation of expected family contribution and the various grants and loans a student would receive, as well as "unmet need," costs that the school knows the family probably cannot pay that must be covered if the student is to come or remain in study. That is an absolute barrier for some students, and it forces others to take extra jobs or high-cost nonguaranteed loans or prompts their parents to take out parent PLUS (Parent Loan for Undergraduate Students) loans, which can become a permanent risk to the economic future of often vulnerable parents.[50] Those are higher-interest loans that can never be forgiven and that easily become a lifetime burden for low-income parents told that it is the only way for their child to go to college. These are threats both to academic success and to the economic future of families. They are a special threat to Black families. But they often become the only alternative. All of these factors tend to push many families toward low-cost local mediocre community colleges serving a low-income area in which students are unlikely to finish and transfer successfully to four-year colleges and students often lose years and much forgone income, as well as piling up debts in the process.[51] For families without resources but living in a web of intergenerational wealth, in contrast, help from grandparents and other relatives can perpetuate those advantages.

The main impacts of the "Reagan revolution" in national higher education policies were a reduction in the cost coverage of grants to low-income students and an attack on affirmative action. In its first year the Reagan administration created regulations that raised the required family contribution and lowered the amount of aid as a serious recession caused state governments to slash college budgets.[52] It cut Pell Grants by $500 million that year.[53] The administration asked for even more cuts but Congress turned them back.[54] Gaps between costs and aid mushroomed. At first it seemed like a temporary recession-based reduction, but it turned out to be the beginning of a large long-term change.

Research suggests that money is not the central problem students of color face within four-year colleges. There are roughly similar effects across racial lines for similarly situated students. The crucial effect seems to be on the decision to go not to four-year public colleges but to community colleges or for-profit colleges or no college at all, perhaps going into military service and hoping eventually to get college support after service from the GI Bill, although the odds are against successfully completing college at later ages and stages of life. It is hard to study the choice effect because most of the higher education data sets are about students already enrolled in higher education (making it far less difficult to collect data) and most high school data are not connected to follow up data showing whether the students go to and persist in college. Community colleges, though extremely important for students of color, are notoriously underfunded and understudied. A large share of students say money had a big impact on their choice of college, and there are large numbers of students who go to schools that are substantially less selective than ones they are qualified for.[55]

Recruiters for for-profit colleges often target students of color with promises of admission with no requirement for money from the students but students are immediately signed up for Pell Grants and guaranteed student loans to pay the college. A 2020 report showed that the two largest single sources of bachelor's degrees for Black students were actually for-profit colleges, one of which did all instruction online.[56] Degrees from these colleges often count for very little in the job market, and students often leave with high debts and no degrees. Many veterans of color eligible for substantial aid after wartime service do not use these benefits, or they spend them at costly and ineffective for-profit colleges, which recruit strongly.[57]

Data collected from freshmen at hundreds of four-year colleges and universities in 2016 showed that most students worry about financing college (56 percent), and an eighth (13 percent) have major worries. One-quarter of Latino students (24.7 percent) and 22.0 percent of Black students report "major" concerns about their ability to pay for college, compared with 9.2 percent of White first-time, full-time students.[58] According to the report, "In 2016, a record 15% of freshmen felt they could not afford their first-choice institution—that's a 60% increase from 2004. In addition, the proportion of first-time, full-time students rating 'not being offered aid by their first choice' as a very important factor in selecting their college has more than doubled from 4.4% in 1984 to 11.5% in 2016."[59]

A major study of a number of national data sets disclosed that there were a large number of low-income students in low-income communities with high test scores, but that most of them did not go to the selective schools that their scores indicated they were eligible for. Many applied to schools far below the level at which they could be admitted. At the other extreme, students from upper-income families with lower scores typically did not even apply to non-selective schools or community colleges, but tended to follow systematic strategies to get into at least somewhat selective schools and to try "reach" institutions. The study showed that high-achieving poor students, if they were able to enroll, were just as successful academically as similar students with higher incomes at competitive schools. In fact, because of financial aid, they actually, on average, paid less to go to considerably better schools, since those schools had far more aid to distribute. The study found that those low-income highly qualified students who did go to the excellent colleges were more likely to have attended strong high schools or magnet schools where there was a critical mass of well-prepared college-bound classmates and better advising and college connections. Very talented students in isolated high-poverty schools or outside large metros tended not to apply to any competitive colleges in spite of their personal achievements and talent.[60] In important ways, they live and try to learn in a different society regardless of their personal capacity.

Only about a seventh of the low-income high achievers are students of color. Among low-income high-achieving students, there are more Asians than Black, Latino, and Native people combined. This is partially because an income measure does not measure the kind of human capital that Asian immigrant children with low-paid but highly educated recent immigrant parents possess, or the fact that they attend, on average, far less impoverished and more integrated schools because they are able to live in more integrated communities (two big reasons why poverty is not a good proxy for race in admissions or aid).

The exact influence of the cost is hard to know because these students and families have multiple forces at work, and students who do not go to four-year colleges tend not to be studied. We have limited knowledge of the constellation of forces that determine whether and where students apply and less about those who do not go. But being in a setting where no one applies to demanding colleges, where the parents and people in the community have limited information and a good deal of misinformation, and where knowledge about need-based scholarships and how to get them is rare greatly lowers students' chances. The great majority of low-income highly talented students of color who do apply is in a relatively small number of schools and regions where there is a critical mass of such students. Such schools tend to be known by recruiters, and the families tend to get better information.

The overall direction of conservative college policy had deep impacts. The conservative view was that higher education was, basically, a private good and those receiving it should pay much more for it and the state governments should continue to cut their taxes and reduce financing of public colleges. In exchange, state legislatures gave the campuses broader authority to raise tuition without state approval. The basic idea was that the universities could continue to operate as before with much less money from the state, but that instead of getting state money, the universities should tax their own students by rapidly increasing tuition.[61] The same aging generation that had a much better deal on college access and costs supported repeated tax cuts that forced more students to bear substantial long-term debts for what previous generations had been given with state funding holding down students' costs. That has continued now for nearly four decades, with tuition increasing far faster than family incomes and aid falling further behind. The biggest tuition increases coincide with recessions, when state funds fall quickly because states, unlike the federal government, are not permitted to run deficit budgets and colleges attempt to avoid disruptive cuts by raising the costs. The net impact is to cut funds that often come from relatively progressive taxes on the adult population and move to targeted flat-rate "taxes" in the form of tuition increases that are much bigger barriers for low-income families, particularly those without resources from relatives.

During the 1970s, when the Pell Grant first took hold, the cost of college was virtually unchanged for the decade. States were expanding college spaces across the country, welcoming what was by far the largest generation in history of students of color. But over time, aid covered much less of the rising costs. A number of state governments stopped expanding college spaces, increasing competition and forcing more students into two-year colleges or for-profit campuses that ran up student debt, often without graduating the students or giving them real qualifications for jobs. The Master Plan for California higher education, which influenced many states, limited four-year college access to the top third of students, using measures that often strongly reflected the resources of students' families and schools, perpetuating inequality. The plan was not adjusted to provide for a larger sector of students as the need grew, intensifying competition.

Federal college funding reached a high point, providing 23 percent of the revenue of public colleges, in 1965. By 1985 it had dropped to 13 percent.[62] The combination of inflation, recession, tax cuts, declining funding, and soaring tuitions produced a fateful change in college access in just a few years: "The steady decline in the share of higher education revenue provided by families as incomes rose and costs stayed stable, came to an abrupt halt after 1979."[63] Families with rising real incomes found it easier over time to pay costs that were often shrinking in constant-value dollars in the 1970s. The Pell Grant program, which greatly aided low-income families seeking four-year college educations, had sharply increased enrollments by low-income students.[64]

The year 1980 marked a dividing line: "The first half of the 1980s saw a sub-stantial real decrease in the federal grants available to lower income students."[65] The net cost of college for the lowest-income students went up 33 percent from 1979 to 1984.[66] The period from the late 1960s to the early 1970s had brought a substantial increase in college going by students in the lowest income quar-tile, but it fell substantially from 1981 to 1984.[67] The drop was particularly dramatic for low-income African Americans.[68] During the 1980s the overall share of low-income students fell significantly and the share of students above middle income climbed 12 percent.[69] A College Board report summa-rized the change: "In the 1970s there was little, if any, real growth in college prices. Since 1980, however, college prices have been rising at twice and some-times three times the Consumer Price Index."[70] It was a period in which incomes were not growing for less educated adults and often shrinking in real terms. There were significant racial consequences.

There has been research for many years showing that the price of tuition has a clear effect on college going.[71] The problem was that in the next two de-cades family incomes grew less than half as fast as costs, and aid covered a smaller share. The problem was most severe for lower-income families, whose incomes were growing even slower as the economy became more unequal.[72] In those two decades, tuition at public four-year universities went up 114 percent while incomes grew an average of 20 percent, even less for low-income families. For the families in the lowest fifth in terms of income, the cost went up to an impossible 62 percent of family income from 38 percent in 1975.[73] This was a sharp break in the history of public higher education.

There was an expanding supply of four-year public colleges with almost no increase in real costs from the 1960s through the 1970s. Then the country made a fateful turn to something very different. Opportunities became more critical for life chances as incomes became more linked to education levels, but access became less abundant and far more expensive. Only the most affluent families were unaffected. Middle-income families were demanding aid.

The racial impact of these colorblind policies was severe. During the period from 1960 to 1975, there had been a dramatic increase in the share of Black high school graduates going to college after high school. For a brief period in the 1970s, what had been a large gap in the share of high school graduates going to some college almost disappeared, only to grow sharply in the first Reagan administration and to remain wide into the next century.[74] In 1976 the college participation rates of eighteen-to-twenty-four-year-old Blacks and whites were actually the same. By 1988 a wide gap had opened.[75] Later the participation rate of Black and Latino students would rise again, but the gap in completion became even larger as students of color completed at higher rates than before but fell further behind white and Asian rates that were rising faster. The gaps between costs and aid grew fast in the periodic recessions when state budgets fell, and the higher tuitions and fees adopted in financial emergency situations such as severe recessions remained after a return to normal.

The share of total federal aid shifted from mostly grants to mostly loans and from overwhelmingly need-based grants to far less focused aid through loans and tax subsidies as well as institutional aid.[76] The value of the maximum Pell Grant fell from a peak of about 80 percent of the total cost of attendance in the early 1970s to less than 40 percent by 1999[77] and has continued to fall since. For upper-income families who started way ahead and whose incomes increased more rapidly as the economy became more unequal, the increases were much more manageable. For families with low income and less secure employment and without wealth or significant savings or relatives who could help, the trends were grim and the choices narrowed or disappeared.

Blocking Civil Rights Enforcement in Higher Education

In power, conservatives worked to dismantle or end civil rights enforcement. Color-conscious remedies are not only permissible but mandatory when institutions have been unconstitutionally created and operated on a racial basis, as was true in the seventeen former slave states with a long history of mandatory segregation where most Black students lived. When the Reagan administration took office, federal civil rights officials were in the midst of a large conflict with the University of North Carolina over a continuing failure to comply with the 1964 Civil Rights Act in one of the most important universities in the South. When the Reagan administration backed down and yielded to the intense pressure, it was an important signal that less would be required of historically all-white Southern public colleges.[78] The Carter administration had negotiated plans with the state governments of the South, most of them aimed at greatly increasing nonwhite enrollment in the historically white colleges and upgrading and integrating the historically Black campuses, which had always been treated badly. The Reagan administration, however, held that as long as the states implemented specific elements of the plans, such as creating new programs at historically Black colleges and universities, that was all that would be required even if they fell far short of the goal or minority representation in white schools even declined. This change reduced compliance with the Civil Rights Act to something more like a ritual rather than actually ending the historical debt of the schools. There would not be any serious revival of the systemic desegregation efforts in higher education in the next four decades.

The federal government was under a series of federal court orders up to the mid-1980s to continue enforcing the Civil Rights Act in higher education and school desegregation. Even before the federal courts dropped the cases, the Reagan administration was moving strongly away from the race-conscious goals. By 1985 the Office for Civil Rights head, Assistant Secretary Harry Singleton, called the goals in the state higher education plans "something these schools are striving for" but said, "It is not mandated that they have to meet them." He said it was better to give attention to "steps and measures," to see whether the campuses had done the specific things required, such as building new facilities or giving the Black colleges more programs, not to focus on the result. He said that if, after doing those things, they fell short, "I don't think that I would find that negative." If the numerical goal were actually enforced, he said, that would make it a quota and "that's not what we are about." A number of major states were reaching the point where decisions would be made about whether they had done enough, though no state had reached its goals. Former Office for Civil Rights acting director Frank Cioffi had concluded that no state "even approximated what might be considered the elimination of the vestiges of dual systems." Civil rights lawyers called for the administration to initiate fund cutoffs to force further compliance.[79] Federal actions are always watched closely by higher education leaders, and these were clear signals that there was slight risk to any enforcement action.

The big change meant that even if the schools met none of their enrollment objectives under the Carter administration plans or were even moving backward, nothing further would be required, the states would be found in compliance, and the rights that students of color had gained under the Civil Rights Act would no longer produce leverage for progress. There were still large and obvious differences between the historically white and Black universities. The administration, however, chose the route of concluding that various states had done enough and that they should be released from enforcement proceedings, much the same approach it advocated for public schools.

The basic idea of the administration was that there had been historical violations sometime in the past, but if there were some positive actions, it would turn things back to local control. In contrast to civil rights groups' support for race-conscious policies that focused strongly on numbers and actual institutional changes and were based on the belief that the country was far from resolving all the continuing effects of generations of discrimination, the idea was that there was a risk of too much federal intervention and that things had changed sufficiently to trust local leaders and institutions even without statistical evidence of real change. Race-conscious policies were seen as something to be shut down as soon as possible.

The Reagan and Bush administrations did nothing significant for further integration of colleges. The one dramatic use of the Civil Rights Act's powerful threat to cut off federal funds for discrimination came out of an investigation of an Asian complaint against the University of California at Berkeley. The claim was discrimination against Asians. The university had decided to increase the importance of the nonmathematics part of the SAT relative to the math scores in its admissions decisions. Since Asian students had higher scores in math, they claimed that the action was discriminatory, though the faculty had given other grounds. Facing a federal threat, the university reversed course.[80] Not long after that, Asians became the largest racial group among Berkeley students. The move to lower the emphasis on math might have been a plus for access by Black, Latino, and American Indian students. In any case the action on behalf of Asians was color conscious, looking at probable statistical results. The enforcement used power from the Civil Right Act, action going deep into university prerogatives in setting admissions requirements, but not to protect underrepresented minorities. There were, of course, many increases in admissions requirements around the country as standards were raised in high schools and colleges that had negative impacts on students of color. None of those were sanctioned.

The Turn Away from Poverty-Conscious College Aid Politics

The impact of the great shift from state government to student and family funding of a much larger share of college costs, together with reduction in the Pell Grant's coverage of college costs, has continued now for almost four decades. In the three decades from 1989 to 2019, the average cost of four-year public colleges in the U.S. tripled, with an accelerating increase after 2000. In 2019–20, the average in-state tuition and fee price in the public four-year sector is about three times as high in inflation-adjusted dollars as it was in 1989–90. Median real family income, however, rose only 19 percent in that thirty-year period,[81] and the bulk of that income went to higher-wage earners with higher levels of education.[82] For people without postsecondary education, which includes the great majority of adults of color, there was no significant increase in income adjusted for inflation for more than four decades. There was a sharp decline in the real value of the minimum wage, which was frozen for long periods, including the 1980s and the period from 2009 to 2021.[83] The minimum wage sets the floor for millions of low-income workers, particularly in the South and other areas without state minimum wages, areas with anti-union state laws blocking unionization to raise wages.

The Pell Grant, by far the largest source of aid for low-income students, declined drastically in terms of its ability to cover the cost of college. In the 2019–20 school year it covered, on average, only 28 percent of the cost of attendance at a four-year public college (including room and board) and only 12 percent of the cost of attending a private college.[84] Over time the gap between the cost of college and the available maximum Pell Grant became so massive that bringing it back to covering the share of average four-year public college cost that it had covered in the early 1970s became inconceivable to policy makers. When there was money in the budget, a small portion of the gap would be closed, and then it would open wider again when a recession came and state budget problems triggered another round of big tuition increases. Lyndon Johnson and Senator Claiborne Pell talked about making four-year colleges affordable for the poor. By the time of Clinton, the discussion was more about affording community colleges. This issue was widely debated in the 2020 Democratic presidential primaries, and President Joe Biden's plan for free community college failed in Congress.

Ignoring Race and Class Effects and Blaming Victims: The "Excellence" Movement

A fateful change in the basic assumptions of education policy for public schools at both the national and state levels in the 1980s had long-lasting impacts. The basic federal education laws, the Elementary and Secondary Education Act of 1965 and the Higher Education Act of 1965, had given primacy to providing money to schools of concentrated poverty and low-income students. In addition, there were a variety of special programs about preschool, reading, libraries, and so on. There was no substantial effort to control local schools, except if there were civil rights violations during Democratic administrations. A large program of assistance to special education was developed. In addition to the school programs, there were a variety of efforts to aid teens, families, and communities. In the 1980s the ground shifted and the new dominant theories blamed the schools and the teachers, saying that they had let their standards fall and were using "excuses" about race and poverty. The basic strategy was to assume that all schools could have equal success and to change those that failed through sanctions. In addition, efforts emerged to foster nonpublic schools outside district control, emphasizing choice and market theory. It was a radical shift of perspective in a period during which business dominated politics, and it was a massive political success for decades.

The biggest shift in the whole framework of public school policy came with the *Nation at Risk* report in 1983,[85] which painted a dark picture of the nation's public schools, insisted that the focus on race and class had been a mistake, and promised to fix things by raising the standards and sanctioning failure, replacing a color-conscious, class-conscious set of policies with policies that assumed that both were irrelevant or worse. The *Nation at Risk* report inaccurately claimed that the American educational system was decaying and student performance was declining, and it said the result was that the once leading nation was "being overtaken by competitors throughout the world." It held that "the educational foundations of our society are presently being eroded by a rising tide of mediocrity that threatens our very future as a Nation and a people." (In fact, there was no evidence that significant decline was taking place, but the claims were widely and uncritically accepted as fact.)[86] The report contained a few statistics suggesting, for example, a drastic decline in SAT scores without the obvious adjustment for the large expansion of the share of the student population being tested in a test that was not mandatory and required a significant cost—a change that would lower the average scores as less prepared students were included.

The country, the report said, had "lost sight of the basic purposes of schooling and of the high expectations and disciplined effort needed to attain them." The schools were being diverted by pressure to solve "personal, social, and political problems that the home and other institutions either will not or cannot resolve," and those diversions "often exact an educational cost."[87] It combined the threat of the ruin of the nation with a new explanation and program. The report was built around a claim that the U.S. had once had higher standards and had lost them, losing focus on demanding requirements and assessments. It called on state and local authorities to upgrade standards, require more math and science training, toughen grading practices, and raise college admissions requirements. The issues of racial inequality in education was ignored.

When the *Nation at Risk* report dominated national news and generated new political responses across the country, even though the federal government proposed spending no more federal money, President Reagan and conservatives embraced it. State commissions to address it were quickly organized, triggering a tidal wave of state legislation. The agenda called, among other things, for an increasingly demanding set of course and exam requirements for high schools, particularly for requiring more science and math courses to obtain high school degrees. What Johnson had seen as critical supports for communities victimized by discrimination, conservatives dismissed as signs of governmental weakness. The U.S., the report said, was falling behind in a global economy where "knowledge, learning, information and skilled intelligence are the new raw materials of international commerce."[88] The solution was to require more. With strong business support, these reforms moved quickly. Within fifteen months, "over 250 state task forces had been created" and "forty-four states raised graduation requirements . . . and twenty-seven states adopted measures to increase instructional time."[89]

The report cited the failure of a substantial share of students to reach cut points on exams as evidence of failure. Schools were not being tough enough. The agenda left middle- and upper-class communities virtually untouched but demanded that Black and Latino schools achieve equal results. Business leaders talked about what kind of workers they needed and what should be required. Almost all the states adopted the call for more math and science requirements in high schools.

The report held that the schools had given too much attention to the social goals that had come into education in the civil rights era, saying that distractions had "compromised" the commitment to "high quality" as schools were "called upon to provide solutions to personal, social, and political problems that the home and other institutions will not or cannot resolve." Such demands "exact an educational cost as well as a financial one."[90] The obvious solution was to drop those costly concerns and get back to traditional standards and be tough about them.

The *Nation at Risk* report cited a national Gallup Poll that showed that 75 percent of Americans favored much more demanding requirements, especially four years of high school math and a full academic curriculum for college-bound students. Educational failure, the report said, accounted for "a steady 15-year decline in industrial productivity, as one great American industry after another falls to world competition."[91] One of the state reform efforts was led by Arkansas governor Bill Clinton, who became the leader of the National Governors Association, working closely with President George H. W. Bush and then, as president, creating a strong bipartisan movement.[92] The ideas set out in the Reagan administration report, which was much more an ideological statement of a probusiness reform than a research-based document, were adopted as bipartisan policy by the time of the Clinton administration and would guide education policy until the last year of the Obama presidency, a period several times longer than the Kennedy-Johnson years. They were colorblind.

These ideas were central to several major reforms. The first was Goals 2000, a bipartisan reform that created high standards that were to be achieved by the end of the century together with some new funds. Those standards included having all students achieve at a high level and eliminating the racial achievement gap.[93] Advocates hailed the law: "America finally has a national education strategy. That strategy is called standards-based reform. Virtually every state in the union has developed, or is in the process of developing, new academic standards that specify what students are expected to know and be able to do in the core academic subjects at key grade levels . . . and an accountability system."[94]

When the year 2000 arrived, none of the major goals had been achieved and some outcomes had gotten worse. The racial achievement gaps actually widened. This was a period in which, according to the Organisation for Economic Co-operation and Development, the U.S. was the only major industrialized country not to show an increase in high school graduates. There had been a sharp cut in student aid and the racial gap in college access grew in the 1980s.

President Clinton echoed the dominant theory in the last year of his term: "All successful schools have followed the same proven formula: higher standards, more accountability, and extra help so children who need it can get it to reach those standards. I have sent Congress a reform plan based on that formula. It holds states and school districts accountable for progress, and rewards them for results. . . . It is time to support what works and stop supporting what doesn't."[95] He wanted more of the same, and advocates from both parties doubled down on the tests and accountability strategy.

President George W. Bush built his 2000 campaign around a high-stakes testing policy from Texas, which led to a broad bipartisan reform agreement for a new law at the end of 2001 using a slogan stolen from the Children's Defense Fund—No Child Left Behind (NCLB). Though it was just a year after the failure of Goals 2000, the new law was much more demanding and specific about requiring all schools and school districts to have test gains at specific grade levels and to have all subgroups, including Latinos, Blacks, and low-income students, at the "high-proficiency" level in state tests in twelve years. All schools were required to make "adequate yearly progress" toward those goals for each subgroup each year. The required gains were actually the largest for the schools that started the furthest behind. If they failed to reach those standards in more than two years, they faced escalating sanctions, including loss of funds, takeover of the school, removal of faculty, dissolution of the school, and conversion to a charter school.

It was the most dramatic federal intervention in the internal operation of schools in U.S. history, and the annual success on the two required tests became all important, producing massive investments in test-prep materials and teaching to the test. The law required that data be published on all schools for all subgroups every year. These unprecedented data (which were a feature strongly supported by civil rights groups) quickly showed schools of color immediately falling behind a very demanding set of requirements. The schools that first faced sanctions were disproportionately segregated high-poverty schools.[96] The intense pressure put on such schools and the way the schools were publicly blamed and the teachers' future threatened made teachers less interested in teaching in those schools and more likely to want to leave for a less pressured and sanctioned school. In many of the schools threatened with sanctions, the teachers were forced to teach highly scripted units specifically aimed at the materials covered in what had become very high-stakes tests.

When President Obama was elected in the midst of the worst economic crisis since the Great Depression, it was already apparent that vast numbers of schools were failing to meet the required levels of progress and that almost all would eventually fail to meet the deadlines for all groups of students to be proficient—in spite of intense efforts. The schools were facing economic crises as tax revenue fell sharply, and many had to lay off teachers. Obama had gigantic problems to face but also a huge amount of "bailout" funds that were intended to revive the economy by pumping in federal stimulus dollars. Some $5 billion was designated for school funding, including flexible money, and the NCLB system was in collapse.

Obama's administration embraced the basic ideas of the Clinton-Bush policies but doubled down again by trying to put greater pressure on teachers and to foster removal of unsuccessful teachers, measured by student test scores. The National Academy of Sciences gathered experts who explained why such measures were invalid given all the variance among students, all the out-of-classroom influences shaping learning, and the limits of what was measured.[97] The administration's effort produced intense critiques and resistance from teachers' organizations. Many experts were convinced that using year-to-year test scores could not produce a valid measure for many reasons, including the fact that next year's class for an individual teacher could be very different from last year's, the evidence that out-of-school differences outside teachers' control had major effects, the fact that there were no specialized state or national tests in many specific subjects, and the fact that students' success could be influenced by their experience in other classrooms. Many teachers were punished or lost jobs on the basis of what were widely viewed as illegitimate ratings.[98] When the *Los Angeles Times* published online the "growth scores" of all teachers, it produced uproar in the nation's second-largest district. The move was praised by Obama education secretary Arne Duncan but was later shown to have damaged the district in a number of ways.[99] The effort produced major pushback from teachers' organizations, and the administration eventually backed off.

Unable to enact a new federal law or repeal the NCLB, which was requiring sanctions on an impossible level and heading toward virtually universal failure in meeting the final twelve-year deadlines, the Obama administration offered the schools a lifeline and waivers from NCLB sanctions if they implemented Obama reforms, which included ending the limits many states had on charter schools (in spite of the absence of evidence that charter schools performed better). The policies called for moving toward accountability of individual teachers, based on findings of the damage weak teachers did to the success of students. The policies were intended to respond to the difference individual teachers made to student achievement and to open the way for action. The Obama administration had doubled down on the assumptions in its initiatives with the Race for the Top and related programs that focused on driving achievement, pressuring teachers, and getting rid of those who were unsuccessful. There was strong pressure on states to adopt one of the models of the Common Core curriculum and testing, which were intended to drive instruction to a more complex level.

A general exhaustion with the standards movement led to a sharp reversal in federal education policy late in the Obama administration when the NCLB policies were unceremoniously dropped and Every Student Succeeds Act was passed in 2015 with huge bipartisan majorities. By that point there was no desire to extend the high-stakes federal accountability policies into another decade. The NCLB died unmourned in 2015 when a massive bipartisan majority in Congress enacted the new law, which basically turned control of federal school aid funds back to state and local education authorities under state plans approved by the secretary of education, who was given very limited power.[100] The Obama administration tried to maintain some significant federal leverage by issuing regulations that would have the force of law. Early in the Trump administration, however, the Republican Congress struck down the new regulations and left power concentrated in the states without significant equity requirements.[101] Most states continue to follow some version of test-based accountability, and some major states, including Florida and Texas, the third and second largest, continue to grade schools publicly and exert sanctions on the basis of test scores, as if differences in student background and previous preparation did not matter.

The new federal law simply transferred the money and the dominant authority over policy to the state governments and required them, in their own policies, to broaden accountability to include at least one outcome other than test scores.[102] The Obama administration, near its end, issued regulations attempting to create some modest federal accountability for use of the funds,[103] but those were quickly repealed in the early Trump administration, leaving the states with the responsibility. To add to the problems of the dominant reform models, investigations of charter schools' closures and failures by the inspector general of the Education Department disclosed many costly mistakes and failures of accountability in the rush to expand charters as a solution to public school problems.[104] State governments, with few exceptions, had never been leaders on issues of racial equity and civil rights. "States' rights" was the slogan of the Southern civil rights resistance. A return to state control was unlikely to initiate action against racial differences in educational opportunity.

Interestingly enough, at the end of the Obama administration, Secretary of Education Duncan resigned and was replaced for the last months by John B. King Jr. King made a point of emphasizing the need to do something about the profound segregation of U.S. schools. He asked Congress for funds to support voluntary integration efforts but was rejected. He said, "Diversity is no longer a luxury; it's essential for helping our students get ready for the world they will encounter after high school and, increasingly, throughout their lives."[105] His initiative received considerable attention. Ironically, understanding seemed to have gone full circle—from a major, multidimensional enforcement and support effort in the 1960s, to a systematic turn away and a denial that issues of race needed to be considered and a confidence that the standards-and-sanctions approach would work, to a recognition, once again, that the country was going through a fundamental demographic transition and badly needed tools to make it work out. The last-minute effort was futile in terms of gaining resources from a conservative Congress. King's very brief term ended with the swearing in of a new president, Donald Trump, whose campaign and popular bitter attacks on immigrants of color showed the need to address the country's deep racial divisions. King would soon be replaced by Betsy DeVos, a major GOP donor and a powerful supporter of for-profit charter schools and vouchers for private religious schools.[106] Her basic claim was that the market could be the solution. In his 2020 State of the Union address, Trump belittled "government schools" and called on Congress to "give one million American children" vouchers and "pass the Education Freedom Scholarships and Opportunities Act—because no parent should be forced to send their child to a failing government school."[107] A possible turning point came in 2020, the year of the nation's largest social protest movement, the Black Lives Matter movement, and of the pandemic and the rise of the progressive movement in the Democratic Party.

Lessons of Four Decades of Colorblind Policy

You can pretend that color doesn't matter, and you can design laws that simply require that everyone succeed, and you can enact sanctions to punish them when they do not. Often it will be a popular position. You can dream that creating schools that compete like grocery stores would solve the problems because you see magic in anything described as a market (but you would have to ignore the vast differences between the grocery stores in affluent suburbs and poor inner-city communities, where the market has often provided nothing but convenience stores and liquor stores selling salty snacks). You could claim that those who insist on talking about race are looking for excuses rather than facing real problems. The most remarkable thing about the decades from 1980 to 2020 has been the consistency and durability of colorblind policies and market-oriented solutions that simply ignored the impacts of concentrated poverty and racial stratification. Part of this, of course, is the ideology of individualism that is deeply rooted in white America and has great influence across the society. It is an ideology that is strongly held in the face of obvious group-based inequalities. Since there was abundant evidence, over and over again, that the policies were not working, the underlying reality must be that most policy makers and education officials found it comfortable to repeatedly talk about high standards and requirements and to promise new programs with new names embodying the same basic assumptions while doing nothing to require any real redistribution of educational opportunity or threaten the privileges of the privileged. In terms of major progress on racial and ethnic inequalities, the decades of colorblindness have, in many ways, been lost decades.

While the denial continued, research showed more and more powerfully that race and poverty mattered greatly—and the country passed through a great demographic transition. Among the young it was the rapid decline and, finally, the disappearance of the white majority and the emergence of Latinos as the society's largest minority, the largest group of students in the West. Although the Latino migrants were eager for education for their children and knew too well what happens to poorly educated people in the U.S. labor market, their children arrived too late for the civil rights era and grew up in the full bloom of colorblind policy. Their children were increasingly segregated in highly impoverished schools with teachers who did not want to be there, schools repeatedly punished by the sanctions of the "excellence" policies. In some states in the Trump period, they experienced growing hostility. After the civil rights–Great Society period of vibrant growth and unprecedented help for poor children to go to college, we experienced a major reversal of civil rights policies and a continuing shrinkage of the ability of financial aid programs to actually make it possible for the students of color who succeeded in spite of their inferior schools to go to four-year colleges.

There is no evidence that we are going to make strong progress in closing the self-perpetuating racial and class divisions in our society indirectly, by denial, or without focus on the realities of a society where race is directly linked to unequal opportunity. It is a society with profound self-perpetuating structures of inequality where people at the top do not see any serious problem. We are not going to get out of it, our history and our research tell us, unless we decide that equality is our goal and we begin again to use the resources of government to consciously pursue it. To get to a better place and to escape the profound racial polarization of the Trump experience, educators and policy makers must overcome resistance and lend support in the necessary transformations, measure the results, and keep trying until we find what works in different settings.

The default in our society is the continuation of separation and inequality and the invisibility of the special problems of people of color and people who live and learn in isolated, concentrated poverty. We learned some big lessons a half century ago, but although the civil rights and education policies were successful, they were fiercely resisted. We first abandoned the policies and then forgot they were needed. Then we announced over and over again that we had other solutions, enacting and doubling down on the Reagan-era assumptions. Substantial forces in our politics assumed our stratification was normal and systematic inequality was the fault of the people at the bottom and the institutions that worked with them.

A Progressive Turn?

President Trump fell to Joe Biden's multiracial coalition in 2020. A surging progressive movement in the Democratic Party led to the most far-reaching race-conscious platform in generations after a year of historic protests demanding racial justice in hundreds of American communities. Joe Biden had been nominated because of Black support and, in spite of a centrist political history, moved far to the left in his agenda. But the Democrats won only an extremely narrow Congressional majority. The program that emerged in his first year emphasized powerful investment in early education, support for young families, and child care—very important to families of color. Biden's call for free community college was not adopted, and the only major higher education legislative commitment was to a modest increase in the very inadequate Pell Grant. Facing many demands for social and environmental programs, neither secondary nor higher education turned out to be top priorities. Biden did appoint administrators strongly supporting public schools and civil rights, but they faced what seemed the most conservative Supreme Court majority in nearly a century, a majority inclined to oppose race conscious civil rights. Issues of racial equity were open, but it was the beginning of a long battle.

Coming out of decades of colorblindness and deepening inequality in our changing and polarized society, we need a recommitment to actually achieving racial equity. There were policies and programs that made big changes in the civil rights era. As we think about the situation today and in the next generation, there is a great deal to be done and many examples, both race conscious and race sensitive, that can make a difference for racial equity. How to make real progress is the subject of the final chapters.

6

Deep Changes for Real Gains

THIS BOOK STARTS with truths and trends, with history and current disputes, with aspirations for higher education and the harsh realities of a polarized, separated society. It begins with the fact that access and success in college are profoundly unequal, and that the current policies of government and higher education are not solving the problem. If that is true, what can we do? Facing the walls limiting access to college, we need high schools that have a serious path to college and the preparation students need to have a real chance for success; we need strong affirmative action for admissions to selective colleges and strong recruitment and support of students of color by less selective and open-access colleges; we need counseling and support for students and families making choices, and we need much stronger financial aid, student support, and information systems that make real choice possible for families and students. We need large changes.

We have necessary bits and pieces addressing these needs, good experiences at some colleges and in some programs, but large gaps remain and we are still doing many things that seriously increase inequality. In many institutions, the old plan or some of the old programs—often made colorblind—are still in place, but there has been little thought and leadership about looking deeper or going further to solve inequalities. Families need knowledge about preparing for and applying to college and a great deal of support in navigating the confusing processes of applying for aid and estimating real costs and debts. The basic systems of federal and state aid need review. Some have become detached from original visions or have simply fallen so far below changing needs that they are ineffectual. Colleges need resources to help students who confront challenges not built into traditional aid formulas. These things will be most effective to the extent that they are color conscious or at least color sensitive, designed with real understanding of the conditions facing students and families of color. When race-targeted assistance, public or private, is not possible, we need to implement multiple strategies that are designed with enough sensitivity to the social and educational realities to be workable for many students of color. We do not have a system that only needs a few tweaks. We have one that will perpetuate racial stratification unless changed substantially. Students of color need access to better schools and classes, the resources and knowledge to make genuine choices, and the most important resources to make segregated schools of concentrated poverty more equal.

There are no easy answers. There has been a profound failure of our high schools, our higher education systems, and our policy makers, who have not only persisted in policies that have failed but actually adopted policies that made things worse. The existing policies work reasonably well for middle-class white and Asian students but not for most students and families of color. Institutions and expectations have been built around existing policies. Colleges may have staffs that are liberal politically, but they are institutionally conservative, leaving unexamined policies and processes that don't work for students of color and students in poverty. If we continue on the existing path, we will perpetuate inequality and, in many places, we will have high schools and colleges that deny real opportunity to much of the rising generation. Often no one will say much about it because education leaders are optimistic about how much good their institutions are doing and reluctant to raise "divisive" issues. As our population changes, if we do not face inequalities and change outcomes, we will not develop the potential of a growing part of the next generation and we will reinforce intergenerational inequality, weakening our economy and society.

Higher education surfaced as a leading issue in the 2020 campaign for the first time in a long time. Normally policy changes in higher education are incremental and are not visible national issues. The 2020 Democratic campaign put a great deal of attention on relieving student college debt and offering "free college" to students. These are both very expensive commitments and likely to be enacted, if at all, with limitations. They do not control the cost of college or solve the debt problems of the future. Since there is rarely a serious buildup of national pressure for college reform and the higher education policy system is too oriented to institutional interests rather than students needing deep help, it is important that reforms are adopted that work for the cause of equity. The Biden administration opened with presidential proposals for providing low-income students the actual support needed for two years of community college and for targeted help to institutions serving students of color. Many congressional Democrats favored more dramatic intervention and major moves to forgive indebtedness from college loans. Joe Biden had pledged to double the Pell Grant but actually asked only for a $550 increase in the maximum award. One reason college aid has been so inadequate is that it involves millions of students and is very expensive. Since community college is, by far, the least costly and is already much better funded by the Pell, it is possible to reach far more people at that stage. But since completion and transfer levels are low, particularly for students of color, compared with those enrolling at a four-year campus, and many students from weak high schools leave during the first year, the question of relative benefits must be raised.

The stakes of college affordability have always been high but continue to rise. Most college-age students will soon be nonwhite, and the cohorts of college-age students are shrinking since a peak almost a decade ago because of a long pattern of declining birth rates and immigration. Although growing areas are still unable to meet the demand for college spaces, especially on the competitive Sunbelt campuses, many small colleges and universities in low-growth areas are having trouble filling their classes but lack a tradition of serving or marketing to students of color. The current production of graduates is far short of the long-term needs of the economy. Today's patterns of access and college completion are leaving students of color behind, deepening racial stratification. For a long time, the inadequacies of our schools and colleges in serving national needs have been covered up by population growth and immigration and students of color were often treated as if they were expendable. With record-low birthrates and low immigration, we are faced with the obvious need to draw on the only large untapped resource—young people of color who are not currently making it to college and graduating. The only alternative is decline, with the country falling further behind peer nations in preparing its young. The existing practices and policies are falling seriously short. The last time we made major progress on racial equity was a half century ago, and we abandoned much of what worked.

We need to figure out how to restore our lost leadership in educating our people. We've changed from a society that massively invested in expanding affordable college opportunities for the baby boom generation to one failing to offer fair chances to the growing sector of students. There are many efforts trying to address different aspects of the problems, but we are falling short. Most universities have affirmed the goal of racial and economic diversity, but public policy and actual decisions within many campuses have veered in a different direction. Even though the society was moving toward extreme economic inequality, state and federal officials decided to invest much less national wealth in higher education and to change the policies in ways that shifted aid from the most disadvantaged to families with more resources, which left many families without resources looking at closed college gates. Many private colleges have diverted their financial aid dollars into offering discounts to nonpoor students to keep up enrollment.

The traditional idea that education was a public good gave way in the 1980s to the idea that higher education enriched students and families must pay much more for it. The price was continuously raised; taking inflation into account, it rose much faster than family income. That amounted to a decision to increase the relative access of the well-to-do and to make access virtually impossible for many lower-income students. Those highly consequential decisions about who could afford college were posed largely as necessary year-to-year decisions by college authorities trying to preserve their programs and faculty as state budgets fell. Both liberal and conservative state governments participated in these changes. It was a long and largely quiet structural change.

Our failure is not because of a lack of desire and effort by families of color. The desire for college is very deep among all parts of our society. There is high initial enrollment in some kind of college by the great majority of high school graduates. Millions sacrifice income and spend money trying to go to college but get nothing. The extreme inequality in opportunities and resources for students of color and their families, inferior separate schools, and much more serious financial barriers to college contribute to substantial gaps by race and ethnicity. Although there are many statements about progress for all and closing gaps, there are virtually no race-specific strategies apart from affirmative action, and that only affects the small share of highly selective campuses and faces a negative Supreme Court. Almost any general policy for higher education that does not have such specific equity goals is likely to increase gaps since those with the best preparation, knowledge, and connections will be the most likely to tap the opportunity. To increase racial equity, we must address the race-related causes and set racial goals, specifying methods and accountability for reaching equity.

Our society and our institutions foster and perpetuate inequality. Different possibilities are built on the continuing effects of past and present discrimination. People of color feel that antiminority discrimination. Most whites do not.[1] Our normal institutional structures and practices reward those with more information and resources, who are predominantly white and Asian. Research shows that easily measurable discrimination continues and that people of color are treated differently by key institutions. These are not superficial or easily changed forces—they are elemental. They reflect such universal forces as parents with power wanting to ensure the best feasible chance for their own children and the fears and prejudices attached to racial and ethnic change, very evident in the rise of Trump and attacks on affirmative action.

College enrollment trends reflect the reality that markets or market-like educational processes tend to favor those with the most resources, the most skills, the most money, and the best information—all of which reflect previous advantages. To make substantial changes in the outcomes, there must be policies making access for the historically excluded groups an explicit goal and there must be policies shaped with an understanding of the nature of the obstacles students of color and their families face. Reducing inequalities requires understanding the serious but often unintended consequences of policies that fail to reflect racial differences and that lack a clear goal and a strategy to address as many of the serious barriers as possible. These are not problems that can be cured by a single big national policy, although the right federal and state policies, incentives, and resources would be invaluable. There are roles for education leaders and policy makers but also for related social and economic institutions. The nonprofit sector and business are also needed. Racial inequality in America is an old, tough, multidimensional, and resilient monster. It feeds on inaction and denial. There are many fronts on which real improvements are possible, but likely only if that is a priority.

Unequal preparation for college starts in homes, neighborhoods, the experiences of students, and the highly unequal offerings from educators and others who support their learning. When you explore the research showing the costs and complexity of changing even single elements in the large and complicated web of inequality, it is not at all surprising that groups of students hitting multiple barriers often fall far behind those who come from families with resources, communities with power and money, and schools with outstanding curricula and teachers and powerful connections with colleges. How many successful families, for example, could provide what they want for their children if they suddenly lost the income needed to live in an area with schools that would not prepare their children adequately for higher education? What if they cannot pay rent or mortgages because they have no savings and lose jobs during a recession? What if that means a disruptive move in the midst of a school year?

To arrive at sensible policies, policy makers and the public need to understand the seriousness of the multiple barriers that families of color face today. When President John F. Kennedy submitted what became the 1964 Civil Rights Act, he said that we must be able to put ourselves in the shoes of Blacks in the

South. When that understanding happens, as it did in Martin Luther King Jr.'s greatest movements, changes that usually seem unnecessary to most become matters of urgent moral necessity, things that arouse the concern of millions. To power large changes, we need that sensibility. Our social future is related to the ability of colleges and policy makers to make the decision not to issue statements, which are good but usually harmless, but to keep working until the outcomes change. Leaders need to understand, as the great majority of families of color clearly do, that normal processes create or sustain barriers that deny most students of color a fair chance and perpetuate inequality in our colleges.

One of the changes needed is to reject the idea that it makes any sense to separate policy discourse into separate public school and higher education silos. Our institutions and most of our research and policies separate these institutions that people must connect for success. Today some form of postsecondary education is more necessary for middle-class life than high school graduation was in the mid-twentieth century. If we think that schools and colleges are two separate worlds, we will miss the dangerous gap into which many students of color fall. Middle-class families now think about education as including some kind of college. That is the assumption of their high schools and their communities. Although there is extremely high desire for college in all communities, many communities of concentrated poverty and disadvantage lack a workable path, understanding, and support.

The country's African American, Latino, and American Indian families need serious help in developing their talents and finding success in the economy to get and hold jobs able to support a family living in a safe and decent place with good schools and neighborhood conditions for the successful development of their children. We do not have that now; we are very far from it. Since so many educational advantages are rooted in income, wealth, and parent education, any policies that improve life for families of color are likely to have a beneficial impact. Since our society is so stratified by race and income, educators are one of the only groups who regularly encounter people from many strata at crucial times in their lives, see the consequences of unequal opportunity, and have some wisdom to add to general policy debates. Overcoming the obstacles can change the lives of students and their children.

The communities where problems are most extreme, Black and Latino concentrated-poverty areas and Native American communities, often face a deadly combination of several formidable social, economic, and educational barriers to the path to college. Of course, there are always things that could help the students and schools left behind but little sign that they are being done well on any scale. Privileged families and schools often have organized and well-supported strategies to guarantee opportunities to their children and safety nets when they run into trouble. To make preparation for college more fair, we must consider a range of possible solutions to the various obstacles. It is a delusion to think that colleges or high schools can solve all of these problems by themselves and that their normal manner of operation will produce fair results.

Serious analysis of large economic and social reforms is beyond the scope of this book, but readers must always keep in mind that the education issue is nested inside and deeply affected by the stratification of the larger society and by the extreme economic inequality we live with. The country surrendered in the War on Poverty during the Reagan administration, and Democrats turned more toward middle-class issues under Carter, Clinton, and Obama. The serious proposals of the Biden administration to sharply reduce children's poverty, to give grants to families with children, to provide childcare, and to generally ease pressures on lower-income families were a welcome change. Poverty harms education in powerful ways, and concentrated poverty in neighborhoods and schools magnifies the damage. Similarly, if the federal minimum wage is doubled, as has been done in some states, the situation of families at the bottom will significantly improve. If children can move from dangerous to stable homes in safe neighborhoods with resources, things will change. Schools are very important, but most Americans overestimate the power of schools and underestimate the need for social policies and income redistribution. Schools, by themselves, face enormous burdens created by family and community poverty. This makes it all the more important that access to the schools most connected to college opportunity becomes much fairer.

Our society often overestimates the value and fairness of markets as we turn both public schools and higher education into more of a market. The market-like school and college strategies that were born in the Reagan era failed. Markets can be very efficient in allocating resources for maximum production and profit, but left on their own, they tend to perpetuate and magnify initial advantages. People mix up economic efficiency with justice, but they can be two very different things, which is why we do not turn to corporations to build parks or have government manufacture computers. Americans tend to think that the education system can make things fair, but in fact, education systems are deeply connected to the rest of society and tend to reflect its inequalities unless intentionally changed. Racial inequality is an elemental feature of our society. People affirm the idea of equal opportunity but often work to make their families more equal than others. Those groups at the top of the socioeconomic pyramid give their children the greatest educational advantages, and the families at the bottom are typically consigned to the weakest schools and have little power to change things. Educational institutions always believe that they need more funds, so there is always competition for the most important scarce resources, and the competition is normally won by those serving the most powerful. Experienced, well-trained teachers are a basic asset, but we don't have policies that keep them where they are most needed and we normally have contracts that enable them to leave nonwhite schools of concentrated poverty just when they have the experience that makes them more effective. Such factors are why it takes strong and focused interventions and persistent leadership to make things less unfair. Breaking this system of intergenerational inequality is the reason so many civil rights conflicts have been about making the myth of equal education real. It is why *Brown v. Board of Education*, which recognized a system of inherent inequality and required change, was the greatest Supreme Court decision of the twentieth century.

A strong and opposing tradition in America plays on fear and extracts power by promising to protect racial advantages. There has been a long tradition in American politics, particularly in the South, of conservatives winning power by emphasizing racial fears, such as that Blacks will take things away and commit violence, to persuade lower-income whites to vote against their economic interest to support continued white control.[2] The Trump election was a classic example.[3] The Trump administration had transferred billions to the most wealthy and corporations through tax changes and implemented a variety of policies to hurt the poor by cutting food aid, housing assistance, and health insurance, as well as denying basic services to legal permanent residents who do not yet have citizenship. It got the votes of many whom its policies hurt by playing on the fear of immigrants and other groups. There was an ugly racial streak in its agenda. Deportation policies created fundamental insecurity for millions of families with at least one undocumented parent, disrupting the lives of children and, of course, their success in schools. Racial justice policies in education were undermined. In education there were efforts to transfer funds to private schools and for-profit colleges while cutting back on civil rights regulations and enforcement.

Though education policy cannot, by itself, change the social structure, it can have a substantial role. It has to be designed and implemented by leaders who are sensitive to the realities of unequal opportunities, not blaming them on the students, their parents, and the teachers in poorly supported schools. When social and economic policies increase the gaps, the burden on the schools becomes that much greater. When disadvantaged families get better jobs and incomes or are able to live in communities with better schools, it makes a difference.

Socioeconomic stratification has often been ignored in the design of education in recent decades, although social and economic inequalities outside the schools are directly related to unequal outcomes of schooling across the world.[4] I focus on education policy, in part, because both liberals and conservatives see education as critical. Education is supposed to be the answer, according to the American dream, and the schools have an enormous reach since nine-tenths of children are socialized to education in public schools. There are few opportunities to change the realities outside the schools. In America's deeply polarized political system, substantial economic change requires a rare social movement of the sort that occurred only twice in the twentieth century—in the 1930s and in the 1960s. The progressive movement in Democratic politics in 2020 called for large changes but achieved only the smallest possible majority in Congress. Most of time we have had only education as a major tool for creating equity, and most of the time education policy did not address racial inequality seriously. At worst, it legitimizes inequality by treating the consequences of better opportunities as personal merit justifying special advantages for those who have had better preparation.

Many scholars who live and work in the academy know the transformative possibilities of higher education and understand some of the barriers that distribute those opportunities so unfairly. The power of a professor in a great university to open opportunities, to help with jobs and professional school access, and to make connections for a student, for example, is considerable. If your only choice is a community college because of the costs, there are many fewer opportunities regardless of your talent. Who gets into the most opportunity-rich schools with the most powerful credentials makes a difference, but it usually reinforces previous advantage, mostly white and Asian advantage. My central interest is making higher education a stronger, broader channel for equality. I have seen students who never had a fair chance before college make stunning gains when well taught and supported, but most students of color never get such a chance. They were concentrated in high schools that offered them no real path to a strong college, they are often far behind before starting college, and they often enroll in a college of limited capacity.[5]

Too many policies claiming to address the deep and persistent inequality were based not on the students' real needs and experiences but on the ideas of those at the top. There are enough examples of amazingly resilient students who succeed against the odds to make many in higher education and in government feel that things are in hand and we're on the right track if they do more of the same without big changes, but the basic patterns continue. The happy examples, widely publicized, obscure the unacceptable persistence of systemic inequality. The historical record shows that when we acted as if race was irrelevant in our society, the remedies did not work and sometimes actually, unintentionally, punished students and schools of color. Giving colleges rewards for the highest graduation rates, for example, sounds like a good policy but, unless carefully shaped, it will award resources to the colleges with the best-prepared students and deny or even sanction colleges working with many struggling low-income students of color, increasing inequality. It can reward exclusion of students never given a fair chance to develop their talents. We have to think critically about how requirements, supports, and systems come together in shaping opportunities for different groups and allocating resources.

Those of us who think of our universities as something very good have to cope with the various ways they are becoming instruments for the perpetuation and even the deepening of stratification and inequality.[6] The world's best system of higher education is perpetuating inequality in the most unequal advanced economy. In the middle of a vast demographic change in the society, it is adapting far too slowly to a population that has changed far faster than the schools and colleges.

In fact, it seems to be slipping backward.

We have focused so much on the first wall, admissions—which does indeed separate many students of color from the most powerful college opportunities—that we have not concentrated on the second and third walls that undermine the good intentions of the institutions for those who could make it through the admissions gate. The second wall is extremely unequal preparation by race. The third is financial barriers that make college impossible for many families of color. There is not just a fence around opportunity; it is a maze with trapdoors, and a maze requires multiple strategies. Simple colorblind approaches mean failure; they assume a society that does not exist. To have a more successful, more equitable society, we must recognize the realities of race, decide to change the outcomes, and use the best research and ideas we can bring together to dismantle a deeply rooted and destructive system. The last time the U.S. decided to do this, there were large and rapid changes. As the millions of young Americans who came into the streets of hundreds of our cities in the plague year of 2020 to protest discrimination so clearly recognized, it is time for another period of large changes.

7

Strategies

THIS BOOK ARGUES that we must have solutions that are designed to overcome problems of race and class. We need solutions whose fundamental goal is to equalize opportunity in preparation for college and to bring down the financial wall around college choice and college persistence. Neither can be done by simply pursuing feasible universal policies that purport to solve the problems for everyone. The reality is that we are not a single society where a universal policy will have common effects.

The basic policy change during the civil rights revolution was a change from antidiscrimination policies that set up procedures that sounded equitable to a realization that inequalities so grounded in our society would not change much with these methods. The shift was from process to a central focus on outcomes. If Black or Latino or Indian people didn't vote, something was wrong. Normal processes of local control had to be suspended in those regions until the outcomes changed, and policy changes had to be evaluated in terms of their outcomes. We need something like that in our high schools and colleges. If we are not making progress in terms of the outcomes for large segments of our society, something is very wrong and the leaders of our institutions need to make serious plans to change it, plans measured not by good intentions but, basically, by the results. Do the students of color in your state or your institution have a growing probability of success in enrolling, persisting and graduating? If the plan is serious, it must be measured and it must be treated as a first-order consideration in hiring, supervising, assessing, and promoting leaders. Government and governing boards must play a central role in encouraging and supporting such efforts and intervening if they fall short or, worse, there is discrimination at work. This chapter is about strategies and tools, but it is not a checklist, and it is important always to keep a focus not on lists or slick reports but on actual results.

Many sensible-sounding proposals don't work or even can make things more unequal. If, for example, we eliminate tuition for community colleges but do not cover the great majority of student costs other than tuition—room and board, transportation, health care, childcare, parking, books, lab fees, and so on—something that sounds like a universal solution will mean help for students and families who can cover the other costs but nothing for those who cannot. Community colleges appear to be similar but are, in reality, as unequal as high schools, often highly segregated by race and class in large metro areas, and have sharply differing outcomes. Many students from weak high schools drop out after a term or two in community college, so they would receive little benefit, while middle-class students who go to strong community colleges and persist would get free tuition over a much longer period and receive a more highly regarded degree. The vast scope of residential segregation means that many students of color end up in low-achieving commuter colleges where successful transfer to a good college is uncommon. Free tuition for a well-prepared student from a good high school at a strong community college offering courses that are truly equal to entry-level university courses, a college with strong connections to a major university, can be a good bargain. By the same token, free entry for a poorly prepared student from a weak high school to a community college from which few transfer can lead to a quick dead end. Or if the student needs money for transportation, childcare, living expenses, books, and equipment, the free tuition may be much too small a subsidy to make a difference. If we assume that students will receive some assistance from their families but a disproportionate share of students of color must actually give assistance to families while they are studying, there will be severe race and class differences between those who are helped and those who are harmed by such policies.

The most efficient way to reach students of color before college is through policies aimed directly at the conditions disproportionately affecting students of color. Such policies could include giving students of color the right to transfer to stronger high schools than those they are assigned to because of residential segregation or, better yet, changing the assignment rules so that many would simply be assigned to better schools, often white and Asian schools with a middle-class majority. Access to a school with a strong middle-class enrollment, experienced teachers, and strong connections to college can change a student's life. Where there are magnet schools offering special programs, there should be targeted outreach and recruitment to communities of color. Admissions to such schools should be on the basis of choice and lottery, not screening and not giving the advantage to those who find out about options first through contacts. Seats should be set aside to ensure that the students from communities of color get a reasonable share. That cannot be done for individual students under current Supreme Court law, but seats can be set aside to ensure that all areas, including communities of color, are represented. It is perfectly legal to set goals to represent sectors of the overall community and to pursue any means that do not rely on the race of each student. Outreach programs and opportunities to take college classes or summer programs at college during high school can create information and contacts. These were standard elements of many successful desegregation plans for public schools and previously segregated colleges, and they should be adopted again.

There are, of course, limits to the possibilities built into residential segregation, school district boundary lines, and current law, so within many districts even the best policies would leave substantial segregation and create an urgent need to support programs in segregated settings that provided as many as possible of the assets and practices of the middle-class white and Asian schools, which will be discussed later.

The problem is that many direct race-conscious policies are prohibited or face serious legal challenges. The Supreme Court ruled in the 2007 *Parents Involved* decision that it is illegal to assign students to high schools on the basis of a student's race, even when the assignment's goal is to produce lasting integration.[1] Since that time, three Trump appointments to the Court have shifted it a good deal further to the right, threatening affirmative action, which has been upheld since 1978 by a single vote on the Court. However, there still may well be ways to pursue intentional integration. While the Supreme Court has forbidden race-conscious assignment of individual students to public schools, it has agreed that integrated education is a "compelling interest" and that other race-conscious methods of zoning attendance areas, for example, are permissible. Some school districts have done careful analysis of the racial segregation patterns of their communities and structured choice programs to create integration by giving preferences to neighborhoods.[2] The courts have also said that when there is proof of intentional policies that produce segregation, it is unconstitutional and remedies that assign students and teachers by race to repair the damage by creating integrated schools are legal. Civil rights advocates believe that there are many places where local authorities have pursued policies producing segregation that could be documented if the appropriate investigation were done. In 2020, for example, the California attorney general found that a suburban San Francisco district had discriminated against students of color.[3] There are a variety of practices—including setting attendance boundaries, creating special schools for students with high test scores, developing choice systems in ways that foreseeably increase segregation, and instituting transfer and transportation policies that undermine integration—that foster segregation and inequality and are largely unexamined. In our complex metropolitan society, we need complex strategies to untangle systems that have foreseeable segregative effects.

Affirmative action is threatened now, and there is no good substitute. Affirmative action in college admissions has been in place for more than a half century, and the great majority of selective colleges continue to use it and see it as necessary. It has made vital changes in those campuses and trained generations of leaders. A national survey of more than 1,500 admissions officials in 2015 produced responses from colleges and universities enrolling 2.7 million students, colleges that reviewed more than three million applications in a year.[4] The institutions varied widely, and their shares of students of color and low-income (Pell Grant) students reflected the national average in spite of the disappointing response rate. The sample overrepresented highly selective colleges.[5] Given the fact that this survey was supported by leading national higher education organizations, including the admissions officers group, and there were repeated follow-ups to raise response rates, it was the best information that could be obtained. The data showed that three-fifths of highly selective campuses considered race in admissions.[6] Leaving out the nine states where it was forbidden in public colleges by state affirmative action bans, the share was significantly higher, about three-fourths. Among the campuses that considered race, 74 percent said that they also had special funding for those students and they also had special consideration for students with low socioeconomic status. A much smaller share of the colorblind campuses had special admissions consideration for students with low socioeconomic status.[7] In other words, those schools practicing affirmative action usually were also affirmatively seeking low-income students. When asked what was most effective in producing actual diversity, those considering race pointed to comprehensive review, race-based recruitment and "yield initiatives," making tests optional, and racially targeted financial aid.[8] They were not seen as alternatives but as necessary complements.

Affirmative action is critical but may not survive the current Supreme Court, and decades of research have not found a workable substitute.[9] Sean Reardon and associates point out, in their analysis of using socioeconomic status or income as alternatives, that it would be very costly and inefficient in enrolling significant numbers of students of color because, though income is correlated with race, income is only one element in a complex of factors that determine applications and admissions to college—factors like course taking, information on campuses and net costs, the financial status of the family, the kind of aid offered, and a number of others. Since few colleges are able to meet full need in financial aid policies; admitting low-income students is much more expensive for the colleges than admitting higher-income students of color, who require less aid; and in a colorblind system they have to admit far more low-income students to get the same number of students of color, it is an extremely costly alternative that few colleges could afford.[10] Another major study by Mark Long explored scores of variables and examined extensive data on Texas admissions records to see whether there were any variables that would provide a strong proxy, or indirect way, to ensure impact on racial diversity. Single variables had weak relationships, and even using improbable combinations of multiple variables, he found that any combination would be significantly less likely to admit students of color and that the students of color who were admitted through emphasis on variables such as family income or socioeconomic status would, on average, be less qualified and less likely to graduate.[11] The fact is that alternatives would be far more costly, would involve formulas hard to explain to the public, would be far less effective, and would yield less successful students of color. This is why the great majority of selective colleges have continued to practice affirmative action for many years. If affirmative action is lost, research shows, a bad situation will become significantly worse.

Seeking racial diversity by focusing on income is very inefficient in reaching students of color because admission of low-income students is never only by income; it is low income plus meeting the school's academic qualifications. Low-income Black, Latino, and Indian students tend to be in weak high schools, so they are unlikely to meet the academic part of the admissions process. Focusing on income plus qualifications is likely to identify white and Asian students who are far less segregated, who attend significantly stronger schools, and who have better-prepared parents. In addition, the most well-prepared students of color are usually those who are not poor and are attending somewhat better schools, and many of them who are fully capable of success on campus will not be selected. Middle-income students of color are better off in terms of money, but research shows they still face discrimination. And the wealth gap, very important for college support, is much larger than the income gap. Duke professor William Darity notes that Blacks are more than an eighth of the population but have only about a fortieth of the wealth and that only a race-specific remedy would make much difference.[12]

There has been far less concentration on remedies focusing on the distinctive characteristics of the financial wall affecting students of color. Families of color, on average, have lower incomes, even controlling for educational credentials. They are much less likely to have financial support from their extended families and much more likely to be expected to help support other relatives. On average, families of color have less credit and lower credit ratings and are far less likely to be homeowners and have equities they can draw on. Students of color are more likely to be in single-parent families and in families that have high housing cost burdens and no discretionary savings. They are much more likely to have a parent incarcerated or an undocumented parent unable to get an on-the-books job, facing possible deportation. Parents who are less familiar with college are much more likely to assume that scholarships are for either athletic skill or high grades and test scores and to be less familiar with need-based scholarships, so they often do not apply for the aid that is available. Parents who are divorced, separated, or never married are less likely to cooperate in filing the financial information needed for scholarship eligibility. Marriage, family stability, and health are related to education. It is a self-perpetuating cycle.

When higher education integration efforts began, there were often special scholarship programs and summer programs set up for African American, Latino, or Native American students. Traditionally individual campuses have had many specialized scholarships set up by donors or policies for students from particular backgrounds. Such scholarships send a strong message about commitment to reaching that particular group of students and helping create a critical mass that makes the campus more appealing and less socially isolated for them. There have been few tests of the legality of such scholarships since the Supreme Court has moved toward principles that see race-conscious policies favoring integration as illegal.[13] In response to a fear of legal battles and possible losses, many of the race-targeted scholarships were changed to a colorblind approach, except where they were part of an approved remedy for a history of discrimination. Civil rights groups believe campuses were too ready to abandon race-specific funding and summer programs when criticized by conservative groups. When universities cannot create special programs on the basis of a student's race, they can, for example, create special summer training programs in African American culture, Latino history, or tribal languages or traditions. It is important for universities to exercise imagination, draw on their special powers, and ask their lawyers to work to defend what they need to create, not to tell them what it would be safest not to try. Lawyers usually want to minimize risk, but some risks need to be taken and lawyers can play a much more creative role.

Affirmative action has been on legal life support since the 1970s.[14] The Trump administration moved the Supreme Court further to the right with the 2018 appointment of Justice Brett Kavanaugh, who had worked against affirmative action in the George W. Bush White House.[15] He replaced Justice Anthony Kennedy, who had written the opinion saving affirmative action in the 2016 *Fisher v. University of Texas* case. Affirmative action will be coming back to the Court.[16] With President Donald Trump's successful placement of three far-right justices on the Court, the barriers to any kind of race-conscious policy are likely to rise. The same conservative group that had twice lost Supreme Court cases against the University of Texas affirmative action program responded to Trump's election in 2016 with active prosecution of a case against Harvard University, an effort supported by the Trump administration.

Affirmative action may be prohibited by the Supreme Court, but that does not mean it is not needed. If a half century of precedents are cast aside, that reversal may be itself reversed if the Court's membership changes in the future. This book focuses primarily on what is actually needed, not what is feasible at this point, if there are to be large gains. Targeted scholarships for students of color, substantial enough to actually enable students from families with few resources to attend college, together with active information and recruitment efforts in segregated communities, would be optimal. When that is not possible, it is important to think about initiating scholarships that are not reserved for these students but are color sensitive, designed to work in the real circumstances families of color face. For example, the University of Texas, during a period when its plan was blocked in the 1990s, designed a special program called the Longhorn scholarships. They targeted schools that had high poverty levels in areas where communities of color were concentrated. A university official would go into a high school and announce at an assembly that there were scholarships reserved just for that school. That did not exclude the small number of other students in the school, but it did greatly increase the probability that the students selected would be Latino or Black. There is no legal barrier to scholarships targeting, for example, students with a different home language or children of immigrants or students from communities of concentrated poverty or students from single-parent families. By the same token, if there were to be a serious commitment to equalizing opportunity for high school students of color, there are race-conscious tools that would be the most efficient and effective ways to do it and race-sensitive strategies that would be more likely to help make progress than the status quo.

If affirmative action falls, inequality will deepen significantly, as it has in states with competitive campuses where affirmative action has been banned. The large move against standardized admissions tests at a number of major universities, including the University of California system, during the pandemic has increased applications from students of color intimidated by ratings systems that seem to require a certain SAT score. If affirmative action falls, so may standardized admissions testing, spurred, in part, by the conservative claim that test scores are an adequate measure of "merit" and that any deviation from test-based admissions amounts to discrimination. How such changes would translate to admissions and actual enrollment over time is unknown.

Beyond Affirmative Action

Although affirmative action is a critically important tool for the nation's selective colleges, the great majority of U.S. colleges are not highly selective and do not have significant affirmative action plans. Many of these campuses also lack financial resources that enable them to award financial aid packages in which grants and loans cover the students' full cost of college when their families have few or no resources to make up the difference. Very few U.S. colleges award packages that meet full need. They assume that the unmet need after maxing out federal and state grants and loans will be met somehow. This works for students and families who can connect with other resources, such as help from grandparents or other relatives with means. It often fails for students of color whose extended families have few resources and many needs.

Colleges now spend much of the money they give in scholarships as discounts to students without financial need. The objective is to compete for qualified students who can pay a significant part of the costs, especially in a period of declining cohorts of potential students. To be serious about diversity may require shifting some of those funds to deeper scholarships by redefining need in ways that better reflect the situations of many students of color. This could be a serious fund-raising goal, and colleges could attempt to coordinate packages with funds from off-campus donors not subject to potential restrictions against race-targeted efforts.

In the 1980s American political and educational leaders began making decisions that resulted in rationing higher education by cost and cutting funding for expanding capacity. In some states, decisions were made that required most students with weak preparation to begin in community colleges, which typically had weak records of successful transfer and bachelor's degree completion. Such decisions produced a shortage of four-year public college spaces, especially in growing areas, although four-year campuses lead to much stronger results for students than community colleges. Higher education, which is highly valued but politically weak, lost out in state budgets to surging health care and prison costs, forcing the great public institutions to either seriously cut back or force students and families to pay a much higher share of rapidly rising costs. Such decisions came year by year with sudden, big changes in recessions when state budgets plummeted, and ended up changing the entire system. Campuses became far less affordable. Around the same period, there was a sharp turn against the race-conscious and class-conscious policies of the civil rights era in both educational and social policy. In 1996 the successful California referendum to forbid affirmative action was supported by the national GOP, and its success led to action in several other states.[17] This combination of policies was a perfect recipe for intensifying stratification by race and class.

The turn to the right in the 1980s brought to an end a long period of broad public belief that education, including higher education, was a crucial public investment. Since the middle of the nineteenth century, the expansion of free public education through high school had been seen as a fundamental public investment in our communities' future. The postwar U.S. created the most extensive higher education system the world had seen. The ideas of low cost and relatively easy access, and many practical as well as traditional fields, remained central. States had invested heavily in expanding and upgrading their colleges and were the basic source of funds. Many of the proliferating community colleges were free or virtually free, and so were some colleges and universities, most of which had tuitions set low enough that many students could "work their way through college."

Since the 1980s antitax era, higher education had to be increasingly financed privately. The market by itself increases inequality.

It turns out that families with enough money can buy access to a prestigious college education and the future benefits that flow from it. It is one of the most powerful ways of transmitting intergenerational advantage. When the best secondary schooling is, for all practical purposes, for sale on the upper ends of the white housing market, those students whose families start out at the bottom in communities with limited human capital and additional obstacles must attend schools that rarely prepare anyone for success in a good college. These differences are, of course, strongly related to race.

The student body presidents at Yale, the University of Southern California, Stanford, and the University of California, Los Angeles, wrote about it in 2019:

> Many high school students from high income families have the resources to attend elite private schools, take personalized SAT/ACT prep courses, go on resume-boosting travel programs, embark on cross-country tours to "demonstrate interest," and employ professional college counselors to strengthen their application materials. . . . High school students at under-funded public schools do not receive the same access to high-quality college prep resources as do their peers at public and private schools in wealthier ZIP Codes. . . . The real scandal is about the millions of kids who will never have an equitable chance in an extremely complex, competitive and costly process.[18]

These students can see it. The rest of us must. The reality is that the higher education system, in general, operates in a way that legitimizes highly unequal opportunities and results. Just look at the racial situation more than a half century after the civil rights era. Among young adults in 2017, twenty-five to twenty-nine years old, 42 percent of whites and 59 percent of Asians had college diplomas. But only 23 percent of Blacks, 19 percent of Latinos, and 16 percent of American Indians had degrees. For graduate and professional degrees, the inequalities were far worse.[19] This is where we are going without a plan; this is the default.

Colleges want to do something positive for students of color but have a lot of cross pressures and limited resources. Other demands often have higher priority. In a society where there has been no committed focus on new policies for racial equity for decades, it is not surprising that colleges tend to be satisfied with limited initiatives. In recent decades the priority in higher education policy has gone to ensuring access for middle-class families, ensuring adequate budgets for colleges, and, for a growing number, maintaining the enrollment they need to keep operating. Institutions struggling to survive within limited budgets often do little to meet the costs of extending major help to disadvantaged students of color or students in poverty. Colleges survived budget cuts and recessions by shifting cost to students and parents since they could not get sufficient money from government. Politicians faced strong middle-class demands, and, as a result, the aid that was available was increasingly spread out to middle-class families. The number of state representatives and senators of color is growing as demographic change continues. It will be important to work with them on serious plans for race-sensitive financial aid.

Although color-conscious policies like affirmative action admissions and aid are by far the most direct and efficient ways of increasing access and success for students of color, and it is important to make that point and pursue such policies, it is important to also pursue other means for two basic reasons. The first is that there are major political and legal barriers to color-conscious action in the U.S. now. The second is that there are many areas of policy that, if properly focused, could provide needed assistance to students of color while helping many others as well. Although those policies would be indirect and far less efficient in reaching students of color, they could lend help especially if they are color-sensitively designed. That means that the aid must be deep enough to be of genuine help to students of color and, when setting preconditions for receiving or keep the aid, must recognize the special problems those students often face. It is wonderful when a helicopter comes to rescue people drowning in a flood, but if the rope is too short to reach some of them, it is not a rescue at all for them. When we design policies that are workable for people with relatively modest or typical needs, they can be a cruel mirage for those who need much more and have nowhere else to turn. That is why sensitivity to actual racial conditions is so critical.

Understanding the nature of the racial inequalities does not mean that we know how to cure them. Anyone who studies evaluation research knows that often seemingly plausible solutions or promising experiments do not actually work at scale. Guesses and hunches and well-meaning programs and policies not based in the students' and families' realities will not work. This is a reason why it is so important to have people who come from communities of color involved in policy making. This chapter suggests fruitful paths and policies that have evidence of positive impacts. There are no simple single answers, but there are a number of policies and practices that would increase the chances that students of color and their families could find their way through the succession of walls that separate them from good college opportunities. Multiple barriers require multiple solutions and innovations as well as serious, sober evaluations of the efforts. It is always important to press for best policies whether or not they are feasible now.

The following recommendations focus largely on things that are in the control of or are deeply related to schools and colleges. These policies are not panaceas but can significantly help. Until another period of general social reform arrives, the educational institutions are the primary avenue for improving equity. If they face barriers to race-conscious plans, they must skillfully target resources in a way that is more likely to reach students of color.

Preparation

High school preparation for college is blatantly unequal, and those inequalities have been largely ignored in national higher education policy. Spending a day visiting what are supposed to be the same classes in a high-poverty urban high school and an affluent suburban high school would show any reasonable observer that, though the schools may be only a few miles apart, we are talking about different worlds in terms of the skills needed for college success. Since the federal government became a major actor in education in the 1960s, the educational programs have been focused on elementary and preschool, with the belief that there are developmental stages early in life that are critical for long-term gains, which can change long-term outcomes even in higher education. The great bulk of hundreds of billions of dollars of targeted federal school funding since the creation of the first general federal aid to education in 1965 has been directed toward elementary education and the expansion of preschool education. The Biden administration is investing heavily in preschool. The diagnosis was that with more resources at the beginning of schooling, we would break through inequality. In reforms, most focus has been on test scores in the early grades. It turned out, however, that though it was possible to accelerate early learning, the effect normally faded or disappeared if the students were sent to the kind of weak schools that most students of color attend after the initial program. In spite of large increases in preschool programs, intense focus on basic skills, and increased course requirements, the high school outcome gaps, particularly in reading, remain huge. Anyone who has raised children is likely to concede that supporting them right at the beginning and neglecting them in adolescence would never be an effective strategy, but this fact has been largely ignored.

By high school, students of color are, on average, far behind, in a harsher community environment, and often dealing with adolescence under very difficult circumstances. Transforming high schools is hard. They are big and highly differentiated, with faculty focused on their subjects, not student problems. In strong high schools there are courses that can give college credit and courses explicitly designed to fit into college curriculum and meet prerequisites for admissions. Such high schools have strong connections with colleges. High schools that students of color attend usually have less experienced and expert teachers. Their students who go to college often go to community colleges in Black, Latino, and Indian communities with low completion and transfer rates. Strong high schools have a much stronger focus on key precollegiate skills in areas like analytic writing, research, computers, and advanced math and science, as well as a good array of AP classes. College recommendations from those schools matter because of the track record of earlier students. Few students of color get access to such powerful high schools. The means are complex, but the goal should be clear: giving students of color the same kind of preparation for college that most white and Asian high school youths receive.

There are basically three strategies to deal with the problem of starkly different high school opportunities—get students of color access to better schools that are already successful, create excellent new diverse magnet schools, or, to the extent possible, replicate in the schools segregated by race and poverty the kinds of opportunities routinely provided in the good middle-class schools. All are needed.

The integration strategy grew out of *Brown v. Board of Education*, the civil rights movement, and the experience across the South. In American society, six decades under the "separate but equal" doctrine of the 1896 *Plessy v. Ferguson* decision had produced blatantly unequal segregated schools. Civil rights lawyers brought proof of that history into courts across the South. After decades of struggle, the unanimous Supreme Court decided that separate schools were "inherently unequal" and did irreversible damage. Enforcing the 1964 Civil Rights Act produced substantial desegregation in the seventeen states with segregation laws in the late 1960s and early 1970s. The change brought important gains for the civil rights generation of young people of color.

When the federal government first became a significant force in education in 1965, it set the high-poverty schools as the focus for federal funding, attempting to equalize segregated schools. The idea was that more money and a requirement of parental involvement would strengthen these schools and their teachers. Hundreds of billions of dollars of federal school aid have been concentrated on poor schools. Policy evolved from transferring money to an extreme of federal control and unreasonable demands under the No Child Left Behind and Race to the Top policies, but then switched back to extreme decentralization in 2015. The federal aid provided significant resources to try out wave after wave of popular reforms. The high schools, however, were virtually forgotten, receiving only one-twentieth of the federal funds.[20] When serious changes in high schools were mandated in the 1980s "excellence" policies, they were usually about demanding more courses and tests without significant additional resources or any structural changes in the schools. At the state and local levels, high-stakes test-based accountability has been dominant for more than a third of a century, built around the idea that standards and sanctions could produce more equal outcomes. By the time Congress adopted the Every Student Succeeds Act in 2015, that approach had failed in federal policy.

In the civil rights era, the early period of major federal school aid embedded federal efforts in a multidimensional reform agenda to aid the poor and their communities through the War on Poverty, Medicaid, and expanded social supports. Later efforts were largely detached from social policy as conservative governments reduced and eliminated social programs and dismantled civil rights. Although research had suggested since the 1960s that the schools had limited power and that out-of-school forces in the family, peer groups, and differential teacher quality mattered greatly,[21] these insights were mostly disregarded in the following decades as racial issues were ignored. The context of the schools and the profound inequalities in our society were largely ignored or addressed in ways that increased the harm.

In the early 1970s the federal government began seriously measuring changes in test scores on a national level through the National Assessment of Educational Progress, often called the "Nation's Report Card." In a half century of intense focus on changing test results, the central targets were elementary schools. The test scores for high school seniors have shown little progress in four decades, especially in language arts, in spite of all the additional course requirements, and the racial gaps have remained large.

For college access and success, the stakes in high school are extremely high. For many students of color who have not been attending strong schools before high school, it is their only chance to prepare for college and deal successfully with the admissions process. There are clear and powerful links between what students learn and accomplish in high school and whether they will be able to go to a good college where they are more likely to graduate. Students who go to schools with the best teachers, the best-prepared classmates, and strong connections with colleges have major advantages. Students of color need the skills that successful students have, connect them to stronger networks, and increase their capacity for success in classes. Since families without college experience usually have little understanding of the process of college choice and financial aid, counseling is critical but largely lacking.

Accessing Better Schools

Since we have had little success in making schools segregated by race, ethnicity, and poverty equal over the 125 years since *Plessy v. Ferguson*, we should try to get as many students of color as possible access to high schools that already have the key ingredients for a viable path to college while we work on upgrading the schools that do not or creating additional successful schools. In the civil rights era there were court orders for mandatory transfer of students and teachers of color to better schools. With the much more conservative courts terminating integration plans, the basic methods available now are changing attendance boundaries and school locations, increasing magnet schools, and expanding and redirecting choice options with strong civil rights policies. Almost nine-tenths (86 percent and 88 percent, respectively) of Blacks and Latinos surveyed in 2019 and three-fourths (76 percent) of whites favored magnet schools. Eighty-one percent of Blacks and 58 percent of whites said they favored locating "more low-income housing in suburbs and other higher income areas" as a way to achieve integration.[22] Certain policies permitting transfers to other school districts can also significantly increase access. In spite of some notably successful and long-lasting efforts under good court orders, these plans have been largely terminated.

Desegregation is something we know could actually be done because we did it in many places for decades and it had substantial benefits, significantly lowering inequality of preparation and raising success in college. It was far from perfect, but it had, on average, solid long-term benefits. The simplest way to give students more challenging and effective high school educations is to let those who would otherwise be assigned to failing schools attend schools with a solid level of success, with stronger and diverse teachers and curriculum, fair treatment, college orientation, and positive connections with colleges. Getting the students inside better schools, of course, is not enough. There must be policies to diversify faculty and train teachers and to avoid segregation of tracks within diverse schools and to support students' success in more challenging coursework.

Various forms of school choice have been the most plausible strategies for increasing access to strong schools since the Supreme Court decisions of the 1990s led to the dissolution of most major plans mandating desegregation. Magnet schools with diversity policies are the most important positive choice example, but in the post-desegregation era, many magnet schools have lost their integration policies, with the best schools often adopting colorblind test-based admission policies, creating less access for African American and Latino students and making them increasingly places for children of more privileged white and Asian families. In a 2019 Gallup Poll, most Americans said segregation was a serious problem and favored additional steps toward integration: "Most popular among the proposals is the creation of magnet schools, which about four in five Americans (79%) favor. Americans also support . . . redistricting school boundaries to diversify districts (60%)."[23] Restoring and improving magnet school methods of providing parents with information, recruiting, and reaching desegregation goals that worked in the desegregation era would surely open up many spaces in strong schools.[24]

Since segregation is mostly between cities and suburbs and among suburbs, not within cities, anything that can create access for students from inferior schools to stronger schools in other districts would be very useful. We have had a half century of experience in regional voluntary transfer plans where students can cross school district lines to attend schools their families see as more desirable in other districts. The scale was usually modest. A voluntary city-suburban plan, the Metropolitan Council for Educational Opportunity, was created in Boston in the mid-1960s and has transferred about three thousand students per year to more than thirty suburban school districts. There has been an enormous demand for participation in the plan, which has a huge waiting list. Many of the students have gone on to success in good four-year colleges and to good jobs in the Boston area.[25] None of the dozens of Boston suburbs involved has departed from the voluntary cooperation in a half century. This is a limited approach that is difficult to initiate but works well in practice.

A much larger voluntary transfer plan existed for several decades in the metro Saint Louis area as a settlement to a major school desegregation case. Under that settlement agreement, the suburban school districts in Saint Louis County agreed to become at least 25 percent nonwhite, a major information office was established for parents, and many steps were taken in the suburban districts. There were notable gains in student achievement, graduation, and college going.[26] State legislation in Wisconsin established the 220 Program, which made it possible for thousands of Milwaukee students of color to go to school in suburban districts.

One of the most positive outcomes of civil rights litigation, regional magnets are a creative voluntary transfer mechanism in the long-standing Connecticut *Sheff* case. Although the federal constitution says nothing about education, many state constitutions do have specific language about it. This is true in Connecticut, one of the richest states with the poorest central cities in well-to-do metros. The state supreme court concluded that separating students by districts in the highly segregated metro violated the state constitution, and it ordered the state to develop a solution. The centerpiece of the solution was a system of regional magnet schools in the three large metro areas, a system that succeeded in lowering segregation through desirable voluntary transfer opportunities that created large waiting lists and strong test scores.[27] The plan has no forced transfers and excellent educational options and would be feasible in many metros with state or federal funding.

There are special schools that offer strong precollegiate programs within central cities, such as the exam schools of New York City and Boston Latin, with extremely talented peer groups, outstanding faculties, strong history, and stellar connections with colleges. In Dallas the city's arts magnet Booker T. Washington is in such demand that there was a major scandal of illegal entry by suburban families giving false addresses or even renting places in the city to get access.[28] A number of formerly integrated magnet schools became selective exam-driven schools[29] after desegregation plans were terminated. The San Antonio School District has had considerable success in attracting students from the suburbs. Magnet schools should be required to adopt diversity policies, as should high school–level charter schools that depend on public funding for their existence.

The other choice framework that could increase access is voluntary transfer. A standard component of many desegregation plans for many years was systems permitting some number of voluntary transfers that would increase diversity at the receiving school, combined with public funding of transportation for the transfer students. In light of the 2007 *Parents Involved*[30] Supreme Court case forbidding assigning individual students to schools solely on the basis of their race or ethnicity without a court order, such plans would have to be designed in terms of neighborhood diversity, linguistic diversity, and other strategies that are still legal. Interdistrict transfer is law in a number of states but with limitations that undermine its impact or actually foster segregation. In Arizona such colorblind transfers are legal but have facilitated white flight, and the same thing has happened under Massachusetts law, as many whites have transferred out of Springfield.[31] Voluntary transfer plans will not end segregation in U.S. schools, but they could, if they were seriously pursued, and if more intentionally integrated magnets were established, open the door to the strong existing schools for large numbers of students excluded by residential segregation and boundary lines.

Making decisive progress in creating access to better schools and expanding the number of them would require serious national leadership and resources and, if possible, plans at the regional level. Universities and colleges could contribute by creating strong, diverse campus-sponsored schools linked to the colleges with strong college orientations. Fair choice plans require free transportation; otherwise they become an additional inequality for poor families. It was clear in the civil rights era that the most effective plans embraced entire metropolitan areas, set clear goals, and had resources for expanding choices, marketing options, retraining faculty and staff, working with community and housing officials, and having clear objectives and accountability. If we want to have the kind of schools that would give much more equal preparation for college on a national scale, it would have to be a national goal supported by education and civil rights officials and be seen as a clear responsibility for education leaders. Such an effort could become a basic building block of more successful multiracial communities and businesses aided by young people ready to live and work in diverse settings. State initiatives could be of significant assistance.

Our cities and suburbs are always changing, and racial change in communities—resegregation of suburbs and middle-class families moving into gentrifying cities—offers possibilities as well as threats. Segregation is a product of flows of people in and out of neighborhoods and schools. So is integration. If the flows can be significantly altered, different and better outcomes are possible. In the suburban situations, crafting school offerings and policies to attract and hold both older and newer groups could produce integrated schools and help stabilize diverse communities. Gentrification can also produce integration under appropriate school and housing policies. Good school policies would aim to bring in the children of young professionals, often mostly white or Asian, and good housing policy would aim at enabling many long-term residents to remain and participate in improving schools.

There are large costs when suburban communities change from diverse to resegregated as housing markets change and whites are steered away or, in cities, when more affluent whites displace low-income Blacks or Latinos. In both cases, combined school and housing strategies can produce a more stable and positive outcome, including schools that can provide better lasting opportunities to prepare for college and for life.

Thinking about even limited efforts to access better schools from the perspective of access to higher education, the results could be substantial. Currently only a small fraction of students of color, in California about one in twenty, attend the top fifth of high schools (in terms of scores). If even 10 percent more students of color could attend schools with strong preparation for college, the colleges could face a tripling of the number of well-prepared students of color who would be far more likely to succeed in their colleges. The reality is that for the past half century of historic racial change in our society, many successful integration efforts have been shut down by judicial or political decisions and little serious work has been launched. Racial issues have been ignored and generations of school officials have issued plans promising to end racial gaps that left the gaps in place. When even small incentives have been available, there has been active school district interest in pursuing positive possibilities.

Just getting students through the door of better schools is, of course, not enough. Real success requires more. It is possible to stratify students within diverse schools that often have few teachers and administrators of color and little training in race relations. Bigger gains come from integrating and training the staffs of the schools and modifying the curriculum to reflect the contributions of all groups. Schools need to avoid classroom segregation and include students of color in the challenging courses, while giving them any needed support to make up for inferior training they may have received in the lower grades. Large structural changes require multidimensional adaptions.

Current school integration efforts rely on voluntary choice programs operated in a way that fosters diversity. Sometimes that can happen just by opening a magnet school or transfer opportunities where demand for the school is racially balanced. Generally, however, it does not happen, and colorblind choice plans often accelerate the departure of whites from schools with rising nonwhite enrollments, give the worst choices to the groups with the least information and fewest contacts, undermine lasting diversity, and deliver the best choices to the most organized and affluent families. To provide better choices to the students of color, the following elements are vital: a clear plan for diversity as a basic goal, targeted recruitment and admissions preference for the less represented groups or neighborhoods in the school, a strong system of informing and counseling parents about the choices and the system, a lottery system that does not give preference to those who first find out and get in line, support for "outsider" students who transfer into a school, a diverse faculty and staff for the school, good free transportation to make it possible for families from other areas to choose the school even if they cannot provide their own transit, and welcome and fair treatment for students transferring into the school. These schools must not use a selection process, such as strong reliance on standardized tests, which will perpetuate and even increase gaps through selective access to superior schools. Schools of choice can, of course, have demanding curricula but must not deny an opportunity to less privileged students to show that they can master and benefit from those crucial opportunities.

Many communities, especially in the South, did these things with considerable success for decades under desegregation plans, so they are feasible policies. The schools were diverse and they often created a substantial increase in strong opportunities. The Supreme Court decision in the 2007 *Parents Involved* case made it more difficult to accomplish stable and substantial integration. But the decision recognized the importance of integration and allows policies that consider the race of neighborhoods or communities positively and there is no bar to setting aside spaces on the basis of home language or neighborhood poverty. The basic problem is not that it cannot be done or doesn't work but that parents from the privileged groups often oppose any limitation on their children's access to the most preferred schools. Many school districts have stopped trying to implement diversity and even moved toward test-based admission in the most desirable schools, including magnets, thus cutting access for students of color.[32] When a school district turns a successful diverse magnet into an elite exam school, it intensifies stratification and the selection mechanism tends to legitimize it. Advocates of college opportunity for students of color must challenge such changes.

The conservative Supreme Court has pushed federal policy backward. With the federal courts blocked off as a source of gains at present, some civil rights organizations are turning to state courts. Unlike the federal Constitution, many state constitutions have education clauses that offer possible levers for dealing with segregation and equalization. Most states have seen school funding lawsuits. In the civil rights era there were a number of states with laws or policies that worked to end segregated education, but many of them were discarded or quietly ignored as the country turned in a conservative direction. A major breakthrough came with the *Sheff* case[33] in Connecticut a quarter century ago when the state supreme court ruled that the state was obligated to take action to overcome the segregation caused by district boundaries in its metropolitan areas. There are currently major statewide cases under way in Minnesota[34] and New Jersey.[35] As the country polarizes more deeply politically and the Democratic Party becomes more liberal, there are at least a small number of important states where such strategies could become viable and powerful. In U.S. policy making, successful state models often influence long-term agendas.

Bringing Down the Wall of Systematically Unequal College Preparation

The logical alternative to increasing access to stronger schools is to make existing weak high schools more effective in preparing students of color for college. What the students need is not hard to outline. How to achieve it in schools facing multiple barriers of inequality is deeply challenging. Most students of color are in weak, doubly segregated schools that need to be upgraded in several ways. There are many extremely inadequate schools, which are the only option for a number of students even though they lack a viable path to college. The bad schools include the nation's "dropout factories," whose major product is devastating failure for their more than 740,000 students.[36]

Many high schools in communities of color are simply failing to prepare students or, as some would see it, are full of students lacking the basic skills needed to learn at a serious precollegiate level. Much of the problem of acting out in disruptive ways in classes, for example, relates to failure to achieve in school. Students who consistently fail face a difficult, embarrassing situation as adolescents and sometimes take it out on teachers and classmates. Obviously, anything that can be done to intervene to prevent failure and flunking and to provide better counseling and support for students who often face difficult situations in their homes and communities will likely improve outcomes and aid teachers.

High schools are big, complex institutions divided by academic departments and resistant to change. Teachers usually have class after class of students during the day. They don't get to know many individual students and cannot deal with the out-of-school problems. High schools in poor, segregated neighborhoods confront all the problems faced by low-income adolescents in families with problems who live in communities with few opportunities, insecure housing, local violence, untreated health and substance abuse problems, and many temptations. Too often they are expected to deal with all those problems with completely inadequate social work and counseling support, and with fewer support services than privileged students in elite public and private schools receive.

Basic Issues of High School Inequality

Colorblind policies often compound the problems faced by the schools serving students of color, blaming the schools for the racial gaps in outcomes. Standards were raised and the students and schools were punished if they could not keep up with middle-class schools. Additional curriculum and testing were imposed without consideration of the inadequate preparation to meet even the old standards. Little was done to increase faculty capacity while sanctions for not attaining unreasonable test scores punished nonwhite schools. Many were closed and communities lost their schools because of a school's test scores. Education leaders of color were criticized as using "excuses" when they raised issues of poverty and inequality and hailed when they directed enormous resources to test preparation and raised scores on the tests in math and language arts. Since many of those gains reflected an increase in test-taking skills and strategies for practicing for a particular test rather than an actual increase of knowledge, the students were not given a real path to college. The successful test strategies of a small group of schools segregated by poverty and race were pointed to as proof that the inequality could be solved if only the schools all worked harder, and they were accepted as a reason for ignoring the systemic racial inequality.[37] When that became national policy in No Child Left Behind, it failed.

Often apparent successes turn out to be deceptive. They do not fail because of ill will but, fundamentally, because the structure of inequality is deeply rooted and the treatments many schools can offer are limited. Successes in schools of concentrated poverty often require extraordinary leaders who dedicate great energy for years to selecting, training, and supporting a strong staff. Such leaders are rare. In some districts, most or all of the high schools do not.

To build more equal opportunity to prepare for college, we must remember the array of forces that subtract from the chances of students of color: (1) Because of growing up in homes with minimal economic and social resources and great stressors, students are far behind before their first day of school. (2) They attend the weakest preschools and elementary schools. (3) Isolation in segregated, concentrated-poverty neighborhoods and schools for most students of color limits resources and opportunities and increases risks. (4) Lack of wealth and housing market and mortgage discrimination isolate the families from strong schools and districts. (5) Children of color have more chronic untreated medical problems. (6) They have the least experienced teachers, often from the least rigorous colleges. (7) Their peer groups are far less prepared. (8) The students face more residential instability and homelessness. (9) They have more exposure to violence and crime. (10) The transition to high school often is difficult and produces rapid failure. (11) School suspension disproportionately affects young men of color. (12) The schools often must cope with overwhelmed single parents or grandparents and family disorganization. (13) Families have far less information about college. (14) Choice systems typically favor middle-class families and students. (15) There are few teachers of students' own race or ethnicity. (16) Students face discrimination by teachers and school staff. (17) There is disproportionate incarceration, and there are few supports for reentry in the regular high schools. (18) Children of immigrants often face the threat or reality of losing parents by sudden deportation. (19) Schools are not organized to produce the levels of academic English and basic study, research, and writing skills needed in college. (20) Schools often lack the needed level of AP and honors programs that prepare for college study. (21) High schools usually have weak relationships with colleges and severely inadequate counseling resources.

Long before students of color and their families are thinking seriously about college, there are many policies that could improve their chances. Any programs that help the education, the income, and the availability of decent housing for the parents would improve the situation of the children. Attention to nutrition and health care makes obvious differences. Anything that can be done at the school level, such as in-school clinics, screenings for chronic problems, guidance on nutrition, places to study, and so on, can be important.

Every part of education before college matters. Strong preschool programs with expert teachers can provide a much better start. Most preschool for students of color, especially those in high-poverty areas, is not strong and does not have lasting impact. There should be strong pressure not just to expand the numbers but also to raise the quality enough to make a difference. For the huge number of children raised in non-English-speaking homes, positive programs for language development in both languages can be very important. For all schools, having teachers who are well trained and experienced makes a substantial difference. Serious school progress requires capable leadership, collaboration among teachers, and the ability to hold a stable staff.

Students of color often enter high school with much lower levels of preparation and knowledge, and the children from concentrated-poverty schools tend to lag far behind. If these students are to have success in high school and be reasonably prepared for college, they need and deserve major help, including (1) an organized effort to prevent failure in the first year of high school, which is very common for these students; (2) care for significant health and psychological problems that are the result of often harsh adolescence experiences; (3) early and continuous counseling about what is needed to get to college or a good job; (4) strong precollegiate courses with support when students fall behind; (5) much better access to schools with a proven record of preparing students for college; (6) strong social work support for dealing with severe home and neighborhood problems, gangs, foster child status, and so on; (7) alternatives to suspension and expulsion; (8) criminal justice reform emphasizing alternative community-based sentencing and educational reentry programs for ex-offenders; (9) positive relationships between schools and parents; (10) the closure or fundamental reform of dropout factory schools, where many drop out and almost none are prepared for college; (11) positive college experiences during high school.

Most of these needs have not been identified as serious priorities in the larger society. Since the schools and the students start far behind, it would require special additional resources and priorities for these schools. In a society in which high schools are profoundly different in privileged and disadvantaged communities in many ways that relate directly to college preparation, the goals discussed here are really efforts to give all children access to things that higher-status white and Asian children already usually receive in their schools, homes, and communities. The truth is that it is an enormous task to provide the things that are built into middle-class schools in schools segregated by race and poverty and often sanctioned by education authorities as "failures" under accountability systems that blame the schools.

What the schools need are the things the middle-class schools have. Sufficient resources, strong teachers, a positive peer group, and leadership are key. To manage a challenging school, you need a talented and experienced principal, but such principals tend to go to schools with more support and fewer challenges where they will be praised rather than pressured and blamed for problems that often come from outside the school.[38] Those leadership issues and teacher recruitment, training, and retention must be addressed. High priority must be given to recruiting, rewarding, and retaining strong principals dedicated to this work.

Teachers are critical, but there is a systemic pattern of teachers leaving high-poverty nonwhite schools as they gain experience and seniority.[39] The work in classrooms with poorly prepared students, limited parental support, more students with counseling needs, and less prestige is harder, and teachers get less credit for it as recognition and honors go to high schools with high-achieving students. Those of us who have taught in leading colleges know that the students are so talented that it is a pleasure and they achieve great things for which we get part of the credit. Teaching students who lack skills and preparation is a more demanding job where there are often few rewards.

Under accountability systems linked to average student test scores, both teachers and administrators have a strong disincentive to stay in troubled schools because their average test scores will be considerably lower even if individual teachers make real gains during the school year. Students of color from homes and communities with fewer educational resources are more likely to lose a significant part of the year's learning gains over the summer when they do not have the options of many more affluent students.

What subject-matter teachers value is the opportunity and time to collaborate with colleagues and good, experienced administrators running the school; they appreciate professional respect, order, and rational evaluation that takes into account that teachers in different schools and classes are dealing with students who come into class with very different preparation and resources.[40] Many want the stimulation of teaching advanced classes. It is hard to imagine equal opportunity until the teacher inequality is solved. You cannot have strong college preparation without strong teachers, and teachers dealing with higher-order skills do not want to spend their time on basic skills that students lack.

Desiree Carver-Thomas and Linda Darling-Hammond's 2017 study of the national Schools and Staffing Survey data showed a devastating difference in staffing schools of color. They conclude, "The turnover rate is about 70% greater than that in the quartile of schools with the fewest students of color. . . . Mathematics and science teacher turnover rates are 90% higher. . . . Special education teachers are more than 80% more likely to turn over."[41]

The colorblind assumptions that the social realities they are dealing with can be ignored and that sanctions will produce equal outcomes seriously undermined the creation of conditions leading expert teachers to stay in troubled schools. Stable faculties are a necessity in implementing major reforms. Reforming institutions as complex as high schools requires years of collaborative work that is almost impossible without long-term commitment by leaders and teachers. Administrators and teachers working in schools where teachers regularly leave for better assignments face conditions that often doom reform efforts. When we have so many schools that teachers want to leave, should we follow policies that keep the students there?

Turning a Dangerous Transition into a Good Start

For students far behind, the start of high school is often a dangerous and demoralizing time, just as is the transition to college, especially to community college, when you are unprepared. It is a time when cumulative inequalities hit the wall. Schools should create a transition to high school that helps prevent failure in the freshman year. Rather than blaming the students' previous schools or the students themselves for their educational shortcomings, the schools need to help students catch up. Research at Johns Hopkins and elsewhere in ninth-grade transition programs indicates that strong moves to strengthen academic preparation can help. A basic goal is to create a special focus on new students and real contact with faculty members who can get to know them. This requires institutional change on a number of fronts, including dealing with the fact that the least experienced teachers tend to be assigned to ninth-grade classes, which are the least advanced and prestigious assignments.[42] Reorganization and funding to support such focused effort is badly needed and should be built into the basic operation of schools. Sometimes this could involve creating "ninth-grade academies" that systematically focus on equipping students with stronger basic skills and preparing them for the demands of high school courses. Students who come into high school with weak preparation can quickly get into trouble and fall between the cracks, with no one paying much attention until the failures accumulate and overwhelm the students. This has led to restructuring experiments like the Talent Development High School Model, which creates an intense focus on more contact with students and academic catchup.[43] The basic need is for a planned, coherent, and positive transition that gives students a real second chance, not the message that they are failures. Without a positive start, a good end is unlikely.

A major 2019 evaluation of a systematic program to produce a better ninth-grade experience showed clear benefits in substantially lowering the racial gap in failing courses and grades in the first year of high school.[44] The U.S. Department of Education financed a random-assignment study of a high school transition strategy called Building Assets and Reducing Risks in eleven high schools across the country. The effort, which included much more collaboration, monitoring, and contact between teachers and students, had significant effects in cutting failure in courses and raising grades, especially for students of color and those from poor families. Students reported more positive relationships and engagement. Teachers praised the increased collaboration. The evaluation found significantly reduced racial gaps in ninth-grade academic success. It is possible to build a better bridge into high school success.

Diversifying Faculty

There is significant research evidence that the performance of students of color is enhanced by the presence of faculty of color.[45] In a difficult period of life in a very polarized society, having professionals and models from your race can help. Diverse schools are an attempt to build a fair multiracial community in a segregated society. It matters that a diverse adult population in the school reinforces that goal. This was apparent back in the civil rights era when the Supreme Court defined faculty desegregation as an essential part of a desegregation plan, agreeing with federal education authorities.[46] Yet a recent Bookings Institution report concludes a half century later, "Teachers in the U.S. are even more segregated than students."[47]

Creating a diverse faculty should be an integral part of high school and district operations, and it would have a positive impact. In contrast to earlier eras, when teaching was one of the only professional options for students of color, there is a serious shortage of teachers of color now, especially male teachers of color. White students are typically in schools with less than one-tenth teachers of color, compared with nonwhite students, for whom the average is about one-third (32 percent).[48]

When there were court-ordered desegregation plans, faculty desegregation was an integral part of the plans, and many contained provisions for affirmative action. Today most of those plans have been dismantled, and the search for teachers of color and their distribution to all schools is often neglected. There is a formal process but little oversight or enforcement. Seniority transfer rights written into union contracts and assessments that punish teachers in high-poverty schools are added barriers that could be corrected by legislation, better contracts, and more positive assessment and support mechanisms. Students of color attending a demanding high school benefit from and deserve the support of faculty of color.

Under desegregation orders, teachers were simply transferred as part of the plan and vice versa. Lacking that power, the main alternative has been to raise salaries or create special bonuses for taking on harder assignments, sometimes referred to as "combat pay." These programs have had little success. An effort by economist Eric Hanushek to estimate how much it would cost to convince experienced teachers to stay in those schools came up with very large numbers.[49] One major analysis concludes that poor working conditions, poor leadership, lack of positive collegial relationships, and other social factors facilitate departures of experienced teachers.[50] Unfortunately, these conditions are often much worse in the schools of color. One of the challenges of making high schools more equal is making substantial changes to the treatment of teachers in schools serving students of color. Teachers have freedom to leave; it is often a contractual right related to seniority. There is more opportunity in fields with a shortage of teachers, including math and science. Keeping teachers requires changing school operations and evaluation systems. When teachers are blamed for outcomes rooted in out-of-school realities and not credited for the difference they make, the negative cycle is reinforced and good teachers and administrators exit.

Resegregation feeds on itself. A Georgia study showed that as white enrollment in schools declined, the departure of experienced teachers accelerated.[51] A national sample of teachers who are members of the National Education Association showed that teachers were more likely to leave schools as they became increasingly nonwhite but that teachers were very positive about working in integrated schools.[52] So policies to keep schools integrated are policies to keep strong faculty. Teachers prefer schools with strong and experienced administrators. But administrators, like teachers, tend to leave high-poverty nonwhite schools. So once again, segregation impedes something that segregated schools truly need.

A fundamental side effect of the high-stakes colorblind testing and accountability model was the creation of a massive disincentive for talented teachers and administrators to work in the schools that needed them most. Because schools were valued (or threatened) according to their test scores, and test scores are strongly related to family income and parent education, there was a strong incentive to avoid the schools likely to have the lowest test scores and the weakest peer groups and to go to schools that looked far better on test rankings, often suburban white and Asian schools. Home seekers' and realtors' use of websites that report school test scores as if they were a measure of the school's quality rather than of the socioeconomic background of students tends to steer middle-class families away from the disadvantaged schools. These are classic examples of a well-meaning colorblind policy, publishing standardized testing results and enforcing "accountability," that compounds rather than solves an urgent problem. The pressure on absolute test scores rather than the difference that schools made for students is systematically unfair to schools dealing with students who were far behind when they arrived.

Recruiting and holding strong teachers and administrators in the schools where they are most needed should be a major consideration in evaluating and rewarding superintendents. If schools are to be equalized, we need systems that recognize and reward the contributions of teachers and administrators, not punish them for working with students who haven't previously had a fair chance.

Integration of faculties is a priority. We segregate students and often do not train the white teachers in race relations and multiculturalism, though many begin in a nonwhite school. The need for more teachers of color has been a constant theme for a half century, but efforts have been insufficient and we have adopted some policies that work directly against more diversity. Some of the negative colorblind policies have been built into the Higher Education Act's requirements of strong success in teacher exams for education schools to retain federal aid. That policy has encouraged pretesting that has blocked many students of color from enrolling in teacher training programs in spite of their strong motivation and commitment. Since standardized test scores are strongly linked to parents' socioeconomic status, this emphasis on tests blocks entry of many potential teachers of color who would be more likely than white teachers to relate to the students in the segregated schools and stay in those schools. The National Academy of Sciences and the ethics statements of the testing profession say that we should not use single high-stakes tests to make major life decisions for students.[53] This is an area in which the assessment process should be reviewed. Giving preference to higher-scoring students who understand nothing of the racial and class context and are unlikely to stay in schools of color is a defective approach.

Equalizing the Curriculum

The curriculum of high schools must provide sufficient classes and subjects to meet state and district high school graduation requirements. Those required courses are guaranteed a virtually universal enrollment, and all counselors know they must be on students' schedules. Other than that, however, there is a lot of variance among high schools, which try to offer classes meeting the interests and needs of a wide range of students. In terms of the practical operation of schools, class sections are offered depending on enrollment, and teachers can only specialize in a certain subject, such as chemistry, when there is enough enrollment to pay for the teachers' time. If there are many students enrolling in a class, more sections will be offered and there may be honors classes. If few are enrolling, it may be dropped or cut down to a single class section.

In other words, the curriculum and teacher specialization respond to the market demand for courses in the school, which reflects the background of the school's attendance area and reinforces stratification. It is not a decision about whether there is enough demand to support a specialist in the subject and how to divide the teaching hours for teachers when there is insufficient demand. Given the complexity of schedules, if there are few sections of calculus, for example, they may often conflict with other requirements in students' schedules and many students may be denied the opportunity to take the class. From the perspective of students who need that course, it amounts to discrimination since, through no personal fault, they cannot get a valuable kind of preparation. But from the perspective of the school, it seems a logical response to the number of students signing up for a course. Much of high school curriculum is shaped by the "market" demand. This, which has very different racial impacts given high school segregation, is another illustration of the consequences of market mechanisms that reflect and reinforce racial gaps. The schools with the best-prepared students have the best selection of classes that prepare them for college and the schools where the students need the most help have the fewest. What looks like a fair, colorblind, market-oriented process closes vital doors for many students of color.[54]

Such patterns have been noted, but little has been done for a long time. Research a generation ago had similar findings. In other words, the problems are deeply rooted, continue after being documented, and are not being resolved. For example, though improvement of math and science performance was a fundamental goal of the reforms of the 1980s and 1990s, a major federal report in 1995, a quarter century ago, showed that there were wide racial gaps and that they were strongly related to out-of-school differences and education in unequal schools.[55] It warned, back then, that large racial gaps "would subsequently affect the quality and quantity of human resources in this country because their populations have been growing at a much faster rate than the white population." Looking at the school variables, the most important were the school's average socioeconomic status, the track the student was in, being in a precollegiate (academic) program, and being enrolled into challenging classes. Students of color were more than five times as likely as white children to be in concentrated-poverty schools[56] where "teachers have lower morale and less positive attitudes about students and are less responsive to student needs."[57] You can use the same sentences a generation later. There is no self-corrective mechanism in place to avert these consequences.

Today schools are far more segregated by race and poverty, and Black students now are not getting fair access to the precollegiate courses.[58] Now we have many more students of color taking more advanced math and science courses and many more enrolling in some kind of college after high school, but achievement levels have changed little and the college completion gap has actually increased. A major study of the Michigan Merit Curriculum, for example, showed that the requirement for more math courses had produced more completion of Algebra 2 but no gain on either test scores or college going. The authors suggested that it might be because of inequality among the schools or the fact that the financial barrier to college was the real problem.[59] A 2021 examination of California high schools showed that white and Asian students were more than twenty times as likely as Latino and Black students to be enrolled in a top-quintile high school in the state. The intensely competitive University of California provides access for only the top one-eighth of California's students, so the extraordinary difference in access to the highest-achieving high schools is a major barrier.[60]

Unless there are serious changes, there will be similar reports a quarter century from now. The real curriculum reflects social structure and will not change unless the market approach to course offerings is changed and students of color are not so concentrated in weak schools. Many segregated schools offer courses that sound like they are precollegiate but actually are taught and graded at a far less advanced level because many students are not prepared for the level of instruction found in schools with better-prepared students. That can create an image of preparation that can turn into a crashing disappointment when students arrive on campus and discover how less prepared they are than students from stronger schools. The students who excelled in weak schools often feel cheated when they arrive at a university and compare their preparation with that of more privileged classmates. If you are in a situation where you do the maximum you are asked for and find out in the real world of college that you were, in an important way, lied to and denied the chance to develop your full potential, you are experiencing another sharp, cutting edge of a system of self-perpetuating inequality.

Advocates, school boards, and state officials sometimes address the weakness through mandates for more advanced course work that can either create more obstacles for poorly prepared students or water down the level of instruction so that students will pass. We have been increasing course requirements since the 1980s without getting parallel learning gains on the National Assessment of Educational Progress. It is much easier for schools to report completion of more college prep courses than to actually operate courses at the level needed for the students to be prepared.

Obviously, there are real academic advantages to taking and passing more demanding courses.[61] There is, for example, a significant increase in enrollment in four-year colleges for students taking stronger courses.[62] At a minimum there should be the opportunity for such courses taught at an authentic level in all high schools. As long as schools are fundamentally unequal, this will rarely happen. Schools would need to make the investments to recruit and hire appropriate faculty and to offer strong courses even if the school has few students prepared for them. This would, of course, be expensive. It costs more to create a genuinely equal preparation at a strong precollegiate level in a disadvantaged school. The alternative is to accept another serious barrier to college that has nothing to do with the individual student.

Cut Suspensions and Educate the Incarcerated

One of the basic problems of high school for students of color, especially Black, Latino, and Indian males, is the high rate of temporary exclusion through school suspension and much longer exclusion through juvenile incarceration in prison and other facilities. Students who are suspended experience serious harm to their academic future and a greater likelihood of dropping out of high school. There has been widespread reform and a dramatic reduction in suspension in recent years, but the massive racial disproportions remain, and the Trump administration undermined the antisuspension policies.[63] Even restoring those policies, however, is far from sufficient.

Many schools have adopted in-school alternatives to suspension. The steps that are essential now are to continue monitoring and use treatment rather than incarceration sanctions.[64] Though alternative schools account for less than 1 percent of total students, they disproportionately serve Black students, especially boys; Latino boys; and boys with disabilities. The situation is especially severe for those sent for disciplinary purposes: 75 percent of the disciplinary transfers in 2015 were African American and Latino. Surprisingly, although these children often have serious behavioral problems, these schools have fewer counselors and social workers than regular schools.[65] These schools are often dead ends for students who might have been made ready for community colleges and certificates or degrees that would greatly enhance their prospects.

Prisoners often come from our most devastated communities with very weak schools. When ex-offenders come out of incarceration, there needs to be a real second chance. School districts, probation offices, and social service agencies need plans to avoid practices that just load young people with no alternative into the criminal economy. Young men of color with criminal records have a very hard time making it in the job market. There are good models of alternative community-based sanctions and of good training programs. The vast expansion of imprisonment took place in a time of conservative insistence on the punitive nature of punishment and neglect of the reality that offenders come back to communities. If they have lives that are revolving doors in and out of jail, never connecting with a decent job or able to support their families, they will continue to be drags on communities and society, including their many children. We are now in the process of the early release of offenders who have been prepared for nothing. The situation is so bad and costs so high that a modest but important bipartisan reform process is under way, and schools are a key part of any good answer.[66]

Even if ex-offenders were attending a reasonable high school before incarceration, they are often sent to dead-end alternative schools where few graduate when they return. It is very important to arrange for students with good records in incarceration and nonviolent offenses to reenter regular public schools or community colleges. A better practice is to keep them out of imprisonment in alternative sentencing that includes an educational focus.

President Barack Obama's administration created an experimental program to give Pell Grants for college courses to a number of incarcerated students in 2016. One of the increasingly harsh reforms of the 1990s had barred such use. The experiment produced a rapid and growing response from students and colleges and quickly resulted in many students receiving postsecondary certificates and some students receiving college degrees. In a country where young men of color with little education and a criminal record often can't connect to the job market, it makes sense on many levels to help as many as possible get on a path to college, or some form of postsecondary credential, rather than an endless cycle of costly imprisonments. The benefits would extend to their families and communities. We should engage community colleges and universities on scale to offer college-level course and possible degrees to prisoners. We have thrown away the future of many young students of color. Colleges can help open more futures.

Institutional Changes

The great institutional reform of secondary education in the twentieth century was the creation of large comprehensive high schools, bringing students together from large areas in low-density communities and from various neighborhoods in metro areas, in order to offer a full range of courses. This was an obvious improvement from schools without the enrollment needed to offer a range of genuine precollegiate courses. In large high schools where teachers work in subject-matter departments, the basic focus is on the substance of the subject, and each teacher instructs several classes. This seems to work well in schools with students ready for the courses and not needing special support.

There can be remarkable and varied opportunities and choices in the best schools. For unprepared students far behind grade level who are coming from weak elementary and middle schools, being on their own in a big comprehensive high school can be a very difficult situation where they can often be lost between the institutional cracks and make poor decisions about courses with no one paying attention in schools with very limited counseling resources.

A movement to create small schools took hold, especially in New York City schools, and then was suddenly treated as a large national solution with the powerful backing of the giant Gates Foundation. Many school districts responded quickly to the ideas and the foundation's dollars. As the movement quickly spread with little preparation, some of the inherent problems of creating small schools, often in parts of the same big school or building, became apparent, and the assessment results were highly disappointing, leading the Gates Foundation to concede failure and withdraw the targeted effort. Ironically, however, strong research on the original New York school sites did show benefits, at least in the way those schools had been developed and operated there.[67] By then, however, the findings of failure had taken the air out of the movement. Many districts had jumped at the idea that simply cutting school size would make a strong academic impact, but it did not. It turned out that the key ingredient in New York was the idea that students facing a variety of academic and personal problems need personal contacts and support in a less threatening setting where high school faculty move beyond subject-matter teaching to develop significant relationships with a smaller group of students. The actual benefits reflected the changes in contacts and the missions of teachers. When implemented in this way, small schools can have benefits, though they do, in their very smallness, suffer from the inability to offer the full range of courses found in a strong comprehensive or magnet school.

Comprehensive Services

Using the schools as a site to deliver services hard to obtain in many communities has been a recurring idea. Students face a variety of health problems, from untreated chronic issues to simpler problems, such as poor uncorrected vision, that harm academic work. Unless they are covered by Medicaid and accessible in their communities, students often do not receive care for problems that affect their school performance. There have been decades of small experiments with schools that offer in-school clinics and other services.[68] From 1990 to 2003 there was an organization called the Collaborative for Integrated School

Services at Harvard. Now the Harvard Education Redesign Lab is advocating similar approaches, and there are local efforts in a number of communities.[69] A 2000 analysis reported that there were forty-nine different initiatives across the country, thirty-six of which claimed academic gains, with a significant number reporting fewer suspensions, more parent involvement, and other improvements.[70] More recently there have been a number of community schools offering a variety of services.[71] Although seemingly a simple idea, it requires a great deal of coordination among a number of agencies that have their own sites and procedures, professional training, budgets, and primary goals. These efforts need support and administrative commitment from local officials and agencies outside the schools. They probably would have the best chance of making a major impact within a much broader antipoverty initiative or targeted federal or state program. The schools, on their side, often feel overwhelmed with meeting existing commitments. This highlights the difficulty of replicating, piece by piece, the resources that middle-class families already have. It is important to make this part of school reform and to try to combine resources from a variety of programs and external support to expand the capacity of struggling schools to help struggling students and their families. When it can be done, it can be an important resource. There is, however, a great deal of work to do to achieve serious implementation and uncertain academic impacts.

The ultimate version of multidimensional collaboration came with the development of the Harlem Children's Zone, which grew out of a center for children and families founded in 1970. In 1999 the Zone devised a plan to try to serve thousands of children and families in a twenty-four-block area in central Harlem, the heart of Manhattan's African American community in an area with three thousand children. The program included the Baby College, designed to help parents with preschool children develop their talents. The goal was to help entire families, including by providing adult education and employment services as well as health care and social work support. By 2009 it was running twenty programs "using more than 1,500 staff members and reaching about 8,200 young people." The Zone was spending more than the city's public schools in its Promise Academies and another $5,000 a year per student for all of its supplemental services, and it operated in a beautiful new school.[72] President Obama hailed the Harlem Children's Zone as a national model in his 2008 presidential campaign, calling it "an all-encompassing, all-hands-on-deck, anti-poverty effort that is literally saving a generation of children."[73] Obama pledged to make it a national model and replicate it in twenty cities.

The Zone was featured as a major solution in the widely distributed documentary *Waiting for Superman*, which presented it as a transformative success.[74] The Zone received strong Wall Street backing of about $15 million per year until the Great Recession and had a large endowment fund.[75]

The history of educational reforms shows that many have little measurable impact on academic success. The Zone's schools, according to an important analysis, did not show test results better than the typical charter schools in New York, which did not have the multiple services attached. According to a Brookings Institution analysis of the overall educational impact of the Zone, it was in the middle level of New York charter schools. An analysis by Harvard scholars of the Zone's own charter school, which had the students for twelve hours a day and a longer school year, indicated that there were significant gains, but another analysis, by Stuart Yeh, showed that there were high levels of teacher burnout and attrition and that, given the scarcity of teachers willing to work that intensely, it was not a viable model of widespread use. An enormous long-term effort involving exceptional expenditures, it certainly provided much better services for children and families in a small area, but its educational impact was uncertain and its feasibility as a model was low.[76]

The federal government began to issue planning grants to replicate the efforts in 2010 and then awarded five-year implementation grants to forty-seven organizations, universities, and other organizations to try to create "Promise Neighborhoods." The initial grants had a maximum of $6 million and a limited duration. Many communities that submitted plans did not receive grants. There were no new grants for several years until 2016 and 2017. The funding was very modest compared with the annual budget of more than $70 million for the Harlem Children's Zone.

A 2014 report to Congress on the program by the U.S. Government Accountability Office concluded that there was little reliable data and few concrete accomplishments to date.[77] Although the Harlem Children's Zone was a far better funded effort developed over a period of several decades, it still faced obstacles inherent in coordinating multiple interventions with large staffs in communities with populations that deal with many problems and move in and out of the community. At best, this kind of ambitious effort, which tries to create middle-class opportunities in a community segregated by race and poverty and populated by many families dealing with their own multiple crises, is a costly and long-term enterprise. Doing this on a large scale nationally would involve large expenses and require strong local leadership and buy-in by local agencies and the schools. Such projects that have comprehensive goals recognize the multidimensional barriers that families face. They are, in their nature, hard to evaluate because of their complexity and long time horizons. How do you judge the value of individual elements of a multidimensional plan, and how can you access the dimensions of leadership needed to create real coordination, raise and administer resources, and sustain the complexity over time? A comprehensive community development effort launched near the end of the Johnson administration, Model Cities, only got through the planning stages, was rejected by the Nixon administration, and was shut down.[78] These multidimensional efforts respond to real needs but are extremely complicated and require talented leaders and major funding over a long period of time in a political system that runs on short-term cycles and favors simple, politically attractive efforts. The Harlem Children's Zone is clearly an important model showing the challenge of making up for all that the children and the community face.

Making Counseling Actually Available

Students of color often need academic, personal, and college counseling and social worker support. Compared with students from families and communities with more resources, these students often have the least information and often lack advice at home or in the community about preparing for college. They may face discrimination or disinterest from other students and even some teachers in their school. There is evidence that good counseling can help keep students in school and expand their prospects. Many students need advice and support in dealing with problems of abuse and violence, foster care, homelessness, substance abuse, probation, threats of family deportation, and many other personal challenges. There is extremely limited counseling and social work available in most high-poverty high schools, and little of counselors' limited time is devoted to college counseling. There has been little financial aid counseling, though putting together the information and forms families need to file to get essential aid can be all-important in college choice. Experiments show substantial impacts on college applications, aid, and college enrollment from targeted efforts to increase information and to build into school operations the steps that middle-class families typically take on their own. In Oakland, for example, the Future Centers in some schools produced substantial increases in four-year college enrollment.[79] Getting admission and aid is a complicated process, and students need information and advice throughout. It is very important that those schools have dedicated college counselors. Surprisingly, many counselors have no training in that field. Usually budgets focus on teachers in classrooms and the policy makers, coming from contexts rich in information and networks of support, truly do not understand the tightropes many students face in the process and the ease with which opportunities can be lost.

Transforming Dropout Factory Schools

There are high schools that are toxic for students' future, schools where a large percentage of students drop out and few have any success in college. Schools that persistently show such results should be closed or reorganized, reformed, and closely monitored. Students should be given information and counseling about transfer alternatives. There has been substantial progress in reported graduation levels for students of color in more recent years thanks to a major movement that began around 2000 and has had many organizations involved, but there are some questions about methods including "credit recovery," which allows students to make up failed classes online or in summer programs. Putting pressure on graduation rates has the great advantage of forcing a focus on the kinds of students who need help and were sometimes transferred or pushed out to raise average test scores, but the response can be counterproductive if it is based on shortcuts that produce good statistics but undermine college preparation. The 2015 Every Student Succeeds Act directs the states to pay special attention to the weakest schools.

Two of the common responses to such pressure have been closing the schools and converting them to charter schools—neither a good response. The school closure method was widely used, for example, in Chicago, where research has shown that the closures hurt the neighborhoods and that the students often were transferred to equally weak or worse schools, disrupting the lives of many students in ways that made things worse. A major study found significant negative impacts on the achievement scores of the students who were displaced in the largest school closure effort in the country, in Chicago in 2013.[80] The research shows that charter schools typically perform no better than similar public schools and the process of making them into charters subtracts resources from the public schools. What is needed is major transformation of weak schools by a deep, lasting reform that develops and supports strong principal and staff collaboration or converts them into effective magnet schools with a trained faculty, drawing diverse students from a wide area.

Helping Students from Immigrant Families
and Non-English-Speaking Homes

The U.S. has its highest share of people born in other countries in a century. With about a fifth of students growing up in non-English-speaking homes, it is very important for high schools to help these students. Though they can often speak English fluently, understanding and writing, critical for college, can pose challenges. Most immigrants since 1980 have been Latino and Asian, the first predominantly nonwhite immigration in American history. Asian parents, on average, have arrived with much higher levels of education than Latino immigrant parents, who, on average, have arrived with elementary education. More than 70 percent of the students from non-English-speaking homes speak Spanish at home, and most are in highly segregated schools of concentrated poverty. Although more than nine-tenths of Latino students are citizens born in the U.S. and speak English, many have parents who are undocumented. Millions of young people have been living in very threatening circumstances in the U.S., fearing loss of parents or deportation to their parents' country.[81] Since Latino students now account for more than a fourth of all U.S. students and are demographically replacing declining white enrollments in many districts and states, it is extremely important that the schools understand and relate effectively to these students, their families, and their communities. Since the students have, on average, attended weak schools highly segregated by ethnicity, poverty, and sometimes home language, and their parents often lack the language skills and education to participate effectively in schools, the schools play a critical role in addressing their special educational needs and communicating with the parents, who often have little or no information about the higher education system.

Strong academic English for college-level work is one important goal for the students. The high schools need staff who can communicate to parents and others in their native language. Students may be strongly motivated by ethnic studies courses emphasizing the history and culture of their group. There are special programs such as Puente that provide academically oriented classes and programs within comprehensive schools to create a critical mass of students to support each other in academic work and help them aim at college. Parents often have little information about college, financial aid, and prerequisites, so it is important to reach out with information and to answer questions and clear up misinformation on cost and aid.

Providing College Experiences and Contacts during High School

The high schools that educate privileged students tend to have strong connections to college. Those students live in communities where knowledge about getting ready for college is abundant, with parents who have gone to college. Such students have grown up in the assumption that they will as well. Everything about the high school is designed to produce a clear highway to college. High schools for students of color tend to be very different. Most of the parents do not have knowledge about college, and the teachers and staff are often much less optimistic about their students' destinies. The assumption often is that students who graduate and go on will go to the local community college, where few successfully transfer to universities.

There are a number of AP courses in many middle-class schools, for which many colleges will give college course credit, giving the students a head start toward college completion. These courses tend to be far more available in schools with well-prepared students. They can further increase inequalities. Many students from leading high schools apply to college with several AP courses completed with high test scores. AP course grades are often counted higher, raising GPA and class rank, which is very important for admissions. There are efforts in many communities to offer more AP courses, but often few students pass the tests at the level required to receive college credit.

Students need to know of broader possibilities, how to prepare for them, and how to access them. There are a variety of programs beginning with the long-standing Upward Bound summer college experiences, one of the programs created long ago by the War on Poverty. Volunteer groups and mentors try to connect and inspire students and give them some key precollegiate skills. The Puente program identifies students willing to commit to extra effort and creates and supports a college-bound group in a high school with many Latino students. It has shown clear benefits. There are a variety of programs that try to create early interest in science or teaching. Unfortunately, these programs have resources to reach only a small fraction of students.[82]

One method to connect students directly is the dual enrollment plan available in some states and districts, which allows students to take classes in local colleges for credit at no cost, proving to students that they can do college work. One important option is the Early College high schools or middle schools, often located on college campuses. These programs make college visible and accessible and build students' confidence and motivation to apply. There are positive evaluations of their benefits. There are many such organizations, and, of course, those that are well developed, evaluated, and organized represent the best bet. Many programs are often disproportionately used by successful white and Asian students, increasing rather than reducing gaps. There need to be efforts focused on students of color to create the kind of knowledge and connections middle-class white and Asian students and families usually have.

Using Housing Policy to Increase Opportunity

Housing policy is outside the purview of most education policy considerations, but so many of the issues this book discusses are directly linked to where students grow up and go to school. Compared with costly and imperfect educational programs, it might be much more effective, when possible, to move entire families to areas with good schools where the students will be put in a radically different setting, not as outsiders but as residents. That is what white families with means do. In recent years there has been powerful research by leading economists documenting the large lifetime harms of growing up in segregated, high-poverty neighborhoods. Students growing up in such neighborhoods experience far less success in later life, controlling for other factors.[83] Separate and unequal neighborhoods are the building blocks of unequal schooling, and policies for housing diversity could increase opportunity. Across American society, school opportunity heavily depends on where you live in terms of specific school attendance boundaries, and the lines that divide the many school districts in our metro areas mean that if you know a family's address, the school district, and the family's race, you can make a reasonable estimate of the level of school opportunity their children will receive. Housing prices and housing marketing strategies are strongly related to school districts and schools. Successful families of color usually own homes in area with weaker schools than white or Asian families with similar incomes because of limited information and discrimination in the real estate and mortgage lending professions.

Anything that can be done to make it possible for families of color to live in these neighborhoods can create access to better schooling opportunities. There is a small percentage but a significant number of Black and Latino families who can afford to purchase homes in areas with strong schools but often do not live there. Housing counseling and vigorous action against racial steering and discrimination could help. Housing segregation produces a lack of knowledge, contacts, and information about schools.

Subsidized housing is a small share of the housing market, but it is very important for low-income people of color and their children. Typically, subsidized families live in segregated areas with weak schools. The largest federal program for building subsidized housing gives builders a large subsidy to construct low-income housing, but a recent study of where this housing was going in Southern California showed that it was being built in areas with very weak schools.[84] Fair-share regional plans, in which each jurisdiction has some responsibility for affordable and subsidized housing provided and marketed to families of color as well as local residents, could make a difference for many children. There are a few communities and even states that do require some affordable housing in any substantial new development. The important thing for school opportunity is that housing is placed in an area with strong schools.

A requirement that the housing, which typically includes both state and federal subsidies, be located in areas with strong schools and be marketed equitably to families of color would be a positive move for college preparation for students of color, producing students whom colleges would be eager to admit. State governments could adopt such standards for projects receiving state subsidies. Unfortunately, under the Trump administration there was a serious retreat on fair housing regulations.[85] President Joe Biden revived efforts and appointed a new secretary of Housing and Urban Development, Marcia Fudge, who, as a member of Congress, sponsored legislation providing aid for school integration initiatives.

What we need in our changing cities and metro regions is collaboration between school and housing and civil rights agencies. Since the first great migrations of people of color into our urban communities about a century ago, we have experienced such vast resegregation of thousands of what were, for a time, diverse communities and schools without building any major positive strategies to produce better outcomes and lasting integration. Resegregation has consistently been harmful, destabilized communities, and led to disinvestment, frustrating the hopes of both longtime residents who want to stay and newcomers of color who want the kinds of opportunities and schools that white and Asian middle-class families usually have. Stably integrated communities and schools have better and more positive outcomes on many levels. With coordination between housing and school authorities, gentrification could produce effective diverse schools, enable more of the established residents to stay, and provide more opportunities for city students of color. There have been possibilities and some efforts for collaboration for decades but very little investment of resources and leadership sufficient to produce positive outcomes.[86] A serious housing policy connected to school opportunities could change lives, open up communities and schools to excluded families, and help support integration.

Bringing Down the Wall of Cost

Step by step, without any overall plan, we have arranged the financing of college opportunity in America in a colorblind way that perpetuates racial and class inequality. We've locked ourselves into a system based on grants that are far too small for poor families, loans that are both too big to pay back and not enough to cover costs. It's a system of complexity and lack of information that forecloses key opportunities and creates burdens that affect the entire lives of students, especially students of color. It is a system that serves the short-term interest of almost all colleges but undermines the long-term interests of American society. It is a system that is patched together and tries to cover up the selfishness of a society where people in the prime of life elect officials who keep their taxes down but will not finance the kind of affordable educational opportunity for young people that they earlier received. It reflects a political bargain between kinds of higher education institutions and shows that policy makers see helping middle-class voters as the highest priority. It creates a maze for families and fosters misinformation that confuses and dispirits many young people seeking higher education. Money should not determine outcomes, but money does. People of color have much less money. The changes needed are large and start with a clear set of basic principles and priorities discussed at the end of this chapter. The most fundamental is that all groups of students, regardless of their family income, should have genuinely equal opportunity to attend four-year public colleges and universities for which they are qualified.

If we allocate college access and choice on the basis of family resources and then greatly increase the cost, it creates a massive, often impassable wall excluding a great many students of color. We live, of course, in a capitalistic society. If you do not have the money or the credit, you cannot buy the product, and if you do not pay back as required by a contract, you will face major long-term problems in many aspects of life. This is understood in business, but making higher education into a business is an entirely different thing. Should market conditions limit young people who do not understand the papers they are signing, the choices they have, and how they may strongly influence their lives, sometimes radically limiting their opportunities? Should we make this the only choice for families of color who have dreams but the fewest resources?

Part of the conservative triumph that took hold in the Reagan years was to radically limit the role of government in U.S. society and transfer functions to the market in the belief that government was incompetent and markets would produce better outcomes. This happened to higher education in ways that made lasting changes. The big changes were largely colorblind. They said nothing about race but did particular damage to the prospects of students of color.

Traditionally, educational opportunity has been a highly important public goal in a country where the public sector is much more limited than in most peer nations. Education has been seen as central to progress. One of the remarkable actions in the midst of a terrible civil war was to set aside public land to fund public higher education. State universities and colleges have long been central elements in each state. The U.S. leadership in creating mass higher education has been analyzed as a central part of the enormous success of the country in the post–World War II period.[87] Today, in a global economy where higher education is crucial for both individuals and nations, it is vital to consider the social consequences of policy and understand that raising the education level is a priority for the entire nation, not just for individuals. Losing that focus can make the higher education system a force to perpetuate inequalities and limit the development of our greatest untapped asset—young people locked at the bottom who could have very productive lives. Multiplying the cost of college since 1980 has done bad damage. For some it has just slammed the door.

In an economically polarized country where most of the young now are from sectors that were historically excluded or poorly educated, the consequences of raising the economic wall are stark. To assume that the market will make this work is to assume the absurd. The market raised prices, benefited those with more assets and information about its complexities, and often used the resources of each institution in a way that maximized its total return, not the achievement of social goals or its own mission statement. Since 1980 the U.S. has converted public higher education from a heavily subsidized state activity into a market, greatly cutting the value of grants to poor students and moving subsidies to the middle class. Through unregulated student grants and loans, it fueled the development of a large for-profit sector, largely marketed to students of color but producing very disappointing results and large debts for both students and the government.[88] In this process, what had been a strong focus of federal policy on the poor and racial minorities has been greatly diminished. Money, by itself, cannot fix the problem of inequality, but there is a money wall around college education that made it worse. The conservative revolution in higher education policy has not worked out well for students of color or the institutions that serve them. In fact, it hasn't worked well for much of the middle class either. These problems helped push the issue into the highest level of national politics in 2020 and the early Biden administration.

The cost barriers take many forms, starting well before students even apply to college. Families with resources tend to live in areas with stronger schools (except families of color who face real estate and mortgage lending discrimination). Their children tend to have more AP and honors courses. They can invest in test-prep courses and multiple test taking to maximize scores. They often visit campuses. Some get active help in preparing applications. The costs of entrance exams and applications to multiple colleges can be prohibitive for low-income families (and schools often provide no help or information on applying for fee waivers). It is difficult for many families to figure out how to provide the needed information at the necessary time to qualify for financial aid. The impacts cumulate.

Educators think of education as an investment, not as a product, as a great opportunity, not an albatross. From the early days of the Land-Grant College Act, there was the idea of creating higher education on a much broader basis than was the tradition in European societies, education that was affordable, practical, and accessible. In the 1960s and 1970s there was a great expansion of public college spaces available at relatively modest costs and the creation of a major role for the federal government in making college available to poor students and ending the history of racial segregation in separate Black and white public colleges in nineteen states. Rates of access to college converged. There are many debates among economists about the degree to which financial aid and college costs shape opportunity for students of color. There are a variety of simultaneous changes affecting students across time, but the basic sequence is notable: "In 1970, before Pell Grants, African-American high school graduates attended college at a rate that was 7.12 percentage points below the rate for whites; but Pell, along with other policies, helped remedy this differential in five short years. By 1975, there was nearly equity in college enrollment rates for high school graduates, with African-American and white high school graduates differing by less than one percentage point, while Hispanic high-school graduates actually had a higher rate than whites (by 3.2 percentage points)."[89]

The Reagan administration cut the share of college costs funded by the Pell Grant and opened a significant gap that has grown now for four decades. The 1980s began a major shift from the idea of affordable colleges and strong financial aid as a right to the conception of college as a personal investment and a shift from the focus on grant aid to poor students to reliance on loans, and there was far more focus on tax subsidies for middle-class students. The coverage of college costs for the poor declined radically during the Reagan-Bush-Clinton twenty years and never recovered. In 1981, under President Jimmy

Carter's last budget, "the maximum Pell Grant covered about 80 percent of the costs of attending a public four-year college; by 1999, it covered about 40 percent."[90] The Obama administration was able to use the stimulus funds in the recovery from the Great Recession to significantly increase the Pell Grant at the outset but was unable to maintain the gains as college costs rose and the budget tightened, though it expanded tax subsidies for student debt. (Tax subsidies, though just as costly as grants, are much easier to enact since they don't show up in the budget and do not have to be appropriated each year. They become entitlements.) The conservative attitude toward college aid was apparent in President Trump's budget proposals. In his first year, Trump had called for sharp cuts in the TRIO student support programs, a freeze on the Pell Grants, and a $487 million cut in Work-Study dollars. When the budget was settled, however, the TRIO and Work-Study program funds were restored. In his second budget proposal, the president called for a big cut of $4 billion in student aid programs. He called for ending the federal subsidy for loan interest payments during college, speeding up repayment times, and ending the public service policy that forgave loans after a decade or more of public service work. Trump proposed a long-term freeze in Pell maximums, ignoring the inflation in college costs.[91] These Trump proposals did not become law but reflected the conservative attitude. The Biden administration entered with very different priorities, and Biden proposed a $550 increase in the Pell maximum in the Build Back Better plan, a significant gain but much less than the doubling he had promised.

Soaring Costs Raise the Wall

College has become an extremely expensive opportunity for most Americans, and if you do not have or cannot get the money, you cannot participate. If families do not understand how to get the available money or are not ready to deal with major debts, their choice is limited. You may decide not to go to college or "underchoose," enrolling in a college that is far less demanding and prestigious than you are academically eligible for. You may leave college without completing because you cannot pay the bills or because you've taken on so much work off campus that you cannot keep up with your studies or you cannot get the grades needed to renew the aid.

One of the keys to the situation's racial impact is that white and Asian students, on average, come from families with vastly larger wealth to draw on in supporting their students. Incomes differ substantially by race, but the gaps in family wealth, also very important for college investments, have been truly vast. The U.S. Federal Reserve reported on the statistics for 2019, before the pandemic: "Black and Hispanic families have considerably less wealth than White families. Black families' median and mean wealth is less than 15 percent that of White families, at $24,100 and $142,500, respectively. Hispanic families' median and mean wealth is $36,100 and $165,500, respectively."[92] Families and extended families, especially grandparents, with wealth have many ways to help support students and new graduates, provide safety nets, and help launch them as adults. Relatives often provide assistance. If you have a network of resources, you are in a fundamentally better position than if you had a network without resources and with family members who needed help from you.

Data collected from freshmen at hundreds of four-year colleges and universities in 2016 showed that most students worry about financing college (56 percent) and an eighth (13 percent) have major worries. The study discovered, "One-quarter of Latino (24.7%) and 22.0% of Black students also have 'major' concerns about their ability to pay for college compared to 9.2% of White first-time, full-time students."[93] Additionally, "In 2016, a record 15% of freshmen felt they could not afford their first-choice institution—that's a 60% increase from 2004. In addition, the proportion of first-time, full-time students rating 'not being offered aid by their first choice' as a very important factor in selecting their college has more than doubled from 4.4% in 1984 to 11.5% in 2016."[94]

Cost, or perceived cost, helps determine whether students go to college and what kind of college they decide to go to. This is particularly clear for students of color. In national surveys of college freshmen, students of color report cost as the number one consideration in college choice. Often these students apply to only one college, and often it is the lowest-cost nearby community college. Students and families without information often do not know the differences among colleges, have little information about costs and none about "net cost," and understand little or nothing about the complex financial aid system. Often they think that the only way for a student without very high grades to get a scholarship for college is to be selected for a sports team or to go into the military and become eligible for the GI Bill after service. A 2019 Gallup survey of admissions directors showed that they saw financial aid as having a very powerful impact on students' choices. When asked whether student debt worries were causing students not to enroll, 82 percent of admissions officials said yes, 72 percent at public and 91 percent at private colleges.[95]

The combination of high costs, fears of debt, and lack of information leads many students who could go to four-year public colleges to go to the local community college. They or their parents made that choice without any understanding of the great additional risk they are taking in going to a college where students are far less successful in completing a bachelor's degree. (There are also many, largely unstudied, students who do not go to college at all because of perceptions of costs. They do not get into the data sets used in devising and assessing college policies, data that only include students who enroll somewhere. Some of them join the military in hope of an eventual college degree, but delaying college tends to seriously diminish the probability of finishing.)

Marta Tienda points to the disproportionate level of Latino enrollment in community colleges compared with whites with similar qualifications and notes the "formidable personal obstacles to completing a degree" among these students, who "are more likely to combine work and school, often assuming family responsibilities while enrolled."[96] Patricia Gándara and Frances Contreras explain in *The Latino Education Crisis* how money worries affect decisions: "Many believe that college is for 'rich kids,' not kids like them and that no matter how well they do in school, it will not be a realistic possibility. Many low-income students are reluctant to place the burden of financial support on their parents, and even feel torn about the idea of not entering the workforce directly after high school to help the family financially. Lack of money shapes students' thinking about what is possible and limits their ambition and the choices they make."[97]

One notable impact of the severe economic problems caused for lower-income families by the pandemic of 2020–21 was a substantial decline in college going by low-income students, many of whom probably had to help out with families facing devastating economic losses.[98] This was especially true for families of color who faced disproportionate job loss and the necessity of students taking dangerous "essential services" jobs to help support the family. The decline was dramatic for schools serving lower-income students, while the highest-ranked colleges experienced a large surge of applications in the midst of the pandemic.[99] The pandemic demonstrated the medical and economic advantages of white and Asian families in many ways as more-educated workers could work safely at home while others lost jobs and small businesses and took dangerous jobs requiring unprotected risks. The college-going statistics showed the same pattern. It was a sharp reversal from the increasing enrollment of low-income students before the pandemic.

As previously mentioned, many lower-income students fully qualified for admission to four-year colleges end up instead in community college with far less chance of eventually getting the bachelor's degree the vast majority of students aspire to. It is often called "underchoosing," but families facing a lack of money often see no real choice. A 2018 report by the National Student Clearinghouse found that of 1 million students starting at a community college, only 60,000 got associate's degrees or certificates and successfully transferred to another school and 350,000 others transferred without a degree. The transfer rates differed widely by race, with half of Asian and white students transferring to a four-year campus but only a fourth of Blacks transferring, and a third of Latinos.[100] When students or parents made a decision based on cost, it often reduced long-term prospects. An examination of transfers of community college students from segregated high schools to the vast California Community College system showed extremely high attrition in the first year and extremely low transfer rates.[101] Students from weak segregated high schools often enroll in the nearby community colleges, which have low transfer rates, another reflection of geographical segregation. Community college levels of success are stratified too much like those of high schools. Seemingly routine choices can have huge consequences.

Research shows that the students who are most likely to finish start college right after high school and go to a four-year institution. Many students of color decide to take a pass and go into the military in the hope that they can eventually go to college with the benefits available to veterans. In the contemporary military, that has often meant repeated postings to combat zones. One of the failures of most higher education policy discussions and reports is a lack of information about the college-age population that did not go to college at all or the young people who think military service is their only chance but never collect after wartime experiences. Starting college late lowers completion rates because of the break in study, disruptive experiences, family duties, and other obstacles. Unfortunately, only a small share of veterans attain a bachelor's degree through the program in spite of generous benefits, and a substantial share of those who enroll go to low-quality, for-profit colleges.[102]

Loan Effects Are Not Race Neutral

The shift from grant aid to low-income students to guaranteed federal loans was primarily motivated by the political need to help middle-class students who could not afford the soaring costs of public colleges as state governments cut taxes and cut higher education funding, authorizing colleges to raise tuition to make up for the losses. It was an intergenerational shift of burden as a generation that had received low-cost college education cut its taxes and shifted the costs to the next generation. Guaranteed student loans for the middle class were not intended to replace the funding of students from poor families, but they have shifted the balance of federal expenditures, including tax expenditures, away from the poor. The arrival of conservative federal and state governments in the 1980 election, which cut state and federal revenues, also cut grant funds' role just as a serious recession and tax cuts hit the states, triggering big tuition increases. The problem was that the grant aid for poor students, which had in its early years covered most of the cost of a four-year college, fell greatly as a share of the actual cost of going to college, so poor students faced the need to rely on student loans, larger loans for typical students of color than white students.

Students of color start with poorer families, often with an obligation to help others in the family. They typically take longer to finish college because they have been less prepared in inferior schools. Many who go to a weak, often for-profit, school end up with a credential that is not respected in the job market, which gravely weakens their ability to repay the debt. Those who receive degrees with similar titles often have less success getting jobs and lower average salaries if they get them, reflecting continuing job discrimination. These factors tend to make it far more difficult, and often impossible, to pay the loans. Because the law makes it extremely difficult to forgive student loans in bankruptcy, unlike the vast majority of other debts, there is often no exit. So a seemingly colorblind policy can have drastic long-term impacts that limit students' future lives.

Dartmouth professor Jason Houle concluded that fifteen years after college, Black graduates had almost twice as much average student debt. Analyzing graduates from 2001 to 2005, he found that "student debt contributed to a substantial minority of the black-white wealth gap in young adulthood."[103] A study by Brandeis researchers found that after twenty years, white graduates had, on average, paid off 94 percent of their loans but Black graduates still owed 95 percent of the original amount as interest and penalty payments mounted. Forty-three percent of white students took no loans but only a fourth of the Blacks graduated without debts.[104] Additionally, a study by Mark Huelsman of Demos followed students for twelve years after graduation.[105] The study concluded that white students were far better off financially and much more likely to have received outside help in dealing with the costs. Whites were about three times as likely as Blacks to receive substantial inheritances or gifts.

Student loans, Huelsman concluded, had "benefitted some, and been harmless for others, but . . . left a trial of financial wreckage for many."[106] The racial differences were stark. White males had paid off an average of 44 percent, but most Black males had defaulted on repayment and were facing collection processes and the typical Black woman owed 13 percent more than the original loan. The impact of defaulting "can ruin credit and prevent them from getting an apartment or a job, and can wipe away a portion of paychecks, tax refunds, or Social Security payments."[107] A system that has enabled many students with more family resources to finish college and pay off loans often leaves students of color in a quagmire.

Race-Based Scholarships

One of the most important factors in dealing with the financial needs preventing students of color from enrolling in high-quality, four-year institutions is understanding the depth of students' financial need and the inability of colleges to provide aid packages that even come close to meeting the full costs students face. Many colleges, when implementing affirmative action or carrying out their duties to remedy a history of racial discrimination, developed special scholarships targeting Black, Latino, or Indian students. If you want to break down stereotypes and fears among potential students of color, most of whom need substantial financial aid, an excellent step is to advertise special sources of funding, as Arthur Hauptman and Patricia Smith conclude: "The most obvious and direct strategy for helping minority students is to expand the number of, and funding for, programs that help only minority students. In a similar fashion, a portion of the aid available through certain programs might be limited, or earmarked, to minority groups of students. . . . It is also the case that targeted programs of this sort tend to provide higher levels of support services for the aided students. . . . Therefore, it may be the case that minority-only programs would result in greater persistence of minority students."[108]

A 2007 study drew data from a variety of sources and reported that these programs were widespread and had "grown steadily":

The number of states reporting they have programs that are either race-conscious or race exclusive have grown steadily. In 1984, 16 states reported at least one program. Most of these states reported specialized programs for both African Americans and Native Americans. The total number of states reporting programs grew to 31 in 1996–2001. In 2003, 30 states reported having these programs even though legal challenges were being raised by this time. It is also important to note that the number of race-exclusive grant programs also increased substantially during the period . . . , as did the total number of programs. Most states with a program had more than one such program. Between 1984 and 2001 the number of race exclusive programs grew from 22 to 55 and this number only dropped to 53 by 2003. In contrast the number of states that had race-sensitive programs grew from 5 in 1984 to 15 in 2000 and dropped to 12 by 2003. These trends in the number of state programs that consider race as part of the award criteria reveals that the emphasis on race-conscious programs has increased.[109]

These programs represented a special invitation to students of color to consider colleges trying to overcome a history of white segregation and to take a chance in a setting where they might be isolated and feel uncomfortable at first. It was using money to overcome history.

The logic of the programs was that it was both far cheaper and more effective to reach enough students of color to create campus diversity through a program that was reserved for them and advertised to them. The regular need-based scholarships had not done the job. Racially targeted scholarships were included in many remedial plans required under the 1964 Civil Rights Act to remedy generations of discrimination in states with racially separate higher education systems. These seemed to be sensible strategies, and there had been a history of colleges operating many scholarships left by donors for specific nationality groups or regions. As the attack on race-conscious efforts grew, these scholarships came under attack, especially in conservative administrations.

The appointment of conservative judges changed the courts, and there was a strong conservative majority on the Supreme Court by the end of the 1980s. Any kind of race-conscious policy was challenged by federal civil rights officials during conservative administrations and by conservative legal action groups. There were threats of federal regulations declaring grants designed for minority students illegal during the George H. W. Bush administration.[110] In 1994 a program for Black students at the University of Maryland was struck down by the Fourth Circuit U.S. Court of Appeals.[111] Though that decision was binding only for that circuit, it had a national impact, especially after review was denied by the Supreme Court.[112] The decision was cited by the George W. Bush administration in its guidance to colleges. Following this decision, action was taken against colleges by conservative administrations and legal action groups that sent colleges threats of litigation.

The basic idea in the legal and political attack on race-conscious policies is a radical colorblind individualism, as if there were no group differences that needed to be taken into account. In fact, opponents claim, it is illegal to consider any systemic differences that are clearly related to race unless policy makers can prove that they originated in intentional decisions to discriminate against an entire group on the basis of race. From a civil rights standpoint, trying to prove what was in the mind of officials making decisions that hurt people of color is an almost impossible challenge unless officials confess or a damning document is found. The important thing is to change the outcome of deeply entrenched practices that have the clear effect of perpetuating unequal college opportunity. The most committed ideological opponents simply argue that the consequences do not matter; considering race is simply always wrong, by definition. During a break in my testimony in the University of Michigan affirmative action case, for example, I stopped by the table of the opposition lawyers and asked them why they were doing this case, given the extreme segregation and inequality of schools in Michigan, which limited any fair chance for preparation for college for most Black students. They responded with an absolute principle of colorblindness, regardless of consequences.

In 2019 leading lawyers working for prominent national higher education organizations advised colleges to minimize or end race-specific programs to avoid legal risks. They noted that there were "strict legal standards" limiting any use of race in providing student aid. "Consequently, race- . . . [or] ethnicity- . . . exclusive aid, if used, should be a very limited portion of the overall institutional aid program and be justified by documented evidence showing a strong need" to avoid serious risk to the institution.[113] In other words, what had been seen as an essential part of successfully integrating colleges was now a risk of litigation against your school. It was a very clear example of the imposition of a colorblind policy limiting or ending race-targeted remedies that worked.

Bankruptcy

Bankruptcy is a drastic process in which someone facing debts that are impossible to repay gets a lawyer and goes to court. The court examines the facts and, if they meet legal standards, distributes available resources to debtors and cancels the other obligations, giving the bankrupt person a chance at a new start. It is, of course, devastating to the person's credit rating and has many other negative consequences, but it frees the person from endless harassment from competing creditors, each trying to get something from a person who doesn't have enough to pay, even to the point of seizing part of his or her income or retirement funds. It is a new start that gives the person a second chance at economic survival and eventual success. It's considered a necessary element in a market economy. President Trump, to cite an example, used this process several times in his business career. Ironically, the federal law, supported at the time by Senator Biden, was written to make it less possible to be released from a student loan than from the purchase of a yacht, an expensive car, a purebred race horse, or a personal airplane. He later reversed his position and his administration favored change.

Congress decided in 1976 to forbid discharge of college loan debt for a period unless the former student could prove "undue hardship."[114] In a key federal court decision in 1981, "undue hardship" was defined in such extremely limited terms that it was virtually impossible to meet and almost no cases were filed, no matter how desperate the former student's situation was.[115] By 2005 both federally insured and most private loans to students were virtually excluded from relief in bankruptcy proceedings.[116] This created a situation in which student debt was more crushing and permanent than any other major debt, even though it was taken on by young people for a good purpose and they made their best efforts to repay it. Given the extreme difficulty a large share of Black and Latino borrowers had trying to pay these debts, they could limit economic possibilities for the rest of their lives. The costs of bringing a case and the probability of losing meant, according to one study, that "99.9 percent of all bankruptcy filers with student loans do not even attempt to discharge them, such is the perceived difficulty of doing so."[117] The differential impact of the bankruptcy law is yet another part of the financial wall around college. A basic idea of the bankruptcy provisions was to protect the government and, later, private banks from defaulted loans, a colorblind idea, but in our racially polarized society with huge economic gaps, the policy had racial consequences, harming the future especially of young men of color and their families. The reality was that, for example, most Black men and a third of Latino men ended up in default and faced both crushing impacts on their credit ratings and endless harassment about unpayable debts.

For-Profit Colleges

The development of federal policy built around scholarships and loans for low-income students, without initial academic requirements for the students or serious supervision of the institutions whose students were funded, opened up the possibility for rapid development of colleges owned by investors and committed to maximizing profits by obtaining the maximum federal grant and loan money from students while providing minimal services, using dollars for advertising and enrolling students, and paying big dividends. Often they heavily targeted students of color for recruitment, told them they would be admitted without tests or qualifications and they needed no cash of their own, and offered little or no explanation when signing students up for Pell Grants and the maximum federally insured student loans.

The for-profit colleges were a boom-and-bust story that, for a considerable time, soaked up a disproportionate share of federal aid money with deeply disappointing outcomes. The existence of an open-access funding process for anything that called itself a college meant that it was possible for private investors to create "colleges" with few permanent faculty members and none of the costly overhead of libraries, student support, residential facilities, or major athletics, building their entire operation around federal aid and loans signed over by heavily recruited students, some responding to glowing national television ads. It was an open door for high profits and academic fraud. Schools became hot, high-leverage investments as they developed a large cash flow with limited start-up costs, sprouting instant pop-up "campuses" near freeway exits across the country. The concentration was on signing up students and getting them to, at the outset, sign papers for the maximum federal student loans and grants. Students signing an array of forms to register at the college may well not have had any understanding that they were incurring substantial debts that could never be forgiven even if they never got any degree.[118]

A major Senate investigation in 2012 found massive abuses.[119] The report found that the federal government was spending about a fifth of its massive aid budget on these schools, the largest owned by Wall Street corporations and hedge funds that were racking up annual profits of almost 20 percent a year although more than half of the students they enrolled were gone without any degree or certificate within about four months. The schools invested massively in recruitment and little in student support services, and they relied overwhelmingly on part-time faculty members. They rarely charged less than the maximum possible federal aid, and they enrolled about two of every five service veterans using the GI Bill funds in these institutions. Their former students had a very high default rate, costing the federal government billions annually.[120] These schools left large numbers of students of color, especially Black ones, facing long-term debts and defaults. The Obama administration took dramatic action against some of the largest chains in 2015 and 2016 by cutting off the eligibility of their students for federal aid, which produced an almost instant collapse of hundreds of campuses that had no reserves and were almost completely financed by an ongoing flow of federal dollars. President Trump appointed Betsy DeVos, a major investor in for-profit colleges, as secretary of education and the Obama rules were reversed.[121] For-profit colleges were the result of other colorblind policies that created a disproportionate impact on students of color. Under DeVos, Obama's decision to forgive student debts incurred at these schools was reversed, but President Biden, in turn, forgave hundreds of millions in debts.

Many colleges are diverting institutional aid from helping low-income students to foster enrollment by students who can pay much of the costs through institutional policies and financial strategies that are "colorblind" but work against students of color. Very few U.S. colleges have sufficient funds to underwrite the total cost of attendance needed to finance college for low-income students. Many colleges, particularly since 2010, have experienced problems meeting enrollment goals to generate enough tuition and fees to meet the colleges' financial needs. Instead of using their funds to aid poor students, many use much of that money to give tuition discounts, in effect partial scholarships, either to students who are able to help increase the college's selectivity in terms of high test scores or to students whose families are able to pay at least a substantial part of the tuition, helping the colleges' budgets. Many colleges are also giving priority to high-paying students, especially out-of-state or foreign students. Admissions offices, in a 2019 survey, were trying to increase enrollment of out-of-state and international students who could pay high tuitions. Fifty-seven percent of public admissions leaders said that they were trying to increase of out-of-state enrollments.[122] Both of these policies tended to work against students of color and in favor of white students, as did preferences offered in many private colleges for children of alumni and substantial donors. None of these policies said anything about race, but they channeled aid and access to higher-income, more white and Asian groups.

College in the high-tuition era is a complex market where expertise matters, and it is especially risky for those with little information. While some families have ample savings, including tax-sheltered savings accounts that have enabled them to accumulate value tax-free for their children or grandchildren, most families and most students have few savings and millions have no net worth— they owe at least as much as their assets. The financial condition of families in terms of wealth, or net worth, varies much more dramatically than income, and so do resources available from other relatives. A policy that will work for all the major sectors of the country has to come to terms with those differences.

As they prepare for college, students and parents need to understand the real costs, the impact of college type on completion, the fact that there is financial aid available on the basis of need, and as much as possible about selecting colleges and applying for them. They need to understand about campus jobs, the tradeoff between finishing and working too much, what can be done about day care, parking, and many other important issues for students with limited budgets. They need to understand that AP classes and joint high school–college programs can produce significant credits before enrollment, cutting the overall cost. Unfortunately, they are most likely to get good information about these issues in strong middle-class high schools and communities. Policies that help to equalize the information gap through college counseling and support could help.

The central financial obstacle is that the basic need-based federal program, the Pell Grant, now covers far too little of the actual cost of attending a four-year public university, but the most visible political issue is student debt. The Democratic Party presidential campaign for 2020 brought into sharp focus the promises of various candidates to forgive debt and to provide "free college." Usually this means no tuition for all students or for some categories of students with greater need and fewer resources. Some colleges or state governments have already provided free tuition for families up to certain income levels or free tuition to two-year colleges, many of which had free or nominal tuition in earlier periods. Sometimes continuing the free tuition requires that students maintain a certain level of grades or credit hours completed to remain eligible in the following years. President Biden promised to double the Pell Grant and took a modest step in that direction.

The free tuition movement has generated remarkable interest since 2017; it is simple, it addresses an obvious problem, and it eliminates the rising "sticker price" that has discouraged many low-income students and their families from applying to college. But tuition is not enough. We must address the total cost of college attendance. Eliminating tuition overall means, of course, spending money on aid for many students who do not need it, something that should come after we have genuinely effective aid for students who cannot succeed in college without aid that goes far beyond tuition. Free tuition would become an entitlement, and it would be hard for government to control future tuition changes. Many countries have had free tuition but extremely unequal outcomes, as had California's community colleges, which had free tuition for many years. The University of California had a long tradition of free tuition until Governor Ronald Reagan's administration, though there were growing fees. So did the City University of New York until the city's great fiscal crisis in the 1970s. Obviously, free tuition would be only part of a solution, but it would certainly be well worth considering how to do it with the right definitions and targeting so it would be part of an effort that would genuinely take down the wall of cost for the least advantaged families and students. The racial effect depends on how policy is designed and administered.

The full cost of college attendance includes books and supplies, transportation, and, most important, room and board and related costs such as health care and childcare. Economists often talk about the cost of lost income while studying. Many low-income students of color are in a situation where they get no help from home and have to contribute. Students from weak high schools may also need to take fewer credit-bearing courses, at least until they acquire the needed experience and skills, increasing costs and prolonging their time to graduation. Too many scholarships require a certain grade point average, which may be a serious obstacle, especially at the outset of college, for students from the weak high schools that educate most students of color, or those who need to spend a great deal of time working. If aid is expanded but still means that families without significant assets cannot close the gap, it may not work or may create severe stress. Students often feel pressed from all sides.

The politics of federal aid to students is dominated by institutions. Student aid is more essential to colleges as tuition has become a larger share of their income and students cannot come without aid. Since the federal government decided a half century ago to aid higher education for most colleges primarily by aiding their students' ability to pay costs, all colleges are concerned about how aid systems work. All types of institutions want more aid for their students, including the public and the private ones, the research universities and the second- and third-tier schools, the community colleges, the graduate and professional schools, the technical schools and business schools, and the for-profit schools. There is also an enormous demand for help from worried middle-class families and for relief from the debts former students have already incurred, which are shadowing their life choices. Immense amounts of money are involved, and the result has been a set of compromises that give something to everyone and, over time, shift aid from the poor to the middle class, from appropriations to tax subsidies. In this process, expectations and entitlements have grown up that make changes difficult. It doesn't work well, but it is deeply rooted and hard to change. It will take serious leadership turning the spotlight on the structural costs of the status quo to break the traditional pattern, which has a long record of failure to achieve equity for students of color.

Priorities

If we are to make financing higher education more equitable, the most basic change should be the establishment of a clear priority—making attendance at a four-year public university by qualified students possible independent of income and wealth and making that unambiguously clear to students and families, thus attacking both the cost barrier and the perception barrier that lead families to "underchoose" or not go at all. The first step would be a large increase in the Pell Grant so that it would cover significantly more than half the total cost of attendance at a four-year public university. (It covered about 80 percent at its peak but now only about a third.) The Pell, together with manageable guaranteed student loans and a modest contribution from work and family if they can afford it, should make it possible to get a bachelor's degree in a public university. All students and parents should be counseled in advance about the ability to sign up for a program in which their total loan payment would be a modest fraction of their adult income in excess of basic necessities for a fixed number of years. It might be best to make this the default arrangement unless students explicitly choose a traditional method after being instructed about the implications and risks. The Pell Grant, together with state aid for extremely low-income families with no net assets, should cover the full cost of attendance at least for the first year. There should be incentives for states and institutions to help make this happen and rewards to states and institutions that significantly equalize access independent of income and wealth. Financial aid offices should have a pool of discretionary funds to deal with the extraordinary problems that many low-income students of color face. For community college students, coverage of the nontuition costs of attendance, which are often far higher than tuition, is particularly important.

None of this will work well without a greatly enhanced system of counseling in schools where most of the parents are not college graduates. Students whose parents are graduates and who are usually in schools with a real path to college have, on average, much better understanding of the steps they must take to go to college. Low-income high schools tend to have very limited counseling and counselors have many other responsibilities. There should be funding for trained college counselors focusing exclusively on college in all high schools.

There are a number of efforts but not national policy to cover the costs of entrance exam testing and application fees for those with financial need. Testing companies and colleges have procedures for exemption from the fees, but few students and parents know about them. These costs can prevent families and students from accessing opportunities that could change their lives. Aid should be provided and the procedures for receiving exemption from fees for testing and applications made simple and widely publicized. For example, students receiving free lunches or families on food stamps should be automatically told that they are covered.

Financial aid forms are complicated even for parents who are professionals, and aid applications have deadlines that must be met or there will be no aid. Parents need good early information explaining that most aid is based on need, not cut points on grades or tests. Mistaken beliefs can have devastating impacts. Schools and community organizations should provide help for parents in filling out financial aid forms, advice that could be provided in part by bringing in parents and others with business and financial experience. Many parents who are not homeowners or have not gone to college themselves see student debts as impossibly large. It is very important that parents have an opportunity to discuss this and receive information about the earnings gains that typically come with college degrees. Parents also urgently need information about the danger of enrolling their children in for-profit institutions with bad completion rates, maximum indebtedness, and virtually worthless degrees. All colleges need to provide much better financial aid information, explained as simply as possible on their websites. In a country where about a fifth of children are growing up in homes where another language (Spanish in the great majority of cases) is spoken, their families need concrete information in their language and people to talk to.

The Work-Study program was created during the War on Poverty to enable poor students to earn part of the cost of their education with on-campus work heavily subsidized by the federal government. Over time it has moved away from its original goals. It has been poorly funded and allocated to individual colleges without regard to relative need, with a disproportionate amount going to selective private colleges. Little goes to community colleges where the poorest students are concentrated. It should be allocated more on the basis of need and considerably expanded since on-campus work, appropriately time-limited, is the best work option. Working with faculty can be especially positive for academic integration into the heart of a campus. These programs should be expected to enroll a substantial share of low-income students of color in these valuable opportunities.

There needs to be more flexibility in financial aid administration. If students are admitted and enrolled but financially destroyed by a family tragedy, there needs to be flexible funding available that campus professionals can use to keep the student enrolled. If a student is not eating enough, cannot buy books or materials, has no computer, or has no place to sleep, full participation is not possible. Flexible money is needed to address the kinds of problems middle-class people almost never encounter. It is also essential to help meet problems that Sara Goldrick-Rab and colleagues have documented, reporting hunger for a significant number of college students.[123]

To deal with the wall of financial need, we need a system of aid that is built around the real situation of students from low-income families, often families with serious problems, rather than a colorblind one that starts out with middle-class assumptions. The fundamental reality is that the financial aid system is not adequate in general for lower-income families and has not been adjusted for the special and different situations of families of color. Failure to make those adjustments can have effects ranging from discouragement to simple exclusion to lifelong debt and can prevent successful students from completing their course of studies, exposing them to serious risks. If we are to take down the third wall around college opportunity for students of color, it must be a central goal informed by and administered with real understanding of our students of color, their schools, their families, and their communities.

These priorities should come before any focus on debt relief for students who have already graduated. Those students were victims of governmental decisions to shift costs from the states to the students, and they are an angry and powerful political constituency, as was apparent in the 2020 presidential campaign. Debt relief is an important goal for their families' future and it deserves action, but it does nothing to increase the access of students from impoverished families. It should not be funded before there are funds for the truly essential resources that allow poor people to attend.

Another thing that is badly needed is continued, vigorous action against for-profit campuses that offer minimal services and that have few students graduate and get jobs. That should include action against such colleges that suddenly shift to nonprofit status to avoid being closed by regulators. It is also important to amend the bankruptcy law and regulations, under consideration in 2021.

During the 2020 presidential campaign, there were promises made about reducing debts for college graduates carrying heavy burdens. Since this generation has larger college debts than any earlier generation and many are experiencing fewer choices in their lives for homeownership and other basic goals, this is a very popular pledge and a very expensive one. This is treated as a college aid policy, but it is actually a debt relief policy that would only be available to former college students. The largest debts often come from the most competitive colleges, whose graduates tend to have considerable economic success. Such relief would obviously be immensely useful to many young graduates, but this should not be considered as college aid unless it is a promise going forward. For it to be equitable, there ought to be debt assistance as well for families not fortunate enough to have college training and debts but owing other public agencies.

My major concerns are twofold. One is that free tuition is not nearly enough for low-income students who face all the other costs, especially on residential campuses, and it would be only a tiny part of the true cost of attendance at many low-cost community colleges. Assuming that there are limits to the budget, the fact that much of the money would go to people who don't need it and that it would become an entitlement that would be very hard to change are large problems. At worst, if it did not cover other expenses, it would not permit students from families with no resources to go but would be a nice subsidy for many who can well afford the costs. If this were to be done on scale as it is in some peer nations, it would require a massive continuing commitment. It would be a good step toward a fundamentally different system that made all education as free as the public schools are.

The reality is that the financial aid system is not adequate in general for lower-income families. Its colorblind assumptions in a profoundly unequal society raise damaging barriers for families of color. Basic rethinking and big changes are needed. Many students of color come from families who lack any significant resources to help them and often need help beyond normal assumptions during their college career. There are millions of U.S. families who regularly report that they have virtually no cash in the bank even for small expenditures, families who have no or negative net worth, and their children feel obligated to help when they cannot afford either the time or money it takes to help or they take truly serious financial risks that may well damage their future. We need to start with the realities of the lives of families of color in our changing and stratified society and rebuild policies in ways that actually work.

Conclusion

We are failing to educate and to give success in higher education to the large majority of students of color. Most college-age students in many parts of the country now are people of color, and this will be true nationally in the near future. These students are an absolutely necessary part of our future, and the future of our country will be weakened if we fail to develop our most important resource, a large share of the potential talent of this generation. Our failure perpetuates a profoundly stratified society that opens us to dangerous racial divisions. We haven't had serious civil rights reforms to equalize opportunity for a half century, and we have moved dangerously backward on education equity. We have let our colleges become powerful instruments that perpetuate stratification. This book argues that this can only be resolved by recognizing the powerful racial barriers that still stand and addressing them directly if possible, or with informed sensitivity if it is not. If we do not do that, we are likely to make an unacceptable situation worse.

Some major higher education and public school policy changes, however, have actually increased barriers and inequality.[124] Dramatically raising tuitions; ending school desegregation and equitable magnet school plans; ending free transportation to desirable schools of choice; reversing federal policy guidance that supports voluntary integration and efforts to limit school suspensions; shifting more net expenditures to private school subsidies; creating course requirements that block some students from graduating; closing schools and disrupting communities without providing better alternatives—all these are among the negative changes. Those trying to decrease the gaps and increase equity need to work to reverse such policies as well as initiate new, positive programs and policies.

Research documents deep, multidimensional racial barriers to college for students of color. Unless policy recognizes the realities and tries to change them, success is very unlikely. Colorblind policies will often deepen inequality since they rest on a fundamentally inaccurate understanding of our society.

It may seem absurd to some readers to read so much about policies unlikely to be adopted in the foreseeable future. This book was written after the Supreme Court had been pushed even further to the right by President Trump's appointments, obviously imperiling affirmative action, voting rights, and other central race-conscious policies. At the same time, we have the first administration in a half century that has seriously spoken out on issues of persisting racism following the nationwide demonstrations in 2020. The book starts not from the question of feasibility but from the question of necessity. Are we to have a reasonably fair opportunity for students of color and for our society to develop the talents of a huge sector of American society that has never had genuinely equal opportunity? The responsibility of the researcher, especially the civil rights researcher, is different—to tell the truth, using the best available research, no matter how overwhelming the resistance to a solution might seem. This is exactly one of the reasons why academic freedom is so important.

There are rare historical moments when society recognizes that something must be done and then the improbable becomes possible. Knowing how large and how interrelated the problems are should make people realize that affirmative action in college admissions by itself must be defended but is a very limited overall policy and that we need to think far more broadly. Anyone who has been in the college access discussions for a number of years knows that the same ideas, sometimes with different names and slight modifications, constantly appear, decade after decade, are embraced, and do not work. Recognizing and addressing the underlying realities, even partially, could be far more successful. Often discussions are ended by the argument that the federal courts will not sustain color-conscious policies, but that should never be the end of the discussion. Conservatives took up the cause of reversing broad civil rights policies when there was a virtual consensus in their favor, and we are now living in a judicial setting framed by their success. Supporters of high school and college opportunity can do no less. They should start with what is actually needed to solve deeply embedded racial inequities and then strategize about how to change the laws or win court approval for policies that are essential if colleges are to realize their declared missions of opening knowledge and preparation to all groups, fairly.

We need policies that upend, not legitimize, stratification. We need vision like the vision that gave us *Brown* and the great reforms of the 1960s. We have much greater wealth and knowledge now, but we've been stuck within failed concepts and parameters. Millions of Americans have been treating college opportunity as if it were a zero-sum game in which someone has to lose for every new one who wins. But college is a positive-sum game in which all can win and society can become stronger.

After nearly a half century of studying, working on, and evaluating civil rights policies and racial change, I am deeply saddened at how little progress we have made. It is disturbing to see how satisfied most successful Americans and leaders are with the racial status quo. The reality is that discrimination and subordination have always been basic features of our society. Now, at the last stage of a white majority, it has become self-evident that our only choices as a society are elevating people of color or declining as a society. Our educational institutions are on the front line in shaping our future. They are falling far short. The implicit choice is to continue the status quo with minor adjustments.

I do not belittle or disparage the intent and the dedication of the many people and groups who have launched initiatives and created new possibilities for groups of students. It is hard work, and things would be worse without these efforts. But the reality is that though the major institutions and policy makers almost always affirm the values of diversity and fairness and they often sponsor programs and defend existing policies such as affirmative action, they don't change normal operations or institutional culture significantly. They seldom seriously evaluate the results. They assume that because of their good intentions and because some people of color support an initiative, it is effective and sufficient. Appointing a person of color as vice provost or assistant superintendent for equity doesn't solve it, especially if that person is not given power and resources to make serious changes.

Our government and institutions rarely hold anyone seriously accountable for the continuing failures. If someone manages a campus or a school district into a deficit, that leader is likely to be replaced. If we continue a deficit of opportunity and attainment for people of color, nothing happens at many levels, except occasional reports and modest program ideas and committees. The same ideas and almost the same words come back time after time.

Good intentions are not enough. The danger is that we make a list of good things we are doing, mostly on a modest scale, and move on. We have been doing that for decade after decade, and we have failed to make real progress since the only serious period of reform a half century ago. What we need now are serious plans, regular accounting, evaluation that identifies choke points, and leadership that addresses them strongly enough to show real and continuing progress. This is not a second-order problem. It is a leading part of defining and producing the kind of society we need. We can do much better.

American schools and colleges are not producing fair outcomes. Public schools and colleges affirm equal opportunity but operate in old ways in extremely stratified communities. Few students of color get the best opportunities, and many the worst. Stacks of plans over many years helped some students but failed to change the basic reality. We need more. We are devising policies that ignore race as if we were in another, imaginary, society. Colleges are comfortable making statements but often do not notice how they are falling further behind a racially changing society. The policies produced by the Biden government strongly addressed childhood poverty but allocated only a tiny portion of their vast new expenditures to colleges and nothing to the problems of unequal high schools. The plan allocated 2.3 percent for higher education. The 8 percent increase in the Pell Grant is positive but far too small. Free community college was deleted. In the competition for funds, higher education lost out and high schools were ignored, as often happens in state budget battles. We need a stronger vision, a higher priority, knowledge of racial realities, and to recognize that we need institutions and policies adequate to our new society.

James D. Anderson
University of Illinois Urbana-Champaign

GARY ORFIELD'S BOOK *The Walls around Opportunity: The Failure of Color-blind Policy for Higher Education* makes an extremely convincing case for our need to adopt race-sensitive policies in order to disrupt, if not end, America's long history of racially segregated and unequal education. Race-sensitive policies instituted by federal and state governments are especially necessary to counter the courts' myopic attitudes to pressing problems of resegregation and inequality in the nation's public education system (Anderson 2007). The romantic view of our nation as the inheritor of a colorblind constitution that forbids the use of race-sensitive policies is due in significant part to our tendency to abstract both law and policy from the nation's history of systemic racism. Our contemporary education policy is predicated in general on the belief that a series of federal court cases and civil rights acts ended our history of racially separate and unequal schooling, and that our present is not significantly shaped by a past of segregation and inequality. The primary focus of this commentary is on how contemporary walls around college opportunities for minoritized students are a direct consequence of the nation's history of segregation, desegregation, and resegregation. The first part focuses on the intergenerational denial of high school opportunities for Black students in the American South and the ways in which such gross denial of secondary opportunity built a brick wall around college and, by extension, economic opportunities for the vast majority of the U.S. Black population. The latter part of this commentary looks more broadly at the long-standing harmful effects of institutionalized segregated schooling on minoritized students outside the South. In both parts the primary aim is to demonstrate how our past of segregation and inequality frames the context for race-sensitive policies to disrupt and overturn our long history of segregated and unequal education.

The denial of high school education in the American South serves as a classic illustration of the intergenerational effects of racial segregation and inequity in secondary education. At the beginning of the twentieth century, 90 percent of Africans Americans resided in the South, and the vast majority remained until the great out-migration in the 1960s. Still, in 2019, of the 46.8 million people who identify as Black in America, 56 percent lived in the South, while the Northeast, Midwest, and West were home to 17 percent, 17 percent, and 10 percent, respectively. Hence, the history of systemic racism in relation to college opportunities for Black Americans begins with the repression of high school opportunities in the South and extends to rising segregation and inequity in the Northeast, Midwest, and West. Throughout the first half of the twentieth century, African American youths in the South were largely excluded from public secondary education. In the early twentieth century, the Southern expansion of public secondary opportunities for white students was attended by a concerted effort to deny high schools for Black students. This denial of opportunity, sustained for generations by white-controlled state and local governments, was integral to the systematic campaign to align access to education with policies and practices of Black subordination. For instance, the number of four-year public high schools for white students in Georgia increased from 4 in 1904 to 122 in 1916. At that time Georgia had no four-year public high schools for the state's Black students, who constituted 46 percent of the state's secondary-school-age population. This was not merely an isolated condition of inequality in one state but a complex system of segregation and inequity extending throughout the South. Similarly, in 1916 Mississippi, South Carolina, Louisiana, and North Carolina had no four-year public high schools for African American children. African American children constituted 57 percent of Mississippi's secondary school population, 57 percent of South Carolina's, 44 percent of Louisiana's, and 33 percent of the high-school-age population in North Carolina. The states of Florida, Maryland, and Delaware each had only one public high school for African American students in 1916. Needless to say, access was extremely limited, depending on location and public means of transportation, something that was seldom provided for African American children before the *Brown v. Board of Education* decision in 1954 (Anderson 1988, 1995).

This pattern continued into midcentury. On the eve of World War II, 77 percent of the high-school-age Black population in the South was not even enrolled in public secondary schools and even fewer attended on a regular basis. The system of subordination was even more dramatic in states with the largest proportions of Black students of high school age. In Alabama, Arkansas, Georgia, and Louisiana, more than 80 percent of the Black high-school-age populations was not enrolled in public secondary schools in 1940. More than 90 percent of Mississippi's Black high-school-age population was not enrolled in public secondary schools at the onset of World War II. The war naturally made the situation worse. From 1940 to 1946 the enrollment of African American students in public secondary schools in the South decreased by over 30 percent. By 1948 enrollment trends were again increasing, but more than two-thirds of African Americans of high school age in the 1950s were not enrolled in public high schools. In countless ways the long-standing denial of access to high school education was a key driver in the racial wealth gap, the college attendance gap, and the intergenerational accumulation of knowledge on how to navigate secondary and collegiate education. For example, African American World War II veterans were unable to take full advantage of the GI Bill because of the very low rates of high school completion. In 1940 only 12 percent of African Americans aged twenty-five to twenty-nine were high school graduates, compared with 41 percent for whites in the same age category. The primary cause of this disparity was the deliberate failure of state and local governments to make high schools available for Black students (Anderson 2004).

By the mid-twentieth century, the mounting importance of a high school education made this history of systemic racism more oppressive with respect to the economic futures of African American youths. In the larger society, public secondary schooling emerged as a central part of American life and culture and was perceived by parents as vital to their children's future. The transformation of public secondary education during the first third of the twentieth century symbolized the extent to which schooling had become a strategic part of the national experience by 1950 and was attended by white students en masse. The public high school emerged as an arena of expanding educational opportunities in which publicly and privately supported schemes to locate the talented burgeoned, and scholarship and loan programs for high school graduates were provided with equal enthusiasm. The launching of the *Sputnik* satellite by the Soviet Union in 1957, regarded as the shock of the twentieth century, accelerated the search for talent in American high schools. African Americans, however, were largely excluded from the post-*Sputnik* talent search in Southern public high schools and, by extension, from the education and economic opportunities resulting from high school completion. As the public high school, only marginally a factor in American life at the dawn of the twentieth century, became the "people's college" by the mid-twentieth century, the expanded opportunities for whites were attended by a system of intergenerational exclusion for Black students dating back to the expansion of secondary education in the early twentieth-century South (Anderson 1988).

The 1954 *Brown v. Board of Education* decision failed to achieve substantial desegregation in Southern high schools until 1968. Rather, it sparked a racially separate and unequal system of secondary education designed mainly to allay the *Brown* mandate. The white South in general reacted strongly to the *Brown* decision. Even before the decision was handed down, two contrasting strategies of counterreform were emerging in the South: moderation and massive resistance. Proponents of both strategies were equally committed in principle to a defense of segregation, but they employed different methods to circumvent desegregation and equal access. The more moderate segment of the white South embraced the strategy of moderation or self-reformation, at once conservative in its scheme to preserve racially separate and unequal schooling and moderate in its flexible response to the new demands created by the *Brown* decision. The tactic of moderation, through token compliance and school equalization programs, sought to avoid or at least delay sweeping federal interventions and Black demands for full desegregation and equality. The "massive resistance" strategy, constructed by reactionaries who insisted that any change would set in motion the dissolution of white supremacy, trumpeted defiance. In 1949 Alabama, for example, adopted the moderation plan of its Governor's Committee on Higher Education for Negroes, a plan to provide for the "equalization" of high school facilities for Black youths. However, the bond issue to finance the recommendations for equalization was not approved. In South Carolina, white-controlled state and local governments maneuvered first to postpone implementation of *Brown* and then to determine the token level of desegregation that African Americans would accept in order to sustain traditional Jim Crow schooling. South Carolina's main tactic of delay was to offer African Americans money to "equalize" school facilities, hoping to mount a successful defense of racial segregation with an offer of more equal public high school facilities. To secure Black support for its efforts to avoid racially desegregated schools, South Carolina allocated between 1951 and 1954 about $120 million, of which 61 percent was spent on school construction for Black children, who were just under 44 percent of the state's total school enrollment in 1954 (Synnott 1989).

Ultimately, neither moderation nor massive resistance transformed high school opportunities for African American families and students. In 1960, the eighth grade was the terminal grade for the vast majority of the South's Black schoolchildren. Mississippi, with over 80 percent of its Black population having completed fewer than nine years of school, ranked first in the nation in the denial of high school opportunities to African American children. South Carolina and Georgia, with 79 and 75 percent, respectively, followed. The African American high school generation of the 1960s was the first to have even limited access to universal secondary education. The 1960s expansion of high schools for Black students was part and parcel of the South's scheme to provide just enough equalization of facilities to circumvent the *Brown* mandate to desegregate its racially segregated schools. Although the quality of such things as textbooks, libraries, physical infrastructure, curriculum offerings, and science labs continued to reflect the racially separate and unequal conditions dating back to 1900, even the limited and unequal expansion of high schools positively affected secondary attainment among African American students. The equalization strategy, to the dismay of the architects of Jim Crow schooling, was also attended by a significant expansion of desegregated schools. Following a decade of "moderation" and "massive resistance," the passage of the 1964 Civil Rights Act and Supreme Court decision in *Green v. County School Board of New Kent County* (1968) compelled the South to accelerate compliance with the *Brown* mandate to desegregate its schools. Consequently, beginning in the late 1960s, Black families and their high-school-age students experienced increased access to public high school opportunities.

The relatively sudden availability of better high school opportunities, whether provided by the South's post-*Brown* equalization strategy or compelled by court-ordered desegregation in 1968, immediately resulted in significant increases in secondary school attainment. By 1970, 31 percent of African Americans twenty-five years old and over had graduated from high school, and among younger people (twenty to twenty-four years old), 62 percent were high school graduates. By 1997, 86 percent of African Americans ages twenty-five to twenty-nine were high school graduates, continuing an upward trend in the educational attainment that began with access to universal secondary education in the late 1960s. Indeed, between 1987 and 1997, the gap in high school completion between African Americans and whites in the twenty-five-to-twenty-nine age group narrowed to the point where there was no significant statistical difference. Given the widespread denial of public high schools to Southern Black students from 1920 to 1960, the progress made between 1960 and 1997 represented substantial growth in high school attainment. In the twenty-five-to-twenty-nine age category, the high school completion rate for

African Americans virtually quadrupled from 1960 to 1997, from 21 percent to 86 percent, even as some critical measures of access, such as transportation, accreditation, physical plants, and curriculum, remained largely separate and unequal. The expansion of secondary opportunities enabled African Americans to act on cultural values and aspirations long repressed by Jim Crow laws and institutional arrangements (Anderson 1988, 2004). Further, the educational attainment in desegregated schools was also substantial. As Rucker Johnson (2019) has demonstrated convincingly, the expansion of desegregated schooling in the 1970s and 1980s was substantially successful in raising the academic achievement and educational attainment levels for African American students in the South.

The enlargement of secondary school opportunities in general and the expanded opportunity to attend desegregated schools in particular resulted in the greatest achievement gains by Black students in the twentieth century. Southern Black students, having lagged behind in the availability of high school opportunity for most of the twentieth century, began contributing to overall attainment and achievement in the 1970s and 1980s. The National Assessment of Educational Progress began reporting results by race and Hispanic origin in 1971. For African American, as well as Latinx, students, the annual reports show a pattern of substantial change from about 1971 to 1988. Among seventeen-year-olds, for example, the Black-white gap in average reading scale scores was cut by more than half, from 52 points when the assessment was first administered in 1971 to 21 points in 1988. In math, for seventeen-year-olds, the gap was reduced from 40 points in 1973 to 20 points in 1990. Scholars studying gaps in academic achievement by race and ethnicity focused on the convergence of the Black-white test score gap in the 1970s and 1980s (Hedges and Nowell 1998). The debate over convergence in those decades stands in marked contrast to the debate over the widening of the racial achievement gap that characterized the 1990s.

The debate over that gap paid little attention to the two previous decades of academic progress and thus failed to explain how a long stretch of achievement convergence transformed relatively suddenly into a widening of the achievement gap. It seems quite clear that the significant upsurge in attainment and achievement was driven by the struggles of Black communities to capitalize on the expansion of public high school opportunities created by the post-*Brown* equalization schemes and court-ordered desegregation. Meanwhile, state and local governments waged subterranean resistance to desegregation, did little more than comply with formal civil rights law and court decisions, and, above all else, failed to develop race-sensitive policies to sustain and en-hance the progress so clearly evident from 1970 to 1990. Instead, Southern state and local governments concentrated on schooling, economic, and political matters that undermined campaigns for desegregation. After 1990 the drifts toward resegregation were not only reinforced by racism and indifference but also intertwined with economic and political policies that sustained inequality (Thuesen 2013; Erickson 2016). The lack of race-sensitive policies designed to capitalize on the substantial achievement of the 1970s and 1980s and the underlying failure to monitor and account for efforts to desegregate meant that progress was ultimately transformed into regression. By the 1990s the debate over Black achievement had shifted from test-score convergence to the widen-ing achievement gaps, and despite ebbs and flows in mathematics and reading assessments, the focus on the widening achievement gap has persisted over the past three decades. Clearly, we have not seen in those years the kind of achievement gains that we witnessed in the 1970s and 1980s.

The decline in achievement paralleled the emergence of school resegrega-tion in the South and across the nation. Following the *Green* ruling by the Supreme Court in 1968, the South became the most successfully desegregated region in the country. However, in the early 1990s a series of anti-desegregation rulings by the Supreme Court enabled many school districts to abandon de-segregation plans. More specifically, the Supreme Court rulings in *Dowell v. Oklahoma City Board of Education* (1992) and *Freeman v. Pitts* (1992) enabled the incremental withdrawal of desegregation supervision. Such rulings al-lowed states and local school districts to take measures that had resegregative effects and, on balance, undermined the development of court-ordered deseg-regation that the South had achieved from 1968 to 1990 (Reardon and Yun 2005; Reardon et al. 2012). By the early twenty-first century, both scholarly and news headlines about schooling in the American South focused on the region's transformation from relatively successful desegregation in the late twentieth century to the onset of resegregation at the dawn of the twenty-first century (Boger and Orfield 2005; Hannah-Jones 2014, 2017). Over the course of the twentieth century, the South experienced seventy years of school segregation, twenty years of mainly court-ordered desegregation, and then ten years of resegregation. This transformation brought the region into the twenty-first century, during which a process of resegregation and inequality has taken a firm hold and erected new walls around college opportunities for Black stu-dents. Recently, we have witnessed the end of hundreds of desegregation orders and plans across the South and the nation at large. The existence of formal court rulings and civil equality statutes (e.g., *Brown* and the Civil Rights Act of 1964) is insufficient to halt or reverse the current trends of resegregation. Without the intervention of race-sensitive policies designed to establish and sustain desegregation and equality, the South and the nation are headed toward education apartheid in a nation becoming more ethnically diverse with each passing year (Frankenberg et al. 2019).

We know from the long history of school segregation in the Northeast, Midwest, and West (hereafter referred to as the Northern states) that formal laws of equality will not translate axiomatically into the kind of race-sensitive policies necessary to disrupt and uproot institutionalized segregation and inequality. In places where formal laws forbidding race discrimination date back to the late nineteenth century, we find the greatest concentration of contemporary segregated schooling. Indeed, today New York remains the most segregated state for African American students and California is the most segregated state for Latinx students (Frankenberg et al. 2019). The long history of enduring school segregation and inequality in Northern states serves as a classic example of how structural racial segregation fails to respond to formal laws of equality in the absence of race-sensitive policies designed to disrupt and uproot institutionalized inequality.

Northern states in the antebellum era established laws of racial segregation to deny or restrict education for Black students. During the Reconstruction era, Northern states in general enacted laws banning racial separation in schools. For example, the Pennsylvania legislature in 1881 enacted a law repealing the racially separate school provision of the state's School Laws (Franklin 1974). In spite of the 1881 law banning racially separate schools, the public schools in Philadelphia remained vastly segregated by race. The city's experience is emblematic of the larger pattern of Northern school segregation—that is, antebellum Jim Crow laws—the enactment of formal laws of equality in the post-Reconstruction era, and the steady rise of racially segregated schooling underneath the laws that theoretically banned such segregation. As Northern states established public schools during the antebellum era, the new laws governing public education initially excluded African Americans in the overwhelming majority of school districts. In some states and many local districts, African American children were excluded from public education until after the Civil War. In the few places where they gained access to public education during the antebellum era, they did so in racially segregated schools. Indiana and Illinois limited public schools to white children by state statutes until 1869. Ohio initially limited its public schools to white children and then in 1849 permitted separate schools for African American children. Michigan and Minnesota also permitted separate schools for African American children. In New Jersey, Pennsylvania, and New York, African Americans gained access to public schools on an almost exclusively segregated basis. The Massachusetts legislature, which outlawed public school segregation in 1855, represented an aberration of the racial segregationist trends in Northern states. No other state during the pre–Civil War era replicated Massachusetts's decision to end public school segregation (McCaul 1987; Gerber 1976; Franklin 1974; Kousser 1986).

During the quarter century following the Civil War, most Northern states reversed their pre–Civil War segregationist mandates and enacted legislation prohibiting public school segregation. It is important to note, however, that an underlying commitment to access and equality (substantive equality) did not accompany the postwar campaigns for legal or formal equality. Rather, institutionalized forms of school segregation and racial subordination accompanied the legal reforms for constitutional equality. In point of fact, school segregation and racial inequality persisted in Northern school districts in open defiance of state laws banning racial segregation. As Davison Douglas (2005) has argued, by the time of *Brown*, Northern school segregation was more extensive than at any time since the Reconstruction era. Although the formal legal devices that drew the color line were discarded after the Civil War, these changes scarcely scratched the surface of the broader and deeper commitment to preserving school segregation and inequality. In most places African American students in Northern states remained fundamentally as they were before the Civil War, confined to racially segregated and unequal schooling. Indeed, a 1967 report by the U.S. Commission on Civil Rights entitled *Racial Isolation in the Public Schools* concluded that 75 percent of Black elementary students in America's cities were enrolled in schools that were nearly all Black, meaning 90 percent or more Black enrollment (Franklin 1974).

In spite of post–Civil War laws banning school segregation, Northern states and local school districts proceeded to develop institutional arrangements and cultural norms that fostered racially segregated schooling. While some of what came to be known as de facto segregation was caused by residential segregation, the continuous denial of access and equality resulted mainly from a variety of devices used to maintain racially separate and unequal public schooling. In some school districts, state officials placed African American children in separate buildings on the grounds of a predominantly white school or in separate classrooms in an otherwise racially desegregated school. Some teachers insisted on racial separation within the classroom, requiring segregated seating arrangements in racially mixed classrooms. Many Northern school districts with desegregated school buildings excluded Black students from a variety of extracurricular activities such as athletics, school band, plays, and talent contests. A favorite method of preserving school segregation was the use of racially gerrymandered school district lines accompanied by discriminatory transfer policies that permitted only white students to transfer. Such actions constituted a Northern version of massive resistance to desegregation and racial equality, one that unfolded decades before the South would construct its own version of massive resistance during the immediate post-*Brown* era (Douglas 1997, 2005).

Northern states developed institutional mechanisms to preserve segregation and inequality that would last from the post–Civil War era to today. Two memoirs, one by Robert Carter and the other by Charles J. Ogletree, provide an up-close and personal view of Northern institutional arrangements and customary practices that served to segregate and isolate students of color. In *All Deliberate Speed*, Ogletree (2004) provides an autobiographical and social examination of the post-*Brown* era in his home town of Merced, California. His lived experiences provide a window into the contradictions between formal civil equality laws and institutionalized inequality in Northern public schools. Similarly, Carter's (2005) autobiography provides an inside and nuanced understanding of the contradiction between legal mandates for equality and the persistence of inequality as he analyzes both the limited vision of *Brown* and the "Silent Covenants" that fortified and sustained perpetual segregation and inequality. While recounting his struggles to overcome barriers of racial discrimination during his K–12 school years in Merced in the 1960s, Ogletree recalls a standard form of institutionalized inequality, the practice of channeling students of color into lower academic tracks. In Ogletree's words, "The public school teachers I encountered had developed rather firm views concerning the inability of black and brown children to compete successfully in the rigorous math and science courses. The teachers routinely tracked black and brown students, relegating them to lower level and less challenging courses. Moreover, once students were placed in a lower academic track, it was nearly impossible for them to be placed in a more rewarding and challenging academic track" (2004, 33).

When Carter's family moved to East Orange, New Jersey, during his school years in the late 1920s, Carter quickly discovered a traditional form of racial resegregation within his school building. As he recalled, "The swimming pool in the school was available to black students only at the close of school on alternate Fridays, by gender. To protect the white children from contamination the blacks might have left in the pool, it was then drained, cleaned, and refilled for the use of white students the following Monday. White students had to pass a swimming test to secure the requisite credits in physical education required for graduation. This test was not required for black students. We could secure the necessary physical education credits without exhibiting skill in swimming" (2005, 12).

The perpetuation of institutionalized racial segregation in defiance of formal laws of equality persisted long after *Brown*. In 1973, in the case of *Keyes v. School District*, the NAACP Legal Defense Fund confronted the question of whether Northern school segregation was contrived or was merely the reflection of housing patterns and racially neutral school attendance zones. In Denver local officials had deliberately rigged the Park Hill area to confine its African American children to racially segregated schools. The Supreme Court ruled that the school district could not disclaim responsibility for policies that were "intentionally segregative" and that served, as effectively as any Jim Crow statute might have, to segregate 38 percent of the city's African American school population (Orfield 1978). Among the policies cited were the building of a new school in the center of a predominantly Black residential area instead of on the fringe in order to foster desegregation; gerrymandering school attendance zones so as to contain African American children within the Park Hill district while excluding white students from the district; establishing optional zones on the outer edge of the Black community so that white students nearby were free to choose schools other than those in the predominantly Black district; and excessively using mobile classrooms so that children in crowded African American schools would not have to be assigned to available classrooms in predominantly white schools (Orfield 1978).

The *Keyes* case helped pull the rug out from under Northern school segregation. Similarly, in 1974 a New York district court held that New York City had made decisions "knowing that they would encourage segregation" and had failed to take available steps to reverse segregative tendencies. A 1976 decision by the California Supreme Court found Los Angeles guilty of racial segregation in its school system. Finally, in April 1979 the Department of Health, Education, and Welfare declared that Chicago's school board, since the 1950s, had created, maintained, and exacerbated an unlawfully segregated school system. The institutionalized practice of school segregation in all cities was very similar. Just as Denver did, Chicago located new permanent and temporary facilities in such a manner as to contain Black students within racially segregated schools. The transportation of students, including student transfer programs and busing, was used to maintain segregation. The assignment of teachers and other professional staff was done in a manner that further intensified racial segregation (Orfield 1978; Kluger 1975).

The Northern transition from antebellum systems of explicit racism sanctioned by law to systems of institutional racism in the context of constitutional equality foreshadowed regional and national developments in the post-1954 era, as well as contemporary trends in school resegregation. Together they help us to understand why the post-*Brown* era epitomizes a modern phase in the evolution of constitutional equality that was ultimately constrained by the bureaucratic and organizational dynamics of institutional racism and the underlying cultural norms of racial segregation and inequality. The troubled legacy that has become central to *Brown*'s heritage is the long-standing struggle to bridge the fundamental contradiction between constitutional equality and the day-to-day reality of institutionalized racial segregation and inequality that exist in spite of and in defiance of the law. Reconciliation between formal equality and institutionalized discrimination will require the appropriate race-sensitive policies to transform day-to-day segregation and inequality into equity and social justice.

Although the primary focus of this commentary is on the history of segregation and inequality as it pertains to Black students, it is important to note that students of color in general have similar historical experiences with racism and inequality. The historical educational subordination of Latinx students is very similar to the treatment of African American students. However, most Latinx students lived outside the Jim Crow South and in states where laws generally did not sanction racially separate and unequal schools. Rather, Spanish-surname students were placed in separate but unequal schools or classrooms based on the primary rationale of language deficiency and perceptions of skin complexion.

In a comparative study of the segregation of Black and Chicano students in Oxnard, California, David Garcia (2018) compels us to rethink the usefulness of the historical distinction between de facto and de jure segregation. By examining the residential and school segregation in Oxnard, Garcia demonstrates convincingly that the segregation of Black and Mexican children in the city's schools resulted from deliberate planning by the local government and was as intentional as any segregation mandated by Jim Crow laws. In doing so, he reframes the conventional understanding about the origins, purpose, and intent of de facto school segregation. Clearly, the Oxnard plan of classroom

and school-building resegregation within officially desegregated schools constituted a pattern of de facto segregation in the pre-*Brown* era that was as deliberate and official as de jure racial segregation. In *Strategies of Segregation*
Garcia unearths California's long-standing practices of de facto school segregation based on language and complexion and helps us to understand that California's problems of school segregation are symptomatic of a long-term, statewide trend of Mexican students quietly becoming the most segregated
minority population of students in the state.

In histories of Latinx school segregation, scholars before and after Garcia
document historical struggles against markedly poor-quality segregated schools.
Guadalupe San Miguel (1987) wrote one of the earliest books to document that
Texas, the first state in which Chicanos organized to seek educational equality,
provided the least education for children of Mexican descent while waging a
strong defense of its separate and unequal schooling. Gilbert G. Gonzalez, in
Chicano Education in the Era of Segregation (1990), links the various aspects of
the segregated school experience, discussing Americanization, testing, tracking,
industrial education, and migrant education as parts of a single system designed
to process the Mexican child as a source of cheap labor. Gonzalez argues that
educational policies of segregation for Mexican children in public schools from
1900 to 1950 developed from Anglo racism and the need to keep Mexicans in a
subordinate socioeconomic position. Richard R. Valencia, in *Chicano Students
and the Courts* (2008), documents the historical educational inequities that Chicano students suffered under so-called de facto segregation.

Similarly, Ruben Donato demonstrates that the segregation of Mexican
students in Kansas, though based on nonlegal mechanisms, was just as effective as de jure segregation. Although the school segregation of Mexican
children in Kansas differed from the segregation of African American children
in the Jim Crow South around issues of race and language, Donato documents
the nuanced and customary ways in which various cities in Kansas arranged
to congregate Mexican students in segregated schools. Hence, the history of
the racial segregation of Mexican students in Kansas informs current and
future struggles for education equality as school segregation and inequality in
today's America, like patterns of de facto segregation in the past, are based
squarely on institutional arrangements that persist over generations in spite of
constitutional provisions, statutes, and court decisions aimed at precluding
such discrimination (Donato 1997, 2007; Donato and Hanson 2017).

The long historical processes of legally mandated and institutionalized patterns of segregated and inferior schooling echo the problems of race and

subordination that are deeply embedded in today's system of education in-equality. America remains a nation of racially segregated and unequal educa-tion. In a recent analysis of the Trends in International Mathematics and Sci-ence Study, known as the TIMSS test, David Berliner disaggregates the test performance by poverty and race. He found that America's white students (without regard for social class) are among the highest-performing students in the world. However, says Berliner, "our African American and Latinx stu-dents, also undifferentiated by social class, were among the poorest perform-ing students in this international sample" (Berliner 2006, 963). For example, among twenty-seven industrialized democracies, the average score for white American students in mathematics ranked them third in the sample, while the average scores for African American and Latinx students ranked them twenty-fifth among the twenty-seven nations; only Luxembourg and Mexico ranked below them. It is doubtful that America's standing among the world's indus-trial democracies will improve as long as the fastest-growing segments of its K–12 populations are Black and Latinx students. Indeed, such disparities are likely to be exacerbated by the developing resegregation of Black and Latinx students because racially isolated schools are least likely to have the kind of rigorous and demanding curriculum that undergirds high performance on standardized exams like the TIMSS test (E. Gonzalez, O'Connor, and Miles 2000).

We know from analyses conducted by the College Board that Black and Latinx students have limited access to rigorous courses such as Advanced Placement (AP) courses, even when their prior academic performance pre-dicts success in such courses. In 2012, 954,070 U.S. students took at least one AP exam. Yet most of the potential AP students do not participate. For in-stance, 60 percent of potential AP students do not participate in any of the AP math courses for which they have high potential. The College Board's measure of AP potential data is based on the nearly two million public school students in the class of 2012 who took the Preliminary SAT/National Merit Scholarship Qualifying Test (PSAT/NMSQT) as tenth or eleventh graders. The strongest predictor of success in AP courses is a student's performance on particular PSAT/NMSQT sections. From the PSAT/NMSQT results, researchers can identify students with a 60 percent or higher likelihood of success in particular AP subjects. Based on its analysis of PSAT/NMSQT results, the College Board concluded that three hundred thousand students in the graduating class of 2012 who were identified as having AP potential did not take any recom-mended AP course (College Board 2013).

Underrepresented students of color make up a disproportionate share of the potential AP population who do not take an available AP subject for which they have potential or attend a school that does not offer AP courses. Among students with high potential for success in AP math course work, as demonstrated by their PSAT/NMSQT performance, only three of ten Latinx students, three of ten Black students, and two of ten Native American students take any AP math courses. Hence, in addition to the 954,070 U.S. students who took at least one AP exam in 2012, there were hundreds of thousands of prepared students in the U.S. who did not take an available AP subject for which they had potential or attended a school that did not offer the subject. This is low-hanging fruit for race-sensitive policies that could remedy the intergenerational harm done to Black and Latinx students and weaken the walls around college opportunity for students of color.

There are many good reasons why students of color should be targeted for greater access to AP classes. They may be able to save on college expenses. If their exam grade is high enough, their college may award credit for the course or allow them to skip college introductory classes. But the best reason for taking AP classes is the rigor of the courses themselves, which contributes to college readiness. AP courses are designed to ensure that students are developing the knowledge and skills they'll need to be successful in college. America's AP students in all subjects develop their knowledge of key concepts and practices essential to each subject, including critical thinking, reading, and writing skills. The performance of AP students on the TIMSS test demonstrates the rigor of AP courses. While the U.S. lags behind industrialized countries that participate in the TIMMS test in physics (ranking eighteenth among industrialized nations), American AP physics students who earned exam grades of 3 or higher outscore all other students in the world. Further, while the U.S. lags behind nearly every industrialized country that participates in the TIMSS test in calculus, U.S. AP calculus students, regardless of exam grade, outscored all other students in the world (E. Gonzalez, O'Connor, and Miles 2000). It should be apparent that the U.S. is not likely to raise its academic standing among the world's industrial democracies without race-sensitive policies designed to improve the preparation of minoritized students. One can only imagine how well we would do as a nation if all segments of our K–12 population had equal access to the best schools, curriculum, and teachers. Even a limited set of race-sensitive policies targeting the students who are left behind will move the nation forward and better prepare students of color for college opportunities.

In summary, America's historical record of institutionalized racially segregated and unequal schooling cries out for race-sensitive interventions that will transform a long past of denial and discrimination into a present of equity and justice. It is quite clear that if we continue to drift in a cloud of colorblind romanticism, resegregation and inequality will characterize the education of the increasing majority of American students. This will continue the long-standing harm to students of color and undermine the economic, social, and democratic prospects of a nation whose K–12 population is becoming increasingly a population of minoritized students with each passing year.

References

Anderson, James D. 1988. *The Education of Blacks in the South, 1860 to 1935.* Chapel Hill: University of North Carolina Press.

———. 1995. "Literacy and Education in the African American Experience." In *Literacy among African-American Youth: Issues in Learning, Teaching, and Schooling,* edited by Vivian L. Gadsen and Daniel A. Wagner, 19–37. Cresskill, NJ: Hampton, 1995.

———. 2004. "The Historical Context for Understanding the Test Score Gap." *Journal of Public Management and Social Policy* 10, no. 1 (Summer): 2–22.

———. 2007. "Race-Conscious Educational Policies versus a 'Color-Blind Constitution': A Historical Perspective." *Educational Researcher* 36, no. 5 (June/July): 249–57.

Berliner, David C. 2006. "Our Impoverished View of Educational Research." *Teachers College Record* 108 (6): 949–95.

Boger, John Charles, and Gary Orfield, eds. 2005. *School Resegregation: Must the South Turn Back?* Chapel Hill: University of North Carolina Press.

Carter, Robert L. 2005. *A Matter of Law: A Memoir of Struggle in the Cause of Equal Rights.* New York: New Press.

College Board. 2013. *The 9th Annual AP Report to the Nation.* New York: College Board, February 13.

Donato, Ruben. 1997. *The Other Struggle for Equal Schools: Mexican Americans During the Civil Rights Era.* Albany: State University of New York Press.

———. 2007. *Mexicans and Hispanos in Colorado Schools and Communities, 1920–1960.* Albany: State University of New York Press.

Donato, Ruben, and Jarrod Hanson. 2017. "'In These Towns, Mexicans Are Classified as Negroes': The Politics of Unofficial Segregation in the Kansas Public Schools, 1915–1935." *American Educational Research Journal* 54 (Supplement 1): 53s–74s.

Douglas, Davison M. 1997. "The Limits of Law in Accomplishing Racial Change: School Segregation in the Pre-*Brown* North." *UCLA Law Review* 44:677–744.

———. 2005. *Jim Crow Moves North: The Battle Over Northern School Segregation, 1865–1954.* New York: Cambridge University Press.

Erickson, Ansley T. 2016. *Making the Unequal Metropolis: School Desegregation and Its Limits.* Chicago: University of Chicago Press.

Frankenberg, Erica, Jongyeon Ee, Jennifer B. Ayscue, and Gary Orfield. 2019. *Harming Our Common Future: America's Segregated Schools 65 Years after "Brown."* Los Angeles: UCLA Civil Rights Project.

Franklin, V. P. 1974. "The Persistence of School Segregation in the Urban North: An Historical Perspective." *Journal of Ethnic Studies* 1 (February): 51–68.

Garcia, David G. 2018. *Strategies of Segregation: Race, Residence, and the Struggle for Educational Equity.* Oakland: University of California Press.

Gerber, David A. 1976. *Black Ohio and the Color Line, 1860–1915.* Urbana: University of Illinois Press.

Gonzalez, Eugenio, K. O'Connor, and J. Miles. 2000. *How Well Do Advanced Placement Students Perform on the TIMSS Advanced Mathematics and Physics Tests?* Boston: International Study Center of Boston College.

Gonzalez, Gilbert G. 1990. *Chicano Education in the Era of Segregation.* Denton: University of North Texas Press.

Hannah-Jones, Nikole. 2014. "Segregation Now: Sixty Years after *Brown v. Board of Education,* the Schools in Tuscaloosa, Alabama, Show How Separate and Unequal Education Is Coming Back." *Atlantic,* May 2014.

———. 2017. "The Resegregation of Jefferson County [Alabama]." *New York Times Magazine,* September 6, 2017.

Hedges, Larry V., and Amy Nowell. 1998. "Black-White Test Score Convergence since 1965." In *The Black-White Test Score Gap,* edited by Christopher Jencks and Meredith Phillips, 149–81. Washington, DC: Brookings Institution Press.

Johnson, Rucker C. 2019. *Children of the Dream: Why School Integration Works.* With Alexander Nazaryan. Boston: Basic Books.

Kluger, Richard. 1975. *Simple Justice: The History of "Brown v. Board of Education" and Black America's Struggle for Equality.* New York: Vintage Books.

Kousser, J. Morgan. 1986. *Dead End: The Development of Nineteenth Century Litigation on Racial Discrimination in Schools.* New York: Oxford University Press.

McCaul, Robert L. 1987. *The Black Struggle for Public Schooling in Nineteenth-Century Illinois.* Carbondale: Southern Illinois University.

Ogletree, Charles J. 2004. *All Deliberate Speed: Reflections on the First Half Century of "Brown v. Board of Education."* New York: W. W. Norton.

Orfield, Gary. 1978. *Must We Bus? Segregated Schools and National Policy.* Washington, DC: Brookings Institution.

Reardon, Sean F., Elena Tej Grewal, Demetra Kalogrides, and Erica Greenberg. 2012. "Brown Fades: The End of Court-Ordered School Desegregation and the Resegregation of American Public Schools." *Journal of Policy Analysis and Management* 31 (4): 876–904.

Reardon, Sean F., and John T. Yun. 2005. "Integrating Neighborhoods, Segregating Schools: The Retreat from School Desegregation in the South, 1990–2000." In *School Resegregation: Must the South Turn Back?,* edited by John Charles Boger and Gary Orfield, 1564–1596. Chapel Hill: University of North Carolina Press.

San Miguel, Guadalupe, Jr. 1987. *"Let All of Them Take Heed": Mexican Americans and the Campaign for Educational Equality in Texas, 1910–1981.* Austin: University of Texas Press.

Synnott, Marcia G. 1989. "Federalism Vindicated: University Desegregation in South Carolina and Alabama, 1962–1963." *Journal of Policy History* 1, no. 3 (July): 292–318.

Thuesen, Sarah Caroline. 2013. *Greater Than Equal: African American Struggles for Schools and Citizenship in North Carolina, 1919–1965.* Chapel Hill: University of North Carolina Press.

Valencia, Richard R. 2008. *Chicano Students and the Courts: The Mexican American Legal Struggle for Educational Equality.* New York: New York University Press.

COMMENTARY

Stella M. Flores
University of Texas at Austin

HOW DO WE REDUCE the effects of racial inequality in the nation and in schools that have colorblind policies and practices? This question has been part of the U.S. legal and political fabric since at least the 1896 U.S. Supreme Court decision *Plessy v. Ferguson*, which legalized the separation of the races in public transportation and thus in public spaces more broadly, stating that racial segregation did not violate the Constitution and that federal courts should defer to state policies.[1] Justice John Marshall Harlan, the lone dissenter in this decision, argued that the Constitution is colorblind and therefore that no class of citizen should be excluded from the rights guaranteed by the Fourteenth Amendment. Three years later, however, he joined a decision allowing a Georgia school district to provide no high school education for Black individuals.[2] Although *Plessy* was overturned in 1954 by *Brown v. Board of Education*, this decision set in motion a debate regarding individual versus systemic remedies that included the question whether it was enough to recognize the individual rights of a few Black students to transfer or whether school systems should formulate policies to integrate students, which the Supreme Court held in the 1968 *Green* decision.[3] Ultimately the Court went back to conservative control and returned to their version of a colorblind approach that ultimately forbid systemic remedies to racial segregation.

The spirit of the colorblind approach was noted once again in the 2007 case *Parents Involved in Community Schools v. Seattle School District No. 1*, which barred the use of race as a factor in K–12 public school assignments even when the purpose of the policy was desegregation.[4] In *Parents*, Chief Justice Roberts stated, "The way to stop discrimination on the basis of race is to stop discriminating on the basis of race." He argued against school assignment plans that took race into account for the purposes of desegregation, which illuminates one of the nation's most uncomfortable conflicts: that between its history of formal and informal racial exclusion and its long-held principles of equal opportunity. This highly debated and misunderstood dilemma about the equal treatment of all races and the realities of racial inequality remains at the core of the U.S. education system.[5] The dilemma is further complicated by use (and misuse) of the term *colorblind* as it applies to social and political policies and outcomes.

Gary Orfield's book *The Walls around Opportunity: The Failure of Colorblind Policy for Higher Education* illustrates the historical and contemporary walls facing low-income students of color on the U.S. pathway to higher education. The "walls around opportunity," while once legally enforced, are now seemingly a bit more subtle but may in fact be equally effective in blocking opportunity. Opportunities related to college admissions, financial aid, and the ability to build family wealth appear to be processes and resources that should be legally available to all. They are not, and Orfield provides evidence that one of our most egregious errors as a nation is assuming that these walls of the past have been torn down. We have been living under a colorblind veil of policy that has stalled, and in many cases reversed, educational progress.

This commentary discusses three areas of colorblind processes in educational policy that we must reckon with to move forward as a nation with increased educational opportunity. First, I discuss the myths and multiple layers of colorblind approaches. Included in the lack of attention to the effects of historical exclusion that characterizes such approaches is the lack of policy awareness of the needs and assets of the largest minority group in the nation: Latino students. Next, I discuss the myths and costs of the limited manner in which we have conceptualized financial aid policy—the largest and most expensive college access mechanism, which not only is colorblind but also has transformed into a system of rewarding a narrow definition of merit that is largely tied to generational privileges of race, income, and wealth. Finally, I end with comment on how the educational crises of today and tomorrow are inherently tied to systems of health, justice, and agencies that serve families. In sum, I call for an intersector management of equity that ends with educational opportunity and goes far beyond calls for free tuition and loan forgiveness, however important these calls are in their own right. We will undoubtedly need large changes in policy across multiple sectors. In the interim, we continue to face a context of increasing racial hate crimes, the senseless murders of Black individuals, massive deportation and disruption of immigrant student lives, and the realities of demands to work first and study if there is time in a culture that requires a college degree for any sustained economic security.

The Manipulation of the Colorblind Concept

The definition, motivations, and applications of the colorblind approach have changed over time. By the time the voices of the civil rights movement entered the debate, it was clear that in the colorblind approach, race is ignored for the purposes of excluding people rather than to solidify the rights and opportunities from which minority groups were originally barred. Multidisciplinary research indicates that colorblindness is insufficient in promoting true equity and has no egalitarian effect. Civil rights advocates noted the weaknesses of this approach and called for taking race into account in education and employment in order to ensure that the legal definition of equal rights and privileges as stated in the Constitution was indeed applied.[6] However, it is nearly impossible to change outcomes if the realities of bias and discrimination, historical or current, are ignored or denied.

The legal community, voters, researchers, and educators have continued this debate, most visibly through desegregation cases but also through admissions decisions in higher education. The U.S. Supreme Court ultimately settled the college affirmative action debate on the diversity rationale, which acknowledges that race can be one factor of consideration in admissions decisions made to ensure that all students receive educational benefits by virtue of a diverse student body. However, the Court also noted that the history of racial inequality in the U.S. should not be a factor in justifying these decisions, creating another uncomfortable conflict between acknowledgment of the benefits of diversity and disregard of the history of racial exclusion whereby the benefits of diversity were impossible to achieve. In sum, this was the new compromise reached by the legal community via the 1978 U.S. Supreme Court case *Regents of the University of California v. Bakke,* which has been maintained up to the present, although not without facing numerous forceful challenges that still continue today.[7] Its limits are our biggest higher education elephant in the room. Nonetheless, this approach keeps some form of equity going for now, at least at a limited level.

While policies that purposely created inequality, particularly racial inequality, have not gone unchallenged and have been retracted, Douglas Massey argues that the perceived costs associated with retracting racially exclusionary legislation that benefited whites led to the creation of more subtle methods of maintaining a privileged social position.[8] These alternative methods, though legal, still carried the harmful effects of opportunity hoarding, exclusion, and, in education in particular, promotion of a false narrative of the need to maintain a fair, meritocratic process of equal access to a college education. As policies evolved to become more inclusionary in theory or in law, efforts were ongoing to maintain privilege for the groups in power, which required constant, long-term monitoring of discrimination across sectors.[9] In the bilingual education bans in California and Massachusetts, two cases in which harmful policies were retracted, showing some rethinking of the value of diversity in the schools by voters, the two states' education labor markets were nearly depleted of expertise in bilingual education because of the prior referendums to remove it from the curriculum.

Colorblind policy goes far beyond admissions and has levers at the individual as well as the organizational levels. This plays out in the midst of the greatest demographic transformation in the nation, of which Latinos are a critical force in schools as well as the economy. In essence, we are a nation that looks very different from the one in which colorblind principles were originally applied. The country has now become a profoundly multiracial society in which a majority of public school students are nonwhite, as are a majority of all births. Nevertheless, the courts and voters are increasingly directed toward colorblindness as the dominant and preferred racial ideology for governing spheres of public participation and influence. Voter initiatives to deny the right to consider race as a factor in public hiring and in higher education admissions have been passed in at least nine states.

This approach to race relations, labeled by sociologists as the colorblind racial ideology or the colorblind ideal, is based on emphasizing the irrelevance of skin color or race to character, ability, or worth. In this approach, judgments based on merit and fairness are not considered valid if skin color (or race and ethnicity) are taken into account. Finally, not acknowledging skin color is considered an effective way to avoid racial discrimination altogether. In other words, employing a colorblind approach requires one to ignore past and present patterns of discrimination and to rely instead on an individual's behavior and cultural patterns to explain racial inequality. Eduardo Bonilla-Silva labels this the "new racism," which goes beyond individual prejudice to the institutional practices and mechanisms that form a larger system of racial domination and contribute to the subjugation of individuals based on their race or ethnicity.[10] Colorblind policies help the groups in power feel less responsible for their privilege and harm minority groups by creating distrust, stereotype threat, and other negative outcomes. Ultimately, the practice of ignoring race deemphasizes the long-term effects of inherited and persistent inequality. At the organizational level, Caryn J. Block describes colorblind approaches as strategies for affirming the belief that systems treat individuals similarly regardless of race in order to evade interventions forcing changes that benefit excluded groups.[11] Bonilla-Silva refer to these strategies as the evasion of privilege, whereby people who do not acknowledge institutional racism will also not see the unfair advantages they have received because of their group membership.[12] The consequence of this approach is that, if institutional or systemic racism is not part of the diagnosis, then the only culprit is the individual's traits or behaviors. That is, organizational decision makers are not seen as biased, and disparities thus are a result of the internal traits of a particular racial group.[13] The decades of policies that Orfield describes in this book present a stark portrait of a nation employing colorblind policy with the exception of a few decades.

The irony is that colorblind ideology has had to work hard to survive in a changing society that was largely Black and white to the current multiracial population. As the nation has transformed demographically to one where Latinos are the largest minority in the nation's schools and the majority population of the nation's largest school districts, state legislatures have also reacted with language-, citizenship-, and culture-blind policy initiatives arguing that inclusion of these factors in civil rights or equity policies is harmful to the national identity and its claims of fairness. Latinos experience issues of racial inequality, but within this identity are also challenges relating to migration, language, and citizenship. Latinos are the group most likely to enter community colleges, making them the group most in need of successful transfer policies. They also often have the lowest income of all groups or at least are the group least likely to apply for financial aid. They are a complex group, not a monolith of a population. Some nationality groups do experience the privilege of social class, including whiteness inherited from home countries.[14] Venezuelans, for example, are the largest group to have migrated from Latin America over the last ten years. They also represent the group with highest educational attainment and higher wages as reported by the U.S. Census. Mexican-origin individuals remain at the bottom of college completion rates of all the major Latin American groups despite impressive rates of college entry over the last twenty years.[15]

Language proficiency is a concern for school districts around the nation with at least 10 percent of all students classified as English-language students.[16] Speaking a language other than English and having cultural needs outside of a dominant U.S. culture has unfortunately been transformed into a deficit rather than an asset. The evidence, however, is contrary to these notions, as applying an asset-based approach that integrates home language, culture, and caring guidance is likely to lead to higher educational outcomes for Latino students.[17] Overall, the research tells us that there are culturally and linguistically responsive inroads for increasing educational attainment. For example, among Latinos, some language programming is not a sentence for low educational outcomes, as these students outperformed Latino students who were assigned to English-language programming but were waived out of this instruction by their parents.[18] Overall, being an immigrant increases the odds of having higher educational attainment, but the location from which one migrated is one of the largest determinants of this outcome.[19] Our research also shows that among Latinos who are first-generation immigrants to the U.S.—that is, foreign-born but arriving by the age of fourteen—being a naturalized U.S. citizen is one of the greatest predictors of college completion. Finally, state educational policy that sets opportunities or barriers for college access pathways also plays a role in an individual's chances for college access and success. For Latino students, living in a state with both an in-state resident tuition policy (state dream acts that allow the in-state tuition for undocumented students) and Hispanic-serving institutions increases the odds of both college enrollment and completion.[20] In sum, college success for Latino students, the largest minority group in the nation, is highly dependent not only on individual characteristics such as country of origin, finances, and access to citizenship naturalization paths but also on the opportunity structure of state policy that surrounds a student's college pathway. The move forward is not to deny color, language, and culture but instead for colleges and universities to take into account these factors as assets for a multiracial and globally competitive nation. Race-conscious policy is a step in the right direction. As our student populations diversify, it will be important to not be blind to the language, culture, and citizenship stories students bring to the table. When acknowledged and seen as assets, students are likely to flourish in their academic environments. We have reached a time in history when no policy arena should be unaware of the issues facing Latino students. Understanding their assets will help other populations as well.

The Racial Wealth Gap and the Reproduction
of Privilege and Disadvantage

We have told a very limited story of the definition and purpose of financial aid in this nation. Orfield makes three critical points regarding what is essentially the colorblind approach to financial aid. First, he states the obvious, which our financial aid systems have not sufficiently acknowledged: "Starting without the means or extended family support to pay college bills, even with student loans, may make success impossible."

Simply stated, college success requires sustained financial investment, and there must be acknowledgment of the fragile supports that low-income students of color have in their lives when life issues such as health care crises, joblessness, and lack of wealth to cover catastrophe enter daily life. Once they are over the admissions wall, the financial aid wall is one that comes up every year and during times of crisis. Even if some stability becomes possible for families of color, this maintenance is often tenuous and not enough to secure stability for the next generation.

Second, Orfield states that racial inequality has always been a basic structure of American society, yet we form policy trying to change outcomes as if this were not the case. Access to financial capital to pay for college, whether by family income or inherited wealth, or even through popular programs like the GI Bill as initially constructed, is the vestige of a racially exclusionary system. There have been some dents in this system, but the race to make up for generations of inherited privilege or inequality was never going to be a fair game. Ultimately, not acknowledging the realities of students of color, including their families and their histories, will deter and delay making a significant change in access to and through a college pathway.

Third, Orfield argues that higher education quality is like health care in the United States: "Higher education, like health care in America, provides world-class opportunities, particularly at its higher levels. But it is very complex and the choices are very different at different economic levels. In this system, money matters greatly. . . . The lack of money can be decisive, even when the student has great talent and desire."

Like health care at a prestigious and well-resourced hospital, where one goes to college still matters in terms of the formulation of world-class opportunity. College resources can save a student from financial ruin. Ironically, despite its complex nuances, it can be argued that the financial aid system for higher education in the U.S. is perhaps one of the most evaluated and originally equity-intentioned mechanisms in the nation. From its inception in 1965, when President Lyndon B. Johnson signed the Higher Education Act, the federal aid system in the U.S. became the primary route for financial accessibility to qualifying students. Such systems were not as available in other countries for all students, and these efforts became a solid opportunity structure for families who had not yet sent any generations to college. The system has had to adapt to massive increases in the real cost of college, severe cuts in state funding of higher education, deepening inequality of income and wealth, a greatly increased share of nonwhite students, the fact that few colleges award packages of aid that cover the full cost of four-year college, and a sharp decline in the share of the cost of a four-year college education covered by the Pell Grant. In essence, we are seeing the slow failure of this system for the students it was intended to help. Instead, the system has changed to benefit middle- and upper-class families at the cost of low-income families. Meanwhile, many students, particularly students of color, report that cost is the most important single factor in making their, and their families', decisions about college. Black and Latino families are especially reluctant to take on long-term debt that can never be discharged.

What we have now is a system that has evolved significantly in intention and outcomes, with state, institutional, and even local aid occupying bigger shares of distributed financing for students than originally instituted. The result is that, in the forms of aid available as well as the parties eligible, the financial aid system is becoming one primarily reserved for those deemed solely meritorious as opposed to one based on need. Susan Dynarski and Judith Scott-Clayton, in fact, note that nearly half of the federal aid available now goes to tax incentives for families who would likely have invested in college without additional federal support.[21] Universities, through institutional aid, and state governments, through merit-focused priorities, have also engaged in this behavior of including and rewarding the financially capable for more than a few decades, often using aid to offer discounts to students with high test scores and the ability to pay a significant share of the costs. These colorblind, poverty-blind aid practices based on test scores, which are strongly related to parent income and socioeconomic status, work to perpetuate inequality and ignore social divisions and historical realities in favor of the mythical "merit-based" approach.

The 2019 admissions scandal in which parents allegedly paid large sums for special fraudulent admissions for their children as athletes and for illegal help in testing locations was an extreme case of the power of money, which routinely buys special help in preparing for testing and preparing college applications. In fact, many aspects of the life plans of relatively affluent white families, including their ability to buy homes and get access to superior high schools that are very successful in preparing students for college, are designed to provide intergenerational advantages to their children, perfectly legal advantages but strongly linked to financial resources. While merit is not solely a financial commodity, there is overwhelming evidence that money has the ability to purchase the appearance of merit on the path to and through college, and government aid is a growing component awarding the meritorious.

The result is that our national research and policy discussion on poverty and access to financial aid for higher education has destructively, although perhaps not intentionally, left out the role of racial inequality in knowing of, applying for, securing, and optimizing financial aid for college access and success. While financial aid is the most viable potential mechanism for increasing college attainment, it has now been reconstructed as a tool that benefits those with the ability to pay and fails students of color because of its colorblind, merit-focused, individual-behavior approach.

In sum, we have put forth a myth about the enduring power of financial aid in the U.S.: aid for college is earned through merit, or because of need; is maintained through an individual's hard work; and will lead to college completion regardless of where one goes to college. Not acknowledging the colorblind, inequality-reproducing mechanisms of the current financial aid system is likely to slow down further progress toward increasing the college completion rates of Black, Latino, and Native American students. The following are three myths that do not bode well for underserved students of color.

The Three Myths of Earned Merit and Privilege

Not acknowledging exclusionary practice of the accumulation of "merit" and privilege. In regard to some of the meritorious aid, merit is conceptualized as a family commodity that is earned without prejudice or advantage and is instead an inherent feature. A commonly unquestioned version of merit is that it is a family commodity earned through hard work, innate ability, generational maintenance of skill, good decisions, and systemic integrity. In sum, all who participate in the system are treated and rewarded without discrimination and through logical and honorable processes. If rewards are received because of test scores and good academic performance, one secured these merits without special advantages. This perception ignores over a century of legal exclusion of women and minorities into U.S. higher education among other exclusionary practices.

Only the individual accounting of income matters, not the systemic and structural factors that lead to wealth generation. The second myth is that who deserves, receives, and utilizes aid in its various forms can be fully understood through the lens of income and socioeconomic status alone. This perception ignores the structural mechanisms of wealth generation and maintenance over time. It assumes colorblindness in the systems of the accumulation of capital, education, housing and lending markets, criminal justice, health care, and others within society. In sum, it assumes that the structural mechanisms of U.S. society's engines of educational access are without racial and ethnic biases that could disrupt opportunity.

Only investing in the individual and not the institution; not accounting for differences in institutional and state investment related to low-income populations and populations of color (Minority-Serving Institutions). Countless research studies have documented that where one goes to college matters in regard to odds of completion, wages, and graduate school entry. Institutional investment also matters, and enrollment at any college does not mean equal chances of completion. The assumption that it does rests on the tenet that all colleges and states are created equal—that is, that once a low-income student enrolls in college, his or her chances of completion and success in the labor market are equal to those of others with more information and resources, because the institution is a product of American higher education that will have the capacity to nurture the student into a postcollege life. This is inherently linked with the notion that all states invest in higher education appropriate to their capacity and that state policy will invest in all their student populations and voter bases indiscriminately and with good intention.

Wealth as a form of capital has intergenerational staying power for individuals, and a similar pattern exists for institutions with powerful donors, state legislatures, and global reputations. The evidence of why income is not useful as a metric for reducing poverty on the road to college is overwhelming but underevaluated. It is underevaluated because we have built a system that ignores the cumulative advantage of wealth, networks, and historical advantage, factors that feature in the most effective arms race in college admissions and success to date. Tuition, while critically important, is the top of a pyramid whose foundation is the racial inequality gap in wealth.

The Need for Intersector Collaboration to Reduce Inequality and Overcome the Effects of Colorblind Policy

In 2020 we hit a milestone of reality checks with the acknowledgment of the murders of countless Black individuals, the migration crisis of unaccompanied youths at the border, and, of course, a global public health crisis that disproportionately hit people of color, especially Black and Latino families. Our new policy prescriptions will undoubtedly have to take these circumstances into account unless we choose to regress into another era of exclusion and large numbers of deaths.

Educational outcomes are a product of many systemic levers that are both inside and outside schools. From a research and policy perspective, there are therefore key interconnections throughout that should be considered if we wish to move forward in the right direction. First, health care is now a central part of our lives and critical to any normalization of instruction in schools and colleges. The labor market is constantly changing, and community colleges, the most likely point of entry for low-income and minority students, are experiencing declining enrollment. As the labor market transforms in a revised economy that is dependent on a healthy nation, it will be community colleges that will be the center of retraining and job access for many students of color. Second, high schools will continue to provide the most important learning experience on the road to a college degree, but the delays in instruction and lack of resources to reengage in a pandemic reality mean colleges will need to be ready for a generation of students who have experienced a disruption not unlike that caused by other national catastrophes. These effects are not colorblind. Third, communities of color with a workforce highly dependent on the service industry and limited access to health care will likely experience even greater delays in getting on track to college. Meanwhile, technological innovations destined to transform our economy are still in place. These advancements don't stop because of a lack of access to capital and social support systems.

Public policy has never been so important for moving forward as a nation. At its foundation is racial inequality that has penetrated every social and economic aspect of our nation. To be fair, there have been some great successes in reducing racial discrimination and biases, but we have focused our efforts on broad legal restrictions and individual behavior. We have not acknowledged the colorblindness of our social structures that lead to health, education, and economic outcomes. The fact that colorblindness is a vestige of our most shameful period in history and the fact that no sector can perform successfully without the healthy functioning of the other are two truths that we need to carry forward into the future. The walls of public policy sectors ultimately also need to come down to recover and reinvigorate the nation.

Moving Forward: A Reckoning and an Opportunity for a Nation

A key contribution of this book is the exposure of how we have allowed intergenerational racial inequality to persist in the institutions that are supposed to break these harmful cycles with opportunities for a better life. The idyllic

American high school, the ever-welcoming community college, and the highly sought-after world-renowned university have only been a reality for some students and not for others. Moving forward, we need to acknowledge that students do not come to the table with equal opportunity, equitable pathways to make rational decisions about college choice, or safety nets that prevent life crises from dismantling any progress that has been made despite unequal conditions. We also need to acknowledge that the lack of opportunity has fallen, in no uncertain terms, on the shoulders of Black, Latino, Native American, and some Asian student populations.

Given the evidence of this book, there are two institutions that we can prioritize to make the real changes Orfield suggests in the spirit of true civil rights reform: the public high school and the federal financial aid system.

The Public High School

Desegregation efforts have not been in full force or successful for some time now. We have abundant evidence that racial segregation produces deeply harmful results not only at the elementary school level but also at the high school level. In our research examining the factors that contribute to the racial college completion gap in Texas, we found that racial segregation (the percentage of Black and Latino students concentrated in a public high school) accounted for a majority of this gap.[22] While we focus on test preparation programs and information campaigns, all of which are useful levers for college access, the formidable stain of segregation will likely always prevent other interventions from having the effects they should, given their investment and innovation. A new, reimagined plan of integration in the context of anti-integration environments should be considered, and it may require different strategies across state contexts. This is not impossible if, for example, the federal government were to institute incentives for integration plans rather than sanctions for not meeting accountability standards. Each sector surely has something another sector needs (housing, justice, education, economic development), so a multisector agreement on promoting a plan that leads to integration initiatives could be promising. Higher education could have cohorts of precollege students trained during the summers or in apprenticeship programs during the school year from high schools with fewer resources. The goal doesn't have to be entry into that college but could simply be entry into a similar league of schools with an eye toward graduate school. Integrating college *completion*, not just college access, cultures into high schools sets a tone for where students should aim their sights for the long term. A culture of college completion assumes college entry and instead puts full force into the preparation needed to succeed academically but also in the context of family obligations. Many low-income students of color come with incredible skill sets, and framing these as assets to compete and succeed in the world could transform perceptions of their promise and their own efficacy. Finally, students need to feel safe and welcomed, and all sectors play a part in this, not just schools. Being of color in this nation is still seen as a liability. Degrees don't hide our color.

The Federal Financial Aid System

We have sufficient evidence to know the federal financial aid system no longer prioritizes those in need, given the numerous benefits it provides upper-middle-class families and families with some form of wealth, often inherited from previous generations. This is perhaps the most unfortunate outcome from the perspective of the system's original intent. Simplifying aid programs has proved to be indispensable, as documented by financial aid scholars. Simple solutions seem to be, in fact, quite marketable. However, this is not enough for the diversifying population in the nation. The most effective financial aid interventions have often been formulated for English-speaking families or families with some sense of how the U.S. college system works, even if minimal. However, the nation now has many families of immigrant origin. Even if students are U.S. citizens, a growing number live in mixed-citizenship households. Simplicity is great, but it also needs to be translated into many languages. Each state needs to take responsibility for its family demographics.

Palatability is also very alluring. As Orfield notes, programs that are appealing to voters, such as free college, make important contributions, but the reality that students do not come to the table with equal resources means tuition-free has different impacts for populations with different resources. The reality of those who need financial aid is not just about tuition. It's about survival while going to college. It's about insecure income sources and no wealth. For those battling racial discrimination, gender bias, language proficiency issues, and family responsibilities amid financial insecurity, free tuition means a $100 loan for a $50,000 car. The gap will never close, no matter how palatable the program. Palatability is not enough for college completion. Our tax dollars deserve to be spent on effective, not just popular, initiatives.

Loan forgiveness, however, might be a plan that has both popularity and performance power. Such plans have been around in various forms since at least the 1960s, but their operationalization has become more complicated. My own parents participated in these programs by traveling back to the migrant camps where they once worked near the Midwest to teach migrant children after college. The plans appealed to newly educated minorities of my parents' generation. They knew there weren't many like them—Mexican Americans with college degrees. Having more flexible programs that target communities or students of color during and after college could make an important dent in the psychology of loan receipt and the confidence that loans on their own will not be disastrous financially in the long term. Overall, flexibility in financial aid that fits the realities and motivations of students of color now is critical. Today's students are not only more likely to be low-income and minority, but they are also attending college when tuition is no longer affordable. Higher education success will require we design programs that fit the realities of students entering college today and into the future.

Finally, the reckoning we need overall is to acknowledge we are a nation deeply attached to a colorblind narrative that frankly never worked well for people of color. It is a seductive premise that ironically leads to more racial inequality. Ultimately, there is clear evidence for a need for multisector civil rights policy reform for the purposes of educational attainment. It will first require acknowledging inherited privilege and intergenerational inequality. It will then require setting policy to disrupt inequality in systems while allowing for individual rights to prosperity. Finally, it will require implementing and monitoring that policy for long periods of time. The benefit of this is that civil rights policy doesn't have to be a policy that detracts from rights and wealth. When all populations prosper, it could be the strongest economic development policy we could put forth in the next century.

The Supreme Court's Rejection
of Affirmative Action

AFFIRMATIVE ACTION had been operating for more than a half century in the great majority of America's selective universities before the Supreme Court decided the Harvard and University of North Carolina cases in June 2023. The idea that virtual exclusion of students of color from these powerful institutions was a problem that harmed both the students of all groups and the quality of education and that diversity could be pursued by voluntary affirmative strategies had been defended in the Supreme Court since the first test in the *Bakke* case in 1978. The Court had recognized and, to a significant extent, deferred to the judgment and expertise of the universities about the details of admissions, specifying that race could be only one of multiple admissions factors and that quotas were illegal. Successive cases had sustained voluntary race-conscious admissions processes allowing universities to consider race among other factors, subject to strict limitations. Colleges that had previously enrolled very few students of color had become modestly integrated though access was far from representing the population of color. It was a settled part of admissions and had happened every year on many campuses for many years. Now it was forbidden. The Supreme Court took over the admissions offices.

The Supreme Court has vast authority in the American system of government since it has broad jurisdiction and no other authorities can override its decisions in applying the Constitution. Changing the Supreme Court had been a central promise of Donald Trump's successful campaign in 2016, when he pledged to nominate judges selected by conservative activist groups. His rare opportunity to name three far-right justices in a single term turned a closely divided Court into the most conservative high court in nearly a century. Though his top priority was ending legal abortion, the judges selected were extremely conservative and the fact that there already were three justices who had voted to end affirmative action in previous cases meant that another battle was a certainty.

The decision was the product of politics and triggered strong political reactions. The law had seemed settled after two recent Supreme Court decisions, *Fisher I* and *Fisher II*, rejecting challenges to the University of Texas affirmative action plans in 2013 and 2016. The same anti–civil rights group, led by Edward Blum, brought very similar cases against Harvard and the University of North Carolina to the Court changed by three Trump appointees. (Blum had earlier succeeded in litigation that won a major Supreme Court decision in 2013, ending the most powerful of the Voting Rights Act enforcement provisions.)[1] The facts concerning affirmative action had not changed and there was even more research finding positive impacts of diverse colleges and the lack of workable nonracial alternatives. The lower courts held trials and ruled that both of the challenged plans were constitutional. What had changed was the membership of the Supreme Court. Since the 1970s the Republican Party, which has now selected a majority of sitting Supreme Court justices for fifty-two consecutive years, became focused on changing the ideology of the Court through appointment of conservative justices. Nominees have been carefully screened for ideology, in close relationship with the conservative Federalist Society and GOP officials. Beginning in the 1980s, an increasingly conservative Supreme Court had reversed or limited civil rights policies in voting rights, school desegregation, minority contracting, and other areas, but voluntary affirmative action had survived a succession of battles. In both the Michigan and Texas cases one conservative justice joined with the more progressive justices to save affirmative action. The Trump appointments changed the playing field. The Harvard and UNC cases challenged basic assumptions of civil rights laws that required systemic plans to undo systemic inequality. The campaign to expand civil rights law took hold in the late 1940s, reaching its historic peak in the late 1960s and early 1970s. A clear turn backward took hold under President Reagan. After the blocking of Obama's nominee and Trump's appointments, most experts had expected a partial or complete reversal of affirmative action. The 2016 election, heavily infected with racial stereotypes, had made civil rights a strongly partisan issue. When the decision came it was a stark across-the-board reversal. In the 6–3 decision outlawing affirmative action, all of the GOP appointees voted against the three chosen by Democratic presidents. The majority rejected affirmative action and the principles and data that supported it and virtually ignored the research submitted to the Court. The decision discarded the precedents upholding affirmative action and rejected the strong appeals by leaders, civil rights groups, and experts in higher education. Colleges and policymakers need a realistic understanding of the consequences of the extreme politization of the Court and the control of the extreme right, which is now built in for years to come by the lifetime appointments of the justices.

The Court's opinion by Chief Justice Roberts reflected the attitudes against race-conscious civil rights remedies he had shown in earlier cases. He and Justices Clarence Thomas and Samuel Alito had tried unsuccessfully to repeal affirmative action in the Texas and University of Michigan cases but now had a sweeping victory. The three dissenters, Justices Jackson, Sotomayor, and Kagan, held to the understanding of civil rights law for higher education that had prevailed since the 1960s but were outvoted 2–1 by a determined majority likely to prevail for a generation. (The *Plessy* "separate but equal" decision had lasted nearly sixty years.) The differences were stark, with the new majority holding that affirmative action had been unconstitutional all along. The decision and the dissents showed that the two parts of the Court had fundamentally different understandings of the realities students of color and the universities faced and interpreted the basic constitutional principles in contradictory ways.

Suddenly, practices accepted and praised by the courts for nearly a half century were defined as violations of the Constitution. Long-established practices and academic relationships with communities of color had to quickly change. Continuing what had been normal admissions processes could now subject colleges to severe penalties. The deeply divided and unusually hostile opinions within the Court showed the radical and divisive nature of the change.

Chief Justice Roberts's opinion saw affirmative action as discrimination against whites and Asians to unfairly help Blacks, Latinos, and Native students. The decision held that all the precedents were wrong and this was simply racial discrimination. The decision rejected the idea that in order to change deeply embedded racial stratification it was necessary to consciously plan for and develop tools to bring down racial lines. It dismissed the idea, in the earlier decisions, that the historic respect for the autonomy of colleges supported their right to plan to create integrated student bodies. The extensive evidence presented in briefs filed by researchers and higher education groups across the country showing that diverse campuses and classes enriched the education of all groups of students was not engaged. The Court argued that race was so complex that no one could precisely define the exact level of diversity needed and that race lines were, in any case, too blurry to be overseen by courts, so nothing should be done.

It is important to listen to the words of the decision to be able to understand the intensity of the views of the Court's majority. Chief Justice Roberts's opinion for the Court held that affirmative action was "racial discrimination," it was "odious," it was "pernicious."[2] The Court ruled that for a half century the courts had read the Constitution incorrectly. Rejecting the claim in earlier decisions that the courts should respect the expertise and the academic freedom of universities to provide better education by increasing the diversity of perspectives, the decision said that universities were stereotyping students of color and had failed to justify a truly compelling interest. "Deference," the Court said, "does not imply abandonment or abdication of judicial review."[3] The claimed benefits "cannot be subjected to meaningful judicial review."[4] The opinion argued, "it is unclear how courts are supposed to measure any of these goals."[5] Responding to claims of broad social benefits, the Court held that addressing general "societal inequality" did not justify such policies and that, in terms of other benefits, "the interests that respondents seek, though plainly worthy, are inescapably imponderable."[6] The decision held that "the student must be treated based on his or her experiences as an individual—not on the basis of race." It said: "many universities have for too long done just the opposite." They were favoring some students simply because of "the color of their skin."[7] Two-thirds of the Supreme Court has an extraordinarily hostile view of race-conscious solutions to racial problems and is uninterested in what defenders and researchers in higher education see as the basic facts.

The decision simply saw admissions as a case where merit, which the Court majority implied could be clearly defined by test scores and grades of each individual, should determine outcomes on the individual level. It saw affirmative action in a zero-sum context where every time affirmative action led to the admission of a Black or Latino or Native student it was taking an opportunity from a more "meritorious" white or Asian student, violating the Constitution. College education was conceived as a fixed supply of opportunities for personal attainment, a capital asset, which must be allocated to those who were best prepared. Admission was a right for the highest-ranked individuals. They were seen as the most deserving and the victims of affirmative action. There was no discussion by the majority of the ways in which test scores and grades related more to family resources and access to better schools in more expensive neighborhoods with more advantaged student bodies and stronger teachers. The extensive research submitted to the Court by higher education experts showing gains for white and Asian students from diverse college experiences was ignored by the majority.

The world described by the dissenters could hardly be more different. It was one where student diversity, as had been found in all the earlier cases, was a net benefit for the university and all groups of students because it increased the richness of the experience and preparation for all students destined to live and work in a profoundly multiracial society. They did not see the problem as allocating a fixed quantity of opportunity among individuals but as something that could be improved and expanded by creating campuses that better reflected the overall society and gave students, including whites and Asians, the opportunity to learn across severe social barriers in ways that would enrich their lives. They saw a world of serious and persistent racial stratification of opportunity that had never been equalized. They saw constitutional language as supporting colleges' efforts to solve problems of racial subordination and stereotypes that were much more than individual discrimination. They discussed how systematic social and educational inequality worked against students of color. It was not language designed to protect white students since there was not a context where nonwhite groups controlled and had long subordinated whites as a group. They did not see "merit" fairly defined by test scores and believed it was important to give colleges, the experts in selecting students and creating campus communities, discretion to define merit in much broader ways. Two worlds.

The decision meant that admissions offices had to ignore what many saw as systematic race-based inequalities in preparation for college. The 2023 decision was deeply dismaying to colleges and civil rights organizations who knew well how historic Supreme Court decisions on major issues create great ripples that often go far beyond the particulars of the decision. Most selective colleges, apart from public universities in the nine states that had outlawed affirmative action, were suddenly confronted with the highest court ruling that what they had been doing for a half century had been unconstitutional all along and was strictly forbidden for the future. The colleges' mission statements promised diversity but the policies and practices they used had been forbidden. Now, though the Court's ruling only directly affected admissions decisions, colleges were already seeing threats and receiving letters saying that they must stop non-admissions race-conscious policies in financial aid, in faculty diversity, and even in curriculum even though the Court had not yet said anything about them. General counsels at most colleges are rarely experts in civil rights law or race relations and they often tend to try to prevent litigation by recommending a very cautious policy. And in the half of the nation's states with GOP governments in all branches, there were governors and attorney generals who were pressing colleges to limit teaching about race issues or making affirmative action appointments for faculty and administrations. In some states, including Florida and Texas, faculty members often felt under siege if they wanted to teach or write about race. Faculty and students of color felt threatened. It was a very difficult time.

This book was written with an expectation that the Supreme Court would overturn affirmative action but without knowing what the rationale would be, what openings there might be for modifications, or how colleges and state officials would respond. It is now clear that the Court has not tried to connect the decision with previous cases or begin a gradual pushback but decided on an immediate and radical rejection of the basic assumptions of the civil rights policy of the last half century. So long as this majority remains in place, efforts to reactivate anything like the traditional arguments for affirmative action will be exercises in futility as far as federal courts are concerned. It is also clear now that in conservative states the decision will be taken as carte blanche for far-reaching efforts to dismantle institutions and even prohibit teaching ideas about the history of discrimination, the continuing inequalities, and the possible remedies. Academic freedom to read and to teach is now under attack in some states. It is doubtful that this will be the last major decision reversing civil rights policy from this far-right Supreme Court majority.

Following the decision most selective colleges, except for public universities in the nine states with affirmative action bans, were faced with the need to rapidly change generations of practices before the admissions season in the fall. This was happening at a time when college enrollment had been decreasing for a decade and when the nation's school population had a nonwhite majority and continuing deep inequalities in test scores and grades that had existed since standardized testing began. In the years before the decision there had already been a notable decline in Black access, and many students of color who indicated they wanted to go to college said that they did not expect that they actually could.[8] The pandemic had produced disproportionate losses for students of color and declines in test scores. There was no evidence that the inequalities would solve themselves. Most colleges were highly dependent on tuition income and very few had the resources to cover the full cost of attendance for low-income students. Colleges had a lot to consider. Congress and state legislatures need to face the long-term trend of states supporting a declining share of the cost of college and the resulting rise in tuitions as well as huge gaps in college aid.

This book was designed to both discuss what would be optimal approaches for increasing equity in higher education and redirect attention from excessive focus on admissions policies in selective schools, though they are very important, to areas that are critical for all levels of higher education: preparation and affordability, which are the second and third major walls around opportunity.

Students of color, on average, receive far weaker preparation for college. It is important to understand affirmative action's function as an effort to partially offset the crippling impact of systematically unequal preparation. It was a modest bandage over the massive wound of fundamentally unequal preparation and resources in families, in communities, and in segregated high-poverty schools that serve most Black, Latino, and Native students. Since the Supreme Court dissolved desegregation plans in the 1990s[9] and voluntary public school diversity efforts in 2007,[10] schools have become far more segregated by race and poverty and a huge system of school choice with no equity provisions has emerged, further increasing stratification.[11] With the affirmative action effort dissolved, it is time to turn attention to this systemic inequality. It is important to document the inequalities and to find the best evidence on possible solutions. It may well require colleges to take a more active role in preparing students for college and to work much more closely with secondary education. The final chapter of this book discusses the possibilities of systemic remedies that are unlikely at the federal level under this Court but could be pursued in states whose constitutions and courts provide more ample remedies, as well as other incremental efforts that show evidence of benefits. The book analyzes the gaping holes in the path to college and discusses evidence and experiments that could contribute at each stage in a battered pipeline.

The other major wall discussed in this book is cost, which is the number one concern in college choice for students of color. The high costs and the often unintelligible aid systems are huge barriers that lead many students to not choose better colleges that would give them a much stronger chance for educational success. A basic reason why weak students in top income groups are much more likely to complete college than strong nonwhite students in the bottom income segments is the inability to pay or even to understand the financial terrain on the college pathway. Possible answers are discussed in the last chapters in this book. When one road up a mountain is blocked, another must be opened. Research can light the way and research-based advocacy in this field will be very important to bringing down that heavy wall. We have recently seen a great deal of attention being paid to college debt, but there has been very little focus on the fact that few colleges provide the kind of aid packages that can cover the real cost of attendance for low-income families. The Supreme Court decision is already leading to broadening attacks on even indirect ways to aid students of color. Given the reality of the Trump Court, it is time for a major refocus on the other primary barriers.

One of the early key questions in the wake of the *Students for Fair Admissions* decision was whether it would trigger attacks on other race-related policies that were not included in the Court decision since Supreme Court decisions often have broad effects and create new issues. College aid was a particularly important issue; college costs are the most important consideration for students of color. The Court decision said nothing about race-targeted aid that many colleges used to help attract students of color whose households had significantly lower average incomes and vastly less family wealth. Some conservative states promptly announced that they would end such programs.[12] Particularly striking was the response of the University of North Carolina, which had defended its affirmative action plan in the Supreme Court loss. A month after the decision the UNC trustees adopted a policy that went well beyond what the Court had required. They banned consideration of race in admission and in hiring, which was not part of the ruling, and they forbade the use of "proxies" such as admissions essays, which the Court had explicitly permitted.[13] About half of the states had conservative GOP control of all branches of state government and opinions of state attorney generals would obviously be important. Within weeks suits were filed against West Point[14] and the Naval Academy[15] by the victors in the Harvard-UNC case because the Supreme Court had noted that the military claims of the national security need to have diverse officers trained for a diverse military could be an exception. Any limit on affirmative faculty job searches in colleges would be particularly consequential because faculty diversity is very important for successful student diversity and for the intellectual research diversity that many colleges seek. Faculty of color will be especially important to students of color who are likely to feel threatened as their numbers decline after affirmative action. Already Edward Blum, who had brought the case, has gone further, writing corporate leaders claiming that their plans to integrate their boards were now illegal, though there was nothing in the decision about them. It was clear that the affirmative action opponents saw the decision as only the opening volley in their attacks on vestiges of affirmative diversity policies across many institutions. Those who make policy for colleges or try to defend the rights of people of color must be prepared for a long struggle.

There will now be a wide array of efforts at colleges to overcome the consequences of a devasting loss; that is a worthy though frustrating effort given the defeat the Supreme Court has delivered. When the conservatives lost in civil rights battles for decades, they intensified their fight, engaged in politics, and funded movements in law schools as well as conservative litigation groups. Parallel efforts may be needed by civil rights supporters. It may be, as this book suggests, that when one door closes attention will shift for a time to opening even bigger gates dealing with the extraordinarily unequal preparation our schools provide for students of color or the impossible financial barriers many of their families face. If the struggle for college access and equity is seen as a multifront battle, the goal remains the same but the strategy may be to open other fronts. If there is not to be serious attention paid to helping the students harmed by the extremely stratified and unequal paths to college at the admissions window, there may be movements to change that entire system.

Often, in the history of constitutional law, you can find the view that eventually comes to be dominant in the previous dissents. Sometimes great dissents, such as that of John Marshall Harlan in *Plessy v. Ferguson,* become the only thing truly remembered and honored about a major case. Those troubled by the outcome of the Harvard and UNC cases may want to focus on the words of the dissenters. They described a different society and saw college actions in a completely different light. The strongest dissent came from Justice Ketanji Brown Jackson: "Our country has never been colorblind."[16] She saw fundamental educational benefits to affirmative action: "ensuring a diverse student body in higher education helps everyone. . . . [S]tudents of every race will come to have a greater appreciation and understanding of civic virtue, democratic values, and our country's commitment to equality."[17] She was strongly critical of what the Court's majority had decided, saying that "deeming race irrelevant in law does not make it so in life."[18] The Court was ignoring the reality facing colleges: "The only way out of this morass—for all of us—is to stare at racial disparity unblinkingly, and then to do what evidence and experts tell us is required to level the playing field and march forward together."[19] She said, "the Court has now been lured into interfering with the crucial work that . . . institutions of higher learning are doing to solve America's real-world problems."[20] The Court's "meddling" amounted to "a dismally misinformed sociological experiment" that "will hamper the best judgments of our world-class educational institutions about who they need to bring onto their campuses right now to benefit every American, no matter their race."[21] Justice Jackson's dissent, joined by those of Justices Kagan and Sotomayor, may foretell the future, but, given the existing Court's membership, it would be a distant future.

NOTES

Chapter 1. Colorblind Higher Education Policy in a Racially Stratified Society

1. Sabrina Tavernise, "U.S. Population Grows at Slowest Rate since 1919," *New York Times*, March 26, 2020.

2. Andrew Howard Nichols, *"Segregation Forever"? The Continued Underrepresentation of Black and Latino Undergraduates at the Nation's 101 Most Selective Public Colleges and Universities* (Washington, DC: Education Trust, July 2020).

3. Stephanie Marken, "Half in U.S. Now Consider College Education Very Important," Gallup, December 30, 2019, https://www.gallup.com/education/272228/half-consider-college-education-important.aspx; Jeff Jones and Lydia Saad, "Gallup News Service—Gallup Poll Social Series: Lifestyle," Gallup memo, December 5–8, 2013.

4. In this book, when I talk about people of color, I am referring to Blacks, Latinos, and American Indians, which are often called underrepresented minorities in discussions of college access. This is a very imperfect concept since, for example, the category of Latino is not a color category. Although many call themselves "brown" and many have mestizo, part-Indian, or part-Black color, many others do not. And Asians often do have distinctive skin coloring but are not, as a group, disadvantaged or poor—in fact, in spite of subgroup differences, they are, on average, considerably more educated and affluent than whites. So the term *students of color* in this context means disadvantaged racial and ethnic minorities.

5. Thomas D. Snyder, Cristobal de Brey, and Sally A. Dillow, *Digest of Education Statistics, 2017* (Washington, DC: National Center for Education Statistics, January 2019), table 501.10, https://nces.ed.gov/programs/digest/d17/tables/dt17_501.10.asp.

6. Snyder, de Brey, and Dillow, table 322.20, https://nces.ed.gov/programs/digest/d17/tables/dt17_322.20.asp.

7. William G. Bowen and Derek Bok, *The Shape of the River: Long-Term Consequences of Considering Race in College and University Admissions* (Princeton, NJ: Princeton University Press, 1998), 5.

8. Ira Katznelson, *When Affirmative Action Was White: An Untold History of Racial Inequality in Twentieth-Century America* (New York: W. W. Norton, 2005). Historically Black colleges and universities were an exception.

9. Ezekiel J. Dixon-Roman, Howard T. Everson, and John J. McArdle, "Race, Poverty and SAT Scores: Modeling the Influences of Family Income on Black and White High School Students' SAT Performance," *Teachers College Record* 115, no. 4 (April 2013); John L. Hoffman and Katie E. Lowitzki, "Predicting College Success with High School Grades and Test Scores:

Limitations for Minority Students," *Review of Higher Education* 28, no. 4 (Summer 2005): 455–74.

10. Bowen and Bok, *Shape of the River*, 7.

11. *Adams v. Richardson*, 480 F.2d 159 (1973).

12. David G. Savage, *Turning Right: The Making of the Rehnquist Supreme Court* (New York: John Wiley, 1992).

13. *Hopwood v. Texas*, 78 F.3d 932 (5th Cir. 1996).

14. California Proposition 209, 1996.

15. *Gratz v. Bollinger*, 539 U.S. 244 (2003); *Grutter v. Bollinger*, 539 U.S. 306 (2003).

16. *Grutter v. Bollinger*.

17. *Schuette v. Coalition to Defend Affirmative Action*, 572 U.S. 291 (2014).

18. Catherine L. Horn and Stella M. Flores, *Percent Plans in College Admissions: A Comparative Analysis of Three States' Experiences* (Cambridge, MA: Civil Rights Project at Harvard University, 2003).

19. *Grutter v. Bollinger*.

20. *Fisher v. University of Texas*, 570 U.S. 297 (2013) (known as *Fisher 1*).

21. *Fisher v. University of Texas*, 579 U.S. ____ (2016) (known as *Fisher 2*).

22. Sean F. Reardon, Rachel Baker, and Daniel Klasik, *Race, Income, and Enrollment Patterns in Highly Selective Colleges, 1982–2004* (Stanford, CA: Center for Education Policy Analysis, Stanford University, 2012), http://hdl.handle.net/10919/92633.

23. Lorelle L. Espinosa, Matthew N. Gaertner, and Gary Orfield, *Race, Class, and College Access: Achieving Diversity in a Shifting Legal Landscape* (Washington, DC: American Council on Education, 2015).

24. William C. Kidder and Patricia Gándara, "Two Decades after the Affirmative Action Ban: Evaluating the University of California's Race-Neutral Efforts," in *Alternative Paths to Diversity: Exploring and Implementing Effective College Admissions Policies*, ed. Gary Orfield, Educational Testing Service Research Report Series No. RR-17-40 (Princeton, NJ: Educational Testing Service, 2017), 25–48.

25. *Students for Fair Admissions, Inc., v. President and Fellows of Harvard College*, slip opinion (November 12, 2020).

26. The Trump administration had filed a case against Yale University but it was dropped in the early days of the Biden administration. Anemona Hartocollis, "Justice Department Drops Suit Claiming Yale Discriminated in Admissions," *New York Times*, February 3, 2021.

27. Gary Orfield and Edward Miller, ed., *Chilling Admissions: The Affirmative Action Crisis and the Search for Alternatives* (Cambridge, MA: Civil Rights Project at Harvard University, 1998); Gary Orfield, ed., *Diversity Challenged: Research on the Impact of Affirmative Action*, with Michal Kurlaender (Cambridge, MA: Harvard Education Press, 2001).

28. President Trump issued an executive order against critical race theory. Laws to restrict the teaching of aspects of racial history or critical race theory were proposed in at least sixteen states and quickly adopted in some. Eesha Pendharkar, "Efforts to Root Out Racism in Schools Would Unravel under 'Critical Race Theory' Bills," *Education Week*, June 2, 2021, 8.

29. Juliana Menasce Horowitz et al., "Amid National Reckoning, Americans Divided on Whether Increased Focus on Race Will Lead to Major Policy Change," Pew Research Center, October 6, 2020, https://www.pewresearch.org/social-trends/2020/10/06/amid-national

-reckoning-americans-divided-on-whether-increased-focus-on-race-will-lead-to-major-policy
-change.

30. Sarah Patton Moberg, Maria Krysan, and Deanna Christianson, "Racial Attitudes in America," *Public Opinion Quarterly* 83, no. 2 (Summer 2019): 450–71.

31. Marc Hooghe and Ruth Dassonneville, "Explaining the Trump Vote: The Effect of Racist Resentment and Anti-immigrant Sentiments," *PS: Political Science and Politics* 51, no. 3 (July 2018): 528–34.

32. Ronald Reagan, "Inaugural Address," January 20, 1981, https://www.reaganfoundation .org/media/128614/inaguration.pdf.

33. Charles A. Murray, *Losing Ground: American Social Policy, 1950–1980* (New York: Basic Books, 1984).

34. John E. Chubb and Terry M. Moe, *Politics, Markets, and America's Schools* (Washington, DC: Brookings Institution, 1990).

35. James S. Coleman and Thomas Hoffer, *Public and Private High Schools: The Impact of Communities* (New York: Basic Books, 1987); Anthony S. Bryk, Valerie E. Lee, and Peter Blakeley Holland, *Catholic Schools and the Common Good* (Cambridge, MA: Harvard University Press, 1993).

36. National Commission on Excellence in Education, *A Nation at Risk: The Imperative for Educational Reform* (Washington, DC: Government Printing Office, April 1983).

37. David C. Berliner and Bruce J. Biddle, *The Manufactured Crisis: Myths, Fraud, and the Attack on America's Public Schools* (Reading, MA: Addison-Wesley, 1995).

38. Ronald Edmunds, "Effective Schools for the Urban Poor," *Educational Leadership* 37, no. 1 (October 1979): 15–18, 20–24.

39. William Julius Wilson, *The Declining Significance of Race: Blacks and Changing American Institutions* (Chicago: University of Chicago Press, 1978).

40. This was a favored argument of Justice Clarence Thomas. Shelby Steele, *The Content of Our Character: A New Vision of Race in America* (New York: Harper Perennial, 1998).

41. Richard J. Herrnstein and Charles A. Murray, *The Bell Curve: Intelligence and Class Structure in American Life* (New York: Simon and Schuster, 1994).

42. Jason Stahl, *Right Moves: The Conservative Think Tank in American Political Culture since 1945* (Chapel Hill: University of North Carolina Press, 2016), 199.

43. Jean Stefancic and Richard Delgado, *No Mercy: How Conservative Think Tanks and Foundations Changed America's Social Agenda* (Philadelphia: Temple University Press, 1996), chap. 4.

44. J. Anthony Lukas, *Common Ground: A Turbulent Decade in the Lives of Three American Families* (New York: Vintage Books, 1986).

45. Douglas S. Massey and Nancy A. Denton, *American Apartheid: Segregation and the Making of the Underclass* (Cambridge, MA: Harvard University Press, 1993); John Goering, ed., *Housing Desegregation and Federal Policy* (Chapel Hill: University of North Carolina Press, 1986).

46. Lee Rainwater, *Behind Ghetto Walls: Black Families in a Federal Slum* (Chicago: Aldine, 1970).

47. Allan H. Spear, *Black Chicago: The Making of a Negro Ghetto, 1890–1920* (Chicago: University of Chicago Press, 1967); Richard Griswold del Castillo, *The Los Angeles Barrio, 1850–1960: A Social History* (Berkeley: University of California Press, 1979).

48. Gary Orfield and Carole Ashkinaze, *The Closing Door: Conservative Policy and Black Opportunity* (Chicago: University of Chicago Press, 1991).

49. José E. Moreno, ed., *The Elusive Quest for Equality: 150 Years of Chicano/Chicana Education* (Cambridge, MA: Harvard Educational Review, 1999).

50. Thomas P. Carter and Roberto D. Segura, *Mexican Americans in School: A Decade of Change* (Princeton, NJ: College Board, 1979).

51. Mary Pattillo-McCoy, *Black Picket Fences: Privilege and Peril among the Black Middle Class* (Chicago: University of Chicago Press, 1999).

52. Chandler Davidson and Bernard Grofman, eds., *Quiet Revolution in the South: The Impact of the Voting Rights Act, 1965–1990* (Princeton, NJ: Princeton University Press, 1994).

53. Melvin Oliver and Thomas Shapiro, *Black Wealth / White Wealth: A New Perspective on Racial Inequality* (New York: Routledge, 1995).

54. Robert L. Crain and Rita E. Mahard, *Desegregation Plans That Raise Black Achievement: A Review of the Research* (Santa Monica, CA: RAND, June 1982), https://eric.ed.gov/?id=ED227198; Thomas F. Pettigrew, *A Study of School Integration: Final Report* (Cambridge, MA: Harvard University, August 1970), https://eric.ed.gov/?id=ED044468.

55. Barbara Grutter v. Lee Bollinger, et al., Brief of the American Educational Research Association, the Association of American Colleges and Universities, and the American Association for Higher Education as Amici Curiae in Support of Respondents, 2001, https://escholarship.org/uc/item/69s9b6fs.

56. *Grutter v. Bollinger.*

57. Randall Rothenberg, *The Neo-liberals: Creating the New American Politics* (New York: Simon and Schuster, 1984); Stanley B. Greenberg, *Middle Class Dreams: The Politics and Power of the New American Majority* (New York: Times Books, 1995).

58. Gary Orfield and Nicholas Hillman, eds., *Accountability and Opportunity in Higher Education: The Civil Rights Dimension* (Cambridge, MA: Harvard Education Press, 2018).

59. Eduardo Bonilla-Silva, *Racism without Racists: Color-Blind Racism and the Persistence of Racial Inequality in the United States* (Lanham, MD: Rowman and Littlefield, 2003), 3. Also see Eduardo Bonilla-Silva, "Rethinking Racism: Toward a Structural Interpretation," *American Sociological Review* 62, no. 3 (June 1997): 465–80.

60. PRRI, *Dueling Realities: Amid Multiple Crises, Trump and Biden Supporters See Different Priorities and Futures for the Nation: Findings from the 2020 American Values Survey* (Washington, DC: PRRI, 2020), 54–57, https://www.prri.org/research/amid-multiple-crises-trump-and-biden-supporters-see-different-realities-and-futures-for-the-nation.

61. Alexis de Tocqueville, *Democracy in America* (New York: Vintage Books, 1945), 1:31–56.

62. James Bryce, *The American Commonwealth* (New York: Macmillan, 1895), 2:286.

63. Herbert David Croly, *The Promise of American Life* (New York: Macmillan, 1914), 9–10, https://books.google.com/books?id=3BASAAAAYAAJ&printsec=frontcover#v=onepage&q&f=false.

64. Jennifer L. Hochschild, *Facing Up to the American Dream: Race, Class, and the Soul of the Nation* (Princeton, NJ: Princeton University Press, 1996); Jennifer L. Hochschild and Nathan Scovronick, *The American Dream and the Public Schools* (New York: Oxford University Press, 2003).

65. Lyndon B. Johnson, "Commencement Address at Howard University: 'To Fulfill These Rights,'" June 4, 1965, in *Public Papers of the Presidents* (Washington, DC: Government Printing Office, 1965), 2:636.

66. "Children in Poverty by Race and Ethnicity in the United States," Kids Count Data Center, updated September 2020, https://datacenter.kidscount.org/data/tables/44-children-in-poverty-by-race-and.

67. "Children in Poverty."

68. "Census Bureau Releases New Report on Patterns of Poverty," U.S. Census Bureau, August 27, 2021, https://www.census.gov/newsroom/press-releases/2021/patterns-of-poverty.html.

69. Kristin L. Perkins and Robert J. Sampson, "Compounded Deprivation in the Transition to Adulthood: The Intersection of Racial and Economic Inequality among Chicagoans, 1995–2013," *RSF: The Russell Sage Foundation Journal of the Social Sciences* 1, no. 1 (November 2015): 51.

70. Erwin Chemerinsky, *The Conservative Assault on the Constitution* (New York: Simon and Schuster, 2010), 17–29.

71. "Poll: Most Americans Think Their Own Group Faces Discrimination," National Public Radio, October 24, 2017.

Chapter 2. Cumulative Racial Inequalities and the Path to College

1. National Academies of Sciences, Engineering, and Medicine, *The Promise of Adolescence: Realizing Opportunity for All Youth* (Washington, DC: National Academies Press, 2019), 73, https://doi.org/10.17226/25388.

2. John Fluke et al., *Research Synthesis on Child Welfare: Disproportionality and Disparities* (Washington, DC: Center for the Study of Social Policy, 2011); Pamela Kato Klebanov, Jeanne Brooks-Gunn, and Greg J. Duncan, "Does Neighborhood and Family Poverty Affect Mothers' Parenting, Mental Health, and Social Support?," *Journal of Marriage and Family* 56, no. 2 (1994): 441–55; Rena L. Repetti, Shelley E. Taylor, and Teresa E. Seeman, "Risky Families: Family Social Environments and the Mental and Physical Health of Offspring," *Psychological Bulletin* 128, no. 2 (2002): 330–66.

3. Leonard Pitt, *The Decline of the Californios: A Social History of the Spanish-Speaking Californians, 1846–1890* (Berkeley: University of California Press, 1998).

4. Erwin Chemerinsky, *The Conservative Assault on the Constitution* (New York: Simon and Schuster, 2010).

5. Dan T. Carter, *From George Wallace to Newt Gingrich: Race in the Conservative Counterrevolution, 1963–1994* (Baton Rouge: Louisiana State University Press, 1996).

6. U.S. Bureau of the Census, *The Social and Economic Status of the Black Population in the United States, 1973*, Current Population Reports, Series P. 23, No. 48 (Washington, DC: Government Printing Office, 1974) (with statistics from 1960).

7. Anna Cristina d'Addio, "Intergenerational Transmission of Disadvantage: Mobility or Immobility across Generations? A Review of the Evidence for OECD Countries," Social, Employment and Migration Working Papers No. 52, Organisation for Economic Co-operation and Development, 2007.

8. Jonathan Guryan, Erik Hurst, and Melissa Kearney, "Parental Education and Parental Time with Children," *Journal of Economic Perspectives* 22, no. 3 (2008): 23–46.

9. Institute of Medicine, *Student Mobility: Exploring the Impacts of Frequent Moves on Achievement: Summary of a Workshop* (Washington, DC: National Academies Press, 2010).

10. Anne Case, Darren Lubotsky, and Christina Paxson, "Economic Status and Health in Childhood: The Origins of the Gradient," *American Economic Review* 92, no. 5 (2002): 1308–34.

11. Asian immigrants were prohibited until the 1965 immigrant act and could not come as relatives since they very rarely had relatives here. Those who came after the 1965 reform (apart from Vietnam-era refugees) tended to have education and incomes sufficient for costly travel and moves. They, like the first wave of refugees from Cuba, came with more education and social capital and, sometimes, significant money compared with the Mexican and Central American immigrants, who tended to come from poor, often rural communities with elementary education and very little money. On average the post-1965 Asian immigration was one of the most educated in U.S. history and was not, in contrast to that of Latinos, segregated residentially or in schooling when it arrived. Its members often confront a positive stereotype about their academic talents.

12. "Spotlight: Young Adult Educational and Employment Outcomes by Family Socioeconomic Status," in Joel McFarland et al., *The Condition of Education 2019* (Washington, DC: U.S. Department of Education, National Center for Education Statistics, May 2019).

13. Michelle J. K. Osterman and Joyce A. Martin, *Timing and Adequacy of Prenatal Care in the United States, 2016*, National Vital Statistics Reports 67, No. 3 (Washington, DC: U.S. Department of Education, National Center for Health Statistics, May 30, 2018), https://stacks.cdc.gov /view/cdc/55174.

14. Brady E. Hamilton et al., *Births: Provisional Data for 2018*, Vital Statistics Rapid Release No. 7 (Hyattsville, MD: National Center for Health Statistics, May 2, 2019), 3–5. Latinas, though they face many kinds of inequality, had birth statistics much more like those of whites and other groups.

15. Hamilton et al., 3–5.

16. Center on the Developing Child, *The Science of Early Childhood Development (InBrief)* (Cambridge, MA: Center on the Developing Child, Harvard University, 2007), https:// developingchild.harvard.edu/resources/inbrief-science-of-ecd.

17. Jessica A. R. Logan et al., "When Children Are Not Read to at Home: The Million Word Gap," *Journal of Developmental and Behavioral Pediatrics* 40, no. 5 (2019): 383–86.

18. Joyce A. Martin et al., *Births: Final Data for 2018*, National Vital Statistics Reports, vol. 68, no. 13 (Hyattsville, MD: National Center for Health Statistics, 2019), 5, https://www.cdc.gov /nchs/data/nvsr68/nvsr68_13-508.pdf.

19. Legal Momentum, Women's Legal Defense and Education Fund, *Single Parenthood in the United States—a Snapshot* (New York: Legal Momentum, Women's Legal Defense and Education Fund, March 2014).

20. Jonathan Rothwell, "Black and Hispanic Kids Get Lower Quality Pre-K," *Social Mobility Memos* (blog), Brookings Institution, June 29, 2016, https://www.brookings.edu/blog/social -mobility-memos/2016/06/29/black-and-hispanic-kids-get-lower-quality-pre-k/.

21. Rachel Valentino, "Will Public Pre-K Really Close Achievement Gaps? Gaps in Prekindergarten Quality between Students and across States," *American Educational Research Journal* 55, no. 1 (February 2018): 79–116.

22. James J. Heckman, *Giving Kids a Fair Chance (A Strategy That Works)* (Cambridge, MA: MIT Press, 2013).

23. Lisa A. Dubois, "The Power of Pre-K: Fact or Fiction," *Peabody Reflector*, Summer 2016, 11–15.

24. Dubois, 15.

25. Katharine B. Stevens and Elizabeth English Smith, *Does Pre-K Work? The Research on Ten Early Childhood Programs—and What It Tells Us* (Washington, DC: American Enterprise Institute, April 2016), 37.

26. "Taking on 'Food Deserts,'" White House of President Barack Obama, February 24, 2010, https://obamawhitehouse.archives.gov/blog/2010/02/24/taking-food-deserts; Kelly Brooks, "Research Shows Food Deserts More Abundant in Minority Neighborhoods," *Johns Hopkins University Magazine*, Spring 2014, https://hub.jhu.edu/magazine/2014/spring/racial-food-deserts.

27. Margarita Alegría et al., "Disparities in Treatment for Substance Use Disorders and Co-occurring Disorders for Ethnic/Racial Minority Youth," *Journal of the American Academy of Child and Adolescent Psychiatry* 50, no. 3 (2011): 22–31.

28. Robert J. Sampson and Alix Winter, "Racial Ecology of Lead Poisoning: Toxic Inequality in Chicago Neighborhoods, 1995–2013," *Du Bois Review: Social Science Research on Race* 13, no. 2 (2016): 261–83.

29. Thomas G. McGuire and Jeanne Miranda, "New Evidence Regarding Racial and Ethnic Disparities in Mental Health: Policy Implications," *Health Affairs* 27, no. 2 (March/April 2008): 393–403.

30. Antonia Orfield, Frank Basa, and John Yun, "Vision Problems of Children in Poverty in an Urban School Clinic: Their Epidemic Numbers, Impact on Learning, and Approaches to Remediation," *Journal of Optometric Vision Development* 32, no. 3 (2001): 114–41; Alan Mozes, "Untreated Vision Problems Plague U.S. Preschoolers," *Health Day News*, May 5, 2017, https://consumer.healthday.com/eye-care-information-13/eye-and-vision-problem-news-295/untreated-vision-problems-plague-u-s-preschoolers-722380.html.

31. John Iceland, *Poverty in America: A Handbook*, 3rd ed. (Berkeley: University of California Press, 2013).

32. Dierdre Pfeiffer, *The Opportunity Illusion: Subsidized Housing and Failing Schools* (Los Angeles: Civil Rights Project, 2009).

33. "Children Living in Areas of Concentrated Poverty by Race and Ethnicity in the United States," Kids Count Data Center, updated January 2021, https://datacenter.kidscount.org/data/bar/7753-children-living-in-areas-of-concentrated-.

34. Kristin L. Perkins and Robert J. Sampson, "Compounded Deprivation in the Transition to Adulthood: The Intersection of Racial and Economic Inequality among Chicagoans, 1995–2013," *RSF: The Russell Sage Foundation Journal of the Social Sciences* 1, no. 1 (November 2015): 35–54.

35. "Concentration of Public School Students Eligible for Free or Reduced-Price Lunch," National Center for Education Statistics, May 2018, figure 1, https://nces.ed.gov/programs/coe/pdf/Indicator_CLB/coe_clb_2018_05.pdf.

36. *Keyes v. School District No. 1, Denver, Colorado*, 413 U.S. 189 (1973); Gary Orfield, *Must We Bus? Segregated Schools and National Policy* (Washington, DC: Brookings Institution, 1978), chap. 7.

37. Gary Orfield and Jongyeon Ee, *Segregating California's Future: Inequality and Its Alternative 60 Years after "Brown v. Board of Education"* (Los Angeles: Civil Rights Project, May 2014).

38. William C. Kidder and Patricia Gándara, "Two Decades after the Affirmative Action Ban: Evaluating the University of California's Race-Neutral Efforts," in *Alternative Paths to Diversity: Exploring and Implementing Effective College Admissions Policies*, ed. Gary Orfield, Research Report Series No. RR-17-40 (Princeton, NJ: Educational Testing Service, 2017), 25–48.

39. *Oklahoma City Board of Education v. Dowell*, 498 U.S. 237 (1991).

40. Gary Orfield and Susan E. Eaton, *Dismantling Desegregation: The Quiet Reversal of "Brown v. Board of Education"* (New York: New Press, 1996).

41. *Parents Involved in Community Schools v. Seattle School District No. 1*, 551 U.S. 701 (2007).

42. Gary Orfield and Jennifer B. Ayscue, eds., *Discrimination in Elite Public Schools: Investigating Buffalo* (New York: Teachers College Press, 2018).

43. Leon Panetta and Peter Gall, *Bring Us Together: The Nixon Team and the Civil Rights Retreat* (Philadelphia: Lippincott, 1971).

44. *Milliken v. Bradley*, 418 U.S. 717 (1974); *San Antonio v. Rodriguez*, 411 U.S. 1 (1973).

45. Rucker C. Johnson, *Children of the Dream: Why School Integration Works*, with Alexander Nazaryan (New York: Basic Books, 2019).

46. Erica Frankenberg et al., *Harming Our Common Future: America's Segregated Schools 65 Years after "Brown"* (Los Angeles: Civil Rights Project, 2019).

47. Johnson, *Children of the Dream*, 60.

48. Johnson, 62.

49. Johnson, 64; Nazgol Ghandnoosh, *Black Lives Matter: Eliminating Racial Inequity in the Criminal Justice System* (Washington, DC: Sentencing Project, February 2015).

50. George Judson, "For Schools, Sad Echoes of Hartford," *New York Times*, May 14, 1996, https://www.nytimes.com/1995/05/14/nyregion/for-schools-sad-echoes-of-hartford.html.

51. Susan E. Eaton, *The Children in Room E4: American Education on Trial* (Chapel Hill, NC: Algonquin Books, 2007).

52. Eaton.

53. Raj Chetty et al., "Race and Economic Opportunity in the United States: An Intergenerational Perspective," March 2018, http://www.equality-of-opportunity.org/assets/documents/race_paper.pdf.

54. James S. Coleman et al., *Equality of Educational Opportunity* (Washington, DC: Government Printing Office, 1966).

55. Myron Orfield, "Segregation and Environmental Justice," *Minnesota Journal of Law, Science and Technology* 7 (2005): 147–60.

56. Josephine Louie, *We Don't Feel Welcome Here: African Americans and Latinos in Metro Boston* (Cambridge, MA: Civil Rights Project at Harvard University, 2005).

57. James M. Quane and Bruce H. Rankin, "Neighborhood Poverty, Family Characteristics, and Commitment to Mainstream Goals: The Case of African American Adolescents in the Inner City," *Journal of Family Issues* 19, no. 6 (1998): 769–94.

58. Gary Orfield, "Housing Segregation Produces Unequal Schools," in *Closing the Opportunity Gap: What America Must Do to Give Every Child an Even Chance*, ed. Prudence L. Carter and Kevin G. Welner (New York: Oxford University Press, 2014), 40–60.

59. Joint Center for Housing Studies of Harvard University, *The State of the Nation's Housing, 2018* (Cambridge, MA: Joint Center for Housing Studies, 2018), 3, 36, https://www.jchs.harvard.edu/state-nations-housing-2018.

60. Elizabeth A. Harris, "Homeless Students Lag behind Peers and Face High Dropout Rates, Study Shows," *New York Times*, April 11, 2018.

61. Joint Center for Housing Studies, *State of the Nation's Housing, 2018*, 32.

62. Wendy Sawyer, "Visualizing the Racial Disparities in Mass Incarceration," Prison Policy Initiative, July 27, 2020, https://www.prisonpolicy.org/blog/2020/07/27/disparities/.

63. Michelle Alexander, *The New Jim Crow: Mass Incarceration in the Age of Colorblindness* (New York: New Press, 2010).

64. Jimmie L. Reeves and Richard Campbell, *Cracked Coverage: Television News, the Anti-cocaine Crusade, and the Reagan Legacy* (Durham, NC: Duke University Press, 1994).

65. Ande Nesmith and Ebony Ruhland, "Children of Incarcerated Parents: Challenges and Resiliency, in Their Own Words," *Children and Youth Services Review* 30, no. 10 (September 2008): 1119–30; Danielle Dallaire, Ann Ciccone, and Laura C. Wilson, "Teachers' Experiences with and Expectations of Children with Incarcerated Parents," *Journal of Applied Developmental Psychology* 31, no. 4 (2010): 281–90.

66. Devah Pager, Bruce Western, and Bart Bonikowski, "Discrimination in a Low-Wage Labor Market: A Field Experiment," *American Sociological Review* 74, no. 5 (October 1, 2009): 777–99.

67. Center for Advanced Studies in Child Welfare, *CW360°: A Comprehensive Look at a Prevalent Child Welfare Issue: Criminal Justice Involvement of Families in Child Welfare* (Saint Paul: Center for Advanced Studies in Child Welfare, University of Minnesota, Spring 2018).

68. William Ayers, Bernardine Dohrn, and Rich Ayers, eds., *Zero Tolerance: Resisting the Drive for Punishment in Our Schools: A Handbook for Parents, Students, Educators, and Citizens* (New York: New Press, 2001).

69. David R. Werner, Amy Widestrom, and Sylvester "Bud" Pues, "Prison Education: The Inmate as Student," in *Education-Based Incarceration and Recidivism: The Ultimate Social Justice Crime-Fighting Tool*, ed. Brian D. Fitch and Anthony H. Normore (Charlotte, NC: Information Age, 2012), 61–79.

70. Pager, Western, and Bonikowski, "Discrimination."

71. Elijah Anderson, *Code of the Street: Decency, Violence, and the Moral Life of the Inner City* (New York: W. W. Norton, 2000).

72. Kyle Spencer, "Navigating College," *New York Times*, October 13, 2019, Learning Section, 8; Doug Lederman, "The Incredible Shrinking Higher Ed Industry," *Inside Higher Education*, October 14, 2019.

73. Gail Sunderman, ed., *Holding NCLB Accountable: Achieving Accountability, Equity and School Reform* (Thousand Oaks, CA: Corwin, 2008).

74. Mary Pattillo-McCoy, *Black Picket Fences: Privilege and Peril among the Black Middle Class* (Chicago: University of Chicago Press, 1999).

75. Pattillo-McCoy.

76. Joint Center for Housing Studies of Harvard University, *The State of the Nation's Housing, 2019* (Cambridge, MA: Joint Center for Housing Studies, 2019), https://www.jchs.harvard.edu/state-nations-housing-2019.

77. Daniel Losen, ed., *Closing the School Discipline Gap: Equitable Remedies for Excessive Exclusion* (New York: Teachers College Press, 2015).

78. Christine Sleeter, "Preparing Teachers for Multiracial and Historically Underserved Schools," in *Lessons in Integration: Realizing the Promise of Racial Diversity in American Schools,* ed. Erica Frankenberg and Gary Orfield (Charlottesville: University of Virginia Press, 2007), 171–98.

79. Erica Frankenberg, "Exploring Teachers' Racial Attitudes in a Racially Transitioning Society," *Education and Urban Society* 44, no. 4 (2012): 448–76; Catherine E. Freeman, Benjamin Scafidi, and David L. Sjoquist, "Racial Segregation in Georgia Public Schools, 1994–2001: Trends, Causes and Impact on Teacher Quality," in *School Resegregation: Must the South Turn Back?,* ed. John Boger and Gary Orfield (Chapel Hill: University of North Carolina Press, 2005), 148–63.

80. Jeannie Oakes, *Keeping Track: How Schools Structure Inequality* (New Haven, CT: Yale University Press, 1985).

81. Jeannie Oakes, *Multiplying Inequalities: The Effects of Race, Social Class, and Tracking on Opportunities to Learn Mathematics and Science* (Santa Monica, CA: RAND, 1990).

82. Amy Stuart Wells and Jeannie Oakes, "Potential Pitfalls of Systemic Reform: Early Lessons from Research on Detracking," *Sociology of Education* 69 (1996): 135–43.

83. Carol Corbett Burris and Kevin G. Welner, "Closing the Achievement Gap by Detracking," *Phi Delta Kappan* 86, no. 8 (April 2005): 594–98.

84. Philip Handwerk et al., *Access to Success: Patterns of Advanced Placement Participation in U.S. High Schools,* Policy Information Report (Princeton, NJ: Educational Testing Service, 2008), 9, 16–17.

85. Mark C. Long, Dylan Conge, and Raymond McGhee Jr., "Life on the Frontier of AP Expansion: Can Schools in Less-Resourced Communities Successfully Implement Advanced Placement Science Courses?," *Educational Researcher* 48, no. 6 (2019): 356–68.

86. Freeman, Scafidi, and Sjoquist, "Racial Segregation."

87. ACT and the Education Trust, *On Course for Success: A Close Look at Selected High School Courses That Prepare All Students for College and Work* (ACT and the Education Trust, 2004), https://edtrust.org/resource/on-course-for-success/.

88. Jaekyung Lee, *The Anatomy of Achievement Gaps: Why and How American Education Is Still Losing (and Can Win) the War on Underachievement* (New York: Oxford University Press, 2016), 204–5.

89. Lee, 216–18.

90. Dana Goldstein, "'It Just Isn't Working': PISA Test Scores Cast Doubt on U.S. Education Efforts," *New York Times,* December 3, 2019, https://www.nytimes.com/2019/12/03/us/us-students-international-test-scores.html.

91. Russell W. Rumberger, *Dropping Out: Why Students Drop Out of High School and What Can Be Done about It* (Cambridge, MA: Harvard University Press, 2011); Gary Orfield, ed., *Dropouts in America: Confronting the Graduation Rate Crisis* (Cambridge, MA: Harvard Education Press, 2004).

92. William Bowen and Derek Bok, *The Shape of the River: Long-Term Consequences of Considering Race in College and University Admissions* (Princeton, NJ: Princeton University Press, 1998).

93. National Academies of Sciences, Engineering, and Medicine, *Promise of Adolescence,* 62.

94. Lorrie A. Shepard and Mary Lee Smith, eds., *Flunking Grades: Research and Policies on Retention*, Education Policy Perspectives (London: Falmer, 1989).

95. Rumberger, *Dropping Out*, 161–62.

96. Kerri A. Kerr and Nettie E. Legters, "Preventing Dropout: Use and Impact of Organizational Reforms Designed to Ease the Transition to High School," in Orfield, *Dropouts in America*, 221–42.

97. Catherine Gewertz, "School Counselors Responsible for 482 Students on Average, Report Finds," *Education Week*, February 8, 2018, https://www.edweek.org/teaching-learning /school-counselors-responsible-for-482-students-on-average-report-finds/2018/02.

98. Gewertz.

99. Catherine Gewertz, "School Counselors Boost College, Financial Aid Chances, Study Finds," *Education Week*, December 7, 2016, https://www.edweek.org/teaching-learning/school -counselors-boost-students-college-financial-aid-chances-study-finds/2016/12.

100. Daniel Koretz, *Measuring Up: What Educational Testing Really Tells Us* (Cambridge, MA: Harvard University Press, 2008), 6–7; Daniel Koretz, *The Testing Charade: Pretending to Make Schools Better* (Chicago: University of Chicago Press, 2017), 16–18.

101. Scott Jaschik and Doug Lederman, "2021 Survey of College and University Admissions Directors: A Survey by Inside Higher Education and Hanover Research," *Inside Higher Education*, October 2021, 8.

102. *Briggs v. Elliott*, 132 F. Supp. 776 (E.D.S.C., 1955).

103. *Green v. Board of Education of New Kent County*, 391 U.S. 430 (1968).

104. *Milliken v. Bradley*, 418 U.S. 717 (1974).

105. Ellen Goldring and Claire Smrekar, "Magnet Schools: Reform and Race in Urban Education," *Clearing House* 76, no. 1 (September–October 2001): 13–15.

106. Andrew Ujifusa, "No Measurable Gap between Charters, Traditional Public Schools on National Tests," *Education Week* blog, September 25, 2019, https://blogs.edweek.org/edweek /campaign-k-12/2019/09/traditional-public-charter-schools-NAEP-assessment-no -measurable-gap.html.

107. Gary Orfield and Erica Frankenberg, *Educational Delusions? Why Choice Can Deepen Inequality and How to Make Schools Fair* (Berkeley: University of California Press, 2013).

108. Peter Rich, Jennifer Candipan, and Ann Owens, "Segregated Neighborhoods, Segregated Schools: Do Charters Break a Stubborn Link?," *Demography* 58, no. 2 (2021): 471–98, https://read.dukeupress.edu/demography/article/58/2/471/169350/Segregated -Neighborhoods-Segregated-Schools-Do. For example, the popular Booker T. Washington arts magnet in Dallas and all the city's other magnets require test scores to enter the competitive schools. "Innovations in Education: Successful Magnet High Schools," U.S. Department of Education, September 2008, https://www2.ed.gov/admins/comm/choice/magnet-hs/report _pg24.html#sec24.

109. Orfield and Ayscue, *Discrimination in Elite Public Schools*.

110. Bruce Fuller and Richard Elmore, eds., *Who Chooses, Who Loses? Culture, Institutions and the Unequal Effects of School Choice*, with Gary Orfield (New York: Teachers College Press, 1995).

111. Sean F. Reardon et al., "What Levels of Racial Diversity Can Be Achieved with Socioeconomic-Based Affirmative Action? Evidence from a Simulation Model," CEPA Working Paper No. 15-04, Center for Education Policy Analysis, Stanford, CA, December 2017,

https://cepa.stanford.edu/sites/default/files/wp15-04-v201712.pdf. See also Sean F. Reardon, John T. Yun, and Michael Kurlaender, "Implications of Income-Based School Assignment Policies for Racial School Segregation," *Educational Evaluation and Policy Analysis* 28, no. 1 (2006): 49–75.

Chapter 3. The Tradition of Exclusion

1. National Academies of Sciences, Engineering, and Medicine, *Monitoring Educational Equity* (Washington, DC: National Academies Press, 2019), chap. 5, https://doi.org/10.17226/25389.

2. Winthrop D. Jordan, *White over Black: American Attitudes toward the Negro, 1550–1812,* 2nd ed. (Chapel Hill: University of North Carolina Press, 2012).

3. Gary B. Nash, "Red, White and Black: The Origins of Racism in Colonial America," in *The Great Fear: Race in the Mind of America*, ed. Gary B. Nash and Richard Weiss (New York: Holt, Rinehart and Winston, 1970), 7.

4. Stanley Lieberson, *A Piece of the Pie: Blacks and White Immigrants since 1880* (Berkeley: University of California Press, 1981).

5. Bill Ong Hing, *Making and Remaking Asian America through Immigration Policy, 1850–1990* (Stanford, CA: Stanford University Press, 1993).

6. Helen F. Eckerson, "Immigration and National Origins," in "The New Immigration," special issue, *Annals of the American Academy of Political and Social Science* 367, no. 1 (1966): 4–14.

7. Lawrence A. Cremin, *American Education*, vol. 2, *The National Experience, 1783–1876* (New York: Harper and Row, 1980), 388–89.

8. Cremin, 389–90.

9. Commission on the Reorganization of Secondary Education, *Cardinal Principles of Secondary Education*, Bulletin 1918, No. 35, Bureau of Education, Department of the Interior (Washington, DC: Government Printing Office, 1918), https://eric.ed.gov/?id=ED541063.

10. David L. Angus and Jeffrey E. Mirel, *The Failed Promise of the American High School, 1890–1995* (New York: Teachers College Press, 1999).

11. Lawrence A. Cremin, *American Education*, vol. 3, *The Metropolitan Experience, 1876–1980* (New York: Harper and Row, 1988), 546.

12. U.S. Department of Education, National Center for Education Statistics, *Digest of Educational Statistics, 1980* (Washington, DC: Government Printing Office, 1980), 44, http://archive.org/details/ERIC_ED202085.

13. Ira Katznelson and Margaret Weir, *Schooling for All: Class, Race, and the Decline of the Democratic Ideal* (New York: Basic Books, 1985), 55.

14. Angus and Mirel, *Failed Promise*, 41–43.

15. W.E.B. DuBois, *The Philadelphia Negro: A Social Study* (Philadelphia: University of Pennsylvania Press, 1899); Allan H. Spear, *Black Chicago: The Making of a Negro Ghetto, 1890–1920* (Chicago: University of Chicago Press, 1967).

16. DuBois, *Philadelphia Negro*, 56.

17. Robert Staughton Lynd and Helen Merrell Lynd, *Middletown: A Study in Contemporary American Culture* (New York: Harcourt Brace, 1929).

18. Ruth E. Eckert and Thomas O. Marshall, *When Youth Leave School: The Regents Inquiry* (New York: McGraw-Hill, 1938).

19. Eckert and Marshall, 11, 28.

20. Eckert and Marshall, 47.

21. Eckert and Marshall, 72.

22. Eckert and Marshall, 74.

23. Thomas D. Snyder, Cristobal de Brey, and Sally A. Dillow, *Digest of Education Statistics, 2017* (Washington, DC: National Center for Education Statistics, January 2019), table 104.10, https://nces.ed.gov/programs/digest/d17/tables/dt17_104.10.asp.

24. Raymond E. Callahan, *Education and the Cult of Efficiency* (Chicago: University of Chicago Press, 1962), 1.

25. James Bryant Conant, *The American High School Today* (New York: McGraw-Hill, 1959).

26. Jeannie Oakes, *Keeping Track: How Schools Structure Inequality* (New Haven, CT: Yale University Press, 1985).

27. Dwight D. Eisenhower, "Annual Message to the Congress on the State of the Union," January 9, 1958, American Presidency Project, https://www.presidency.ucsb.edu/documents/annual-message-the-congress-the-state-the-union-10.

28. Michael J. Bennett, *When Dreams Came True: The GI Bill and the Making of Modern America* (Washington, DC: Brassey's, 1996), 243.

29. James MacGregor Burns, *Roosevelt: The Soldier of Freedom, 1940–1945* (New York: Harcourt Brace Jovanovich, 2012), 362.

30. "Education and Training: History and Timeline," U.S. Department of Veterans Affairs, Veterans Benefits Administration, last updated November 21, 2013, https://www.benefits.va.gov/gibill/history.asp.

31. Sarah Turner and John Bound, "Closing the Gap or Widening the Divide: The Effects of the G.I. Bill and World War II on the Educational Outcomes of Black Americans," *Journal of Economic History* 63, no. 1 (March 2003): 145–77.

32. C. Vann Woodward, *Reunion and Reaction: The Compromise of 1877 and the End of Reconstruction* (Boston: Little, Brown, 1951).

33. Henry Allen Bullock, *A History of Negro Education in the South* (Cambridge, MA: Harvard University Press, 1967; repr., New York: Praeger, 1970), 170.

34. Bullock, 171.

35. James D. Anderson, *The Education of Blacks in the South, 1860–1935* (Chapel Hill: University of North Carolina Press, 1988), 137–54; Alfred Perkins, *Edwin Rogers Embree: The Julius Rosenwald Fund, Foundation Philanthropy, and American Race Relations* (Bloomington: Indiana University Press, 2011).

36. Bullock, *History of Negro Education*, 178–82.

37. W.E.B. DuBois and Augustus Granville Dill, *The College-Bred Negro American* (Atlanta: Atlanta University Press, 1910), 23, 45.

38. Thomas P. Carter, *Mexican Americans in School: A History of Educational Neglect* (New York: College Entrance Examination Board, 1970), 9.

39. Kathleen L. Wolgemuth, "Woodrow Wilson and Federal Segregation," *Journal of Negro History* 44, no. 2 (April 1959): 158–73.

40. Adam Green, "How a Brutal Race Riot Shaped Modern Chicago: A Century Later, the City, and America, Are Still Dealing with the Consequences," *New York Times*, August 3, 2019.

41. Roger Daniels, *Coming to America: A History of Immigration and Ethnicity in American Life*, 2nd ed. (New York: Harper Perennial, 2002).

42. Mildred A. Schwartz, *Trends in White Attitudes toward Negroes*, Report No. 119 (Chicago: National Opinion Research Center, University of Chicago, 1967), 19.

43. *Cumming v. Richmond County Board of Education*, 175 U.S. 528 (1899).

44. Anderson, *Education of Blacks*, 194–95.

45. For a chart summarizing the violations proved in federal courts in many cities outside the South, see Gary Orfield, *Must We Bus? Segregated Schools and National Policy* (Washington, DC: Brookings Institution, 1978), 20–22.

46. Karl E. Taeuber and Alma Taeuber, *Negroes in Cities: Residential Segregation and Neighborhood Change* (Chicago: Aldine, 1965).

47. Kriston Capps, "How the Federal Government Built White Suburbia," Bloomberg CityLab, September 2, 2015, https://www.bloomberg.com/news/articles/2015-09-02/how-the-federal-government-built-white-suburbia.

48. Taeuber and Taeuber, *Negroes in Cities*.

49. Susan C. Faircloth and John W Tippeconnic III, *The Dropout/Graduation Rate Crisis among American Indian and Alaska Native Students: Failure to Respond Places the Future of Native Peoples at Risk* (Los Angeles: Civil Rights Project, 2010); Civil Rights Project/Proyecto Derechos Civiles, homepage, accessed August 9, 2021, https://www.civilrightsproject.ucla.edu; U.S. Commission on Civil Rights, *Bordertown Discrimination in Montana: Summary Findings and Policy Implications: A Brief from the Montana Advisory Committee* (May 2019).

50. Charles Wollenberg, *Ethnic Conflict in California History* (Los Angeles: Tinnon-Brown, 1970), 97.

51. Carter, *Mexican Americans in School*, 9.

52. Carter, 10, quoting William McEwen.

53. Wilson Little, *Spanish-Speaking Children in Texas* (Austin: University of Texas Press, 1944); Ruth Connor, "Some Community, Home and School Problems of Latin American Children in Austin, Texas" (MA thesis, University of Texas, 1949), both cited in Vernon Carl Allsup, *The American G.I. Forum: Origins and Evolution*, Mexican American Monographs No. 6 (Austin: Center for Mexican American Studies, University of Texas at Austin, 1982), 167.

54. Carter, *Mexican Americans in School*, 23.

55. U.S. Commission on Civil Rights, *Racial Isolation in the Public Schools* (Washington, DC: Government Printing Office, 1967), 1:2–3.

56. U.S. Commission on Civil Rights, 106–7.

57. DuBois, *Philadelphia Negro*; Spear, *Black Chicago*.

58. Findings from many federal court decisions summarized in Orfield, *Must We Bus?*

59. *Plessy v. Ferguson*, 163 U.S. 537 (1896).

60. Anderson, *Education of Blacks*.

61. Lieberson, *Piece of the Pie*.

62. Richard Kluger, *Simple Justice* (New York: Vintage Books, 1975).

63. *Sweatt v. Painter*, 339 U.S. 629 (1950).

64. Gary Orfield, *The Reconstruction of Southern Education: The Schools and the 1964 Civil Rights Act* (New York: John Wiley, 1969).

65. J. W. Peltason, *Fifty-Eight Lonely Men: Southern Federal Judges and School Desegregation* (New York: Harcourt, Brace and World, 1961).

Chapter 4. The Civil Rights Revolution and the War on Poverty: A Color-Conscious Rights Policy Worked

1. James L. Sundquist, *Politics and Policy: The Eisenhower, Kennedy and Johnson Years* (Washington, DC: Brookings Institution, 1968), chap. 5.

2. Gary Orfield, "Race and the Liberal Agenda: The Loss of the Integrationist Dream, 1965–1974," in *The Politics of Social Policy in the United States*, ed. Margaret Weir, Ann Shola Orloff, and Theda Skocpol (Princeton, NJ: Princeton University Press, 1988), 313–55.

3. Taylor Branch, *Parting the Waters: America in the King Years, 1954–63* (New York: Simon and Schuster, 1988).

4. Raymond Arsenault, *Freedom Rides: 1961 and the Struggle for Racial Justice* (New York: Oxford University Press, 2006).

5. David B. Filvaroff and Raymond E. Wolfinger, "The Origin and Enactment of the Civil Rights Act of 1964," in *Legacies of the 1964 Civil Rights Act*, ed. Bernard Grofman (Charlottesville: University of Virginia Press, 2000), 11.

6. Diane McWhorter, *Carry Me Home: Birmingham, Alabama, the Climactic Battle of the Civil Rights Revolution* (New York: Touchstone, 2001).

7. McWhorter, 373–74.

8. Sundquist, *Politics and Policy*, 266–67; Robert Mann, *The Walls of Jericho: Lyndon Johnson, Hubert Humphrey, Richard Russell, and the Struggle for Civil Rights* (New York: Harcourt Brace, 1996); Charles Whalen and Barbara Whalen, *The Longest Debate: A Legislative History of the 1964 Civil Rights Act* (Santa Ana, CA: Seven Locks, 1985).

9. Frank Newport, "Public Opinion on Civil Rights 50 Years after the Civil Rights Act of 1964," Gallup News release, April 10, 2014, https://news.gallup.com/opinion/polling-matters/169361/public-opinion-civil-rights-years-civil-rights-act-1964.aspx.

10. Michael Harrington, *The Other America* (New York: Macmillan, 1962).

11. Sundquist, *Politics and Policy*, 144–50.

12. Elementary and Secondary Education Act of 1965, Pub. L. No. 89-10.

13. Higher Education Act of 1965, Pub. L. No. 89-329.

14. Numan V. Bartley, *The Rise of Massive Resistance: Race and Politics in the South during the 1950's* (Baton Rouge: Louisiana State University Press, 1999).

15. Gloria J. Browne-Marshall, *The Voting Rights War: The NAACP and the Ongoing Struggle for Justice* (Lanham, MD: Rowman and Littlefield, 2016).

16. Lyndon Johnson, Address on Voting Rights to Joint Session of Congress, March 16, 1965.

17. Frank R. Parker, *Black Votes Count: Political Empowerment in Mississippi after 1965* (Chapel Hill: University of North Carolina Press, 1990), 1.

18. Alexander Keyssar, *The Right to Vote: The Contested History of Democracy in the United States* (New York: Basic Books, 2000), 264.

19. *South Carolina v. Katzenbach*, 383 U.S. 301 (1966).

20. Owen M. Fiss, *The Civil Rights Injunction* (Bloomington: Indiana University Press, 1978).

21. Julian E. Zelizer, *The Fierce Urgency of Now: Lyndon Johnson, Congress, and the Battle for the Great Society* (New York: Penguin, 2015); Sheldon H. Danziger and Daniel H. Weinberg, eds., *Fighting Poverty: What Works and What Doesn't* (Cambridge, MA: Harvard University Press, 1986).

22. Bernard Grofman, ed., *Legacies of the 1964 Civil Rights Act* (Charlottesville: University Press of Virginia, 2000).

23. Gary Orfield, "The 1964 Civil Rights Act and American Education," in Grofman, *Legacies*, 89–128.

24. Stephen Kemp Bailey and Edith K. Mosher, *ESEA: The Office of Education Administers a Law* (Syracuse, NY: Syracuse University Press, 1968).

25. Gary Orfield, *The Reconstruction of Southern Education: The Schools and the 1964 Civil Rights Act* (New York: John Wiley, 1969).

26. U.S. Commission on Civil Rights, *Survey of School Desegregation in the Southern and Border States, 1965–1966* (Washington, DC: Government Printing Office, 1966).

27. Orfield, *Reconstruction of Southern Education*, chaps. 2, 3.

28. Orfield, chaps. 2, 3.

29. *Green v. County School Board of New Kent County*, 391 U.S. 430 (1968).

30. Gary Orfield, *Public School Desegregation in the United States, 1968–1980* (Washington, DC: Joint Center for Political Studies, 1983).

31. Gary Orfield, "Public Opinion and School Desegregation," *Teachers College Record* 96, no. 4 (Summer 1995): 654–70.

32. Rucker C. Johnson, *Children of the Dream: Why School Integration Works* (New York: Basic Books, 2019).

33. Johnson, 59.

34. Johnson, 60.

35. Johnson, 62.

36. Robert L. Crain, "School Integration and Occupational Achievement of Negroes," *American Journal of Sociology* 75, no. 4, pt. 2 (January 1970): 593–606.

37. Jomills Henry Braddock II and James M. McPartland, *More Evidence on Social-Psychological Processes That Perpetuate Minority Segregation: The Relationship of School Desegregation and Employment Segregation*, Report No. CSOS-338 (Baltimore: Center for Social Organization of Schools, Johns Hopkins University, June 1983).

38. Chandra Muller et al., "Race and Academic Achievement in Racially Diverse High Schools: Opportunity and Stratification," *Teachers College Record* 112, no. 4 (2010): 1038–63; Gregory J. Palardy, "High School Socioeconomic Segregation and Student Attainment," *American Educational Research Journal* 50, no. 4 (2013): 714–54.

39. Gordon Willard Allport, *The Nature of Prejudice* (Boston: Addison-Wesley, 1954).

40. Thomas F. Pettigrew and Linda R. Tropp, "A Meta-analytic Test of Intergroup Contact Theory," *Journal of Personality and Social Psychology* 90, no. 5 (2006): 751–83.

41. Bobby D. Rampey, Gloria S. Dion, and Patricia L. Donahue, *NAEP 2008: Trends in Academic Progress* (Washington, DC: National Center for Education Statistics, U.S. Department of Education, April 2009), https://nces.ed.gov/nationsreportcard/pdf/main2008/2009479.pdf; Jacob Vigdor and Jens Ludwig, "Segregation and the Test Score Gap," in *Steady Gains and Stalled Progress: Inequality and the Black-White Test Score Gap*, ed. Katherine Magnuson and Jane Waldfogel (New York: Russell Sage, 2008), 181–211.

42. Daniel Koretz, *Trends in Educational Achievement* (Washington, DC: Congressional Budget Office, April 1986).

43. Gerald David Jaynes and Robin M. Williams Jr., eds., *A Common Destiny: Blacks and American Society* (Washington, DC: National Academy Press, 1989), 326–29.

44. Gary Orfield, ed., *Diversity Challenged: Research on the Impact of Affirmative Action*, with Michal Kurlaender (Cambridge, MA: Harvard Education Press, 2001).

45. Meyer Weinberg, *A Chance to Learn: The History of Race and Education in the United States* (Cambridge: Cambridge University Press, 1977), 281.

46. William G. Bowen and Derek Bok, *The Shape of the River: Long-Term Consequences of Considering Race in College and University Admissions* (Princeton, NJ: Princeton University Press, 1998), 5. See also Marvin W. Peterson et al., *Black Students on White Campuses: The Impact of Increased Black Enrollments* (Ann Arbor: Institute for Social Research, University of Michigan, 1978).

47. Bowen and Bok, *Shape of the River*, 5.

48. Bowen and Bok, 6–7.

49. Bowen and Bok, 7–9.

50. Leon Panetta and Peter Gall, *Bring Us Together: The Nixon Team and the Civil Rights Retreat* (Philadelphia: Lippincott, 1971).

51. *Adams v. Richardson*, 356 F. Supp. 92 (D.D.C., 1973), aff'd, 480 F.2d 1159 (D.C. Cir., 1973).

52. U.S. Office for Civil Rights, "Revised Criteria Specifying the Ingredients of Acceptable Plans to Desegregate State Systems of Public Higher Education," *Federal Register* 43, no. 2 (February 15, 1978): 6658–64.

53. John B. Williams, "The State Role in Achieving Equality of Higher Education," in *Toward Black Undergraduate Student Equality in American Higher Education*, ed. Michael T. Nettles (New York: Greenwood, 1988), 155–56.

54. Williams, 158.

55. Southern Education Foundation, *Redeeming the American Promise: Report of the Panel on Educational Opportunity and Postsecondary Desegregation* (Atlanta: Southern Education Foundation, 1995), A33.

56. Higher Education Act of 1965, Pub. L. No. 89-329.

57. Thomas A. Snyder, Sally A. Dillow, and Charlene M. Hoffman, *Digest of Education Statistics, 2007* (Washington, DC: National Center for Education Statistics, 2008), table 320, "Average Undergraduate Tuition and Fees and Room and Board Rates Charged for Full-Time Students in Degree-Granting Institutions, by Type and Control of Institution: 1964–65 through 2006–07," https://nces.ed.gov/programs/digest/d07/tables/dt07_320.asp.

58. "Upward Bound," in *Encyclopedia of Education*, ed. John W. Groutt and James W. Guthrie, 2nd ed. (New York: Macmillan Reference, 2002), 7:2603–5; Edward J. McElroy and Maria Armesto, "TRIO and Upward Bound: History, Programs, and Issues—Past, Present, and Future," *Journal of Negro Education* 67, no. 4 (1998): 373–80.

59. Associated Press, "Black College Enrollment Has Doubled since 1970," *New York Times*, May 18, 1981, D13.

60. Pew Research Center, *Modern Immigration Wave Brings 59 Million to U.S., Driving Population Growth and Change through 2065: Views of Immigration's Impact on U.S. Society Mixed* (Washington, DC: Pew Research Center, September 2015).

61. Gary Orfield, *Congressional Power: Congress and Social Change* (New York: Harcourt Brace Jovanovich, 1975), chap. 7.

62. *Keyes v. School Dist. No. 1, Denver, Colorado*, 413 U.S. 189 (1973).

63. *Lau v. Nichols*, 414 U.S. 563 (1974).

64. U.S. Commission on Civil Rights, *Toward Quality Education for Mexican Americans* (Washington, DC: Government Printing Office, 1972); Gary Orfield, "The Rights of Hispanic Children," in *Must We Bus? Segregated Schools and National Policy* (Washington, DC: Brookings Institution, 1978), 198–232.

65. *San Antonio Independent School Dist. v. Rodriguez*, 411 U.S. 1 (1973).

66. *Milliken v. Bradley*, 418 U.S. 717 (1974).

67. *Regents of the University of California v. Bakke*, 438 U.S. 265 (1978).

Chapter 5. Colorblindness Reigns: Four Decades of Inequality in a Transforming Society

1. Susan E. Eaton, *The Other Boston Busing Story: What's Won and Lost across the Boundary Line* (New Haven, CT: Yale University Press, 2001).

2. Gary Simons, ed., *Be the Dream: Prep for Prep Graduates Share Their Stories* (Chapel Hill, NC: Algonquin Books, 2003).

3. Patricia Gándara, "A Study of High School Puente: What We Have Learned about Preparing Latino Youth for Postsecondary Education," *Educational Policy* 16, no. 4 (September 1, 2002): 474–95.

4. Fabian T. Pfeffer and Alexandra Killewald, "Generations of Advantage: Multigenerational Correlations in Family Wealth," *Social Forces* 96, no. 4 (June 2018): 1411–42.

5. Samantha Smith, "Why People Are Rich and Poor: Republicans and Democrats Have Very Different Views," *Fact Tank*, Pew Research Center, May 2, 2017, https://www.pewresearch .org/fact-tank/2017/05/02/why-people-are-rich-and-poor-republicans-and-democrats-have -very-different-views.

6. Jackyung Lee, "Two Takes on the Impact of NCLB on Academic Achievement," in *Holding NCLB Accountable: Achieving Accountability, Equity, and School Reform*, ed. Gail Sunderman (Thousand Oaks, CA: Corwin, 2008), 75–90.

7. Jennifer Hochschild and Nathan Scovronick, *The American Dream and the Public Schools* (New York: Oxford University Press, 2003); Jennifer L. Hochschild, *Facing Up to the American Dream: Race, Class, and the Soul of the Nation* (Princeton, NJ: Princeton University Press, 1996).

8. Maria Krysan and Sarah Patton Moberg, "Trends in Racial Attitudes," University of Illinois, Institute of Government and Public Affairs, August 25, 2016, http://igpa.uillinois.edu /programs/racial-attitudes.

9. Dan T. Carter, *From George Wallace to Newt Gingrich: Race in the Conservative Counterrevolution, 1963–1994* (Baton Rouge: Louisiana State University Press, 1996).

10. Helen A. Neville, Miguel E. Gallardo, and Derald Wing Sue, eds., *The Myth of Racial Color Blindness: Manifestations, Dynamics, and Impact* (Washington, DC: American Psychiatric Association, 2016).

11. Charles Peters and Phillip Keisling, eds., *A New Road for America: The Neoliberal Movement* (Lanham, MD: Madison Books, 1985); Stanley B. Greenberg, *Middle Class Dreams: The Politics and Power of the New American Majority* (New Haven, CT: Yale University Press, 1996).

12. Bill Clinton and Al Gore, *Putting People First: How We Can All Change America* (New York: Times Books, 1992), 5, 14–15.

13. *San Antonio Independent School District v. Rodriguez*, 411 U.S. 1 (1973).

14. Joe McGinniss, *The Selling of the President, 1968* (New York: Trident, 1969), 92–95.

15. "'Welfare Queen' Becomes Issue in Reagan Campaign," *New York Times*, February 15, 1976, 51.

16. Peter Baker, "Bush Made Willie Horton an Issue in 1988, and the Racial Scars Are Still Fresh," *New York Times*, December 3, 2018.

17. "Ronald Reagan's 1980 Neshoba County Fair Speech," *Neshoba Democrat*, April 8, 2021, https://www.neshobademocrat.com/stories/ronald-reagans-1980-neshoba-county-fair -speech,49123?.

18. *San Antonio Independent School District v. Rodriguez*, 411 U.S. 1 (1973).

19. Gary Orfield and Susan E. Eaton, *Dismantling Desegregation: The Quiet Reversal of "Brown v. Board of Education"* (New York: New Press, 1996).

20. *Board of Ed. of Oklahoma City Public Schools v. Dowell*, 498 U.S. 237 (1991).

21. *Keyes v. School Dist. No. 1, Denver Colorado*, 413 U.S. 189 (1973).

22. See U.S. Government Accountability Office, *K–12 Education: Better Use of Information Could Help Agencies Identify Disparities and Address Racial Discrimination* (Washington, DC: U.S. Government Accountability Office, April 21, 2016), https://www.gao.gov/products/GAO -16-345.

23. Gary Orfield and Chungmei Lee, *"Brown" at 50: King's Dream or Plessy's Nightmare?* (Cambridge, MA: Civil Rights Project at Harvard University, January 2004), https:// civilrightsproject.ucla.edu/research/k-12-education/integration-and-diversity/brown-at-50 -king2019s-dream-or-plessy2019s-nightmare/orfield-brown-50-2004.pdf.

24. Raj Chetty et al., "Where Is the Land of Opportunity? Intergenerational Mobility in the US," NBER Working Paper No. 19843, National Bureau of Economic Research, Cambridge, MA, 2014.

25. Gary Orfield, "Public Opinion and School Desegregation," *Teachers College Record* 96, no. 4 (Summer 1995): 654–70.

26. Raj Chetty, John N. Friedman, and Jonah E. Rockoff, "The Long-Term Impacts of Teachers: Teacher Value-Added and Student Outcomes in Adulthood," NBER Working Paper No. 17699, National Bureau of Economic Research, Cambridge, MA, December 2011, 47, https://doi.org/10.3386/w17699; Charles T. Clotfelter, Helen F. Ladd, and Jacob Vigdor, "Who Teaches Whom? Race and the Distribution of Novice Teachers," *Economics of Education Review* 24, no. 4 (2005): 377–92; Steven G. Rivkin, Eric A. Hanushek, and John Kain, "Teachers, Schools, and Academic Achievement," *Econometrica* 73, no. 2 (2005): 417–58. See, for example, Hamilton Lankford, Susannah Loeb, and James Wyckoff, "Teacher Sorting and the Plight of Urban Schools: A Descriptive Analysis," *Educational Evaluation and Policy Analysis* 24, no. 1 (2002): 37–62.

27. John Rogers et al., *California Educational Opportunity Report* (Los Angeles: Institute for Democracy, Education, and Access at the University of California, Los Angeles, and University of California All Campus Consortium on Research for Diversity, 2009).

28. Geoffrey Borman and Maritza Dowling, "Schools and Inequality: A Multilevel Analysis of Coleman's Equality of Educational Opportunity Data," *Teachers College Record* 112, no. 5 (2010): 1201–46; Russell W. Rumberger and Gregory J. Palardy, "Does Segregation Still Matter? The Impact of Student Composition on Academic Achievement in High School," *Teachers College Record* 107, no. 9 (2005): 1999–2045; Caroline M. Hoxby, "Peer Effects in the Classroom: Learning from Gender and Race Variation," NBER Working Paper No. 7867, National Bureau of Economic Research, Cambridge, MA, August 2000, https://www.nber.org/papers/w7867; Janet Ward Schofield and Leslie R. M. Hausmann, "The Conundrum of School Desegregation:

Positive Student Outcomes and Waning Support," *University of Pittsburgh Law Review* 66, no. 1 (April 2004): 83–111.

29. *Parents Involved in Community Schools v. Seattle School District No. 1*, 551 U.S. 701 (2007).

30. Eliza Shapiro, "Only 7 Black Students Got into Stuyvesant, N.Y.'s Most Selective High School, Out of 895 Spots," *New York Times*, March 18, 2019; Eliza Shapiro and K. K. Rebecca Lai, "How New York's Elite Public Schools Lost Their Black and Hispanic Students," *New York Times*, June 3, 2019, https://www.nytimes.com/interactive/2019/06/03/nyregion/nyc-public-schools-black-hispanic-students.html.

31. Gary Orfield and Jennifer B. Ayscue, eds., *Discrimination in Elite Public Schools: Investigating Buffalo* (New York: Teachers College Press, 2018).

32. Roslyn Arlin Mickelson and Martha Bottia, "Integrated Education and Mathematics Outcomes: A Synthesis of Social Science Research," *North Carolina Law Review* 88 (2010): 993–1089; Thomas Pettigrew and Linda Tropp, "A Meta-analytic Test of Intergroup Contact Theory," *Journal of Personality and Social Psychology* 90, no. 5 (2006): 751–83; Douglas D. Ready and Megan R. Silander, "School Racial and Ethnic Composition and Young Children's Cognitive Development: Isolating Family, Neighborhood and School Influences," in *Integrating Schools in a Changing Society: New Policies and Legal Options for a Multiracial Generation*, ed. Erica Frankenberg and Elizabeth DeBray (Chapel Hill: University of North Carolina Press, 2011), 91–113; Melanie Killen, David S. Crystal, and Martin Ruck, "The Social Developmental Benefits of Intergroup Contact among Children and Adolescents," in *Lessons in Integration: Realizing the Promise of Racial Diversity in American Schools*, ed. Erica Frankenberg and Gary Orfield (Charlottesville: University of Virginia Press, 2007), 57–73.

33. *San Antonio Independent School District v. Rodriguez*, 411 U.S. 1 (1973).

34. C. Kirabo Jackson, Rucker Johnson, and Claudia Persico, "The Effect of School Finance Reforms on the Distribution of Spending, Academic Achievement, and Adult Outcomes," NBER Working Paper No. 20118, National Bureau of Economic Research, Cambridge, MA, May 2014.

35. Kiah Collier, "Texas Supreme Court Rules School Funding System Is Constitutional," *Texas Tribune*, May 13, 2016.

36. *Hancock v. Commissioner of Education*, 443 Mass. 428, 822 N.E.2d 1134 (Mass. 2005).

37. David A. Stockman, *The Triumph of Politics: The Inside Story of the Reagan Revolution* (New York: Random House, 1986).

38. Ronald Reagan, Inaugural Address, January 20, 1981, Ronald Reagan Presidential Foundation and Institute, https://www.reaganfoundation.org/ronald-reagan/reagan-quotes-speeches/inaugural-address-1/.

39. Meyer Weinberg, "United States," *Integrated Education* 20, no. 6 (1983): 47.

40. Andrew Busch, *Ronald Reagan and the Politics of Freedom* (Lanham, MD: Rowman and Littlefield, 2001), 41.

41. George E. Peterson et al., *The Reagan Block Grants: What Have We Learned?* (Washington, DC: Urban Institute Press, 1986), 20–21.

42. Author was chair of the National Institute of Education desegregation research committee.

43. Middle Income Student Assistance Act, H.R. 11274, 95th Cong., 2nd Sess., 1978.

44. Dick Morris, *Behind the Oval Office: Winning the Presidency in the Nineties* (New York: Random House, 1997), 223–26; Mark Pitsch, "Clinton Proposes Tax Credit for College Tuition," *Education Week*, June 12, 1996, https://www.edweek.org/teaching-learning/clinton-proposes -tax-credit-for-college-tuition/1996/06.

45. Suzanne Mettler, *Degrees of Inequality: How the Politics of Higher Education Sabotaged the American Dream* (New York: Basic Books, 2014), 83.

46. Randall B. Ripley and Grace A. Franklin, *Congress, the Bureaucracy, and Public Policy*, 5th ed. (Pacific Grove, CA: Brooks/Cole, 1991).

47. Donald E. Heller and Patricia Marin, eds., *State Merit Scholarship Programs and Racial Inequality* (Cambridge, MA: Civil Rights Project at Harvard University, 2004).

48. Michael S. McPherson and Morton Owen Shapiro, *The Student Aid Game: Meeting New and Rewarding Talent in American Higher Education* (Princeton, NJ: Princeton University Press, 1998), 39.

49. McPherson and Shapiro, 40–41.

50. Tammy LaGorce, "Retired, or Hoping to Be, and Saddled with Student Loans," *New York Times*, March 3, 2020.

51. Patricia Gándara et al., *Building Pathways to Transfer: Community Colleges That Break the Chain of Failure for Students of Color* (Los Angeles: Civil Rights Project, 2012).

52. Deborah Rankin, "Your Money: Reagan Cuts in Student Aid," *New York Times*, October 24, 1981, https://www.nytimes.com/1981/10/24/business/your-money-reagan-cuts-in -student-aid.html.

53. American Council on Education, *Student Aid in the Reagan Administration: Fact Sheet* (October 1984), 9.

54. Rankin, "Your Money," 30.

55. Caroline M. Hoxby and Christopher Avery, "The Missing 'One-Offs': The Hidden Supply of High-Achieving, Low Income Students," NBER Working Paper No. 18586, National Bureau of Economic Research, Cambridge, MA, December 2012; Derek Thompson, "Why Smart Poor Students Don't Apply to Selective Colleges (and How to Fix It)," *Atlantic*, January 24, 2013, https://www.theatlantic.com/business/archive/2013/01/why-smart-poor-students-dont -apply-to-selective-colleges-and-how-to-fix-it/272490/.

56. "The Top Producers of African-American Graduates," *Diverse*, February 6, 2020, 20.

57. Catharine Bond Hill et al., *Enrolling More Veterans at High-Graduation-Rate Colleges and Universities* (New York: Ithaka S+R, 2019), 4, 10.

58. Kevin Eagan et al., *The American Freshman: National Norms Fall 2016* (Los Angeles: Higher Education Research Institute, Graduate School of Education and Information Studies, University of California, Los Angeles, 2017), 7.

59. Eagan et al., 8–9.

60. Hoxby and Avery, "Missing 'One-Offs.'"

61. Edward B. Fiske, "Reagan Record in Education: Mixed Results," *New York Times*, November 14, 1982, sec. 12, p. 1.

62. Michael S. McPherson and Morton Owen Schapiro, *Keeping College Affordable: Government and Educational Opportunity* (Washington, DC: Brookings Institution, 1991), 21.

63. McPherson and Schapiro, 24.

64. McPherson and Schapiro, 47.

65. McPherson and Schapiro, 32.

66. McPherson and Schapiro, 36.

67. McPherson and Schapiro, 37–40.

68. McPherson and Schapiro, 41.

69. McPherson and Schapiro, 87.

70. College Board, *Trends in College Pricing 2000* (New York: College Board, 2000), 4.

71. Steven W. Hemelt and Dave E. Marcotte, "The Impact of Tuition Increases on Enrollment at Public Colleges and Universities," *Educational Evaluation and Policy Analysis* 33, no. 4 (December 2011): 435–57.

72. College Board, *Trends in College Pricing 2000*, 4.

73. College Board, 15–16.

74. College Board, 19.

75. Deborah J. Wilds, *Minorities in Higher Education: Seventh Annual Status Report* (Washington, DC: American Council on Education, Office of Minority Concerns, 1988), 16–27.

76. College Board, *Trends in College Pricing 2000*, 5, 13.

77. College Board, 13.

78. Robert A. Dentler, D. Catherine Baltzell, and Daniel J. Sullivan, *University on Trial: The Case of the University of North Carolina* (Cambridge, MA: Abt Books, 1985).

79. Gaynelle Evans, "Rights Office May De-emphasize Numerical Goals," *Chronicle of Higher Education*, October 9, 1985.

80. Gary Orfield and Edward Miller, *Chilling Admissions: The Affirmative Action Crisis and the Search for Alternatives* (Cambridge, MA: Harvard Education Press, 1998), 6.

81. College Board, *Trends in College Pricing 2019* (New York: College Board, 2019), 13.

82. College Board, *Trends in Student Aid 2019* (New York: College Board, 2019), highlights.

83. "History of Federal Minimum Wage Rates under the Fair Labor Standards Act, 1938–2009," U.S. Department of Labor, accessed September 23, 2021, https://www.dol.gov/agencies/whd/minimum-wage/history/chart.

84. College Board, *Trends in Student Aid 2019*.

85. National Commission on Excellence in Education, *A Nation at Risk: The Imperative for Educational Reform* (Washington, DC: Government Printing Office, April 1983).

86. David C. Berliner and Bruce J. Biddle, *The Manufactured Crisis: Myths, Fraud, and the Attack on America's Public Schools* (Reading, MA: Addison-Wesley, 1995), 5.

87. National Commission on Excellence in Education, *Nation at Risk*, 5–6.

88. National Commission on Excellence in Education, 7.

89. Robert B. Schwartz, "The Emerging State Leadership Role in Education Reform: Notes of a Participant-Observer," in *A Nation Reformed? American Education 20 Years after "A Nation at Risk,"* ed. David T. Gordon (Cambridge, MA: Harvard Education Press, 2003), 133.

90. National Commission on Excellence in Education, *Nation at Risk*, 6.

91. National Commission on Excellence in Education, 16–18.

92. Maris A. Vinovskis, *The Road to Charlottesville: The 1989 Education Summit* (National Education Goals Panel, September 1999), https://govinfo.library.unt.edu/negp/reports/negp30.pdf.

93. The Goals 2000: Educate America Act, Pub. L. No. 103-227.

94. Robert B. Schwartz et al., "Goals 2000 and the Standards Movement," *Brookings Papers on Education Policy 2000* (2000): 173.

95. William Jefferson Clinton, "Eighth State of the Union Address," Wikisource, January 27, 2000, https://en.wikisource.org/wiki/Bill_Clinton's_Eighth_State_of_the_Union_Address.

96. Gail L. Sunderman, James S. Kim, and Gary Orfield, *NCLB Meets School Realities: Lessons from the Field* (Thousand Oaks, CA: Corwin, 2005).

97. National Research Council, *Getting Value Out of Value-Added: Report of a Workshop* (Washington, DC: National Academies Press, 2008), https://doi.org/10.17226/12820.

98. Linda Darling-Hammond, "Value-Added Teacher Evaluation: The Harm Behind the Hype," *Education Week*, March 14, 2012.

99. "Los Angeles Teacher Ratings," database, *Los Angeles Times*, accessed August 6, 2021, http://projects.latimes.com/value-added.

100. Every Student Succeeds Act, Pub. L. No. 114-95, 129 Stat. 1802, 114th Cong. (2015); Alyson Klein, "The Every Student Succeeds Act: An ESSA Overview," *Education Week*, March 31, 2016, https://www.edweek.org/policy-politics/the-every-student-succeeds-act-an-essa-overview/2016/03.

101. Emma Brown, "Trump Signs Bills Overturning Obama Era Education Regulations," *Washington Post*, March 127, 2017.

102. Every Student Succeeds Act.

103. Alyson Klein, "Obama Administration Releases Final Testing Regulations for ESSA," *Education Week*, December 7, 2016, https://www.edweek.org/policy-politics/obama-administration-releases-final-testing-regulations-for-essa/2016/12.

104. Peter Greene, "Report: The Department of Education Has Spent $1 Billion on Charter School Waste and Fraud," *Forbes*, March 29, 2019; Jeff Bryant, "New Report Spurs Congress to Question up to $1 Billion Wasted on Charter Schools," *Progressive*, April 2, 2019, https://progressive.org/public-schools-advocate/new-report-spurs-congress-to-question-charter-grants-bryant-190402/.

105. Alyson Klein, "Ed. Sec. John B. King, Jr to PTA: Diversity in Schools Benefits All Students," *Education Week*, July 12, 2016, https://www.edweek.org/policy-politics/ed-sec-john-b-king-jr-to-pta-diversity-in-schools-benefits-all-students/2016/07.

106. Patricia Bauer, "Betsy DeVos," *Encyclopedia Britannica*, last updated January 4, 2020, https://www.britannica.com/biography/Betsy-DeVos.

107. Donald J. Trump, "State of the Union Address," February 4, 2020, published in *New York Times*, February 5, 2020.

Chapter 6. Deep Changes for Real Gains

1. Joe Neel, "Poll: Most Americans Think Their Own Group Faces Discrimination," National Public Radio, October 24, 2017, https://prod-text.npr.org/559116373; Juliana Menasce Horowitz, Anna Brown, and Kiana Cox, "Race in America 2019," Pew Research Center, April 9, 2019, 6, https://www.pewresearch.org/social-trends/wp-content/uploads/sites/3/2019/04/Race-report_updated-4.29.19.pdf.

2. V. O. Key Jr., *Southern Politics in State and Nation* (New York: Alfred. A. Knopf, 1949).

3. Christopher Ingraham, "Two New Studies Find Racial Anxiety Is the Highest Driver of Support for Trump," *Washington Post*, June 6, 2016.

4. Stacy Dickert-Conlin and Ross Rubenstein, eds., *Economic Inequality and Higher Education: Access, Persistence, and Success* (New York: Russell Sage Foundation, 2007).

5. Jacqueline M. Nowicki, *K–12 Education: Public High Schools with More Students in Poverty and Smaller Schools Provide Fewer Academic Offerings to Prepare for College*, GAO-19-8 (Washington, DC: Government Accountability Office, October 11, 2018).

6. Paul Tough, *The Years That Matter Most: How College Makes or Breaks Us* (New York: Houghton Mifflin Harcourt, 2019).

Chapter 7. Strategies

1. *Parents Involved in Community Schools v. Seattle School District No. 1*, 551 U.S. 701 (2007).

2. Berkeley, California, and Louisville-Jefferson County, Kentucky, are leading examples. See Lisa Chavez and Erica Frankenberg, *Integration Defended: Berkeley Unified's Strategy to Maintain School Diversity* (Los Angeles: Civil Rights Project, September 2009).

3. Erin Allday and Bob Egelko, "School District in Marin County Agrees to Desegregate in Settlement with State," *San Francisco Chronicle*, August 9, 2019.

4. Lorelle L. Espinosa, Matthew N. Gaertner, and Gary Orfield, *Race, Class, and College Access: Achieving Diversity in a Shifting Legal Landscape* (Washington, DC: American Council on Education, 2015), 3.

5. Espinosa, Gaertner, and Orfield, 10–11.

6. Espinosa, Gaertner, and Orfield, 15.

7. Espinosa, Gaertner, and Orfield, 28.

8. Espinosa, Gaertner, and Orfield, 209.

9. Gary Orfield, ed., *Alternative Paths to Diversity: Exploring and Implementing Effective College Admissions Policies*, Research Report Series No. RR-17-40 (Princeton, NJ: Educational Testing Service, 2017).

10. Sean F. Reardon et al., *Can Socioeconomic Status Substitute for Race in Affirmative Action College Admissions Policies? Evidence from a Simulation Model*, Issue Brief (Princeton, NJ: Educational Testing Service, 2015). See also Sean F. Reardon, Rachel Baker, and Daniel Klasik, *Race, Income, and Enrollment Patterns in Highly Selective Colleges, 1982–2004* (Stanford, CA: Center for Education Policy Analysis, 2012), http://hdl.handle.net/10919/92633.

11. Mark C. Long, "Is There a 'Workable' Race-Neutral Alternative to Affirmative Action in College Admissions?" *Journal of Policy Analysis and Management* 34, no. 1 (September 2014): 162–83.

12. Emily Badger, "Can the Racial Wealth Gap Be Closed without Speaking of Race?," *New York Times*, May 10, 2019.

13. The one major court of appeals case is *Podberesky v. Kirwan*, 38 F.3d 147 (4th Cir. 1994).

14. *Fisher v. University of Texas*, 136 S. Ct. 2198 (2016).

15. Monica Levitan and LaMont Jones, "Scholars Believe Supreme Court Likely to End Affirmative Action with Kavanaugh," *Diverse* (blog), September 13, 2018, https://diverseeducation .com/article/126121/.

16. The cases against Harvard and the University of North Carolina are the leading targets.

17. Lydia Chavez, *The Color Bind: California's Battle to End Affirmative Action* (Berkeley: University of California Press, 1998).

18. Robert Blake Watson et al., "What's Legal in College Admissions Is a Real Scandal," *Los Angeles Times*, August 7, 2019, https://www.chicagotribune.com/opinion/commentary/ct -opinion-college-admissions-scandal-20190809-lfcc5lb75zgivlbtvcil2mp6au-story.html.

19. Thomas D. Snyder, Cristobal de Brey, and Sally A. Dillow, *Digest of Education Statistics, 2017* (Washington, DC: National Center for Education Statistics, January 2019), table 104.20, "Percentage of Persons 25 to 29 Years Old with Selected Levels of Educational Attainment, by Race/Ethnicity and Sex: Selected Years, 1920 through 2017," https://nces.ed.gov/programs /digest/d17/tables/dt17_104.20.asp.

20. James M. McPartland and Will J. Jordon, "Older Students Also Need Major Federal Compensatory Education Resources," in *Hard Work for Good Schools: Facts Not Fads in Title I Reform*, ed. Gary Orfield and Elizabeth H. DeBray (Cambridge, MA: Civil Rights Project of Harvard University, 1999), 102–9.

21. The first national study of racial inequality in schools was commissioned by Congress in 1964 and produced both clear evidence of inequality and powerful indicators that much of the inequality was rooted outside the schools. James Coleman et al., *Equality of Educational Opportunity* (Washington, DC: Government Printing Office, 1966).

22. Justin McCarthy, "Most Americans Say Segregation in Schools Is a Serious Problem," Gallup Poll, September 17, 2019, https://news.gallup.com/poll/266756/americans-say -segregation-schools-serious-problem.aspx.

23. McCarthy, "Most Americans Say Segregation."

24. Gary Orfield and Jennifer B. Ayscue, eds., *Discrimination in Elite Public Schools: Investigating Buffalo* (New York: Teachers College Press, 2018); Jennifer Ayscue et al., *Choices Worth Making: Creating, Sustaining and Expanding Diverse Magnet Schools* (Los Angeles; Civil Rights Project, 2017).

25. Susan E. Eaton, *The Other Boston Busing Story: What's Won and Lost across the Boundary Line* (New Haven, CT: Yale University Press, 2001).

26. Gerald W. Heaney and Susan Uchitelle, *Unending Struggle: The Long Road to an Equal Education in St. Louis* (Saint Louis: Ready, 2004).

27. Gary Orfield, *Connecticut School Integration: Moving Forward as the Northeast Retreats*, with Jongyeon Ee (Los Angeles: Civil Rights Project, 2015).

28. Sharon Grigsby, "Months after Admissions Cheating Scandal, New Signs of Trouble at Dallas ISD's Prestigious Booker T.," *Dallas Morning News*, January 29, 2020, https://www .dallasnews.com/news/commentary/2020/01/29/months-after-admissions-cheating-scandal -new-signs-of-trouble-at-dallas-isds-prestigious-booker-t/.

29. Patrick Wall, "Newark's Rush to Create New Magnet-School Admissions Test Is Raising Eyebrows," Chalkbeat Newark, January 11, 2019, https://newark.chalkbeat.org/2019/1/11 /21106544/newark-s-rush-to-create-new-magnet-school-admissions-test-is-raising-eyebrows -here-s-what-you-need-t.

30. *Parents Involved in Community Schools v. Seattle School District No. 1*, 551 U.S. 701 (2007).

31. W. Richard Fossey, "School Choice in Massachusetts: Will It Help Schools Improve?" (Ed.D. diss, Harvard Graduate School of Education, 1993).

32. Orfield and Ayscue, *Discrimination in Elite Public Schools*.

33. "*Sheff v. O'Neill*," NAACP Legal Defense and Educational Fund, filed April 27, 1989, https://www.naacpldf.org/case-issue/sheff-v-oneill.

34. Erin Golden, "Twin Cities School Segregation Case Proceeds after Ruling on Charter Schools' Lawsuit Involving Public and Charter Area Schools Could Go to Trial in 2020," *Star Tribune* (Minneapolis), June 12, 2019, https://www.startribune.com/school-segregation-case -proceeds-after-ruling-on-charter-schools/511209602/.

35. Rachel M. Cohen, "New Jersey Is Getting Sued over School Segregation," Bloomberg CityLab, January 3, 2019, https://www.citylab.com/equity/2019/01/new-jersey-school -segregation-lawsuit-brown-v-board-housing/579373/.

36. Jennifer C. Kerr, "Big Decrease in Number of 'Dropout Factory' High Schools," AP, November 10, 2015, https://apnews.com/article/365ea65eb9ca4bb6b31fd0723d201cae.

37. Abigail Thernstrom and Stephan Thernstrom, *No Excuses: Closing the Racial Gap in Learning* (New York: Simon and Schuster, 2003).

38. Susanna Loeb, Demetra Kalogrides, and Eileen Lai Horng, "Principal Preferences and the Uneven Distribution of Principals across Schools," *Educational Evaluation and Policy Analysis* 32, no. 2 (June 1, 2010): 205–29.

39. Donald Boyd et al., "Explaining the Short Careers of High-Achieving Teachers in Schools with Low-Performing Students," *American Economic Review* 95, no. 2 (2005): 166–71.

40. Samantha Viano et al., "What Teachers Want: School Factors Predicting Teachers' Decisions to Work in Low-Performing Schools," *American Educational Research Journal* 58, no. 1 (February 2021): 201–33.

41. Desiree Carver-Thomas and Linda Darling-Hammond, *Teacher Turnover: Why It Matters and What We Can Do about It* (Palo Alto, CA: Learning Policy Institute, 2017), v.

42. Ruth Curran Neild and Elizabeth Farley, "Whatever Happened to the Class of 2000? The Timing of Dropout in Philadelphia's Schools," in *Dropouts in America: Confronting the Graduation Rate Crisis*, ed. Gary Orfield, (Cambridge, MA: Harvard Education Press, 2004), 207–20.

43. James J. Kemple, Corinne M. Herlihy, and Thomas J. Smith, *Making Progress toward Graduation: Evidence from the Talent Development High School Model* (New York: Manpower Development Research Corporation, 2005).

44. Johannes M. Bos, Sonica Dhillon, and Trisha Borman, *Building Assets and Reducing Risks (BARR) Validation Study: Final Report* (Washington, DC: American Institutes for Research, 2019).

45. Anna J. Egalite and Brian Kisida, "The Effects of Teacher Match on Students' Academic Perceptions and Attitudes," *Educational Evaluation and Policy Analysis* 40, no. 1 (March 2018): 59–81.

46. *Green v. County School Board of New Kent County*, 391 U.S. 430 (1968).

47. Michael Hansen and Diana Quintero, "Teachers in the U.S. Are Even More Segregated Than Students," *Brown Center Chalkboard* (blog), Brookings Institution, August 15, 2018, https://www.brookings.edu/blog/brown-center-chalkboard/2018/08/15/teachers-in-the-us -are-even-more-segregated-than-students.

48. Hansen and Quintero.

49. Eric Hanushek, John F. Kain, and Steven G. Rivkin, "Why Public Schools Lose Teachers," *Journal of Human Resources* 39, no. 2 (Spring 2004): 326–54.

50. Nicole Simon and Susan Moore Johnson, "Teacher Turnover in High-Poverty Schools: What We Know and Can Do," *Teachers College Record* 117, no. 3 (2015): 1–36.

51. Catherine E. Freeman, Benjamin Scafidi, and David L. Sjoquist, "Racial Segregation in Georgia Public Schools, 1994–2001: Trends, Causes and Impact on Teacher Quality," in *School Resegregation: Must the South Turn Back?*, ed. John Charles Boger and Gary Orfield (Chapel Hill: University of North Carolina Press, 2005), 148–63.

52. Erica Frankenberg, *Are Teachers Prepared for America's Diverse Schools? Teachers Describe Their Preparation, Resources and Practices for Racially Diverse Schools*, with Genevieve Siegel-Hawley (Los Angeles: Civil Rights Project, January 2008).

53. American Educational Research Association, American Psychological Association, and National Council on Measurement in Education, *The Standards for Educational and Psychological Testing* (Washington, DC: American Educational Research Association, 2014).

54. Jacqueline M. Nowicki, *K–12 Education: Public High Schools with More Students in Poverty and Smaller Schools Provide Fewer Academic Offerings to Prepare for College*, GAO-19-8 (Washington, DC: Government Accountability Office, October 11, 2018).

55. Samuel S. Peng, DeeAnn Wright, and Susan T. Hill, *Understanding Racial-Ethnic Differences in Secondary School Science and Mathematics Achievement*, NCES 95-710 (Washington, DC: Government Printing Office, February 1995).

56. Peng, Wright, and Hill, 6–9, 10, 15, 17–18.

57. Peng, Wright, and Hill, 21.

58. Rhonda Tsoi-A-Fatt Bryant, *College Preparation for African American Students: Gaps in the High School Educational Experience* (Washington, DC: Center for Law and Social Policy, February 2015).

59. Soobin Kim et al., "The Impact of the Michigan Merit Curriculum on High School Math Course-Taking," *Educational Evaluation and Policy Analysis* 41, no. 2 (June 2019): 164–88.

60. Gary Orfield and Danielle Jarvie, *Unequal Public Schools Makes Affirmative Action Essential for Equal Opportunity* (Los Angeles: Civil Rights Project, October 2020).

61. Mark C. Long, Dylan Conger, and Patrice Iatarola, "Effects of High School Course-Taking on Secondary and Postsecondary Success," *American Educational Research Journal* 49, no. 2 (April 2012): 285–322.

62. Long, Conger, and Iatarola, 316.

63. Daniel J. Losen, ed., *Closing the School Discipline Gap: Equitable Remedies for Excessive Exclusion* (New York: Teachers College Press, 2015); Erica L. Green and Katie Benner, "Trump Officials Plan to Rescind Obama-Era School Discipline Policies," *New York Times*, December 17, 2018.

64. Government Accountability Office, *K–12 Education: Certain Groups of Student Attend Alternative Schools in Greater Proportion Than They Do Other Schools*, GAO-29-373 (Washington, DC: Government Accountability Office, June 13, 2019); Priscilla Rouse Carver, Laurie Lewis, and Peter Tice, *Alternative Schools and Programs for Public School Students At Risk of Educational Failure: 2007–08*, NCES 2010-026 (Washington, DC: U.S. Department of Education, National Center for Education Statistics, Government Printing Office, 2010).

65. Government Accountability Office, *K–12 Education*.

66. Pub. L. No. 115-391, First Step Act of 2018, December 2018, https://www.congress.gov/115/plaws/publ391/PLAW-115publ391.pdf.

67. Rebecca Unterman, *Headed to College: The Effects of New York City's Small High Schools of Choice on Postsecondary Enrollment*, MDRC Policy Brief (New York: MDRC, 2014); Jack Schneider, "Small Schools: The Edu-Reform Failure That Wasn't," *Education Week*, February 9, 2016, https://www.edweek.org/leadership/opinion-small-schools-the-edu-reform-failure-that-wasnt/2016/02.

68. Joy G. Dryfoos, *Full Service Schools: A Revolution in Health and Social Services for Children, Youth, and Families* (San Francisco: Jossey-Bass, 1994).

69. Denise Superville, "Thriving Students Are the Goal of City, District Partnerships," *Education Week*, September 12, 2018, 10–11.

70. Joy G. Dryfoos, *Evaluation of Community Schools: Findings to Date* (Coalition for Community Schools, 2000), https://eric.ed.gov/?q=ED450204&id=ED450204.

71. William R. Johnston et al., *Illustrating the Promise of Community Schools: An Assessment of the Impact of the New York City Community Schools Initiative* (Santa Monica, CA: RAND, 2020), https://www.rand.org/pubs/research_reports/RR3245.html.

72. Robin Shulman, "Harlem Children's Zone Reaches Out to Youth," *Washington Post*, August 2, 2009.

73. Harlem Children's Zone, "Barack Obama on the Harlem Children's Zone," YouTube video, 5:02, August 6, 2008, https://www.youtube.com/watch?v=Xh5QRMaa_KE.

74. David Guggenheim, dir., *Waiting for Superman* (Paramount, 2010).

75. Mike Spector, "A Harlem Education Project That Won Big Corporate Backing Now Faces Cutbacks as Donors Close Their Wallets," *Wall Street Journal*, January 24, 2009.

76. Michelle Croft and Grover J. "Russ" Whitehurst, "The Harlem Children's Zone Revisited," Brookings Institution Release, July 28, 2010; Will Dobbie and Roland G. Fryer Jr., "Are High Quality Schools Enough to Close the Achievement Gap? Evidence from a Social Experiment in Harlem," NBER Working Paper 15473, National Bureau of Economic Research, Cambridge, MA, November 2009, http://www.nber.org/papers/w15473; Stuart S. Yeh, "A Re-analysis of the Effects of KIPP and the Harlem Promise Academies," *Teachers College Record* 115, no. 4 (2013).

77. U.S. Government Accountability Office, *Education Grants: Promise Neighborhoods Promotes Collaboration but Needs National Evaluation Plan*, GAO-14-423 (Washington, DC: Government Accountability Office, May 2014), https://www.gao.gov/products/gao-14-432.

78. Bernard J. Frieden and Marshall Kaplan, *The Politics of Neglect: Urban Aid from Model Cities to Revenue Sharing* (Cambridge, MA: MIT Press, 1976).

79. Frieden and Kaplan, 11.

80. Molly F. Gordon et al., *School Closings in Chicago: Staff and Student Experiences and Academic Outcomes* (Chicago: University of Chicago Consortium on School Research, 2018).

81. Patricia Gándara and Jongyeon Ee, eds., *Schools under Siege: The Impact of Immigration Enforcement on Educational Equity* (Cambridge, MA: Harvard Education Press, 2021).

82. Patricia M. McDonough, *The School-to-College Transition: Challenges and Prospects* (Washington, DC: American Council on Education, Center for Policy Analysis, 2004).

83. Raj Chetty et al., "Race and Economic Opportunity in the United States: An Intergenerational Perspective," March 2018, http://www.equality-of-opportunity.org/assets/documents/race_paper.pdf (see discussion of this study in chapter 2); Rucker C. Johnson, *Children of the Dream: Why School Integration Works*, with Alexander Nazaryan (New York: Basic Books, 2019).

84. Dierdre Pfeiffer, *The Opportunity Illusion: Subsidized Housing and Failing Schools* (Los Angeles: Civil Rights Project, 2009).

85. Lola Fadulu, "Trump Proposal Would Raise Bar for Proving Housing Discrimination," *New York Times*, August 2, 2019.

86. Gary Orfield, *Toward a Strategy for Urban Integration: Lessons in School and Housing Policy from Twelve Cities* (New York: Ford Foundation, 1981); Gary Orfield and Nancy McArdle, *The Vicious Cycle: Segregated Housing, Schools and Intergenerational Inequality* (Cambridge, MA: Joint Center for Housing Studies, Harvard University, 2006); Deborah L. McKoy, Jeffrey M.

Vincent, and Ariel H. Bierbaum, *Opportunity-Rich Schools and Sustainable Communities: Seven Steps to Align High-Quality Education with Innovations in City and Metropolitan Planning and Development* (Berkeley: Center for Cities and Schools, University of California, Berkeley, 2011).

87. Claudia Goldin and Lawrence Katz, *The Race between Education and Technology* (Cambridge, MA: Belknap Press of Harvard University Press, 2008).

88. Tressie McMillan Cottom, *Lower Ed: The Troubling Rise of For-Profit Colleges in the New Economy* (New York: New Press, 2017).

89. Edward P. St. John et al., *Race-Conscious Scholarships and Persistence: A Study of Students in a State System of Higher Education*, report to NAACP Legal Defense Fund (August 2007), 7, https://doi.org/10.13140/RG.2.1.2493.3367.

90. Henry N. Drewry and Humphrey Doermann, *Stand and Prosper: Private Black Colleges and Their Students* (Princeton, NJ: Princeton University Press, 2001), 248.

91. Danielle Douglas-Gabriel, "Trump and DeVos Call for Massive Cuts to College Student Aid Programs," *Washington Post*, February 13, 2018, https://www.washingtonpost.com/news/grade-point/wp/2018/02/13/trump-and-devos-call-for-massive-cuts-to-college-student-aid-programs/.

92. Neil Bhutta et al., "Disparities in Wealth by Race and Ethnicity in the 2019 Survey of Consumer Finances," FEDS Notes, Federal Reserve, September 28, 2020, https://www.federalreserve.gov/econres/notes/feds-notes/disparities-in-wealth-by-race-and-ethnicity-in-the-2019-survey-of-consumer-finances-20200928.htm.

93. Kevin Eagan et al., *The American Freshman: National Norms Fall 2016* (Los Angeles: Higher Education Research Institute, Graduate School of Education and Information Studies, University of California, Los Angeles, 2017), 7.

94. Eagan et al., 8–9.

95. Scott Jaschik and Doug Lederman, eds., *2019 Survey of College and University Admissions Officers* (Washington, DC: Inside Higher Ed, 2019), https://www.insidehighered.com/booklet/2019-survey-college-and-university-admissions-officers.

96. Marta Tienda, *Hispanicity and Educational Inequality: Risks, Opportunities and the Nation's Future*, Tomás Rivera Lecture Series (Princeton, NJ: Educational Testing Service, March 2009), 24.

97. Patricia Gándara and Frances Contreras, *The Latino Education Crisis: The Consequences of Failed Social Policies* (Cambridge, MA: Harvard University Press, 2007), 293.

98. Todd Sedmak, "High School Class of 2020 College Enrollments Decline 22% Compared to 2019 Class," National Student Clearing House, December 10, 2020, https://www.studentclearinghouse.org/blog/high-school-class-of-2020-college-enrollments-decline-22-compared-to-2019-class/; Heather Long and Danielle Douglas-Gabriel, "The Latest Crisis: Low-Income Students Are Dropping Out of College This Fall in Alarming Numbers," *Washington Post*, September 16, 2020, https://www.washingtonpost.com/business/2020/09/16/college-enrollment-down/.

99. Amelia Nierenberg, "An Application Deluge for Top Colleges, a Drought for the Rest," *New York Times*, February 21, 2021, 4.

100. Ashley A. Smith, "Report: Most Transfer Students Leave College without 2-Year Degree," Inside Higher Education, August 8, 2018, https://www.insidehighered.com/quicktakes/2018/08/08/report-most-transfer-students-leave-college-without-2-year-degree.

101. Mary Martinez-Wenzl and Rigoberto Marquez, *Unrealized Promises: Unequal Access, Affordability, and Excellence at Community Colleges in Southern California* (Los Angeles: Civil Rights Project, February 2012).

102. U.S. Congress, Joint Economic Committee, "10 Key Facts about Veterans of the Post-9/11 Era," updated November 2016, https://www.jec.senate.gov/public/_cache/files/26971be7-ba33-4417-8cbc-c6022e734321/jec-veterans-day-fact-sheet-2016.pdf.

103. Dartmouth College, "Study Finds Racial Disparities in Student Debt Increase after Young People Leave College," press release, December 15, 2019, https://phys.org/news/2018-10-racial-disparities-student-debt-young.html.

104. Lauren Fisher, "White Borrowers? Almost Paid Off. Black Borrowers? Still Indebted," *Chronicle of Higher Education*, September 26, 2019.

105. Mark Huelsman, *Debt to Society: The Case for Bold, Equitable Student Loan Cancellation and Reform* (New York: Demos, June 2019), https://www.demos.org/research/debt-to-society.

106. Huelsman, 2.

107. Huelsman, 15.

108. Arthur Hauptman and Patricia Smith, "Financial Aid Strategies for Improving Minority Student Participation in Higher Education," in *Minorities in Higher Education*, ed. Manuel J. Justiz, Reginald Wilson, and Lars G. Bjork (Phoenix: Oryx, 1994), 94.

109. Edward P. St. John, Britany Affolter-Caine, and Anna S. Chung, "Race-Conscious Student Financial Aid: Constructing an Agenda for Research, Litigation, and Policy Development," in *Charting the Future of College Affirmative Action: Legal Victories, Continuing Attacks, and New Research*, ed. Gary Orfield et al. (Los Angeles: Civil Rights Project, 2007), 183.

110. Mark Pitsch, "Regulations Banning Race-Based Scholarships Proposed," *Education Week*, December 11, 1991.

111. *Podberesky v. Kirwan*, 38 F.3d 147 (4th Cir. 1994).

112. Kimberly J. McLarin, "Impact of Court Ruling on Black Scholarships," *New York Times*, November 2, 1994, https://www.nytimes.com/1994/11/02/us/impact-of-court-ruling-on-black-scholarships.html.

113. Arthur L. Coleman and Jamie Lewis Keith, *Federal Nondiscrimination Law regarding Diversity Implications for Higher Education Financial Aid and Scholarship Policies and Programs* (Washington, DC: College Board, Education Counsel, and National Association of Student Financial Aid Administrators, 2019), 12.

114. Education Amendments of 1976, Pub. L. No. 94-482.

115. *In re Briscoe v. Bank of New York and New York State Higher Education Services Corp*, 16 B.R. 128 (Bankr. S.D.N.Y. 1981).

116. Bankruptcy Abuse Prevention and Consumer Protection Act, Pub. L. No. 109-8 (2005).

117. Huelsman, *Debt to Society*, 23; Ron Lieber and Tara Siegel Bernard, "Bankruptcy Isn't an Easy Fix to Student Debt," *New York Times*, November 8, 2020, 1.

118. Genevieve "Genzie" Bonadies et al., "For-Profit Schools' Predatory Practices and Students of Color: A Mission to Enroll Rather than Educate," *Harvard Law Review* (blog), July 30, 2018, https://blog.harvardlawreview.org/for-profit-schools-predatory-practices-and-students-of-color-a-mission-to-enroll-rather-than-educate/.

119. U.S. Senate, Committee on Health, Education, Labor and Pensions, *For Profit Higher Education: The Failure to Safeguard the Federal Investment and Ensure Student Success* (July 30,

2012), https://www.help.senate.gov/imo/media/for_profit_report/PartI-PartIII-Selected Appendixes.pdf.

120. U.S. Senate, Committee on Health, Education, Labor and Pensions, 2–9.

121. Michelle Hackman, "Trump Administration Revokes Obama-Era Rule on For-Profit Universities," *Wall Street Journal*, June 28, 2019, https://www.wsj.com/articles/trump-administration-revokes-obama-era-rule-on-for-profit-universities-11561763021.

122. Scott Jaschik, "2019 Survey of Admissions Leaders: The Pressure Grows," Inside Higher Education, September 23, 2019, https://www.insidehighered.com/news/survey/2019-survey-admissions-leaders-pressure-grows.

123. Sara Goldrick-Rab et al., *College and University Basic Needs Insecurity: A National #RealCollege Survey Report* (Philadelphia: Hope Center, Temple University, April 2019), https://hope4college.com/wp-content/uploads/2019/04/HOPE_realcollege_National_report_digital.pdf; Ashley A. Smith, "Discrepancies in Estimates on Food Insecurity," Inside Higher Education, April 30, 2019, https://www.insidehighered.com/news/2019/04/30/new-research-finds-discrepancies-estimates-food-insecurity-among-college-students.

124. Gary Orfield and Nicholas Hillman, eds., *Accountability and Opportunity in Higher Education: The Civil Rights Dimension* (Cambridge, MA: Harvard Education Press, 2018).

Commentary: Stella M. Flores

1. *Plessy v. Ferguson*, 163 U.S. 537 (1896).

2. *Cummings v. Richmond Co. Bd. of Education*, 175 U.S. 528 (1899).

3. *Brown v. Board of Education of Topeka*, 347 U.S. 483 (1954); *Green v. County Sch. Bd. of New Kent County*, 391 U.S. 430 (1968).

4. *Parents Involved in Community Schools v. Seattle School District No. 1*, 551 U.S. 701 (2007).

5. Imani Perry, *More Beautiful and More Terrible: The Transcendence of Racial Inequality in the United States* (New York: New York University Press, 2011).

6. Perry.

7. *Regents of the University of California v. Bakke*, 438 U.S. 265 (1978).

8. Douglas Massey, *Categorically Unequal: The American Stratification System* (New York: Russell Sage Foundation, 2007).

9. Massey.

10. Eduardo Bonilla-Silva, "Down the Rabbit Hole: Colorblind Racism in Obamerica," in *The Myth of Racial Color Blindness: Manifestations, Dynamics, and Impact*, ed. Helen A. Neville, Miguel E. Gallardo, and Derald Wing Sue (Washington, DC: American Psychological Association, 2016), 25–38.

11. Caryn J. Block, "The Impact of Colorblind Racial Ideology on Maintaining Racial Disparities in Organizations," in Neville, Gallardo, and Sue, *Myth of Racial Color Blindness*, 243–59.

12. Bonilla-Silva, "Down the Rabbit Hole."

13. Block, "Impact."

14. Cinthia Feliciano and Yader Lanuza, "An Immigrant Paradox? Contextual Attainment and Intergenerational Educational Mobility," *American Sociological Review* 82, no. 1 (February 2017): 211–41.

15. Stella M. Flores, Tim Carroll, and Suzanne M. Lyons, "Beyond the Tipping Point: Searching for a New Vision for Latino College Success in the U.S.," *Annals of American Academy of Political and Social Science* (forthcoming).

16. National Center for Education Statistics, "The Condition of English Language Learners," in *The Condition of Education* (Washington, DC: Institute for Educational Sciences, 2020), 1–4.

17. Patricia Gándara and Frances Contreras, *The Latino Education Crisis: The Consequences of Failed Social Policies* (Cambridge, MA: Harvard University Press, 2007).

18. Stella M. Flores et al., "State Policy and the Educational Outcomes of English Learner and Immigrant Students: Three Administrative Data Stories," *American Behavioral Scientist* 61, no. 14 (2017): 1824–944.

19. Sandy Baum and Stella M. Flores, "Higher Education and Children in Immigrant Families," *Future of Children* 21, no. 1 (2011): 173–93.

20. Flores, Carroll, and Lyons, "Beyond the Tipping Point."

21. Susan Dynarski and Judith Scott-Clayton, "Financial Aid Policy: Lessons from Research," *Future of Children* 23, no. 1 (2013): 67–91.

22. S. M. Flores, T. J. Park, and D. Baker, D. (2017). "The Racial College Completion Gap: Evidence from Texas," *Journal of Higher Education.* https://doi.org/10.1080/00221546.2017.1291259.

Afterword: The Supreme Court's Rejection of Affirmative Action

1. Shelby County v. Holder, 570 U.S. 529 (2013).

2. Students for Fair Admissions v. President and Fellows of Harvard College, 600 U.S. 181 (2023), slip opinion pp. 15, 16, 26.

3 *Students for Fair Admissions,* 600 U.S. 181 (2023), at 26.

4. *Students for Fair Admissions,* 600 U.S. 181 (2023), at 22

5. *Students for Fair Admissions,* 600 U.S. 181 (2023), at 23

6. *Students for Fair Admissions,* 600 U.S. 181 (2023), at 24

7. *Students for Fair Admissions,* 600 U.S. 181 (2023), at 40

8. Scott Jaschik, "The Students Who Aren't Coming," *Inside Higher Education,* May 22, 2023.

9. Gary Orfield and Susan Eaton, *Dismantling Desegregation: The Quiet Reversal of Brown v. Board of Education* (New York: New Press, 1996).

10. Parents Involved in Community Schools v. Seattle School District No. 1, 551 U.S. 701 (2007).

11. Gary Orfield and Erica Frankenberg, and Associates, *Educational Delusions: How Choice Can Deepen Inequality and How to Make Schools Fair* (Berkeley: University of California Press, 2013).

12. Douglas Belkin and Megan Tagami, "Ruling Puts Race-Based College Scholarships at Risk," *Wall Street Journal,* July 8–9, 2023.

13. Mitch Smith, "North Carolina Trustees Vote to Bar Race as Consideration in Hiring or Admissions," *New York Times,* July 29, 2023.

14. Michael Hill, "West Point Sued over Using Race as an Admissions Factor," *Army Times,* September 19, 2023.

15. Nick Anderson, "Critic of Affirmative Action Sues Naval Academy over Race in Admissions," *Washington Post,* October 5, 2023.

16. Brown Jackson dissent, *Students for Fair Admissions*, 600 U.S. 181 (2023), at 2.

17. Brown Jackson dissent, *Students for Fair Admissions*, 600 U.S. 181 (2023), at 23.

18. Brown Jackson dissent, *Students for Fair Admissions*, 600 U.S. 181 (2023), at 25.

19. Brown Jackson dissent, *Students for Fair Admissions*, 600 U.S. 181 (2023), at 26.

20. Brown Jackson dissent, *Students for Fair Admissions*, 600 U.S. 181 (2023), at 25.

21. Brown Jackson dissent, *Students for Fair Admissions*, 600 U.S. 181 (2023), at 28.

BIBLIOGRAPHY

ACT and the Education Trust. *On Course for Success: A Close Look at Selected High School Courses That Prepare All Students for College and Work.* ACT and the Education Trust, 2004. https://edtrust.org/resource/on-course-for-success/.

Adams v. Richardson, 480 F.2d 1159 (1973).

Addio, Anna Cristina d'. "Intergenerational Transmission of Disadvantage: Mobility or Immobility across Generations?" OECD Social, Employment and Migration Working Papers No. 52, Organisation for Economic Co-operation and Development, 2007.

Alegria, Margarita, Nicholas J. Carson, Marta Goncalves, and Kristen Keefe. "Disparities in Treatment for Substance Use Disorders and Co-occurring Disorders for Ethnic/Racial Minority Youth." *Journal of the American Academy of Child and Adolescent Psychiatry* 50, no. 1 (2011): 22–31.

Allday, Erin, and Bob Egelko. "School District in Marin County Agrees to Desegregate in Settlement with State." *San Francisco Chronicle,* August 9, 2019. https://www.sfchronicle.com/bayarea/article/School-district-in-Marin-County-agrees-to-14293740.php.

Allport, Gordon Willard. *The Nature of Prejudice.* Boston: Addison-Wesley, 1954.

Allsup, Vernon Carl. *The American G.I. Forum: Origins and Evolution.* Mexican American Monographs No. 6. Austin: Center for Mexican American Studies, University of Texas at Austin, 1982.

American Council on Education. *Student Aid in the Reagan Administration: Fact Sheet.* October 1984.

American Educational Research Association, American Psychological Association, and National Council on Measurement in Education. *The Standards for Educational and Psychological Testing.* Washington, DC: American Educational Research Association, 2014.

Anderson, Elijah. *Code of the Street: Decency, Violence, and the Moral Life of the Inner City.* New York: W. W. Norton, 2000.

Anderson, James D. *The Education of Blacks in the South, 1860–1935.* Chapel Hill: University of North Carolina Press, 1988.

Angus, David L., and Jeffrey E. Mirel. *The Failed Promise of the American High School, 1890–1995.* New York: Teachers College Press, 1999.

Arsenault, Raymond. *Freedom Riders: 1961 and the Struggle for Racial Justice.* New York: Oxford University Press, 2006.

Associated Press, "Black College Enrollment Has Doubled since 1970." *New York Times,* May 18, 1981, sec. D.

Ayers, William, Bernardine Dohrn, and Rick Ayers, eds. *Zero Tolerance: Resisting the Drive for Punishment in Our Schools: A Handbook for Parents, Students, Educators, and Citizens*. New York: New Press, 2001.

Ayscue, Jennifer, Rachel Levy, Genevieve Siegel-Hawley, and Brian Woodward. *Choices Worth Making: Creating, Sustaining and Expanding Diverse Magnet Schools*. Los Angeles: Civil Rights Project, 2017.

Badger, Emily. "Can the Racial Wealth Gap Be Closed without Speaking of Race?" *New York Times*, May 10, 2019.

Bailey, Stephen Kemp, and Edith K. Mosher. *ESEA: The Office of Education Administers a Law*. Syracuse, NY: Syracuse University Press, 1968.

Baker, Peter. "Bush Made Willie Horton an Issue in 1988, and the Racial Scars Are Still Fresh." *New York Times*, December 3, 2018. https://www.nytimes.com/2018/12/03/us/politics /bush-willie-horton.html.

Bankruptcy Abuse Prevention and Consumer Protection Act, Pub. L. No 109-8, 2005.

Bartley, Numan V. *The Rise of Massive Resistance: Race and Politics in the South during the 1950's*. Baton Rouge: Louisiana State University Press, 1999.

Bauer, Patricia. "Betsy DeVos." *Encyclopedia Britannica*. Last updated January 4, 2020. https:// www.britannica.com/biography/Betsy-DeVos.

Bennett, Michael J. *When Dreams Came True: The GI Bill and the Making of Modern America*. Washington, DC: Brassey's, 1996.

Berliner, David C., and Bruce J. Biddle. *The Manufactured Crisis: Myths, Fraud, and the Attack on America's Public Schools*. Reading, MA: Addison-Wesley, 1995.

Bhutta, Neil, Andrew C. Chang, Lisa J. Dettling, Joanne W. Hsu, and Julia Hewitt. "Disparities in Wealth by Race and Ethnicity in the 2019 Survey of Consumer Finances." FEDS Notes, Federal Reserve, September 28, 2020. https://www.federalreserve.gov/econres/notes/feds -notes/disparities-in-wealth-by-race-and-ethnicity-in-the-2019-survey-of-consumer -finances-20200928.htm.

Board of Ed. of Oklahoma City Public Schools v. Dowell, 498 U.S. 237 (1991).

Bonadies, Genevieve "Genzie," Joshua Rovenger, Eileen Connor, Brenda Shum, and Toby Merrull. "For-Profit Schools' Predatory Practices and Students of Color: A Mission to Enroll Rather than Educate." *Harvard Law Review* (blog), July 30, 2018. https://blog .harvardlawreview.org/for-profit-schools-predatory-practices-and-students-of-color-a -mission-to-enroll-rather-than-educate/.

Bond Hill, Catharine, Martin Kurzweil, Elizabeth Davidson Pisacreta, and Emily Schwartz. *Enrolling More Veterans at High-Graduation-Rate Colleges and Universities*. New York: Ithaka S+R, 2019.

Bonilla-Silva, Eduardo. *Racism without Racists: Color-Blind Racism and the Persistence of Racial Inequality in the United States*. Lanham, MD: Rowman and Littlefield, 2003.

Borman, Geoffrey, and Maritza Dowling. "Schools and Inequality: A Multilevel Analysis of Coleman's Equality of Educational Opportunity Data." *Teachers College Record* 112, no. 5 (2010): 1201–46.

Bos, Johannes M., Sonica Dhillon, and Trisha Borman. *Building Assets and Reducing Risks (BARR) Validation Study: Final Report*. Washington, DC: American Institutes for Research, 2019.

Bowen, William G., and Derek Bok. *The Shape of the River: Long-Term Consequences of Considering Race in College and University Admissions*. Princeton, NJ: Princeton University Press, 1998.

Boyd, Donald, Hamilton Lankford, Susanna Loeb, and James Wyckoff. "Explaining the Short Careers of High-Achieving Teachers in Schools with Low-Performing Students." *American Economic Review* 95, no. 2 (2005): 166–272.

Braddock, Jomills Henry, II, and James M. McPartland. *More Evidence on Social-Psychological Processes That Perpetuate Minority Segregation: The Relationship of School Desegregation and Employment Segregation.* Report No. CSOS-338. Baltimore: Center for Social Organization of Schools, Johns Hopkins University, June 1983.

Branch, Taylor. *Parting the Waters: America in the King Years, 1954–63.* New York: Simon and Schuster, 1988.

Briggs v. Elliott, 132 F. Supp. 776 (E.D.S.C., 1955).

Brooks, Kelly. "Research Shows Food Deserts More Abundant in Minority Neighborhoods." *Johns Hopkins University Magazine*, Spring 2014. https://hub.jhu.edu/magazine/2014/spring/racial-food-deserts.

Brown, Emma. "Trump Signs Bills Overturning Obama Era Education Regulations." *Washington Post*, March 27, 2017.

Browne-Marshall, Gloria J. *The Voting Rights War: The NAACP and the Ongoing Struggle for Justice.* Lanham, MD: Rowman and Littlefield, 2016.

Bryce, James. *The American Common Wealth.* 2 vols. New York: Macmillan, 1895.

Bryk, Anthony S., Valerie E. Lee, and Peter Blakeley Holland. *Catholic Schools and the Common Good.* Cambridge, MA: Harvard University Press, 1993.

Bullock, Henry Allen. *A History of Negro Education in the South.* Cambridge, MA: Harvard University Press, 1967; repr., New York: Praeger, 1970.

Burns, James MacGregor. *Roosevelt: The Soldier of Freedom, 1940–1945.* New York: Harcourt Brace Jovanovich, 2012.

Burris, Carol Corbett, and Kevin G. Welner. "Closing the Achievement Gap by Detracking." *Phi Delta Kappan* 86, no. 8 (April 2005): 594–98.

Busch, Andrew E. *Ronald Reagan and the Politics of Freedom.* Lanham, MD: Rowman and Littlefield, 2001.

Callahan, Raymond E. *Education and the Cult of Efficiency.* Chicago: University of Chicago Press, 1962.

Capps, Kriston. "How the Federal Government Built White Suburbia." Bloomberg CityLab, September 2, 2015. https://www.bloomberg.com/news/articles/2015-09-02/how-the-federal-government-built-white-suburbia.

Carter, Dan T. *From George Wallace to Newt Gingrich: Race in the Conservative Counterrevolution, 1963–1994.* Baton Rouge: Louisiana State University Press, 1996.

Carter, Thomas P. *Mexican Americans in School: A History of Educational Neglect.* New York: College Entrance Examination Board, 1970.

Carver, Priscilla Rouse, Laurie Lewis, and Peter Tice. *Alternative Schools and Programs for Public School Students at Risk of Educational Failure, 2007–08.* NCES 2010-026. Washington, DC: U.S. Department of Education, National Center for Education Statistics, Government Printing Office, 2010.

Carver-Thomas, Desiree, and Linda Darling-Hammond. *Teacher Turnover: Why It Matters and What We Can Do about It.* Palo Alto, CA: Learning Policy Institute, 2017.

Case, Anne, Darren Lubotsky, and Christina Paxson. "Economic Status and Health in Childhood: The Origins of the Gradient." *American Economic Review* 92, no. 5 (2002): 1308–34.

Center for Advanced Studies in Child Welfare. *CW360°: A Comprehensive Look at a Prevalent Child Welfare Issue: Criminal Justice Involvement of Families in Child Welfare*. Saint Paul: Center for Advanced Studies in Child Welfare. University of Minnesota, Spring 2018.

Center on the Developing Child. *The Science of Early Childhood Development (InBrief)*. Cambridge, MA: Center on the Developing Child, Harvard University, 2007. https://developingchild.harvard.edu/resources/inbrief-science-of-ecd.

Chavez, Lisa, and Erica Frankenberg. *Integration Defended: Berkeley Unified's Strategy to Maintain School*. Los Angeles: Civil Rights Project, September 2009.

Chavez, Lydia. *The Color Bind: California's Battle to End Affirmative Action*. Berkeley: University of California Press, 1998.

Chemerinsky, Erwin. *The Conservative Assault on the Constitution*. New York: Simon and Schuster, 2010.

Chetty, Raj, John N. Friedman, and Jonah E. Rockoff. "The Long-Term Impacts of Teachers: Teacher Value-Added and Student Outcomes in Adulthood." NBER Working Paper No. 17699, National Bureau of Economic Research, Cambridge, MA, December 2011. https://doi.org/10.3386/w17699.

Chetty, Raj, Nathaniel Hendren, Maggie R. Jones, and Sonya R. Porter. "Race and Economic Opportunity in the United States: An Intergenerational Perspective." *Quarterly Journal of Economics* 135, no. 2 (March 2018): 711–83.

Chetty, Raj, Nathaniel Hendren, Patrick Kline, and Emmanuel Saez. "Where Is the Land of Opportunity? The Geography of Intergenerational Mobility in the United States." NBER Working Paper No. 19843, National Bureau of Economic Research, Cambridge, MA, January 2014. https://doi.org/10.3386/w19843.

Clinton, Bill, and Al Gore. *Putting People First: How We Can All Change America*. New York: Times Books, 1992.

Clinton, William Jefferson. "Eighth State of the Union Address." Wikisource, January 27, 2000. https://en.wikisource.org/wiki/Bill_Clinton's_Eighth_State_of_the_Union_Address.

Clotfelter, Charles T., Helen F. Ladd, and Jacob Vigdor. "Who Teaches Whom? Race and the Distribution of Novice Teachers." *Economics of Education Review* 24, no. 4 (2005): 377–92.

Cohen, Rachel M. "A Lawsuit Challenges New Jersey on School Segregation." Bloomberg CityLab, November 10, 2015. https://www.bloomberg.com/news/articles/2019-01-03/a-lawsuit-challenges-new-jersey-on-school-segregation.

Coleman, Arthur L., and Jamie Lewis Keith. *Federal Nondiscrimination Law regarding Diversity Implications for Higher Education Financial Aid and Scholarship Policies and Programs*. Washington, DC: College Board, Education Counsel, and National Association of Student Financial Aid Administrators, 2019.

Coleman, James S., and Thomas Hoffer. *Public and Private High Schools: The Impact of Communities*. New York: Basic Books, 1987.

College Board. *Trends in College Pricing 2019*. New York: College Board, 2019.

Collier, Kiah. "Texas Supreme Court Rules School Funding System Is Constitutional." *Texas Tribune*, May 13, 2016.

Commission on the Reorganization of Secondary Education. *Cardinal Principles of Secondary Education*. Bulletin 1918, No. 35. Bureau of Education, Department of the Interior. Washington, DC: Government Printing Office, 1918. https://eric.ed.gov/?id=ED541063.

Conant, James Bryant. *The American High School Today*. New York: McGraw-Hill, 1959.

Cottom, Tressie McMillan. *Lower Ed: The Troubling Rise of For-Profit Colleges in the New Economy*. New York: New Press, 2017.

Crain, Robert L. "School Integration and Occupational Achievement of Negroes." *American Journal of Sociology* 75, no. 4, pt. 2 (January 1970): 593–606.

Cremin, Lawrence A. *American Education*. Vol. 2, *The National Experience, 1783–1876*. New York: Harper and Row, 1980.

———. *American Education*. Vol. 3, *The Metropolitan Experience, 1876–1980*. New York: Harper and Row, 1988.

Croly, Herbert David. *The Promise of American Life*. New York: Macmillan, 1914. https://books .google.com/books?id=3BASAAAAYAAJ&printsec=frontcover#v=onepage&q&f=false.

Cumming v. Richmond County Board of Education, 175 U.S. 528 (1899).

Custred, Glynn, and Tom Wood. California Proposition 209. November 1996.

Daniels, Roger. *Coming to America: A History of Immigration and Ethnicity in American Life*. 2nd ed. New York: Harper Perennial, 2002.

Danziger, Sheldon H., and Daniel H. Weinberg, eds. *Fighting Poverty: What Works and What Doesn't*. Cambridge, MA: Harvard University Press, 1986.

Dartmouth College. "Study Finds Racial Disparities in Student Debt Increase after Young People Leave College." Press release, December 15, 2019. https://phys.org/news/2018-10 -racial-disparities-student-debt-young.html.

Davidson, Chandler, and Bernard Grofman, eds. *Quiet Revolution in the South: The Impact of the Voting Rights Act, 1965–1990*. Princeton, NJ: Princeton University Press, 1994.

Del Castillo, Richard Griswold. *The Los Angeles Barrio, 1850–1890: A Social History*. Berkeley: University of California Press, 1979.

Dentler, Robert A., D. Catherine Baltzell, and Daniel J. Sullivan. *University on Trial: The Case of the University of North Carolina*. Cambridge, MA: Abt Books, 1985.

De Tocqueville, Alexis. *Democracy in America*. Vol. 1. New York: Vintage Books, 1945.

Dickert-Conlin, Stacy, and Ross Rubenstein, eds. *Economic Inequality and Higher Education: Access, Persistence, and Success*. New York: Russell Sage Foundation, 2007.

Dixon-Roman, Ezekiel J., Howard T. Everson, and John J. McArdle. "Race, Poverty and SAT Scores: Modeling the Influences of Family Income on Black and White High School Students' SAT Performance." *Teachers College Record* 115, no. 4 (2013).

Douglas-Gabriel, Danielle. "Trump and DeVos Call for Massive Cuts to College Student Aid Programs." *Washington Post*, February 13, 2018. https://www.washingtonpost.com/news /grade-point/wp/2018/02/13/trump-and-devos-call-for-massive-cuts-to-college-student -aid-programs/.

Drewry, Henry N., and Humphrey Doermann. *Stand and Prosper: Private Black Colleges and Their Students*. Princeton, NJ: Princeton University Press, 2001.

Dryfoos, Joy G. *Evaluation of Community Schools: Findings to Date*. Coalition for Community Schools, 2000. https://eric.ed.gov/?q=ED450204&id=ED450204.

———. *Full Service Schools: A Revolution in Health and Social Services for Children, Youth, and Families*. San Francisco: Jossey-Bass, 1994.

Du Bois, W.E.B. *The Philadelphia Negro: A Social Study*. Philadelphia: University of Pennsylvania Press, 1899.

Du Bois, W.E.B., and Augustus Granville Dill. *The College-Bred Negro American*. Atlanta: Atlanta University Press, 1910.

Eagan, Kevin, Ellen Bara Stolzenberg, H. B. Zimmerman, M. C. Aragon, H. Whang Sayson, and Cecilia Rios-Aguilar. *The American Freshman: National Norms Fall 2016*. Los Angeles: Higher Education Research Institute, Graduate School of Education and Information Studies, University of California, Los Angeles, 2017.

Eaton, Susan E. *The Children in Room E4: American Education on Trial*. Chapel Hill, NC: Algonquin Books, 2009.

———. *The Other Boston Busing Story: What's Won and Lost across the Boundary Line*. New Haven, CT: Yale University Press, 2001.

Eckerson, Helen F. "Immigration and National Origins." In "The New Immigration," special issue, *Annals of the American Academy of Political and Social Science* 367, no. 1 (1966): 4–14.

Eckert, Ruth E., and Thomas O. Marshall. *When Youth Leave School: The Regents Inquiry*. New York: McGraw-Hill, 1938.

Edmonds, Ronald. "Effective Schools for the Urban Poor." *Educational Leadership* 37, no. 1 (1979): 15–24.

Education Amendments of 1976, Pub. L. No. 94-482 (1976).

Egalite, Anna J., and Brian Kisida. "The Effects of Teacher Match on Students' Academic Perceptions and Attitudes." *Educational Evaluation and Policy Analysis* 40, no. 1 (March 2018): 59–81.

Eisenhower, Dwight D. "Annual Message to the Congress on the State of the Union." January 9, 1958, American Presidency Project. https://www.presidency.ucsb.edu/documents/annual -message-the-congress-the-state-the-union-10.

Espinosa, Lorelle L., Matthew N. Gaertner, and Gary Orfield. *Race, Class, and College Access: Achieving Diversity in a Shifting Legal Landscape*. Washington, DC: American Council on Education, 2015.

Fad, Lola. "Trump Proposal Would Raise Bar for Proving Housing Discrimination." *New York Times*, August 2, 2019. https://www.nytimes.com/2019/08/02/us/politics/trump-housing -discrimination.html.

Faircloth, Susan C., and John W. Tippeconnic III. *The Dropout/Graduation Crisis among American Indian and Alaska Native Students: Failure to Respond Places the Future of Native Peoples at Risk*. Los Angeles: Civil Rights Project, 2010.

Filvaroff, David B., and Raymond E. Wolfinger. "The Origin and Enactment of the Civil Rights Act of 1964." In *Legacies of the 1964 Civil Rights Act*, edited by Bernard Grofman, 9–32. Charlottesville: University of Virginia Press, 2000.

Fisher, Lauren. "White Borrowers? Almost Paid Off. Black Borrowers? Still Indebted." *Chronicle of Higher Education*, September 26, 2019.

Fisher v. University of Texas at Austin, 133 S. Ct. 2411 (2013).

Fiske, Edward B. "Reagan Record in Education: Mixed Results." *New York Times*, November 14, 1982, sec. 12.

Fiss, Owen M. *The Civil Rights Injunction*. Bloomington: University of Indiana Press, 1978.

Fitch, Brian D., and Anthony H. Normore, eds. *Education-Based Incarceration and Recidivism: The Ultimate Social Justice Crime-Fighting Tool*. Charlotte, NC: Information Age, 2012.

Flores, Stella M., Catherine L. Horn, William C. Kidder, Patricia Gándara, and Mark C. Long. *Alternative Paths to Diversity: Exploring and Implementing Effective College Admissions Policies.* Edited by Gary Orfield. Research Report Series No. RR-17-40. Princeton, NJ: Educational Testing Service, 2017. https://escholarship.org/uc/item/3vq970qw.

Fluke, John, Brenda J. Harden, Molly Jenkins, and Ashleigh Ruehrdanz. *Research Synthesis on Child Welfare: Disproportionality and Disparities.* Washington, DC: Center for the Study of Social Policy, 2011.

Folger, John K., and Charles B. Nam. *Education of the American Population.* 1960 Census Monograph. U.S. Department of Commerce, Bureau of the Census. Washington, DC: Government Printing Office, 1967.

Fossey, W. Richard. "School Choice in Massachusetts: Will It Help Schools Improve?" EdD diss., Harvard Graduate School of Education, 1993.

Frankenberg, Erica. *Are Teachers Prepared for America's Diverse Schools? Teachers Describe Their Preparation, Resources and Practices for Racially Diverse Schools.* With Genevieve Siegel-Hawley. Los Angeles: Civil Rights Project, January 2008.

———. "Exploring Teachers' Racial Attitudes in a Racially Transitioning Society." *Education and Urban Society* 44, no. 4 (2012): 448–76.

Frankenberg, Erica, Jongyeon Ee, Jennifer B. Ayscue, and Gary Orfield. *Harming Our Common Future: America's Segregated Schools 65 Years after "Brown."* Los Angeles: Civil Rights Project, 2019.

Freeman, Catherine E., Benjamin Scafidi, and David L. Sjoquist, "Racial Segregation in Georgia Public Schools, 1994–2001: Trends, Causes and Impact on Teacher Quality." In *School Resegregation: Must the South Turn Back?*, edited by John Charles Boger and Gary Orfield, 148–63. Chapel Hill: University of North Carolina Press, 2005.

Frieden, Bernard J., and Marshall Kaplan. *The Politics of Neglect: Urban Aid from Model Cities to Revenue Sharing.* Cambridge, MA: MIT Press, 1976.

Fuller, Bruce F., and Richard Elmore, eds. *Who Chooses? Who Loses? Culture, Institutions and the Unequal Effects of School Choice.* With Gary Orfield. New York: Teachers College Press, 1995.

Gándara, Patricia. "A Study of High School Puente: What We Have Learned about Preparing Latino Youth for Postsecondary Education." *Educational Policy* 16, no. 4 (September 1, 2002): 474–95.

Gándara, Patricia, Elizabeth Alvarado, Anne Driscoll, and Gary Orfield. *Building Pathways to Transfer: Community Colleges That Break the Chain of Failure for Students of Color.* Los Angeles: Civil Rights Project, 2012.

Gándara, Patricia, and Frances Contreras. *The Latino Education Crisis: The Consequences of Failed Social Policies.* Cambridge, MA: Harvard University Press, 2007.

Gándara, Patricia, and Jongyeon Ee, eds. *Schools under Siege: The Impact of Immigration Enforcement on Educational Equity.* Cambridge, MA: Harvard Education Press, 2021.

Gewertz, Catherine. "School Counselors Boost Students' College, Financial Aid Chances, Study Finds." *Education Week*, December 7, 2016. https://www.edweek.org/teaching-learning/school-counselors-boost-students-college-financial-aid-chances-study-finds/2016/12.

———. "School Counselors Responsible for 482 Students on Average, Report Finds." *Education Week*, February 8, 2018. https://www.edweek.org/teaching-learning/school-counselors-responsible-for-482-students-on-average-report-finds/2018/02.

Ghandnoosh, Nazgol. *Black Lives Matter: Eliminating Racial Inequity in the Criminal Justice System*. Washington, DC: Sentencing Project, February 2015.

The Goals 2000: Educate America Act, Pub. L. No.103-227 2000.

Goering, John M., ed. *Housing Desegregation and Federal Policy*. Chapel Hill: University of North Carolina Press, 1986.

Golden, Erin. "Twin Cities School Segregation Case Proceeds after Ruling on Charter Schools." *Star Tribune* (Minneapolis), June 12, 2019. https://www.startribune.com/school-segregation-case-proceeds-after-ruling-on-charter-schools/511209602/.

Goldin, Claudia, and Lawrence Katz. *The Race between Education and Technology*. Cambridge, MA: Belknap Press of Harvard University Press, 2008.

Goldrick-Rab, Sara, Christine Baker-Smith, Vanessa Coca, Elizabeth Looker, and Tiffani Williams. *College and University Basic Needs Insecurity: A National #RealCollege Survey Report*. Philadelphia: Hope Center, Temple University, April 2019. https://hope4college.com/wp-content/uploads/2019/04/HOPE_realcollege_National_report_digital.pdf.

Goldring, Ellen, and Claire Smrekar. "Magnet Schools: Reform and Race in Urban Education." *Clearing House* 76, no. 1 (2002): 13–15.

Goldstein, Dana. "'It Just Isn't Working': PISA Test Scores Cast Doubt on U.S. Education Efforts." *New York Times*, December 3, 2019. https://www.nytimes.com/2019/12/03/us/us-students-international-test-scores.html.

Gordon, Molly F., Marisa de la Torre, Jennifer R. Cowhy, Paul T. Moore, Lauren Sartain, and David Knight. *School Closings in Chicago: Staff and Student Experiences and Academic Outcomes*. Chicago: University of Chicago Consortium on School Research, 2018.

Gratz v. Bollinger, 539 U.S. 244 (2003).

Green, Adam. "How a Brutal Race Riot Shaped Modern Chicago: A Century Later, the City, and America, Are Still Dealing with the Consequences." *New York Times*, August 3, 2019. https://www.nytimes.com/2019/08/03/opinion/how-a-brutal-race-riot-shaped-modern-chicago.html.

Green v. County School Board of New Kent County, 391 U.S. 430 (1968).

Greenberg, Stanley B. *Middle Class Dreams: The Politics and Power of the New American Majority*. New Haven, CT: Yale University Press, 1996.

Greene, Peter. "Report: The Department of Education Has Spent $1 Billion on Charter School Waste and Fraud." *Forbes*, March 29, 2019. https://www.forbes.com/sites/petergreene/2019/03/29/report-the-department-of-education-has-spent-1-billion-on-charter-school-waste-and-fraud/.

Grigsby, Sharon. "Months after Admissions Cheating Scandal, New Signs of Trouble at Dallas ISD's Prestigious Booker T." *Dallas Morning News*, January 29, 2020. https://www.dallasnews.com/news/commentary/2020/01/29/months-after-admissions-cheating-scandal-new-signs-of-trouble-at-dallas-isds-prestigious-booker-t/.

Grofman, Bernard, ed. *Legacies of the 1964 Civil Rights Act*. Charlottesville: University of Virginia Press, 2000. https://books.google.com/books/about/Legacies_of_the_1964_Civil_Rights_Act.html?id=J5iKFGQxN-0C.

Groutt, John W., and James W. Guthrie, eds. *Encyclopedia of Education*. 2nd ed. Vol. 7. New York: Macmillan Reference, 2002.

Grutter v. Bollinger, 539 U.S. 306 (2003).

Guggenheim, David, dir. *Waiting for Superman*. Paramount, 2010.

Guryan, Jonathan, Erik Hurst, and Melissa Kearney. "Parental Education and Parental Time with Children." *Journal of Economic Perspectives* 22, no. 3 (2008): 23–46.

Hackman, Michelle. "Trump Administration Revokes Obama-Era Rule on For-Profit Universities." *Wall Street Journal*, June 28, 2019. https://www.wsj.com/articles/trump-administration-revokes-obama-era-rule-on-for-profit-universities-11561763021.

Hamilton, Brady E., Joyce A. Martin, Michelle J. K. Osterman, and Lauren M. Rossen. *Births: Provisional Data for 2018*. Vital Statistics Rapid Release, Report No. 007. Hyattsville, MD: National Center for Health Statistics, Division of Vital Statistics, May 2019.

Hancock v. Commissioner of Education, 443 Mass. 428 (2005).

Handwerk, Philip, Namrata Tognatta, Richard J. Coley, and Drew H. Gitomer. *Access to Success: Patterns of Advanced Placement Participation in U.S. High Schools*. Policy Information Report. Princeton, NJ: Educational Testing Service, 2008.

Hansen, Michael, and Diana Quintero. "Teachers in the U.S. Are Even More Segregated Than Students." *Brown Center Chalkboard* (blog), Brookings Institution, August 15, 2018. https://www.brookings.edu/blog/brown-center-chalkboard/2018/08/15/teachers-in-the-us-are-even-more-segregated-than-students.

Hanushek, Eric A., John F. Kain, and Steven G. Rivkin. "Why Public Schools Lose Teachers." *Journal of Human Resources* 39, no. 2 (Spring 2004): 326–54.

Harlem Children's Zone. "Barack Obama on the Harlem Children's Zone." YouTube video, 5:02. August 6, 2008. https://www.youtube.com/watch?v=Xh5QRMaa_KE.

Harrington, Michael. *The Other America*. New York: Macmillan, 1962.

Harris, Elizabeth A. "Homeless Students Lag behind Peers and Face High Dropout Rates, Study Shows." *New York Times*, April 11, 2018.

Hartocollis, Anemona. "Justice Department Drops Suit Claiming Yale Discriminated in Admissions." *New York Times*, February 3, 2021.

Hauptman, Arthur, and Patricia Smith. "Financial Aid Strategies for Improving Minority Student Participation in Higher Education." In *Minorities in Higher Education*, edited by Manuel J. Justiz, Reginald Wilson, and Lars G. Bjork, 78–106. Phoenix: Oryx, 1994.

Heaney, Gerald W., and Susan Uchitelle. *Unending Struggle: The Long Road to an Equal Education in St. Louis*. Saint Louis: Reedy, 2004.

Heckman, James J. *Giving Kids a Fair Chance (A Strategy That Works)*. Cambridge, MA: MIT Press, 2013.

Heller, Donald E., and Patricia Marin, eds. *State Merit Scholarship Programs and Racial Inequality*. Cambridge, MA: Civil Rights Project at Harvard University, 2004.

Herrnstein, Richard J., and Charles A. Murray. *The Bell Curve: Intelligence and Class Structure in American Life*. New York: Simon and Schuster, 1994. http://catdir.loc.gov/catdir/enhancements/fy0641/95042934-s.html.

Hing, Bill Ong. *Making and Remaking Asian America through Immigration Policy, 1850–1990*. Stanford, CA: Stanford University Press, 1993.

Hochschild, Jennifer L. *Facing Up to the American Dream: Race, Class, and the Soul of the Nation*. Princeton, NJ: Princeton University Press, 1996.

Hochschild, Jennifer L., and Nathan Scovronick. *The American Dream and the Public Schools*. New York: Oxford University Press, 2003.

Hooghe, Marc, and Ruth Dassonneville. "Explaining the Trump Vote: The Effect of Racist Resentment and Anti-immigrant Sentiments." *PS: Political Science and Politics* 51, no. 3 (July 2018): 528–34.

Hopwood v. State of Texas, 236 F.3d 256 (2000).

Horn, Catherine L., and Stella M. Flores. *Percent Plans in College Admissions: A Comparative Analysis of Three States' Experiences.* Cambridge, MA: Civil Rights Project at Harvard University, 2003.

Horowitz, Juliana Menasce, Kim Parker, Anna Brown, and Kiana Cox. "Amid National Reckoning, Americans Divided on Whether Increased Focus on Race Will Lead to Major Policy Change." Pew Research Center, October 2020. https://www.pewresearch.org/social-trends /2020/10/06/amid-national-reckoning-americans-divided-on-whether-increased-focus -on-race-will-lead-to-major-policy-change.

Hoxby, Caroline M. "Peer Effects in the Classroom: Learning from Gender and Race Variation." NBER Working Paper No. 7867. National Bureau of Economic Research, Cambridge, MA, August 2000. https://www.nber.org/papers/w7867.

Hoxby, Caroline M., and Christopher Avery. "The Missing 'One-Offs': The Hidden Supply of High-Achieving, Low Income Students." NBER Working Paper No. 18586. National Bureau of Economic Research, Cambridge, MA, December 2012.

H.R.11274, Middle Income Student Assistance Act. 95th Cong., October 14, 1978. https://www .congress.gov/bill/95th-congress/house-bill/11274.

Huelsman, Mark. *Debt to Society: The Case for Bold, Equitable Student Loan Cancellation and Reform.* New York: Demos, June 2019. https://www.demos.org/research/debt-to-society.

Iceland, John. *Poverty in America: A Handbook.* 3rd ed. Berkeley: University of California Press, 2013.

In re Briscoe v. Bank of New York and New York State Higher Education Services Corp, 16 B.R. 128 (Bankr. S.D.N.Y. 1981).

Ingraham, Christopher. "Two New Studies Find Racial Anxiety Is the Highest Driver of Support for Trump." *Washington Post,* June 6, 2016.

Jackson, C. Kirabo, Rucker Johnson, and Claudia Persico. "The Effect of School Finance Reforms on the Distribution of Spending, Academic Achievement, and Adult Outcomes." NBER Working Paper No. 20118, National Bureau of Economic Research, Cambridge, MA, May 2014.

Jacob, Brian, Susan Dynarski, Kenneth Frank, and Barbara Schneider. "Are Expectations Enough? Estimating the Effect of a Mandatory College-Prep Curriculum in Michigan." *Educational Evaluation and Policy Analysis* 39, no. 2 (2017): 333–60.

Jaschik, Scott. "2019 Survey of Admissions Leaders: The Pressure Grows." Inside Higher Education, September 23, 2019. https://www.insidehighered.com/news/survey/2019-survey -admissions-leaders-pressure-grows.

Jaynes, Gerald David, and Robin M. Williams Jr., eds. *A Common Destiny: Blacks and American Society.* Washington, DC: National Academy Press, 1989.

Johnson, Lyndon B. "Address on Voting Rights to Joint Session of Congress." *New York Times,* March 16, 1965.

———. "Commencement Address at Howard University: 'To Fulfill These Rights.'" June 4, 1965. In *Public Papers of the Presidents,* 2:634–40. Washington, DC: Government Printing Office, 1965.

Johnson, Rucker C. *Children of the Dream: Why School Integration Works*. With Alexander Nazaryan. New York: Basic Books, 2019.

Johnston, William R., John Engberg, Isaac M. Opper, Lisa Sontag-Padilla, and Lea Xenakis.
*Illustrating the Promise of Community Schools: An Assessment of the Impact of the New York
City Community Schools Initiative*. Santa Monica, CA: RAND, 2020. https://www.rand.org
/pubs/research_reports/RR3245.html.

Joint Center for Housing Studies of Harvard University. *The State of the Nation's Housing, 2018*.
Cambridge, MA: Joint Center for Housing Studies, 2018. https://www.jchs.harvard.edu
/state-nations-housing-2018.

———. *The State of the Nation's Housing, 2019*. Cambridge, MA: Joint Center for Housing Studies, 2019. https://www.jchs.harvard.edu/state-nations-housing-2019.

Jordan, Winthrop D. *White over Black: American Attitudes toward the Negro, 1550–1812*. 2nd ed.
Chapel Hill: University of North Carolina Press, 2012.

Judson, George. "For Schools, Sad Echoes of Hartford." *New York Times*, May 15, 1996. https://
www.nytimes.com/1995/05/14/nyregion/for-schools-sad-echoes-of-hartford.html.

Katznelson, Ira. *When Affirmative Action Was White: An Untold History of Racial Inequality in
Twentieth-Century America*. New York: W. W. Norton, 2005.

Katznelson, Ira, and Margaret Weir. *Schooling for All: Class, Race, and the Decline of the Democratic Ideal*. New York: Basic Books, 1985.

Kemple, James J., Corinne M. Herlihy, and Thomas J. Smith. *Making Progress toward Graduation:
Evidence from the Talent Development High School Model*. New York: Manpower Development Research Corporation, 2005.

Kerr, Jennifer C. "Big Decrease in Number of 'Dropout Factory' High Schools." AP, November 10, 2015. https://apnews.com/article/365ea65eb9ca4bb6b31fd0723d201cae.

Kerr, Kerri A., and Nettie E. Legters. "Preventing Dropout: Use and Impact of Organizational
Reforms Designed to Ease the Transition to High School." In *Dropouts in America: Confront-
ing the Graduation Rate Crisis*, edited by Gary Orfield, 221–42. Cambridge, MA: Harvard
Education Press, 2004.

Key, V. O., Jr. *Southern Politics in State and Nation*. New York: Alfred. A. Knopf, 1949.

Keyes v. School Dist. No. 1, Denver, Colorado, 413 U.S. 189 (1973).

Keyes v. School District No. 1, Denver, Colorado, 521 F.2d 465 (1975).

Keyssar, Alexander. *The Right to Vote: The Contested History of Democracy in the United States*.
New York: Basic Books, 2000.

Kidder, William C., and Patricia Gándara. *Two Decades after the Affirmative Action Ban: Evaluating the University of California's Race-Neutral Efforts*. Los Angeles: Civil Rights Project, 2016.

Kids Count Data Center. "Children in Poverty by Race and Ethnicity." Accessed July 27, 2021.
https://datacenter.kidscount.org/data/tables/44-children-in-poverty-by-race-and
-ethnicity.

———. "Children Living in High Poverty Areas by Race and Ethnicity." Accessed July 28, 2021.
https://datacenter.kidscount.org/data/bar/7753-children-living-in-high-poverty-areas-by
-race-and-ethnicity/share//1~any~false~1983~10,11,9,12,1,185,13~14942#1/any/false/1983
/10,11,9,12,1,185,13/14942.

———. *A Shared Sentence: The Devastating Toll of Parental Incarceration on Kids, Families and
Communities*. Baltimore: Anne E. Casey Foundation, April 18, 2016. https://assets.aecf.org
/m/resourcedoc/aecf-asharedsentence-2016.pdf.

Killen, Melanie, David S. Crystal, and Martin Ruck. "The Social Developmental Benefits of Intergroup Contact among Children and Adolescents." In *Lessons in Integration: Realizing the Promise of Racial Diversity in American Schools*, edited by Erica Frankenberg and Gary Orfield, 57–73. Charlottesville: University of Virginia Press, 2007.

Kim, Soobin, Gregory Wallsworth, Ran Xu, Barbara Schneider, Kenneth Frank, Brian Jacob, and Susan Dynarski. "The Impact of the Michigan Merit Curriculum on High School Math Course-Taking." *Educational Evaluation and Policy Analysis* 41, no. 2 (June 2019): 164–88.

Klebanov, Pamela Kato, Jeanne Brooks-Gunn, and Greg J. Duncan. "Does Neighborhood and Family Poverty Affect Mothers' Parenting, Mental Health, and Social Support." *Journal of Marriage and the Family* 56, no. 2 (1994): 441–55.

Klein, Alyson. "Ed. Sec. John B. King, Jr to PTA: Diversity in Schools Benefits All Students." *Education Week*, July 12, 2016. https://www.edweek.org/policy-politics/ed-sec-john-b-king -jr-to-pta-diversity-in-schools-benefits-all-students/2016/07.

———. "The Every Student Succeeds Act: An ESSA Overview." *Education Week*, March 31, 2016. https://www.edweek.org/policy-politics/the-every-student-succeeds-act-an-essa-overview /2016/03.

———. "Obama Administration Releases Final Testing Regulations for ESSA." *Education Week*, December 7, 2016. https://www.edweek.org/policy-politics/obama-administration-releases -final-testing-regulations-for-essa/2016/12.

Kluger, Richard. *Simple Justice*. New York: Vintage Books, 1975.

Koretz, Daniel M. *Measuring Up: What Educational Testing Really Tells Us*. Cambridge, MA: Harvard University Press, 2008.

———. *Trends in Educational Achievement*. Washington, DC: Congressional Budget Office, April 1986.

Krysan, Maria, and Sarah Patton Moberg. "Trends in Racial Attitudes." University of Illinois, Institute of Government and Public Affairs, August 25, 2016. http://igpa.uillinois.edu /programs/racial-attitudes.

La Gorce, Tammy. "Retired, or Hoping to Be, and Saddled with Student Loans." *New York Times*, February 26, 2020. https://www.nytimes.com/2020/02/26/business/retirement -student-loan-debt.html.

Lankford, Hamilton, Susanna Loeb, and James Wyckoff. "Teacher Sorting and the Plight of Urban Schools: A Descriptive Analysis." *Educational Evaluation and Policy Analysis* 24, no. 1 (2002): 37–62.

Lau v. Nichols, 414 U.S. 563 (1974).

Lee, Jackyung. "Two Takes on the Impact of NCLB on Academic Achievement." In *Holding NCLB Accountable: Achieving Accountability, Equity, and School Reform*, edited by Gail L. Sunderman, 75–90. Thousand Oaks, CA: Corwin, 2008.

Legal Momentum, Women's Legal Defense and Education Fund. *Single Parenthood in the United States—a Snapshot*. New York: Legal Momentum, Women's Legal Defense and Education Fund, March 2014.

Levitan, Monica, and LaMont Jones. "Scholars Believe Supreme Court Likely to End Affirmative Action with Kavanaugh." *Diverse* (blog), September 13, 2018. https://diverseeducation .com/article/126121/.

Lieber, Ron, and Tara Siegel Bernard. "Bankruptcy Isn't an Easy Fix to Student Debt." *New York Times*, November 8, 2020.

Lieberson, Stanley. *A Piece of the Pie: Blacks and White Immigrants since 1880*. Berkeley: University of California Press, 1981.

Little, Wilson. *Spanish-Speaking Children in Texas*. Austin: University of Texas Press, 1944.

Loeb, Susanna, Demetra Kalogrides, and Eileen Lai Horng. "Principal Preferences and the Uneven Distribution of Principals across Schools." *Educational Evaluation and Policy Analysis* 32, no. 2 (June 1, 2010): 205–29.

Logan, Jessica A. R., Laura M. Justice, Melike Yumus, and Leydi Johana Chaparro-Moreno. "When Children Are Not Read to at Home: The Million Word Gap." *Journal of Developmental and Behavioral Pediatrics* 40, no. 5 (2019): 383–86.

Long, Heather, and Danielle Douglas-Gabriel. "The Latest Crisis: Low-Income Students Are Dropping Out of College This Fall in Alarming Numbers." *Washington Post*, September 16, 2020. https://www.washingtonpost.com/business/2020/09/16/college-enrollment-down/.

Long, Mark C. "Is There a 'Workable' Race-Neutral Alternative to Affirmative Action in College Admissions?" *Journal of Policy Analysis and Management* 34, no. 1 (September 2014): 162–83.

Long, Mark C., Dylan Conger, and Patrice Iatarola. "Effects of High School Course-Taking on Secondary and Postsecondary Success." *American Educational Research Journal* 49, no. 2 (April 2012): 285–322.

Long, Mark C., Dylan Conger, and Raymond McGhee Jr. "Life on the Frontier of AP Expansion: Can Schools in Less-Resourced Communities Successfully Implement Advanced Placement Science Courses?" *Educational Researcher* 48, no. 6 (2019): 356–68.

Los Angeles Times. "Los Angeles Teacher Ratings." Database. Accessed August 6, 2021. http://projects.latimes.com/value-added/.

Losen, Daniel J., ed. *Closing the School Discipline Gap: Equitable Remedies for Excessive Exclusion*. New York: Teachers College Press, 2015.

Louie, Josephine. *"We Don't Feel Welcome Here": African Americans and Hispanics in Metro Boston*. Cambridge, MA: Civil Rights Project at Harvard University, 2005.

Lukas, J. Anthony. *Common Ground: A Turbulent Decade in the Lives of Three American Families*. New York: Vintage Books, 1986.

Lynd, Robert Staughton, and Helen Merrell Lynd. *Middletown: A Study in Contemporary American Culture*. New York: Harcourt Brace, 1929.

Mann, Robert. *The Walls of Jericho: Lyndon Johnson, Hubert Humphrey, Richard Russell, and the Struggle for Civil Rights*. New York: Harcourt Brace, 1996.

Martinez-Wenzl, Mary, and Rigoberto Marquez. *Unrealized Promises: Unequal Access, Affordability, and Excellence at Community Colleges in Southern California*. Los Angeles: Civil Rights Project, February 2012.

Massey, Douglas S., and Nancy A. Denton. *American Apartheid: Segregation and the Making of the Underclass*. Cambridge, MA: Harvard University Press, 1993.

McCarthy, Justin. "Most Americans Say Segregation in Schools a Serious Problem." Gallup Poll, September 17, 2019. https://news.gallup.com/poll/266756/americans-say-segregation-schools-serious-problem.aspx.

McDonough, Patricia M. *The School-to-College Transition: Challenges and Prospects*. Washington, DC: American Council on Education, Center for Policy Analysis, 2004.

McElroy, Edward J., and Maria Armesto. "TRIO and Upward Bound: History, Programs, and Issues—Past, Present, and Future." *Journal of Negro Education* 67, no. 4 (1998): 373–80.

McFarland, Joel, Bill Hussar, Jijun Zhang, Xiaolei Wang, Ke Wang, Sarah Hein, Melissa Diliberti, et al. *The Condition of Education 2019.* Washington, DC: U.S. Department of Education, National Center for Education Statistics, May 2019.

McGinniss, Joe. *The Selling of the President, 1968.* New York: Trident, 1969.

McGuire, Thomas G., and Jeanne Miranda. "New Evidence Regarding Racial and Ethnic Disparities in Mental Health: Policy Implications." *Health Affairs* 27, no. 2 (March/April 2008): 393–403.

McKoy, Deborah L., Jeffrey M. Vincent, and Ariel H. Bierbaum. *Opportunity-Rich Schools and Sustainable Communities: Seven Steps to Align High-Quality Education with Innovations in City and Metropolitan Planning and Development.* Berkeley: Center for Cities and Schools, University of California, Berkeley, 2011.

McLarin, Kimberly J. "Impact of Court Ruling on Black Scholarships." *New York Times,* November 2, 1994. https://www.nytimes.com/1994/11/02/us/impact-of-court-ruling-on-black-scholarships.html.

McPartland, James M., and Will J. Jordan. "Older Students Also Need Major Federal Compensatory Education Resources." In *Hard Work for Good Schools: Facts Not Fads in Title I Reform,* edited by Gary Orfield and Elizabeth H. DeBray, 102–9. Cambridge, MA: Civil Rights Project of Harvard University, 1999.

McPherson, Michael S., and Morton Owen Schapiro. *Keeping College Affordable: Government and Educational Opportunity.* Washington, DC: Brookings Institution, 1991.

———. *The Student Aid Game: Meeting New and Rewarding Talent in American Higher Education.* Princeton, NJ: Princeton University Press, 1998.

McWhorter, Diane. *Carry Me Home: Birmingham, Alabama, the Climactic Battle of the Civil Rights Revolution.* New York: Touchstone, 2001.

Mettler, Suzanne. *Degrees of Inequality: How the Politics of Higher Education Sabotaged the American Dream.* New York: Basic Books, 2014.

Mickelson, Roslyn Arlin, and Martha Bottia. "Integrated Education and Mathematics Outcomes: A Synthesis of Social Science Research." *North Carolina Law Review* 88 (2010): 993–1089.

Milliken v. Bradley, 418 U.S. 717 (1974).

Milliken v. Bradley, 433 U.S. 267 (1977).

Moberg, Sarah Patton, Maria Krysan, and Deanna Christianson. "Racial Attitudes in America." *Public Opinion Quarterly* 83, no. 2 (Summer 2019): 450–71.

Moreno, José F. *The Elusive Quest for Equality: 150 Years of Chicano/Chicana Education.* Cambridge, MA: Harvard Educational Review, 1999.

Morris, Dick. *Behind the Oval Office: Winning the Presidency in the Nineties.* New York: Random House, 1997.

Mozes, Alan. "Untreated Vision Problems Plague U.S. Preschoolers." *Health Day News,* May 5, 2017. https://consumer.healthday.com/eye-care-information-13/eye-and-vision-problem-news-295/untreated-vision-problems-plague-u-s-preschoolers-722380.html.

Muller, Chandra, Catherine Riegle-Crumb, Kathryn S. Schiller, Lindsey Wilkinson, and Kenneth A. Frank. "Race and Academic Achievement in Racially Diverse High Schools: Opportunity and Stratification." *Teachers College Record* 112, no. 4 (2010): 1038–63.

Murray, Charles A. *Losing Ground: American Social Policy, 1950–1980.* New York: Basic Books, 1984.

Nash, Gary B. "Red, White and Black: The Origins of Racism in Colonial America." In *The Great Fear: Race in the Mind of America*, edited by Gary B. Nash and Richard Weiss, 1–26. New York: Holt, Rinehart and Winston, 1970.

National Academies of Sciences, Engineering, and Medicine. *Monitoring Educational Equity.* Washington, DC: National Academies Press, 2019. https://doi.org/10.17226/25389.

———. *The Promise of Adolescence: Realizing Opportunity for All Youth.* Washington, DC: National Academies Press, 2019. https://doi.org/10.17226/25388.

National Commission on Excellence in Education. *A Nation at Risk: The Imperative for Educational Reform.* Washington, DC: Government Printing Office, April 1983.

Neel, Joe. "Poll: Most Americans Think Their Own Group Faces Discrimination." National Public Radio, 2017.

Nesmith, Ande, and Ebony Ruhland. "Children of Incarcerated Parents: Challenges and Resiliency, in Their Own Words." *Children and Youth Services Review* 30, no. 10 (September 2008): 1119–30.

Neville, Helen A., Miguel E. Gallardo, and Derald Wing Sue, eds. *The Myth of Racial Color Blindness: Manifestations, Dynamics, and Impact* Washington, DC: American Psychological Association, 2016.

Newport, Frank. "Public Opinion on Civil Rights 50 Years after the Civil Rights Act of 1964." Gallup News release, April 10, 2014. https://news.gallup.com/opinion/polling-matters/169361/public-opinion-civil-rights-years-civil-rights-act-1964.aspx.

New York Times. "Full Transcript of Trump's State of the Union Address." February 4, 2020. https://www.nytimes.com/2020/02/05/us/politics/state-of-union-transcript.html.

———. "'Welfare Queen' Becomes Issue in Reagan Campaign." *New York Times,* February 15, 1976.

Nichols, Andrew Howard. *"Segregation Forever"? The Continued Underrepresentation of Black and Latino Undergraduates at the Nation's 101 Most Selective Public Colleges and Universities.* Washington, DC: Education Trust, July 2020.

Nierenberg, Amelia. "An Application Deluge for Top Colleges, a Drought for the Rest." *New York Times,* February 21, 2021.

Nowicki, Jacqueline M. *Public High Schools with More Students in Poverty and Smaller Schools Provide Fewer Academic Offerings to Prepare for College.* GAO-19-8. Washington, DC: Government Accountability Office, October 11, 2018.

Oakes, Jeannie. *Keeping Track: How Schools Structure Inequality.* New Haven, CT: Yale University Press, 1985.

———. *Multiplying Inequalities: The Effects of Race, Social Class, and Tracking on Opportunities to Learn Mathematics and Science.* Santa Monica, CA: RAND, 1990.

Oliver, Melvin, and Thomas Shapiro. *Black Wealth / White Wealth: A New Perspective on Racial Inequality.* New York: Routledge, 2006.

Orfield, Antonia, Frank Basa, and John Yun. "Vision Problems of Children in Poverty in an Urban School Clinic: Their Epidemic Numbers, Impact on Learning, and Approaches to Remediation." *Journal of Optometric Vision Development* 32, no. 3 (2001): 114–41.

Orfield, Gary, ed. *Alternative Paths to Diversity: Exploring and Implementing Effective College Admissions Policies.* Research Report Series No. RR-17-40. Princeton, NJ: Educational Testing Service, 2017. https://escholarship.org/uc/item/3vq970qw.

———. *Congressional Power: Congress and Social Change.* New York: Harcourt Brace Jovanovich, 1975.

———. *Connecticut School Integration: Moving Forward as the Northeast Retreats.* With Jonyeon Ee. Los Angeles: Civil Rights Project, 2015.

———, ed. *Diversity Challenged: Evidence on the Impact of Affirmative Action.* With Michal Kurlaender. Cambridge, MA: Harvard Education Pub. Group, 2001.

———, ed. *Dropouts in America: Confronting the Graduation Rate Crisis.* Cambridge, MA: Harvard Education Press, 2004.

———. "Housing Segregation Produces Unequal Schools." In *Closing the Opportunity Gap: What America Must Do to Give Every Child an Even Chance,* edited by Prudence L. Carter and Kevin G. Welner, 40–60. New York: Oxford University Press, 2014.

———. *Must We Bus? Segregated Schools and National Policy.* Washington, DC: Brookings Institution, 1978.

———. "The 1964 Civil Rights Act and American Education." In *Legacies of the 1964 Civil Rights Act,* edited by Bernard Grofman, 89–128. Charlottesville: University of Virginia Press, 2000.

———. "Public Opinion and School Desegregation." *Teachers College Record* 96, no. 4 (Summer 1995): 654–70.

———. *Public School Desegregation in the United States, 1968–1980.* Washington, DC: Joint Center for Political Studies, 1982.

———. "Race and the Liberal Agenda: The Loss of the Integrationist Dream, 1965–1974." In *The Politics of Social Policy in the United States,* edited by Margaret Weir, Ann Shola Orloff, and Theda Skocpol, 313–55. Princeton, NJ: Princeton University Press, 1988.

———. *The Reconstruction of Southern Education: The Schools and the 1964 Civil Rights Act.* New York: John Wiley, 1969.

———. "The Rights of Hispanic Children." In *Must We Bus? Segregated Schools and National Policy,* 198–229. Washington, DC: Brookings Institution, 1978.

———. *Toward a Strategy for Urban Integration: Lessons in School and Housing Policy from Twelve Cities.* New York: Ford Foundation, 1981.

Orfield, Gary, and Carole Ashkinaze. *The Closing Door: Conservative Policy and Black Opportunity.* Chicago: University of Chicago Press, 1991.

Orfield, Gary, and Jennifer B. Ayscue, eds. *Discrimination in Elite Public Schools: Investigating Buffalo.* New York: Teachers College Press, 2018.

Orfield, Gary, and Susan E. Eaton. *Dismantling Desegregation: The Quiet Reversal of "Brown v. Board of Education."* New York: New Press, 1996.

Orfield, Gary, and Jongyeon Ee. *Segregating California's Future: Inequality and Its Alternative 60 Years after "Brown v. Board of Education."* Los Angeles: Civil Rights Project, 2014.

Orfield, Gary, and Erica Frankenberg. *Educational Delusions? Why Choice Can Deepen Inequality and How to Make Schools Fair.* Berkeley: University of California Press, 2013.

Orfield, Gary, and Nicholas Hillman, eds. *Accountability and Opportunity in Higher Education: The Civil Rights Dimension.* Cambridge, MA: Harvard Education Press, 2018.

Orfield, Gary, and Danielle Jarvie. *Unequal Public Schools Makes Affirmative Action Essential for Equal Opportunity.* Los Angeles: Civil Rights Project, October 2020.

Orfield, Gary, and Chungmei Lee. *"Brown" at 50: King's Dream or Plessy's Nightmare?* Cambridge, MA: Civil Rights Project at Harvard University, January 2004. https:// civilrightsproject.ucla.edu/research/k-12-education/integration-and-diversity/brown-at -50-king2019s-dream-or-plessy2019s-nightmare/orfield-brown-50-2004.pdf.

Orfield, Gary, and Nancy McArdle. *The Vicious Cycle: Segregated Housing, Schools and Intergenerational Inequality*. Cambridge, MA: Joint Center for Housing Studies, Harvard University, 2006.

Orfield, Gary, and Edward Miller, eds. *Chilling Admissions: The Affirmative Action Crisis and the Search for Alternatives*. Cambridge, MA: Civil Rights Project at Harvard University, 1998.

Orfield, Myron. "Segregation and Environmental Justice." *Minnesota Journal of Law, Science and Technology* 7 (2005): 147–60.

Osterman, Michelle J. K., and Joyce A. Martin. *Timing and Adequacy of Prenatal Care in the United States, 2016*. Washington, DC: U.S. Department of Education, National Center for Health Statistics, May 30, 2018. https://stacks.cdc.gov/view/cdc/55174.

Pager, Devah, Bart Bonikowski, and Bruce Western. "Discrimination in a Low-Wage Labor Market: A Field Experiment." *American Sociological Review* 74, no. 5 (October 1, 2009): 777–99.

Palardy, Gregory J. "High School Socioeconomic Segregation and Student Attainment." *American Educational Research Journal* 50, no. 4 (2013): 714–54.

Panel on Educational Opportunity and Postsecondary Desegregation. *Redeeming the American Promise*. Atlanta: Southern Education Foundation, 1995.

Panetta, Leon E., and Peter Gall. *Bring Us Together: The Nixon Team and the Civil Rights Retreat*. Philadelphia: Lippincott, 1971.

Parents Involved in Community Schools v. Seattle School District No. 1, 551 U.S. 701 (2007).

Parker, Frank R. *Black Votes Count: Political Empowerment in Mississippi after 1965*. Chapel Hill: University of North Carolina Press, 1990.

Pattillo-McCoy, Mary. *Black Picket Fences: Privilege and Peril among the Black Middle Class*. Chicago: University of Chicago Press, 1999.

Paul, Catherine A. "Elementary and Secondary Education Act of 1965 (ESEA)." Social Welfare History Project, 2016. https://socialwelfare.library.vcu.edu/programs/education/elementary-and-secondary-education-act-of-1965.

Peltason, J. W. *Fifty-Eight Lonely Men: Southern Federal Judges and School Desegregation*. New York: Harcourt, Brace and World, 1961.

Pendharkar, Eesha. "Efforts to Root Out Racism in Schools Would Unravel under 'Critical Race Theory' Bills." *Education Week* 40, no. 34 (2021): 8.

Peng, Samuel S., DeeAnn Wright, and Susan T. Hill. *Understanding Racial-Ethnic Differences in Secondary School Science and Mathematics Achievement*. NCES 95-710. Washington, DC: Government Printing Office, February 1995.

Perkins, Alfred. *Edwin Rogers Embree: The Julius Rosenwald Fund, Foundation Philanthropy, and American Race Relations*. Bloomington: Indiana University Press, 2011.

Perkins, Kristin L., and Robert J. Sampson. "Compounded Deprivation in the Transition to Adulthood: The Intersection of Racial and Economic Inequality among Chicagoans, 1995–2013." *RSF: The Russell Sage Foundation Journal of the Social Sciences* 1, no. 1 (November 2015): 35–54.

Peters, Charles, and Phillip Keisling, eds. *A New Road for America: The Neoliberal Movement*. Lanham, MD: Madison Books, 1985.

Peterson, George E., Randall R. Bovbjerg, Barbara A. Davis, Walter G. Davis, Eugene C. Durman, and Theresa A. Gullo. *The Reagan Block Grants: What Have We Learned?* Washington, DC: Urban Institute Press, 1986.

Peterson, Marvin W., Robert T. Blackburn, Zelda F. Gamson, Carlos H. Arce, Roselle W. Davenport, and James R. Mingle. *Black Students on White Campuses: The Impact of Increased Black Enrollments*. Ann Arbor: Institute for Social Research, University of Michigan, 1978.

Pettigrew, Thomas F., and Linda R. Tropp. "A Meta-analytic Test of Intergroup Contact Theory." *Journal of Personality and Social Psychology* 90, no. 5 (2006): 751–83.

Pew Research Center. *Modern Immigration Wave Brings 59 Million to U.S., Driving Population Growth and Change through 2065: Views of Immigration's Impact on U.S. Society Mixed*. Washington, DC: Pew Research Center, September 2015.

Pfeffer, Fabian T., and Alexandra Killewald. "Generations of Advantage: Multigenerational Correlations in Family Wealth." *Social Forces* 96, no. 4 (June 2018): 1411–42.

Pfeiffer, Deirdre. *The Opportunity Illusion: Subsidized Housing and Failing Schools in California*. Los Angeles: Civil Rights Project, December 2009.

Pitsch, Mark. "Clinton Proposes Tax Credit for College Tuition." *Education Week*, June 12, 1996. https://www.edweek.org/teaching-learning/clinton-proposes-tax-credit-for-college-tuition /1996/06.

———. "Regulations Banning Race-Based Scholarships Proposed." *Education Week*, December 11, 1991.

Pitt, Leonard. *The Decline of the Californios: A Social History of the Spanish-Speaking Californians, 1846–1890*. Berkeley: University of California Press, 1998.

Plessy v. Ferguson, 163 U.S. 537 (1896).

Podberesky v. Kirwan, 38 F.3d 147 (4th Cir. 1994).

PRRI. "Amid Multiple Crises, Trump and Biden Supporters See Different Priorities and Futures for the Nation," October 19, 2020. https://www.prri.org/research/amid-multiple-crises -trump-and-biden-supporters-see-different-realities-and-futures-for-the-nation/.

Pub. L. No. 89-329, Higher Education Act of 1965. November 9, 1965.

Pub. L. No. 115-391, First Step Act of 2018. December 2018. https://www.congress.gov/115/plaws /publ391/PLAW-115publ391.pdf.

Quane, James M., and Bruce H. Rankin. "Neighborhood Poverty, Family Characteristics, and Commitment to Mainstream Goals: The Case of African American Adolescents in the Inner City." *Journal of Family Issues* 19, no. 6 (1998): 769–94.

Rainwater, Lee. *Behind Ghetto Walls: Black Families in a Federal Slum*. Chicago: Aldine, 1970.

Rampey, Bobby D., Gloria S. Dion, and Patricia L. Donahue. *NAEP 2008: Trends in Academic Progress*. Washington, DC: National Center for Education Statistics, U.S. Department of Education, April 2009. https://nces.ed.gov/nationsreportcard/pdf/main2008/2009479.pdf.

Rankin, Deborah. "Your Money; Reagan Cuts in Student Aid." *New York Times*, October 24, 1981. https://www.nytimes.com/1981/10/24/business/your-money-reagan-cuts-in-student-aid.html.

Ready, Douglas D., and Megan R. Silander. "School Racial and Ethnic Composition and Young Children's Cognitive Development: Isolating Family, Neighborhood and School Influences." In *Integrating Schools in a Changing Society: New Policies and Legal Options for a Multiracial Generation*, edited by Erica Frankenberg and Elizabeth DeBray, 91–113. Chapel Hill: University of North Carolina Press, 2011.

Reagan, Ronald. Inaugural Address. January 20, 1981. Ronald Reagan Presidential Foundation and Institute. https://www.reaganfoundation.org/ronald-reagan/reagan-quotes-speeches /inaugural-address-1/.

Reardon, Sean F., Rachel Baker, Matt Kasman, Daniel Klasik, and Joseph B. Townsend. "What Levels of Racial Diversity Can Be Achieved with Socioeconomic-Based Affirmative Action? Evidence from a Simulation Model." CEPA Working Paper No. 15-04, Center for Education Policy Analysis, Stanford, CA, December 2017. https://cepa.stanford.edu/sites/default/files/wp15-04-v201712.pdf.

Reardon, Sean F., Rachel Baker, and Daniel Klasik. *Race, Income, and Enrollment Patterns in Highly Selective Colleges, 1982–2004.* Stanford, CA: Center for Education Policy Analysis, 2012. http://hdl.handle.net/10919/92633.

Reeves, Jimmie L., and Richard Campbell. *Cracked Coverage: Television News, the Anti-cocaine Crusade, and the Reagan Legacy.* Durham, NC: Duke University Press, 1994.

Regents of the University of California v. Bakke, 438 U.S. 265 (1978).

Repetti, Rena L., Shelley E. Taylor, and Teresa E. Seeman. "Risky Families: Family Social Environments and the Mental and Physical Health of Offspring." *Psychological Bulletin* 128, no. 2 (2002): 330–66.

Ripley, Randall B., and Grace A. Franklin. *Congress, the Bureaucracy, and Public Policy.* 5th ed. Pacific Grove, CA: Brooks/Cole, 1991.

Rogers, John, Sophie Fanelli, David Medina, Queenie Zhu, Rhoda Freelon, Melanie Bertrand, and Jaime Del Razo. *California Educational Opportunity Report.* Los Angeles: Institute for Democracy, Education, and Access at the University of California, Los Angeles, and University of California All Campus Consortium on Research for Diversity, 2009.

Rosenbaum, James E. "Changing the Geography of Opportunity by Expanding Residential Choice: Lessons from the Gautreaux Program." *Housing Policy Debate* 6, no. 1 (1995): 231–69.

Rothenberg, Randall. *The Neo-Liberals: Creating the New American Politics.* New York: Simon and Schuster, 1984.

Rothwell, Jonathan. "Black and Hispanic Kids Get Lower Quality Pre-K." *Social Mobility Memos* (blog), Brookings Institution, June 29, 2016. https://www.brookings.edu/blog/social-mobility-memos/2016/06/29/black-and-hispanic-kids-get-lower-quality-pre-k/.

Rumberger, Russell W. *Dropping Out: Why Students Drop Out of High School and What Can Be Done about It.* Cambridge, MA: Harvard University Press, 2011.

Sampson, Robert J., and Alix S. Winter. "Racial Ecology of Lead Poisoning: Toxic Inequality in Chicago Neighborhoods, 1995–2013." *Du Bois Review: Social Science Research on Race* 13, no. 2 (2016): 261–83.

San Antonio Independent School Dist. v. Rodriguez, 411 U.S. 1 (1973).

Savage, David G. *Turning Right: The Making of the Rehnquist Supreme Court.* New York: John Wiley, 1992.

Schneider, Jack. "Small Schools: The Edu-Reform Failure That Wasn't." *Education Week*, February 9, 2016. https://www.edweek.org/leadership/opinion-small-schools-the-edu-reform-failure-that-wasnt/2016/02.

Schofield, Janet Ward, and Leslie R. M. Hausmann. "The Conundrum of School Desegregation: Positive Student Outcomes and Waning Support." *University of Pittsburgh Law Review* 66, no. 1 (April 2004): 83–111. https://doi.org/10.5195/lawreview.2004.48.

Schuette v. Coalition to Defend Affirmative Action, 134 S. Ct. 1623 (2014).

Schwartz, Mildred A. *Trends in White Attitudes toward Negroes.* Report No. 119. Chicago: National Opinion Research Center, University of Chicago, 1967.

Schwartz, Robert B. "The Emerging State Leadership Role in Education Reform: Notes of a Participant-Observer." In *A Nation Reformed? American Education 20 Years after "A Nation at Risk,"* edited by David T. Gordon, 131–52 Cambridge, MA: Harvard Education Press, 2003.

Schwartz, Robert B., Marian A. Robinson, Michael W. Kirst, and David L. Kirp. "Goals 2000 and the Standards Movement." *Brookings Papers on Education Policy* 2000 (2000): 173–214.

Sedmak, Todd. "High School Class of 2020 College Enrollments Decline 22% Compared to 2019 Class." National Student Clearing House, December 10, 2020. https://www.studentclearinghouse.org/blog/high-school-class-of-2020-college-enrollments-decline-22-compared-to-2019-class/.

SFFA v. President and Fellows of Harvard College, 980 F.3d 157 (2020).

Shapiro, Eliza. "Only 7 Black Students Got into Stuyvesant, N.Y.'s Most Selective High School, Out of 895 Spots," *New York Times,* March 18, 2019.

Shapiro, Eliza, and K. K. Rebecca Lai. "How New York's Elite Public Schools Lost Their Black and Hispanic Students." *New York Times,* June 3, 2019. https://www.nytimes.com/interactive/2019/06/03/nyregion/nyc-public-schools-black-hispanic-students.html.

Sharpe, Rhonda Vonshay. "The Top Producers of African-American Graduates." *Diverse,* February 6, 2020, 20.

"*Sheff v. O'Neill.*" NAACP Legal Defense and Educational Fund, filed April 27, 1989. https://www.naacpldf.org/case-issue/sheff-v-oneill/.

Shepard, Lorrie A., and Mary Lee Smith, eds. *Flunking Grades: Research and Policies on Retention.* Education Policy Perspectives. London: Falmer, 1989.

Simon, Nicole, and Susan Moore Johnson. "Teacher Turnover in High-Poverty Schools: What We Know and Can Do." *Teachers College Record* 117, no. 3 (2015): 1–36.

Simons, Gary, ed. *Be the Dream: Prep for Prep Graduates Scare Their Stories.* Chapel Hill, NC: Algonquin Books, 2003.

Sleeter, Christine E. "Preparing Teachers for Multiracial and Historically Underserved Schools." In *Lessons in Integration: Realizing the Promise of Racial Diversity in American School,* by Erica Frankenberg and Gary Orfield, 171–89. Charlottesville: University of Virginia Press, 2007.

Smith, Ashley A. "Discrepancies in Estimates on Food Insecurity." Inside Higher Education, April 30, 2019. https://www.insidehighered.com/news/2019/04/30/new-research-finds-discrepancies-estimates-food-insecurity-among-college-students.

———. "Report: Most Transfer Students Leave College without 2-Year Degree." Inside Higher Education, August 8, 2018. https://www.insidehighered.com/quicktakes/2018/08/08/report-most-transfer-students-leave-college-without-2-year-degree.

Smith, Samantha. "Why People Are Rich and Poor: Republicans and Democrats Have Very Different Views." *Fact Tank,* Pew Research Center, May 2, 2017, https://www.pewresearch.org/fact-tank/2017/05/02/why-people-are-rich-and-poor-republicans-and-democrats-have-very-different-views.

Snyder, Thomas D., Cristobal de Brey, and Sally A. Dillow. *Digest of Education Statistics, 2017.* Washington, DC: National Center for Education Statistics, January 2019.

South Carolina v. Katzenbach, 383 U.S. 301 (1966).

Spears, Allen. *Black Chicago: The Making of a Negro Ghetto, 1890–1920.* Chicago: University of Chicago Press, 1967.

Stahl, Jason. *Right Moves: The Conservative Think Tank in American Political Culture since 1945.* Chapel Hill: University of North Carolina Press, 2016.

Steele, Shelby. *The Content of Our Character: A New Vision of Race in America*. New York: Harper Perennial, 1991.

Stefancic, Jean, and Richard Delgado. *No Mercy: How Conservative Think Tanks and Foundations Changed America's Social Agenda*. Philadelphia: Temple University Press, 1996.

Stevens, Katharine B., and Elizabeth English Smith. *Does Pre-K Work? The Research on Ten Early Childhood Programs—and What It Tells Us*. Washington, DC: American Enterprise Institute, April 2016. https://www.aei.org/research-products/report/does-pre-k-work-the-research-on-ten-early-childhood-programs-and-what-it-tells-us/.

St. John, Edward P., Anna S. Chung, David Blough, Sharon Wilhelm, and Britany Affolter-Caine. *Race-Conscious Scholarships and Persistence: A Study of Students in a State System of Higher Education*. Report to NAACP Legal Defense Fund. August 2007. https://doi.org/10.13140/RG.2.1.2493.3367.

Stockman, David A. *The Triumph of Politics: The Inside Story of the Reagan Revolution*. New York: Random House, 1986.

Sunderman, Gail L., ed. *Holding NCLB Accountable. Achieving Accountability, Equity and School Reform*. Thousand Oaks, CA: Corwin, 2008.

Sunderman, Gail L., James S. Kim, and Gary Orfield. *NCLB Meets School Realities: Lessons from the Field*. Thousand Oaks, CA: Corwin, 2005.

Sundquist, James L. *Politics and Policy: The Eisenhower, Kennedy and Johnson Years*. Washington, DC: Brookings Institution, 1968.

Superville, Denise. "Thriving Students Are the Goal of City, District Partnerships." *Education Week*, September 12, 2018, 1.

Sweatt v. Painter, 339 U.S. 629 (1950).

Taeuber, Karl E. and Alma Taeuber. *Negroes in Cities: Residential Segregation and Neighborhood Change*. Chicago: Aldine, 1965.

Tavernise, Sabrina. "U.S. Population Grows at Slowest Rate since 1919." *New York Times*, March 26, 2020.

Thernstrom, Abigail, and Stephan Thernstrom. *No Excuses: Closing the Racial Gap in Learning*. New York: Simon and Schuster, 2003.

Thompson, Derek. "Why Smart Poor Students Don't Apply to Selective Colleges (and How to Fix It)." *Atlantic*, January 24, 2013. https://www.theatlantic.com/business/archive/2013/01/why-smart-poor-students-dont-apply-to-selective-colleges-and-how-to-fix-it/272490/.

Tienda, Marta. *Hispanicity and Educational Inequality: Risks, Opportunities and the Nation's Future*. Tomás Rivera Lecture Series. Princeton, NJ: Educational Testing Service, March 2009.

Tough, Paul. *The Years That Matter Most: How College Makes or Breaks Us*. New York: Houghton Mifflin Harcourt, 2019.

Tsoi-A-Fatt Bryant, Rhonda. *College Preparation for African American Students: Gaps in the High School Educational Experience*. Washington, DC: Center for Law and Social Policy, February 2015.

Turner, Sarah, and John Bound. "Closing the Gap or Widening the Divide: The Effects of the G.I. Bill and World War II on the Educational Outcomes of Black Americans." *Journal of Economic History* 63, no. 1 (March 2003): 145–77.

Ujifusa, Andrew. "No Measurable Gap between Charters, Traditional Public Schools on National Tests." *Education Week*, September 25, 2019. https://www.edweek.org/education/no-measurable-gap-between-charters-traditional-public-schools-on-national-tests/2019/09.

U.S. Bureau of the Census. *Census of the Population: 1960.* Vol. 1, *Characteristics of the Population.* Pt. 1, *United States Summary.* Washington, DC: Government Printing Office, 1964. https://www.census.gov/library/publications/1961/dec/population-vol-01.html.

———. "Population Characteristics (P20) Publication Series." Accessed August 17, 2021. https://www.census.gov/library/publications/time-series/p20.html.

———. *The Social and Economic Status of the Black Population in the United States, 1973.* Current Population Reports, Series P. 23, No. 48. Washington, DC: Government Printing Office, 1974.

U.S. Commission on Civil Rights. *Bordertown Discrimination in Montana: Summary Findings and Policy Implications: A Brief from the Montana Advisory Committee.* May 2019. https://www.usccr.gov/pubs/2019/05-29-Bordertown-Discrimination-Montana.pdf.

———. *Racial Isolation in the Public Schools.* Vol. 1. Washington, DC: Government Printing Office, 1967.

———. *Survey of School Desegregation in the Southern and Border States, 1965–1966.* Washington, DC: Government Printing Office, 1966.

———. *Toward Quality Education for Mexican Americans.* Washington, DC: Government Printing Office, 1972.

U.S. Congress, Joint Economic Committee. "10 Key Facts about Veterans of the Post-9/11 Era." Updated November 2016. https://www.jec.senate.gov/public/_cache/files/26971be7-ba33-4417-8cbc-c6022e734321/jec-veterans-day-fact-sheet-2016.pdf.

U.S. Department of Education, National Center for Education Statistics. *Digest of Educational Statistics, 1980.* Washington, DC: Government Printing Office, 1980. http://archive.org/details/ERIC_ED202085.

———. *Digest of Education Statistics, 2007.* Washington, DC: National Center for Education Statistics, March 2008.

U.S. Department of Veterans Affairs, Veterans Benefits Administration. "Education and Training: History and Timeline." Last updated November 21, 2013. https://www.benefits.va.gov/gibill/history.asp.

U.S. Government Accountability Office. *Education Grants: Promise Neighborhoods Promotes Collaboration but Needs National Evaluation Plan.* GAO-14-432. Washington, DC: Government Accountability Office, May 2014. https://www.gao.gov/products/gao-14-432.

———. *K–12 Education: Better Use of Information Could Help Agencies Identify Disparities and Address Racial Discrimination.* Washington, DC: Government Accountability Office, April 21, 2016. https://www.gao.gov/products/gao-16-345.

———. *K–12 Education: Certain Groups of Student Attend Alternative Schools in Greater Proportion Than They Do Other Schools.* GAO-29-373. Washington, DC: Government Accountability Office, June 13, 2019.

U.S. Senate, Committee on Health, Education, Labor and Pensions. *For Profit Higher Education: The Failure to Safeguard the Federal Investment and Ensure Student Success.* July 30, 2012. https://www.help.senate.gov/imo/media/for_profit_report/PartI-PartIII-SelectedAppendixes.pdf.

Unterman, Rebecca. *Headed to College: The Effects of New York City's Small High Schools of Choice on Postsecondary Enrollment.* MDRC Policy Brief. New York: MDRC, October 2014.

Valentino, Rachel. "Will Public Pre-K Really Close Achievement Gaps? Gaps in Prekindergarten Quality between Students and across States." *American Educational Research Journal* 55, no. 1 (February 2018): 79–116.

Viano, Samantha, Lam D. Pham, Gary T. Henry, Adam Kho, and Ron Zimmer. "What Teachers Want: School Factors Predicting Teachers' Decisions to Work in Low-Performing Schools." *American Educational Research Journal* 58, no. 1 (February 2021): 201–33.

Vigdor, Jacob, and Jens Ludwig. "Segregation and the Test Score Gap." In *Steady Gains and Stalled Progress: Inequality and the Black-White Test Score Gap,* edited by Katherine Magnuson and Jane Waldfogel, 181–211. New York: Russell Sage, 2008.

Wall, Patrick. "Newark's Rush to Create New Magnet-School Admissions Test Is Raising Eyebrows." Chalkbeat Newark, January 11, 2019. https://newark.chalkbeat.org/2019/1/11 /21106544/newark-s-rush-to-create-new-magnet-school-admissions-test-is-raising -eyebrows-here-s-what-you-need-t.

Watson, Robert Blake, Trenton Stone, Erica Scott, and Kahlil Greene. "What's Legal in College Admissions Is a Real Scandal." *Los Angeles Times,* August 7, 2019. https://www.chicagotribune .com/opinion/commentary/ct-opinion-college-admissions-scandal-20190809 -lfcc5lb75zgivlbtvcil2mp6au-story.html.

Weinberg, Meyer. *A Chance to Learn: The History of Race and Education in the United States.* Cambridge: Cambridge University Press, 1977.

———. "United States." *Integrated Education* 20, no. 6 (1983): 47.

Wells, Amy Stuart, and Jeannie Oakes. "Potential Pitfalls of Systemic Reform: Early Lessons from Research on Detracking." *Sociology of Education* 69 (1996): 135–43.

Whalen, Charles, and Barbara Whalen. *The Longest Debate: A Legislative History of the 1964 Civil Rights Act.* Santa Ana, CA: Seven Locks, 1985.

Wilds, Deborah J. *Minorities in Higher Education: Seventh Annual Status Report.* Washington, DC: American Council on Education, Office of Minority Concerns, 1988.

Williams, John B. "The State Role in Achieving Equality of Higher Education." In *Toward Black Undergraduate Student Equality in American Higher Education,* edited by Michael T. Nettles, 149–78 New York: Greenwood, 1988.

Wilson, William Julius. *The Declining Significance of Race: Blacks and Changing American Institutions.* Chicago: University of Chicago Press, 1978.

Wolgemuth, Kathleen L. "Woodrow Wilson and Federal Segregation." *Journal of Negro History* 44, no. 2 (April 1959): 158–73.

Wollenberg, Charles. "Ethnic Experiences in California History: An Impressionistic Survey." *California Historical Quarterly* 50, no. 3 (1971): 221–33.

Woodward, C. Vann. *Reunion and Reaction: The Compromise of 1877 and the End of Reconstruction.* Boston: Little, Brown, 1951.

Zelizer, Julian E. *The Fierce Urgency of Now: Lyndon Johnson, Congress, and the Battle for the Great Society.* New York: Penguin, 2015.

INDEX

NOTE: Page numbers in *italics* refer to figures and tables. Note information is indicated by n and note number following the page reference.

Hopwood v. Texas (1996), 5–6
Houle, Jason, 247
housing: civil rights initiatives on, 115; colorblind policies toward, 151, 155; cumulative
racial inequalities with, 47, 53, 54, 60, 68–73;
discrimination in, 4, 14, 70, 71, 73, 102–3, 106–7,
109, 113, 238; educational opportunities and,
4, 14, 27, 54, 60, 68–73, 106–7, 212, 238–39;
exclusion in, 70, 102–3, 106–7, 109, 113;
homelessness without, 60, 72; income and,
27, 70–72; mortgage lending for, 71–72, 238;
research on social and economic effects of,
18–19; segregation by, 18–19, 27, 60, 62–63, 69–71,
73, 98, 100, 102–3, 106–7, 109, 160, 200, 215,
238–39; strategies to lessen segregation of, 200,
238–39; subsidized, 60, 70, 71, 73, 155, 212, 238–39
Huelsman, Mark, 247–48
Humphrey, Hubert, 15
hunger. *See* food and hunger

immigrants: cumulative racial inequalities for,
47, 60; demographic changes with, 148, 190;
education and income of, 310n11; English
education for, 61, 220, 236 (*see also* language
issues); exclusion of, 93–94, 105; national
origins quotas for, 139; nonwhite, 1, 24, 236;
poverty among, 27, 60; racial discrimination
against, 195
Immigration Act (1924), 105, 139
Immigration and Nationality Act (1965), 139
incarceration: conservative policies increasing,
20, 147, 164; criminal justice alternatives to, 220,
229–30; cumulative racial inequalities and, 54,
57, 73–75; education and, 67, 73–75, 220, 229–30
income: cost of college increases vs. increase in,
178; cumulative racial inequalities and, 53, 54–55,
56, 58–61, 87–88, 289–90; exclusion influenced
by, 96–98; finance policies and (*see* financing
higher education); higher education effects on,
2–3, 53; housing and, 27, 70–72; inequalities of,
rising, 35, 148–49, 194, 243–44, 286–90;
integration effects on, 67; minimum wage,
60–61, 149, 178, 194; single-parent, 56. *See also*
low-income students; poverty
Indian Education Act (1972), 141
*Indian Education: A National Tragedy—a
National Challenge* report, 141
Indians: admissions policies specific to, 8, 135
(*see also* admissions policies); civil rights for,
121, 141; educational attainment by, 52, 52, 53,
97, 98–99, 104, 108, 109–10, 207; employment
of, 93; enduring effects of discrimination and
exclusion among, 50–51; enrollment in higher
education, 7, 149; exclusion of, 50–51, 91, 93,
95, 108, 109–10, 113 (*see also* exclusion,
tradition of); financial burdens for, 43;
incarceration of, 74; Indian boarding schools
for, 99; poverty among, 59, 59–61, 87;

race-based scholarships for, 203–4, 248–50;
school choice for, 38; schooling disparities for,
61, 66; single parenting by, 55; terminology
identifying, x; tracking for, 79. *See also* people
of color; students of color; *race-related entries*
individual achievement/individualism, 13–14,
22–23, 91, 146, 150, 153, 185, 250, 289
inferiority, assumptions of, 16, 48, 92, 93, 103–6, 108,
110
IQ tests, 105, 108

Jeanes Fund, 103
Jefferson, Thomas, 51
Johnson, Lyndon and administration: civil rights
support by, 23, 119–21, 123, 126–30, 139–40, 142;
community development initiative of, 234;
educational policies of, 64, 137, 178, 180, 287;
election of, 126, 127; end of presidency of, 116;
Great Society reforms of, 5, 101, 115, 138, 139,
144; immigration policies of, 139
Johnson, Rucker, 66–67, 132, 268; *Children of the
Dream,* 67

Kahlenberg, Richard, 26
Kavanaugh, Brett, 204
Keeping Track (Oakes), 78
Kennedy, Anthony, 6, 7, 204
Kennedy, John F. and administration: civil rights
stance of, 111, 117, 119, 125–26, 142, 192–93;
education policies of, 117; election of, 116–17, 125
Kerry, John, 15
Keyes v. School District No. 1 (1973), 108, 273
King, John B., Jr., 184–85
King, Martin Luther, Jr., 32, 48, 117, 123, 193
Koretz, Daniel, *The Testing Charade: Pretending to
Make Schools Better,* 83–84
Ku Klux Klan, 102, 105, 110, 123. *See also* White
supremacy groups

Land-Grant College Act (1862), 242
language issues, 61, 141, 220, 236, 284, 285–86
The Latino Education Crisis (Gándara and
Contreras), 245
Latinos: admissions policies specific to, 8, 135
(*see also* admissions policies); civil rights for,
121, 140–41; colorblind policies effects on, 186,
282, 284, 285–86 (*see also* colorblind policies);
demographic changes among, 34, 35, 62, 108,
159, 186, 284, 285; educational attainment by,
52, 52, 53, 97, 98–99, 104–5, 108–10, 207, 285–86;
employment of, 2, 93; enduring effects of
discrimination and exclusion among, 51;
enrollment in higher education, 1, 7, 148, 149,
175, 242; exclusion of, 51, 91, 93, 95, 108–10, 113,
282 (*see also* exclusion, tradition of); financial
burdens for, 43, 171, 244, 245, 251, 288 (*see also*
financing higher education); high school
preparation for, 146, 236, 237 (*see also* high

OUR COMPELLING INTERESTS

Advisory Board

Anthony Appiah, Professor of Philosophy and Law, New York University

Saleem Badat, Research Professor in Humanities, University of Kwazulu-Natal

Armando I. Bengochea, Senior Program Officer and Director of the Mellon Mays
Undergraduate Fellowship Program, The Andrew W. Mellon Foundation

Lawrence E. Bobo, Dean of Social Science and the W. E. B. Du Bois Professor of
the Social Sciences, Harvard University

Nancy Cantor, Co-chair, Chancellor, Rutgers University-Newark

Rosario Ceballo, Dean of Georgetown College, and Professor of Psychology,
Georgetown University

Tabbye Chavous, Director, National Center for Institutional Diversity, and
Professor of Education and Psychology, and Associate Dean for Diversity,
Equity, and Inclusion, College of Literature, Science, and the Arts, University
of Michigan

Sumi Cho, Director of Strategic Initiatives, African American Policy Forum

Angela Dillard, Chair of History Department, and the Richard A. Meisler
Collegiate Professor of Afroamerican & African Studies, History and in the
Residential College, University of Michigan

Stephanie A. Fryberg, Associate Professor of American Indian Studies and
Psychology, University of Washington, and University Diversity and Social
Transformation Professor of Psychology, University of Michigan

Patricia Y. Gurin, Nancy Cantor Distinguished University Professor Emerita of
Psychology and Women's Studies, University of Michigan

Makeba Morgan Hill, Executive Director in the Office of the Executive Vice
President for Piedmont Healthcare

Earl Lewis, Thomas C. Holt Distinguished University Professor of History,
Afroamerican and African Studies and Public Policy, and Director, Center for
Social Solutions

Gary Orfield, Distinguished Research Professor of Education, Law, Political
Science and Urban Planning, and Co-Director, Civil Rights Project / Proyecto
Derechos Civiles, University of California at Los Angeles

Scott E. Page, Leonid Hurwicz Collegiate Professor, Complex Systems, Political Science, and Economics, University of Michigan

Eboo Patel, Founder and President, Interfaith Youth Core

George J. Sanchez, Professor of American Studies and Ethnicity, and History, University of Southern California

Claude M. Steele, Lucie Stern Professor in the Social Sciences, Emeritus, Stanford University

Susan P. Sturm, George M. Jaffin Professor of Law and Social Responsibility, Columbia University Law School

Thomas J. Sugrue, Silver Professor of Social and Cultural Analysis and History, New York University

Beverly Daniel Tatum, President Emerita, Spelman College

Doreen N. Tinajero, Project Senior Manager, Center for Social Solutions, University of Michigan

Sarah E. Turner, University Professor of Economics and Education, University of Virginia

Michele S. Warman, Executive Vice President, Chief Operating Officer, General Counsel and Secretary, The Andrew W. Mellon Foundation

Laura Washington, Chief Communications Officer and Vice President for Strategic Initiatives, New-York Historical Society

Alford Young, Jr., Edgar G. Epps Collegiate Professor and Chair of Sociology, and Arthur F. Thurnau Professor of Sociology, Afroamerican and African Studies, and Gerald R. Ford School of Public Policy, and Associate Director, Center for Social Solutions, University of Michigan

Milton Keynes UK
Ingram Content Group UK Ltd.
UKHW031529120324
439228UK00003B/134